Internal Reasons

MIT Readers in Contemporary Philosophy

Persistence: Contemporary Readings, Sally Haslanger and Roxanne Marie Kurtz, eds. (2006)

Disjunctivism: Contemporary Readings, Alexander Byrne and Heather Logue, eds. (2009)

Internal Reasons: *Contemporary Readings*, Kieran Setiya and Hille Paakkunainen, eds. (2012)

Internal Reasons

Contemporary Readings

edited by Kieran Setiya and Hille Paakkunainen

The MIT Press
Cambridge, Massachusetts
London, England

© 2012 Massachusetts Institute of Technology

All rights reserved. No part of this book may be reproduced in any form by any electronic or mechanical means (including photocopying, recording, or information storage and retrieval) without permission in writing from the publisher.

This book was set in Stone Sans and Stone Serif by Toppan Best-set Premedia Limited.

Library of Congress Cataloging-in-Publication Data

Internal reasons : contemporary readings / edited by Kieran Setiya and Hille Paakkunainen.
  p. cm.—(MIT readers in contemporary philosophy)
Includes bibliographical references (p.) and index.
ISBN 978-0-262-01648-3 (hardcover : alk. paper)—ISBN 978-0-262-51640-2 (pbk. : alk. paper)
1. Ethics, Modern. I. Setiya, Kieran, 1976–. II. Paakkunainen, Hille, 1980–.
BJ301.I58 2012
170'.42—dc23

2011016636

Contents

Sources   vii

Introduction: Internal Reasons   1
Kieran Setiya

I   Williams and His Critics   35

1   Internal and External Reasons (1979)   37
Bernard Williams

2   Skepticism about Practical Reason (1986)   51
Christine Korsgaard

3   Might There Be External Reasons? (1995)   73
John McDowell

4   Reply to McDowell (1995)   89
Bernard Williams

5   Internal Reasons (1995)   99
Michael Smith

II   Instrumentalism   125

6   Humean Doubts about the Practical Justification of Morality (1997)   127
James Dreier

7   Why Is Instrumental Rationality Rational? (2005)   147
Troy Jollimore

8   Putting Rationality in Its Place (1993)   167
Warren Quinn

III Kantian Conceptions 193

9 Selections from *The Possibility of Altruism* (1970) 195
Thomas Nagel

10 The Normativity of Instrumental Reason (1997) 201
Christine Korsgaard

11 The Possibility of Practical Reason (1996) 249
J. David Velleman

12 Velleman's Autonomism (2001) 285
Philip Clark

IV Alternatives 301

13 Beyond the Error Theory (2010) 303
Michael Smith

14 Rationality and Virtue (1994) 329
Philippa Foot

15 Reasons and Motivation (1997) 343
Derek Parfit

Bibliography   373
Contributors   379
Index   381

Sources

1. Bernard Williams, "Internal and External Reasons," originally published in Ross Harrison, ed., *Rational Action*, Cambridge: Cambridge University Press, 1979. Reprinted with the permission of Cambridge University Press.
2. Christine Korsgaard, "Skepticism about Practical Reason," originally published in the *Journal of Philosophy* 83 (1986): 5–25. Reprinted with permission.
3. John McDowell, "Might There Be External Reasons?" Originally published in J. E. J. Altham and Ross Harrison, eds., *World, Mind, and Ethics*, Cambridge: Cambridge University Press, 1995. Reprinted with the permission of Cambridge University Press.
4. Bernard Williams, "Reply to McDowell," originally published as "Internal and External Reasons" in J. E. J. Altham and Ross Harrison, eds., *World, Mind, and Ethics*, Cambridge: Cambridge University Press, 1995. Reprinted with the permission of Cambridge University Press.
5. Michael Smith, "Internal Reasons," originally published in *Philosophy and Phenomenological Research* 55 (1995): 109–131. Copyright © Blackwell Publishing Ltd., 1995. Reproduced with the permission of Blackwell Publishing Ltd.
6. James Dreier, "Humean Doubts about the Practical Justification of Morality," originally published in Garrett Cullity and Berys Gaut, eds., *Ethics and Practical Reason*, Oxford: Oxford University Press, 1997. By permission of Oxford University Press.
7. Troy Jollimore, "Why Is Instrumental Rationality Rational?" Originally published in the *Canadian Journal of Philosophy* 35 (2005): 289–307. Reprinted with the permission of the University of Calgary Press.
8. Warren Quinn, "Putting Rationality in Its Place," originally published in R. G. Frey and Christopher W. Morris, eds., *Value, Welfare, and Morality*, Cambridge: Cambridge University Press, 1993. Reprinted with the permission of Cambridge University Press.

9. Thomas Nagel, *The Possibility of Altruism.* © 1970 Thomas Nagel. © 1978 Princeton University Press. Reprinted by permission of Princeton University Press.

10. Christine Korsgaard, "The Normativity of Instrumental Reason," originally published in Garrett Cullity and Berys Gaut, eds., *Ethics and Practical Reason*, Oxford: Oxford University Press, 1997. This version from Christine Korsgaard, *The Constitution of Agency*, Oxford: Oxford University Press, 2008. By permission of Oxford University Press.

11. J. David Velleman, "The Possibility of Practical Reason," originally published in *Ethics* 106 (1996): 694–726. © 1996 by The University of Chicago. Reprinted by permission of the University of Chicago Press.

12. Philip Clark, "Velleman's Autonomism," originally published in *Ethics* 111 (2001): 580–593. © 2001 by The University of Chicago. Reprinted by permission of the University of Chicago Press.

13. Michael Smith, "Beyond the Error Theory," originally published in R. Joyce and S. Kirchin, eds., *A World without Values: Essays on John Mackie's Error Theory*, Dordrecht, Holland: Springer, 2010. © Springer Science + Business Media B. V. 2010. Reprinted by kind permission of Springer Science and Business Media.

14. Philippa Foot, "Rationality and Virtue," originally published in Herlinde Pauer-Studer, ed., *Norms, Value, and Society*, Amsterdam: Kluwer, 1994. This version from Philippa Foot, *Moral Dilemmas*, Oxford: Oxford University Press, 2003. By permission of Oxford University Press.

15. Derek Parfit, "Reasons and Motivation," originally published in *Proceedings of the Aristotelian Society, Supplementary Volume* 71 (1997): 99–130. Reprinted by courtesy of the Editor of the Aristotelian Society: © 1997.

Introduction: Internal Reasons

Kieran Setiya

In book II of Plato's *Republic*, Glaucon locates justice "among the finest goods, as something to be valued . . . both because of itself and because of what comes from it."[1] Unhappy with the Socratic defense of this doctrine in book I, Glaucon confronts it with the challenge of Gyges' ring. What if you had the power to be invisible?

> Now, no one, it seems, would be so incorruptible that he would stay on the path of justice or stay away from other people's property, when he could take whatever he wanted from the marketplace with impunity, go into people's houses and have sex with anyone he wished, kill or release from prison anyone he wished, and do all the other things which would make him like a god among humans. Rather his actions would be in no way different from those of an unjust person, and both would follow the same path. This, some would say, is a great proof that one is never just willingly but only when compelled to be. (*Republic* 360b–c)

We can take this passage to raise one of the most persistent and challenging questions of ethics: "Why should I be moral?" Should I conform to principles of justice only from the threat of punishment or the promise of a good reputation? Is there reason to do so when some act of suitably concealed injustice would gratify my desires?

On closer inspection, however, there is an apparent discrepancy between the topic introduced in Glaucon's first remark, which speaks to the value of justice, and the evidence supplied by the thought-experiment, which is essentially psychological. We are invited to see the tawdry facts of human nature, our pettiness and corruptibility, as refuting a normative claim: that we *should* be loyal to the demands of justice even when we can safely disregard them. This argumentative strategy, of moving from (alleged) psychological to normative fact, is a model and precedent for more recent discussion of moral reasons. In a hugely influential 1979 essay, "Internal and External Reasons," Bernard Williams argued that reasons for action are always "internal," in being constrained by an agent's motivational capacities and "subjective motivational set." If an action would do nothing to satisfy one's desires or to further one's projects, one has no reason to perform it. This doctrine validates the inference from psychological facts about the motivation of agents to claims about the justification of action and so to the verdict that a given agent should or should not concern herself with justice or morality, all things considered. Williams concludes that agents whose subjective motivations are sufficiently antisocial may have no reason whatever to respect the rights and interests of others.

The framing of the dispute about internal and external reasons promised a more tractable way to ask and answer the question, "Why be moral?" But its significance was not confined to that. Along with earlier work, including Thomas Nagel's path-breaking book, *The Possibility of Altruism*, Williams's essay renewed interest in the relationship of action theory and moral psychology to ethics; it helped initiate a broader investigation of non-moral and instrumental reasons; and it offered a fresh perspective on questions about the nature of normativity in general. Each of these lines is pursued in one or more of the selections in this book. Taken together, they offer a comprehensive survey of recent work on internal reasons and a distinctive, focused approach to foundational problems of ethical objectivity, epistemology, and metaphysics. The volume ends with a substantial bibliography. The purpose of this introduction is to clarify the concept of an internal reason in Williams and the associated doctrine of internalism, to sketch how and why internalism has seemed compelling to so many even as it puts pressure on the universality of moral reasons, and to provide a partial taxonomy and map of positions taken up in the rest in the book.

1 What Is Internalism?

Our topic is the justification of action and the corresponding concept of a normative practical reason. Normative reasons for action are considerations that count in favor of doing something. Reasons in this sense need not be decisive—there can be reasons both for and against a single course of action—but reasons always have some weight. What one should do, all things considered, is fixed by the balance of reasons. It is in these terms that we ask, "Why should I be moral?" or "Do considerations of justice provide us with reasons to act?"

Philosophers sometimes contrast normative with motivating reasons, the latter being reasons that explain or motivate action, people's reasons for doing things. There is considerable dispute about the metaphysics of motivating reasons. Are they psychological states? Are they, like normative reasons, facts or true propositions? Are they considerations or putative facts?[2] It is not obvious that these questions are well-posed, or that the various answers put forward are inconsistent. In any case, we need not take them up. All we need for the statement of Williams's view is the idea of motivation by belief and desire, whether it is taken as basic or explained in other terms, and whether we identify motivating reasons with psychological states, with their contents, or with something else.

A further distraction might stem from Williams's title, which distinguishes two sorts of reasons, internal and external, or from his opening remarks, which identify statements of two corresponding kinds. Williams's distinction is not between normative and motivating reasons, but between conceptions of the former. He states his principal conclusion roughly as follows:

The fact that p is a reason for A to ϕ if and only if there is a sound deliberative route from A's beliefs, taken together with his subjective motivational set and the belief that p, to the desire to ϕ.

In asking what this principle means, and whether it is true, we set aside the more obscure and less profitable question of how to classify reasons (are some internal? some external?) if the principle is false. We also depart from aspects of Williams's presentation that are unnecessarily vague or controversial. When Williams sets out his position piecemeal in the opening pages of his essay, he tends to ask whether A has reason to ϕ, not whether some particular consideration, that p, provides such a reason. The formulation above adapts his remarks to this more specific question. In addition to this, Williams assumes that when we reason from belief to desire, we do so by way of the conviction that we have reason to ϕ (this volume, 40, 43). That is consistent with the view proposed above, but is not entailed by it. One can be an "internal reasons theorist" while finding Williams's picture of practical reasoning excessively reflective or intellectual in its appeal to such beliefs.[3]

Williams expands on his position in three ways. First, he insists that sound deliberation cannot rest on errors of fact. In his petrol/gin example (this volume, 38), I believe that the liquid in the bottle is gin when in fact it is petrol. The fact that I am thirsty is not a reason for me to mix the stuff with tonic and drink it, even though the reasoning by which I am moved to do so is in some sense rational. Since it rests on a false belief, deliberation of this kind does not correspond to reasons. Second, Williams stresses the variety of sound deliberation. It includes, but is not confined to, the narrowly instrumental process of forming desires for causal means to one's ends. Among the "wider possibilities for deliberation" are time-ordering, balancing the elements of one's subjective motivational set, and finding constitutive solutions. Imagination plays a role in such activities: "it can create new possibilities and new desires" (this volume, 40). What these forms of deliberation have in common is that they are governed by, and aim at the objects of, one's subjective motivations. In that sense they are broadly, if not narrowly, instrumental. Finally, the subjective motivational set is to be understood inclusively: it "can contain such things as dispositions of evaluation, patterns of emotional reaction, personal loyalties, and various projects, as they may abstractly be called, embodying commitments of the agent" (this volume, 41).

The main argument of Williams's paper is about the necessary conditions for something to be a reason, not what would be sufficient.[4] Nor does it bear on the exclusion of false beliefs. If we make these facts explicit in stating his conclusion, along with the sketch of deliberation from the previous paragraph, we end up here:

Internal Reasons Theory: The fact that p is a reason for A to ϕ only if there is a broadly instrumental route from A's beliefs, taken together with his subjective motivational set and the belief that p, to the desire to ϕ.

Informally: if an action does not answer to one's desires, in the broadest possible sense, there is no reason to perform it. It follows that, if someone does not care about the rights and interests of others, and can get what he wants while ignoring them entirely, he is justified in doing so. Moral reasons do not apply to him. In endorsing this argument, one adopts a neo-Humean or, perhaps more accurately, a neo-Hobbesian account of reasons for action.

Williams's principle is a possible definition of "internalism about reasons." But it is not the only one, nor is it the best. (Hence the pedantic label, "Internal Reasons Theory.") An alternative conception is more common and more illuminating; it is prevalent, though not universal, in the contents of this book.[5] This alternative has the virtue of saying what is common to neo-Humean internalists (Williams, Dreier) and neo-Kantians (Nagel, Korsgaard) who reject the Internal Reasons Theory. What these philosophers share is the conviction that normative reasons have the capacity to motivate the agent whose reasons they are:

Internalism about Reasons: The fact that p is a reason for A to ϕ only if A is capable of being moved to ϕ by the belief that p.

Introduction

The capacity in question here is not the potential to change so that one is susceptible to movement, but the actual possession of susceptibility. An agent who is capable of being moved to φ by the belief that *p* has something in her present psychology that can engage with that belief so as to move her in that way—even if, on a given occasion, she is not so moved.[6]

Something like Internalism is the guiding premise of Williams's argument for the Internal Reasons Theory. This argument begins with the assumption that reasons, even normative reasons, are potentially motivating: "If something can be a reason for action, then it could be someone's reason for acting on a particular occasion, and it would then figure in an explanation of that action" (this volume, 42). How to make this "dimension of possible explanation" more precise? Williams considers and quickly rejects the view that reasons are capable of explaining action all by themselves (this volume, 42–43). After all, an agent may be unaware of the fact that provides the reason, which cannot then account for what he does. When normative reasons explain our actions, they do so by way of a "psychological link." On the other hand, if we conceive this link as the belief that "some determinate consideration . . . constitutes a reason . . . to φ," we lose the force of the explanatory constraint (this volume, 43). Since we can be moved by *any* consideration that we believe to be a reason, the constraint excludes nothing. It does not restrict what can be a reason for A to φ.[7] Is there any way between these two extremes, a version of the explanatory constraint that is neither trivial nor implausibly strong? For Williams, the answer is Internalism: if the fact that *p* is a reason for A to φ, A is capable of being moved to φ by the belief that *p*. We avoid implausibility by insisting that reasons motivate, when they do, through a psychological link. We avoid triviality by treating this link as a belief whose content is the reason, not a belief about reasons, as such.

It is consistent with Internalism that in moving from belief to desire one must recognize the content of one's belief as a reason to act. Since Williams assumes this, he asks "what it is to *come to believe* [that one has a reason]," instead of asking directly how an agent is moved by the belief that *p* (this volume, 43). But it is clear that motivation is the principal topic.[8] This comes out in his earlier remarks about need: "If an agent really is uninterested in pursuing what he needs; and this is not the product of false belief; and he could not reach any such motive from motives he has by the kind of deliberative process we discussed; then I think we do have to say that . . . he indeed has no reason to pursue these things" (this volume, 41). And it comes out again in the culmination of Williams's argument, which asks how and when we can "reach . . . new motivation" (this volume, 45).

Understood in this way, Williams's argument takes the following form. First premise: Internalism about Reasons. Second premise: new motivation, or desire, cannot arise from deliberation when there is "no motivation for the agent to deliberate *from*" (this volume, 45). In effect, A is capable of being moved to ϕ by the belief that *p* only when there is a broadly instrumental path from his beliefs, taken together with his subjective motivational set and the belief that *p*, to the desire to ϕ. Conclusion: if the fact that *p* is a reason for A to ϕ, the conditions of the Internal Reasons Theory must be met.

This way of reading Williams suggests two points of resistance, and that is just what we find. "Externalists" such as John McDowell reject Internalism about Reasons (this volume, chap. 3). Neo-Kantians accept the first premise of Williams's argument but go on to dispute the second. For Nagel, "reasons must be capable of motivating"; the mistake is to assume that "all motivation has desire at its source" (this volume, 195). We can resist Williams's conclusion by finding "structural features" of reason and motivation that are not even broadly instrumental. Agents who possess the corresponding motivational capacities are subject to reasons by which they can be moved in deliberation even though there is no prior motivation for them to deliberate from. If these capacities are shared by all possible agents, they can be the ground of universal reasons.[9] Likewise, for Korsgaard, it is "a requirement on practical reasons, that they be capable of motivating us" (this volume, 56). But it is not a consequence of this that there is no such thing as "pure practical reason." Rather, if moral or other considerations provide us all with reasons to act, "the capacity [to be moved by them] belongs to the subjective motivational set of every rational being" (this volume, 66).

In a later essay, Williams acknowledges this possibility, or something close to it, but doubts that it is realized (Williams 1995, 37). He is not careful to distinguish two views. On the first, commitment to morality is an essential component of our subjective motivational set, with practical reasoning still conceived as broadly instrumental. This is consistent with the Internal Reasons Theory. On the second, commitment to morality is a disposition to engage in non-instrumental reasoning. It may belong to our subjective motivational set, but it does not play the role of a desire. This is consistent with Internalism about Reasons but inconsistent with the Internal Reasons Theory. Williams's carelessness can be excused, in part. If we are interested in the possibility of universal reasons, the distinction

Introduction

between these views is less significant than what they share. Internalism about Reasons supports the inference from sufficient variation in subjective motivational sets to the limited scope of reasons to be moral. What matters most is whether to accept the premises of this inference. It is of secondary importance whether we question the premise about variation by insisting that, while deliberation is broadly instrumental, some desires are universal, or hold instead that capacities for non-instrumental reasoning are essential to being an agent. Either way, the most urgent task of the neo-Kantian is to say what these desires or capacities are, to show that agency is impossible without them, and to specify the reasons they support. This task is taken up, in different ways, by Korsgaard (1996, 2009) and by David Velleman (1989, 2000, 2009).

Korsgaard's treatment of "skepticism" is a useful hook on which to hang some final distinctions. Although she appears to advocate Internalism about Reasons (see above, and this volume, beginning of §VI), her formulations are occasionally hard to make out. When Korsgaard first states internalism in §II, she runs together theories on which the *belief* that one has a reason can motivate action with theories on which the *existence* of the reason implies potential motivation; and she runs together judgments of moral right and wrong with beliefs about reasons, as such.[10] When she settles on a form of "existence internalism"—a claim about the motivational conditions for the existence of a normative reason, not the motivational effects of normative judgment—she qualifies her view ambiguously: "So long as there is doubt about whether a given consideration is able to motivate a *rational* person, there is doubt about whether that consideration has the force of a practical reason" (this volume, 56, my emphasis). At one point, she seems to go further:

In order for a theoretical argument or practical deliberation to have the status of a reason, it must of course be capable of motivating or convincing a rational person, but it does not follow that it must at all times be capable of motivating or convincing any given individual. (This volume, 59–60)

The problem with *Qualified Internalism*, according to which reasons must be capable of moving only rational agents, is that it is subject to such different interpretations. On one reading, "rational agent" means *minimally* rational agent, or agent capable of acting for reasons. Then Qualified Internalism is equivalent to Internalism about Reasons. On another reading, "rational agent" means one who meets standards of perfect rationality, whatever they are, and then Qualified Internalism is almost trivial. Who would deny that, when the fact that p is a reason for A to ϕ and A is incapable of being moved to ϕ by the belief that *p*, she falls short of rational excellence?[11]

A third reading is possible, one that draws on the special connotations of "irrationality." In rejecting externalism, Williams insists that, when we say of someone that he is failing to respond to a reason, we must be "concerned to say that what is particularly wrong with [him] is that he is *irrational*" (this volume, 46). Like other versions of Qualified Internalism, this claim confronts a dilemma. If "irrational" means "less than perfectly rational" or "less than fully responsive to reasons," it falls into near-triviality. On the other hand, if we insist on "irrationality" as a distinctive charge, the principle looks simply false. As McDowell protests:

> [What] is the point of holding out for the right to make an accusation of irrationality . . . if it is not to bluff the person into mending his ways by means of a fraudulent suggestion that he is flouting considerations that anyone susceptible to reasons at all would be moved by? (This volume, 80)

Different authors have proposed different conceptions of irrationality. For T. M. Scanlon, "[irrationality] in the clearest sense occurs when a person's attitudes fail to conform to her own judgments" (Scanlon 1998, 25). When someone does not know that a fact is a reason for her to ϕ she can fail to be moved by this fact without being, in the clearest sense, irrational. For Stephen White, "to call a person's action irrational is to ascribe a certain kind of blame to the person" (White 1990, 412). If someone's failure to be moved by a reason is not culpable, she will not be irrational in the corresponding sense.[12] We need not settle the dispute between these conceptions. What matters is that, on each of them, a failure to respond to reasons may not be irrational, even though it is a failure of rational excellence. In his reply to McDowell, Williams agrees: because it can be used in artificially narrow ways, "it [is] a mistake to pick out 'irrational' as a crucial term in this connection" (this volume, 94).[13]

There is no reason to accuse Korsgaard of making this mistake or of defending a near triviality. On balance, we should take her to advocate Internalism about Reasons and treat the passage above, which denies that reasons "must at all times be capable of motivating or convincing any given individual," as stressing the relative weakness of capacity claims: that A is capable of being moved in a given way is consistent with the presence of interfering factors that ensure that she will not be moved here and now.[14] In this respect, capacities are like dispositions. An object may fail to do what it is disposed to do, on some occasion, because its disposition is "masked."[15] The parallel is revealing. Part of the appeal of Qualified

Internalism, in its subjunctive formulations—"A would be moved . . . if she were rational"—is that it avoids the concept of a capacity, which many find obscure. With dispositions, too, there is an impulse toward subjunctive analysis.[16] In each case, the reductive project is fraught.[17] Whatever its fate, it would be unwise to write a particular theory of agents' capacities into our statement of Internalism. Better to keep the simple formula above. As Korsgaard insists, even unqualified Internalism leaves room for "true irrationality" (this volume, chap. 2, §§IV–V). It does not imply "that rational considerations always succeed in motivating us" or "that people can always be argued into reasonable conduct" (this volume, 62).

In "The Possibility of Practical Reason," Velleman reads Korsgaard differently. He, too, appeals to Qualified Internalism: "reasons for someone to do something must be considerations that would sway him toward doing it if he entertained them rationally" (this volume, 249). As he insists, it does not follow from this that, "if a consideration fails to influence someone, it isn't a reason for him to act"; what follows is merely that "it isn't a reason for him to act or he hasn't entertained it rationally" (this volume, 250).

The inclinations that would make an agent susceptible to the influence of some consideration may therefore be necessary—not to the consideration's being a reason for him—but rather his being rational in entertaining that reason. (This volume, 250)

Despite n. 10, in which Velleman identifies his premise with what others have called 'internalism'—"requiring reasons to have the capacity of exerting an influence"—he must intend the almost-trivial claim that being indifferent to a reason is a rational defect. The premise would otherwise conflict with the kind of "externalism" criticized in the following pages (this volume, 250–252), even though the externalist is said to accept it. For Velleman's externalist, we can be subject to reasons by which we have no inclination whatsoever to be moved: Internalism about Reasons is false. Velleman takes Korsgaard to leave this option open.[18] Hence her critique "suggests a version of externalism" that Williams "prematurely discounts" (this volume, 250–251). As the previous paragraph notes, I think this is a mistake; the misreading is made possible by the ambiguities of Qualified Internalism. At any rate, Velleman's own approach is not "internalist" only in a qualified sense, but in the sense defined by Internalism about Reasons. He believes that certain inclinations are essential to agency: action has a "constitutive aim." If they turn on this constitutive aim, reasons for action may depend on inclination, or the capacity to be moved, without depending on the particular inclinations someone happens to have (this volume, 256–257). That is what Velleman means when he insists that we "do not in fact have to choose between" internalism and externalism, and that they present a "false dichotomy" (this volume, 249, 262). What is false for Velleman, as for Korsgaard, is the dichotomy between Internalism about Reasons and reasons that do not depend on contingent motivation or desire.

2 Why Internalism?

In defending Internalism about Reasons, Williams cites the "dimension of possible explanation . . . which applies to any reason for action" (this volume, 42). A normative practical reason "could be someone's reason for acting on a particular occasion, and it would then figure in an explanation of that action" (this volume, 42). The problem for Williams is that Internalism is only one way in which to make sense of this attractive principle. Weaker readings are possible, and these readings do not support Internalism or the Internal Reasons Theory. According to the weakest interpretation of the explanatory constraint, we can act for normative reasons in that the grounds on which we do things are of the right metaphysical category to be such reasons: they are facts, or putative facts, about our circumstance.[19] In the basic case, we report someone's reason for acting in the form "A is doing ϕ because p," and the schematic letter "p" stands for a sentence that states a true proposition. By itself, the requirement of metaphysical congruence—that normative reasons can be grounds on which we act—does not constrain the content of this fact or its power to motivate A. According to a second interpretation, the explanatory constraint is this: if the fact that p is a reason for A to ϕ, someone or other could be moved to ϕ by the belief that p.[20] Alternatively, if a consideration is a reason for someone to act, the capacity to be moved by it must be consistent with human nature. These premises might be sufficient for Glaucon's argument, given psychological assumptions of corresponding strength. But they do not imply Internalism about Reasons, since they do not imply that reasons must be capable of moving the particular agent whose reasons they are.

Williams later complained, on behalf of Internalism, that it "must be a mistake simply to separate explanatory and normative reasons" (Williams 1995, 38–39). 'Reason' is not just ambiguous between "The fact that p is a reason for A to ϕ" and "His reason for ϕ-ing was that p." Internalism solves the ambiguity by treating normative reasons, reported by the first sentence, as potential explanations of the kind that figure in the second. (This perhaps involves more than the conditional formulation of Internalism about Reasons above.) But again, alternatives are readily imagined. Some hold that agents' reasons must be normative, except when they are false; or that this forms a "regulative ideal" to which reasons-explanations of action approximate.[21] Others hold that agents' reasons for acting are considerations they *take* to be normative reasons for what they are doing.[22] Either way, it is not mere ambiguity that 'reason' appears in both the explanation and justification of action. Finally, normative or "good" reasons might be thought of as grounds on which it would be good to act: good things to have among one's reasons for acting; reasons that conform to relevant norms.[23] Not mere ambiguity, but one can act on grounds that are not good reasons and that one does not take to be. If any of these accounts is right, we can agree with Williams that it would be a mistake to see no relation between normative reasons and reasons that explain action, without accepting Internalism or the Internal Reasons Theory.

None of this implies that Williams's argument is fruitless. On the contrary, its first premise is one that many find plausible. As we have seen, contemporary neo-Kantians share Williams's commitment to Internalism about Reasons. Its second premise has advocates, too: that our capacity to be moved by beliefs rests on their broadly instrumental relation to prior desires is one version of the so-called "Humean theory of motivation." Still, Internalism is and should be controversial. One way to bring this out is to stress its apparent optimism about our rational powers. For the internalist, each of us, no matter how impaired or ill-habituated, has the capacity to be moved by any reason to which he is subject. If we are capable of being moved by reasons in proportion to their weight, the consequence is more dramatic: that those who can act for reasons *at all* can do so perfectly. Why believe it? Why believe that our potential is so sublime, that we cannot be subject to reasons by which we cannot be moved? What is it about the nature of agency, or the metaphysics and epistemology of reasons, that makes such incapacity impossible?

In what follows, I examine three motivations for Internalism about Reasons. The first derives from Williams's reply to McDowell on the possibility of "external reasons." It points to recent debates about the relationship of reasons to ideal rationality and to conceptions of "internalism" rather different from those considered so far. The second argument for Internalism draws on problems in action theory and moral psychology about the nature of motivation and its relationship to mere causality. These issues are central to *The Possibility of Altruism* and to Korsgaard's development of Kantian themes. They blur into a third contention, that externalism about reasons is metaphysically or epistemologically problematic. I end by exploring this claim.

To begin with McDowell. Like Williams, he assumes that deliberation from belief to desire goes through the conviction that one has reason to ϕ.[24] He also accepts Williams's strictures on the power of deliberation to generate such beliefs: "it is very hard to believe there could be a kind of reasoning that was pure in [the relevant] sense—owing none of its cogency to the specific shape of pre-existing motivations—but nevertheless motivationally efficacious" (this volume, 76). How then does he avoid Williams's conclusion and resist the Internal Reasons Theory? By denying that, when the fact that *p* is a reason for A to ϕ, there must be a way to argue from A's present psychology, taken together with the belief that *p*, to the conclusion that he has reason to ϕ (this volume, chap. 3, §4). Being properly responsive to reasons is a matter of habituated virtue, and "from certain starting-points there is no rational route—no process of being swayed by reasons—that would take someone to being as if he had been properly brought up" (this volume, 79).

McDowell's response to Williams could mislead. How can one deny that, when the fact that *p* is a reason for A to ϕ, his being moved to ϕ by the belief that *p* would be an instance of sound deliberation? It is, after all, an instance of being moved in accordance with a reason. The answer is that McDowell does not deny this. Instead, he contrasts deliberation in Williams's sense, the provision of practical arguments that draw on an agent's present commitments, with an alternative usage, on which "deliberating correctly [is] giving all relevant considerations the force they are credited with in a correct picture of one's practical predicament" (this volume, 82).

This yields a sense in which to believe an external reason statement is . . . to believe that if the agent deliberated correctly, he would be motivated (of course not necessarily conclusively) in the direction in which the reason points. But there is no implication, as in Williams's argument, that there must be a deliberative or rational procedure that would lead anyone from not being so motivated to being so motivated. On the contrary, the transition to being so motivated is a transition *to* deliberating correctly, not one effected *by* deliberating correctly; effecting the transition may need some non-rational alteration such as conversion. (This volume, 82)

Being moved by a reason is an instance of correct deliberation. But if I am not so moved, I may be unable to acquire that disposition by deliberating correctly. Internalism about Reasons is false.

It is at this point that Williams comes to his own defense, objecting to McDowell's picture of reasons and correct deliberation. He takes McDowell to be giving an account of reasons on which "A has reason to ɸ" means "if A were a correct deliberator, A would be motivated in these circumstances to ɸ, where a 'correct deliberator' is someone who deliberates as a well-informed and well-disposed person would deliberate" (this volume, 91). The problem is that, if A were a correct deliberator, his reasons might be different. For instance, he would have no need to compensate for the various forms of irrationality to which he is subject. Thus A can have reason to ɸ even though, if he were a correct deliberator, he would have no such reason and would not be moved accordingly; and he may not have reason to ɸ even though, if he were a correct deliberator, he would want to do so. Nor can we solve this problem by counting A's limitations as part of his circumstance, for the circumstance will then be one that no correct deliberator could occupy. By contrast, there is no such problem for the broad instrumentalism of the Internal Reasons Theory.

Although Williams frames his point as one about reason and virtue, with the correct deliberator conceived as an ethically virtuous person, it is in fact quite general. Problems will arise for any view that explains the reasons of a particular situated agent, with his various imperfections, through the motivations he would have if he were to be, instead, ideally rational. Michael Smith calls this conception of reasons and rationality "the example model," since it treats an idealized version of the agent as setting an example for him to follow (this volume, chap. 5). As Smith contends, this model cannot be right. If I were to be fully rational, I would be moved to act in ways that there is no reason for me to act, in my actual circumstance. In the case that Smith describes, I am furious with my opponent after losing a hard-fought game of squash. If I were fully rational, and so not gripped by irrational anger, I would be moved to shake hands with him—but in my actual fury, I would probably lose my cool. There is no reason for me to take that risk. The same example shows that there are reasons to act in ways that I would not care to act if I were fully rational. For instance, there is reason for me to hit the showers right away, which I would not need to do if I were sufficiently rational to ignore or not to feel such anger.[25]

A terminological warning is essential here. Smith means by "internalism" the view that there is an "analytic connection between what we have reason to do in certain circumstances and what we would desire to do in those circumstances if we were fully rational" (this volume, 99). He identifies this view with Williams's doctrine of internal reasons and with Korsgaard's requirement of internalism (this volume, 99). If what was said in section 1, above, is right, these equations are not correct. At any rate, Smith's "internalism" is not Internalism or the Internal Reasons Theory. According to his "advice model" of reasons and rationality, A has reason to φ in circumstance C just in case A would want himself to φ in C if he were fully rational. Here we treat the idealized agent as giving advice to his actual self in the form of desires for what he should do. The advice model does not imply that reasons for A to φ are fixed or constrained by A's motivational capacities.[26] And Smith explicitly rejects, or expands, Williams's broadly instrumental picture of deliberation (this volume, 103–109).

What does all this mean? We presumably do need some account of the connection between reasons, on the one hand, and sound deliberation or ideal rationality, on the other. (This is not to assume priority for either side.) Williams is right to insist on this; and he is right to object to views that treat an idealized agent—one with full rationality, a correct deliberator—as an example to imitate. He goes wrong in assuming that there is no alternative to such views apart from the Internal Reasons Theory. If the advice model is adequate, we can relate reasons to full rationality without being pushed toward Williams's conclusions.

Smith's argument goes further. He contends that Williams's view conflicts with the ordinary concept of a reason. So long as we include in an agent's circumstance the relevant facts of his psychology, it is a conceptual truth that if A has reason to φ in circumstance C, everyone has reason to φ in C.[27] This is consistent with my having reason to satisfy my desires and you having reason to satisfy yours, since our varying desires will count as circumstantial facts (this volume, 113–114). According to the advice model, it is also a conceptual truth that A has reason to φ in circumstance C just in case A would want himself to φ in C if he were fully rational. It follows that A has reason to φ in C only if everyone would want themselves to φ in C if they were fully rational. On the advice model, reasons depend on convergence in the relevant desires of fully rational agents. As Smith points out, such convergence is unlikely on Williams's conception of practical reason.[28] Smith concludes that Williams must give up the first conceptual truth, that if A has reason to φ in C, everyone has reason to φ in

C: he must embrace an implausible relativity in reasons to act (this volume, 109–116).

As an interpretation of Williams, this is deeply controversial. It turns on reading him as an implicit advocate of the advice model.[29] Williams can otherwise respond by accepting the first premise of Smith's argument while disputing the second. He does, after all, have the makings of an alternative to Smith's conception: the picture of reasons and rationality, or sound deliberation, in the Internal Reasons Theory. So long as one's circumstance includes psychological facts, this theory is quite consistent with the non-relativity of reasons: if A has reason to φ in circumstance C, everyone has reason to φ in C.

This fact may seem to revive Williams's objection to McDowell, now posed as a dilemma. What is the connection between reasons and rationality? There are two live options: advice model and Internal Reasons Theory. If we doubt that reasons turn on convergence in the relevant desires of rational agents, as they do on the advice model, we must adopt Williams's view. But this is too quick. There are other pictures of the relationship here. Consider the following:

The fact that p is a reason for A to φ if and only if there is a sound deliberative route from A's psychological states, together with the belief that p, to the desire to φ.[30]

Because it connects reasons with particular deliberative routes, not ideal rationality, this principle avoids the difficulties raised above. Nor does it imply convergence in the desires of sound deliberators. At the same time, it is not a form of the Internal Reasons Theory or Internalism about Reasons. It does not place even broadly instrumental limits on deliberation or tie it to the capacities of particular agents.

The upshot is that, whether we accept Smith's advice model or the minimal principle just described, there is no argument for Internalism or the Internal Reasons Theory from the bare idea of a connection between practical reasons and practical rationality. If Internalism is justified, the reasons lie elsewhere.

A more promising path to Internalism draws on the theory of motivation; its most influential recent source is *The Possibility of Altruism* (Nagel 1970).

Nagel's argument turns on the distinction between "motivated" and "unmotivated" desires. As well as acting for reasons, we can want things for reasons, whether we act on our desire or not. When I want something for a reason, my desire is motivated: I am moved to want whatever it is by other beliefs and desires. Unmotivated desires are ones that lack this kind of explanation.[31]

This distinction bears on the debate about internalism in two ways. First, it can be used to block the argument we found in Williams, above. According to the second premise of that argument, A is capable of being moved to φ by the belief that p only when there is a broadly instrumental path from his beliefs, taken together with his subjective motivational set and the belief that p, to the desire to φ. This can now be read as a principle of motivation for desire. As Nagel points out, however, we can accept a modest "Humean theory," on which intentional action is motivated by desire, without accepting Williams's premise. We need only insist that some of the desires that motivate action are produced in turn by non-instrumental reasoning (this volume, 195–198). Suppose, for instance, that beliefs about my future interests motivate present desires without the help of any prior desire; or that the same is true of explicitly normative beliefs about what there is reason to do. These claims are consistent with the modest Humean theory, inconsistent with Williams's premise. Since standard arguments for the Humean theory support at most its modest form, this premise requires some other defense.[32]

Nagel's second appeal to motivation is more constructive. He gives an example of "deviant causality" for desire:

[It] is imaginable that thirst should cause me to want to put a dime in my pencil sharpener [when I see that the way to get a drink is to put a dime in the slot of a vending machine], but this would be an obscure compulsion or the product of malicious conditioning, rather than a rational motivation. We should not say that the thirst provided me with a *reason* to do such a thing, or even that thirst had motivated me to do it. (This volume, 199)

According to Nagel, mere causation is not enough for motivated desire. It would be wrong to say that I want to put the dime in the pencil sharpener *for a reason*, or on the ground that I am thirsty. My desire is caused but not motivated: it is a mere effect of the relevant belief. A useful comparison here is with Davidson on intentional action.[33] Having argued that, in acting intentionally, one is caused to act by related beliefs and desires, Davidson came to see that mere causation is not enough. In cases of "wayward" or "deviant" causality, an agent is caused to act by the desire for an end and a relevant belief about the means, but the ensuing action is not intentional. Davidson's example: a nervous climber wants to be rid of his companion's dangerous weight, and knows that he can manage this by dropping his rope; he becomes increasingly anxious as a result and this prompts him, carelessly, to let go (Davidson 1980c, 79). Davidson's climber does not let go of the rope intentionally, in order to lose his bothersome companion; his action is involuntary. Without assuming a causal theory of action (which Davidson defends), or that we can give non-circular conditions for non-deviance (which he does not), we can accept the crucial distinction. In acting on the ground that p, one is moved to act by the belief that p, where being moved is not simply being caused. Nagel's thought is parallel: when I want something for a reason, my desire is not merely caused by psychological states, but motivated.

The question is how to explain this contrast. How does mere causation differ from the kind of motivation involved in wanting something for a reason?

> The solution is to confer a privileged status on the relation between ends and means. . . . We may say that if being thirsty provides a reason to drink, then it also provides a reason for what enables one to drink. That can be regarded as the consequence of a perfectly general property of reasons: that they transmit their influence over the relation between ends and means. (This volume, 199)

Thus, for Nagel, motivation differs from mere causation in corresponding to the structure of normative reasons. What makes it intelligible to put a dime in the vending machine—and not in the pencil sharpener—is that this is what it is practically rational for me to do in light of my thirst and the relevant means-end belief. This, in turn, is why such motivation is possible, as the alleged motivation in the deviant case is not.

What does this mean for Internalism about Reasons? If Nagel is right, there is an intimate connection between the capacity to act for reasons, which involves motivation, and the standards of practical reason. At its simplest, the connection might be this:

If A is moved to φ by the belief that p, the fact that p is a reason for her to φ.

More realistically, we should allow for false beliefs and "true irrationality." Even if I am capable of instrumental reasoning, I sometimes reason badly. The most we can say is this:

If A is moved to φ by the belief that p, his being moved in that way is the perhaps-defective exercise of a capacity to respond to normative reasons.[34]

Motivation is distinguished from mere causation in being the expression of such a capacity, though this expression may be flawed: it may depend on false beliefs or only approximate to full or ideal rationality.

Nagel's position is in fact more specific: that the capacity for motivation in desire involves the capacity for instrumental reasoning, practical reasoning from ends to means by way of means-end beliefs. In this respect, he is like James Dreier and Christine Korsgaard. For Dreier, it is a condition of being subject to reasons at all that one accept "M/E," his version of an instrumental principle deriving reasons from desires (this volume, 141–144).[35] For Korsgaard, one cannot *will* an end without being committed to instrumental rationality in its pursuit (this volume, 226–228). These authors differ over the character of instrumental reasoning, its premise and conclusion, but they agree that it is a form of sound deliberation in which all minimally rational agents can engage.

We are one step away from Internalism about Reasons. The conclusion so far is that *some* reasons satisfy the internalist constraint: they connect with capacities possessed by anyone subject to reasons at all. For the internalist, *all* reasons satisfy this constraint. Why believe this stronger claim? Why not a hybrid view, on which some reasons are bound to capacities definitive of agency, while some are not? The need to respond to this question is vivid at the end of Dreier's paper. Having argued that commitment to M/E is a condition of being subject to practical reasons, he contends that no further commitments are required and concludes that there is "a problem about the justification of morality" (this volume, 144). This inference assumes that reasons always correspond to essential commitments of agency, or that if *some* reasons do so, *all* reasons do. The universality of moral reasons would otherwise be unthreatened by their alleged asymmetry with reasons related to M/E.[36]

There are at least two ways to bridge this gap. The first is to argue piecemeal that other putative reasons correspond to capacities of minimally rational agents. If in doing so we span the territory of plausible reasons, there will be no need to appeal to reasons for which Internalism fails. This is one way to understand the strategy of Nagel's book.[37] Still, we can ask what motivates this project. Why attempt to connect all reasons with capacities of minimally rational agents? Why worry if it can't be done?

Working in the background, I believe, is a more abstract argument, rarely made explicit.[38] This argument rules out the possibility of a hybrid view and makes the step from *some* to *all* intelligible. It can be conceived as a "function argument" in the spirit of Aristotle, though without his more contentious claims. Recall that, for Aristotle, human beings have a defining function or activity, which is the use of reason, and whatever has a function finds its good in performing that function well. There are standard objections. Is it right to speak of a human function? Does the argument conflate what is good *for* an *F* with being good *as* an *F*? Even if they are sound, however, these objections do not undermine the functional use of 'good'.

Excellence: When *F*s have a defining function or activity, a good *F* is one that performs that activity or function well.

If the function of a clock is to tell the time, a good clock is one that does so both legibly and reliably. If the defining activity of a thief is to steal others' property, a good thief is one who gets away with the loot. Whatever its application to humanity, or its relevance to what is good for *F*s, this principle seems true. We can use it to argue as follows. If Nagel and others are right, the propensity for instrumental reasoning is essential to minimally rational agents. Agency is, in the relevant sense, a functional or purposive kind: it is defined by an activity. It follows that being good as an agent is performing this activity well. There is nothing more to the excellence of agency, as such. Assuming that such excellence amounts to ideal rationality, or to sound deliberation—apart, perhaps, from the exclusion of false beliefs—it follows in turn that there is no room for hybrid views. If some reasons are tied to capacities definitive of agency, agency is a functional kind all of whose standards are so aligned.

As an argument for Internalism, this line of thought is not airtight. It assumes a particular structure in the function of agency: not just that agents are defined by an activity—doing things for reasons—but that agency has a target, like means-end coherence, of which it can fall short.[39] It belongs to the nature of agents to be directed by, or tend toward, an aim or ideal that is realized by degree. It is from this structure, in conjunction with Excellence, that we infer what a good agent would be: not just one who acts and reasons well—which is trivial—but one who meets the aim or ideal that is the target of agents, as such. This is the standard of practical rationality.

That agency has a target of the relevant kind—whether means-end coherence or something else—is not beyond dispute.[40] Even if it is true, however, there is a residual gap. We can resist Internalism by denying that the target of agency is fixed by the capacities of minimally rational agents. According to a more flexible alternative, such agents must *approximate* the possession of certain capacities, and the function of agency is set by the capacities we must approximate, not those we actually have. It is the ideal capacities whose target aligns with practical reason, and if one falls short of them, one can be subject to reasons by which one is incapable of being moved.

In "The Explanatory Role of Being Rational," Michael Smith defends a view of just this kind.[41] He argues that, in order to act for reasons, we must be minimally capable of putting means to ends. When one acts intentionally, however, one does not manifest only this minimal power. Instead, one manifests the capacity for means-end coherence to whatever degree one has it (Smith 2009, 67–72). It belongs to the nature of agency to approximate full means-end coherence, which is thus a dimension of ideal rationality (Smith 2009, 73). Further standards may apply to the causation of belief and desire (Smith 2009, 73–79). Smith's broader picture is made explicit in "Beyond the Error Theory" in terms that resonate with those above (this volume, 309–311). The standards of practical reason conform to Excellence, with the sense of "function" that of functionalism in the philosophy of mind. Mental states are functional kinds defined by roles that must be realized by their instances, at least to some degree; these roles are at the same time measures of ideal rationality.[42]

A similar approach is taken by Ralph Wedgwood, without the reductive ambitions of standard functionalism. For Wedgwood, it is "constitutive of mentality [that] thinkers have a disposition to conform to the basic requirements of rationality that apply to them" (Wedgwood 2007, 27). This follows from his account of concept- and attitude-possession (Wedgwood 2007, chap. 7). Wedgwood's picture looks in one way stronger than Smith's, in one way weaker. It looks weaker in that it speaks only to "basic" requirements of rationality. It looks stronger in that it requires the full possession of relevant dispositions. In both respects, however, the simple formulation is misleading. Wedgwood insists that basic rational dispositions are defeasible and that in having them one must be sensitive to defeating conditions (Wedgwood 2007, 169–171). Since any reason might play a defeating role, basic rationality involves the disposition to respond to reasons in general. He also qualifies the need for rational dispositions in the constitution of agency and thought.

In saying that possessing [a] concept requires having a disposition to use the concept in a certain basically rational way, I need not claim that this disposition must be *perfectly* rational; I need only claim that this disposition must to a greater or lesser degree *approximate* to such perfect rationality. (Wedgwood 2007, 171)[43]

We end up with another version of the claim that agency has an implicit function: it tends to conform to the requirements of ideal rationality, and so to be responsive to reasons except in the case of false belief.

What these theories share with Internalism is a picture of agency as a functional kind defined by a target: an aim or ideal to which it is directed, or to which it tends approximately to conform. From this picture, we extract the standards of agency by the application of Excellence; and we think of practical rationality as the excellence of agency, as such. This more inclusive view might be labeled *Ethical Rationalism*, with Internalism about Reasons a specially uncompromising form.[44]

Along with the question of Internalism, ethical rationalists differ on the content of practical reason. For some—like Dreier and Williams, respectively—it is narrowly or broadly instrumental.[45] Instrumentalism lends itself to the psychological reduction of normative reasons. But Rationalism does not require it. Along with Wedgwood's non-reductive view, there is the form of Internalism on which it is a condition of agency to act "under the guise of the good" or to be disposed to do so, where reasons consist in irreducible evaluative facts.[46] Other forms of Rationalism are neither instrumentalist nor committed to irreducibility. For neo-Kantians like Korsgaard and Velleman, agency is more than instrumental, its standards reaching beyond means-end coherence perhaps as far as the content of morality.[47]

In "Why Is Instrumental Rationality Rational?" Troy Jollimore objects to Rationalism in its instrumentalist form. For Jollimore, instrumental failure is distinctive, since it offends against a principle we must accept if we act for reasons at all (this volume, 151–152). But practical reason is not generally so constrained. In arguing for these claims, he draws in part on a comparison: the epistemological contrast between principles of logic and standards of evidence (this volume, chap. 7, §III). It is irrational to violate the former, since in doing so one offends against requirements any thinker must accept. It does not follow that there are no further principles of theoretical reason, ones to which we should conform, but which possible thinkers may ignore. If this holds in epistemology, why not also in the practical sphere?

Although its explicit target is narrow, Jollimore's argument does not turn on the specifics of instrumentalism. It suggests that while some requirements are special, in that we must accept them or be disposed to follow them, simply because we are agents or thinkers, it is a mistake to infer that these requirements exhaust the content of practical or theoretical reason. Perhaps we can even explain the special requirements, and their distinctive character, in terms of requirements to which Rationalism does not apply. This is Jollimore's approach, drawing on a potentially vexed distinction between "objective" and "subjective" reasons. Even if his explanation is wrong, however, the challenge remains. We can press the ethical rationalist to defend a corresponding rationalism in epistemology, despite the apparent possibility of the pervasively evidence-insensitive, or to explain why practical and theoretical reason are not to be treated alike.[48]

One weakness of this challenge is that, even if it is persuasive—which is very much in dispute—it does not tell us where the argument for Rationalism goes wrong. Is it a mistake to suppose that agency has a target, an aim or ideal that it tends to realize? That the principle of Excellence is true? That standards of practical reason are standards for agency, as such? These questions deserve more sustained attention than they have so far received.

A final source of Internalism and Rationalism lies in concerns about the metaphysics and epistemology of normative reasons. Smith's exploration and defense of Ethical Rationalism in "Beyond the Error Theory" turns on hostility to "Moorean non-natural qualities." On Parfit's reading, Williams's argument for the Internal Reasons Theory takes a similar form. Parfit cites passages in which Williams complains about the obscurity of external reasons (this volume, 358–359).

What is it that one comes to believe when he comes to believe that there is reason for him to φ if it is not the proposition, or something that entails the proposition, that if he deliberated rationally, he would be motivated to act appropriately? (This volume, 45)

I do not believe . . . that the sense of external reason statements is in the least clear. (Williams 1995, 40)

On this interpretation, the principal virtue of the Internal Reasons Theory is that it promises an "analytic reduction" of claims about what there is reason to do: the meaning of these claims can be captured in non-normative psychological terms.

At the same time, Parfit sees that the relationship between Internalism and reductionism is not straightforward. There is room for "Non-Reductive Internalism," while "[some] Externalists hold analytically reductive views" (this volume, 350, 360). Parfit's terminology does not map neatly on to ours. His "externalists" agree that "if we knew the relevant facts and were fully rational, we would be motivated to do whatever we had reason to do" (this volume, 345). They differ from his "internalists" in appealing to requirements of "substantive" and not just "procedural" rationality.

To be substantively rational, we must care about certain things, such as our own well-being. . . . To be procedurally rational, we must deliberate in certain ways, but we are not required to have any particular desires or aims. (This volume, 345)

Parfit's distinction is obscure. If procedural rationality is understood in broadly instrumental terms, Parfit's "internalism" is close to the Internal Reasons Theory and is not shared by neo-Kantian internalists like Nagel and Korsgaard. This definition is too narrow. If, on the other hand, procedural rationality is not tied to the subjective motivational set, what rules out a procedural requirement of being moved by facts about our own wellbeing, or that of others? In which case, Parfit's "internalism" does not sufficiently constrain the content of reasons to act. Whatever we make of this dilemma, Parfit's insight about reductionism applies as well to Internalism and Ethical Rationalism. As we saw above, such claims do not imply the reducibility of reasons or values. And reductive views, analytic or otherwise, need not take internalist or rationalist forms.

This makes for an apparent puzzle. How do concerns about irreducible normativity favor reductive versions of Rationalism and Internalism over other reductive views? One answer is that they do not: there are independent pressures toward Rationalism and reductionism; these pressures merely converge. But there may be more to say. In objecting to all forms of reductionism, Parfit contends that "normative [and] natural facts . . . are as different as the chairs and propositions that, in a dream, Moore once confused" (this volume, 361).

> It may seem that, by appealing to claims about normative concepts, we could at most refute analytical naturalism. . . . That, I believe, is not so. Reductive views can be both non-analytical and true when, and because, the relevant concepts leave open certain possibilities, between which we must choose on non-conceptual grounds. But many other possibilities are conceptually excluded. Thus it was conceptually possible that heat should turn out to be molecular kinetic energy. But heat could not have turned out to be a shade of blue, or a medieval king. . . . Similar claims apply, I believe, to Reductive Internalism, and to all other forms of naturalism. (This volume, 361)

Parfit's argument here is dialectically unimpressive, since it begs the question against reductionists. But it may nonetheless be sound: Parfit is surely right that we sometimes know a priori, in whatever way we know the truths called 'analytic', that being F is not the same as being G. For reductionists, part of the appeal of Ethical Rationalism is in helping to defuse such a priori skepticism. The reductionist will contend, first, that reductive naturalism is not ruled out by the meaning of 'good F' where Fs have a defining function or activity. We do not need "Moorean non-natural qualities" in order to make sense of good thieves, good thermometers, and good roots.[49] He then insists that agency, too, is a functional kind, and that standards of practical reason are standards for agency, as such. It is the application of Excellence to agency that makes room for reductionism about reasons.

If this is what pushes us toward reductive Rationalism, we may be led elsewhere: to the Aristotelian naturalism of Philippa Foot. In "Rationality and Virtue," she too assimilates acting well to the pattern of Excellence, but she takes the function or activity that bears on human agency to be "the way of life of the species" (this volume, 333). Like other animals, we have characteristic parts and operations, and these parts and operations are good, as such, so far as they perform their function in our lives. Such assessment is no more mysterious than the assessment of good roots in an oak tree, or good eyesight in an owl. In each case, the standards are fixed by what the members of a species need (this volume, 333–335). The same conceptual structure can be applied to practical reasoning, or agency, as an operation in the life of human beings. It, too, can be assessed as good of its kind by the extent to which it plays its role in our lives, meeting our distinctive human needs (this volume, 335–337). The standards that emerge from this assessment are standards of good practical reasoning, or practical rationality, and thus of what there is reason to do. It is a further claim, which Foot finds plausible, that the traditional virtues of character can be vindicated, in terms of human need, as forms of excellence in responding to practical reasons. As she contends, "the teaching and observing of rules of justice is as necessary a part of human life as hunting together in packs with a leader is a necessary part of the lives of wolves, or dancing part of the life of the dancing bee" (this volume, 336).

Foot develops her account more fully in other work.[50] But even this sketch reveals that one can share the broad metaphysical picture of Rationalism, on which the standards of agency and thus of practical reason are understood through Excellence, without accepting that these standards are fixed by the nature of agency alone—regardless of the form of life in which that agency embeds—and without accepting Internalism about Reasons. Foot's rejection of Internalism appears in her discussion of the "shameless individual" who has no motive for acting justly when it does not benefit him to do so. Although there is "no way in which we can touch his life," since he cannot be moved by the facts to which justice appeals, those facts still count as reasons for him to act (this volume, 338).[51]

Along with the metaphysics of Excellence and doubts about "Moorean non-natural qualities," we find more directly epistemological arguments for Internalism and Ethical Rationalism. In "The Possibility of Practical Reason," Velleman complains that the externalist "must at some point provide practical reasoning with a substantive standard of success" and "will then have to justify his normative judgment that an agent ought to be swayed by consideration of the specified features"; Velleman doubts that this can be done (this volume, 255). That practical reasoning should achieve its "formal object"—performing "the privileged action," the one that satisfies the standards of practical reason—is true but uninformative. We need to specify the object in question. The problem is that, in doing so, we make a substantive judgment. This judgment can be questioned; and where a normative judgment can be questioned, a justification is required.[52] Velleman cannot see how the externalist can meet this demand. He does not support his normative judgments empirically. Nor are they plausibly seen as analytic truths (this volume, 255). And so their epistemic basis is obscure.

In responding to Velleman, Philip Clark objects to the inference from an object's being substantive rather than formal to its being a specification of particular, non-normative properties (this volume, 291–297). The object of an activity can be described in terms that are at once substantive and generic. Even if this is right, however, rejecting Velleman's inference is not enough. That practical reasoning aims at the good may be a substantive truth not open to epistemological challenge.[53] But as Velleman insists in a similar context, it cannot be applied to action without a criterion of the good, and "this criterion will once again require justification" (this volume, 252). The demand for justification can be directed at any evaluative claim, at claims about the good no less than claims about practical reason. To show that one provides a standard for the other is not to show how this demand can finally be met.

More troubling is that Velleman's skepticism about externalist judgments draws on a questionable epistemology. What Velleman finds problematic are normative beliefs that are not self-evident, lack empirical support, and cannot be derived from the analysis of normative concepts. It is not obvious, however, that internalists avoid such beliefs. Are their claims about agency and practical reason self-evident or analytic truths? What is the epistemic status of Excellence? Meanwhile, most externalists allow for justified beliefs whose contents are neither empirical nor analytic, and will protest that Velleman begs the question. They may go further, arguing that beliefs of this kind appear in normative epistemology: empirical science cannot do without them.[54]

There is room for a milder version of Velleman's concern, which could be framed constructively. Ethical Rationalism draws a connection between the facts about reasons and how we respond to them that might explain how the correlative beliefs can be non-accidentally true. This holds for non-reductive Rationalism as well as for reductive forms.[55] Can this possibility be explained in other ways? By Foot's appeal to human nature and human need as standards of practical reason? By Parfit's resolutely non-reductive, non-naturalist, and non-rationalist view?

These questions take us from the philosophy of practical reason and the action-theoretic foundations of Internalism to some of the deepest and most troubling issues in the epistemology of normative thought. In doing so, they lead beyond the remit of this book. The dispute about Internalism and Ethical Rationalism is not in the end extricable from disputes about the metaphysics of normativity and the nature and possibility of non-empirical knowledge. What we gain from the present approach is not a way to avoid these problems, but a source of potential constraints on their solution that attends to the peculiarities of practical reason. Thinking about Internalism is a way to connect one of the most immediately gripping questions of ethics—"Why be moral?"—with questions of agency and epistemology that are more difficult to access but no less profound.

Acknowledgments

For help in writing this introduction, I am grateful to Marah Gubar, Simon Keller, Jessica Moss, Evgenia Mylonaki, Karl Schafer, Nishi Shah, James Shaw, Robert Steel, Joshua Stuchlik, to participants in my spring 2010 seminar on reasons for action at the University of Pittsburgh, and especially to Hille Paakkunainen.

Notes

1. Cooper 1997, 999, 358a; translation by G. A. Grube and C. D. C. Reeve. Henceforth cited in the text.

2. For psychological theories, see Davidson 1980a, Smith 1987; for anti-psychologism, Dancy 2000.

3. This objection is made, to Williams and others, in Setiya 2010; it is related to issues in action theory that collect around the question whether we act intentionally "under the guise of the good."

4. For this concession, see Williams 1995, 35.

5. Even Williams may prefer this definition; see Williams 1995, 35–37, discussed in the text below.

6. In Aristotelian terms, the capacity is a matter of second potentiality, not first. We return to the nature of capacities and to the logical strength of capacity claims, below.

Introduction

7. Williams's expression of this point is slightly odd. He writes that the agent who believes that some consideration is a reason "appears to be one about whom, now, an *internal* reason statement could truly be made: he is one with an appropriate motivation in his *S*" (this volume, 43). But he cautions that "it does not follow from this that there is nothing in external reason statements" (this volume, 43). It would be more perspicuous to say: it does not follow from this that external reasons meet the explanatory constraint, or that the distinction between internal and external reasons is undermined.

8. As it is explicitly in Williams's "Reply to McDowell" (this volume, chap. 4).

9. Nagel's position on the universality of prudential and altruistic reasons is more circumspect. He does not assert that the motivational capacities that make us susceptible to such reasons are essential to agency; but "if we were not so constituted, we should be unrecognizably different, and that may be enough for the purpose of the argument" (Nagel 1970, 19).

10. In both respects, she echoes Nagel 1970, 7–8. The distinction between judgment and existence internalism exploited here is due to Darwall 1983, 54.

11. For this reading of Korsgaard, and the corresponding objection, see Parfit's essay in this volume, 350. The weak version of Qualified Internalism is sometimes attributed to Williams, whose argument for the Internal Reasons Theory then looks question-begging; see Hooker 1987.

12. White's view is developed in Setiya 2004, which connects the appeal to irrationality with Internalism about Reasons—though its terminology is different. See also Pettit and Smith 2006, 153–157; Setiya 2007, 96 n. 34.

13. Scanlon finds this mistake in Foot's (1972) argument against the universality of moral reasons (Scanlon 1998, 28–29). (Foot has since revised her view; see Foot 2001, 13–14.) More generally, Troy Jollimore contends that a focus on irrationality gives false appeal to instrumentalism (this volume, chap. 7). For recent discussions that lean on the special connotations of "irrationality," see Wedgwood 2003, 214–215; Svavarsdóttir 2006, 63–64.

14. On the role of interference, see Korsgaard in this volume, 71 n. 9. Along with the passages cited above, the reading of Korsgaard as unqualified internalist makes sense of her partial agreement with Williams in chap. 2, §VI and her invocation of Nagel in chap. 2, §VII. Korsgaard's commitment to Internalism is explicit in her second essay in this volume, chap. 10.

15. The terminology derives from Johnston 1992, 233.

16. A canonical version appears in Lewis 1997.

17. For powerful objections, see Bird 1998; Fara 2005. The defects of subjunctive analyses are related to the so-called conditional fallacy (Shope 1978).

18. Though Velleman recognizes that Korsgaard is not herself an externalist, and that, in structure at least, her view is very close to his; see this volume, chap. 11, nn. 14, 32, citing Korsgaard, this volume, chap. 10.

19. A point much emphasized by Dancy (2000).

20. See, for instance, Parfit, "Reasons and Motivation" (this volume, 369–370 n. 28).

21. Joseph Raz defends a "classical approach" to agency on which "intentional action is action done for a reason; and . . . reasons are facts in virtue of which those actions are good in some respect and to some degree" (Raz 1999b, 23). See also Dancy 2000, 9: "to explain an action is . . . to show that it would have been [what there was most reason to do] if the agent's beliefs had been true." Dancy later calls this "a regulative ideal for the explanation of action" (Dancy 2000, 95). McDowell makes a related claim, about approximate rationality in reasons-explanation (McDowell 1998, 328).

22. This position is shared by many. See Williams in this volume, 40, 43; Darwall 1983, 205; Bond 1983, 30–31; Velleman 2000a, 140–142; Korsgaard in this volume, 206; Broome 1997; Raz 1999a, 8; Dancy 2000, 97.

23. Setiya 2007, 30–31; Setiya 2010, 92.

24. At least, he notes this feature of Williams's view and does not question it (this volume, 74–77).

25. For similar arguments, see Hubin 1996; Johnson 1999, §III; and Sobel 2001; an ancestor is Shope 1978.

26. Thus it does not capture the dimension of possible explanation, as Williams intends it. For this point, see Johnson 1999 and Sobel 2001. (A further remark on terminology: Johnson uses "internalism" in roughly the same way as Smith, for the general idea of a connection between reasons and ideally rational desire; Sobel restricts "internalism" to versions of the example model, contrasting it with the "ideal advisor account.") In a later discussion, written with Philip Pettit, Smith sees that the advice model does not imply Internalism and treats this as a separate element of Williams's view (Pettit and Smith 2006, 149–150).

27. See also Scanlon 1998, 73–74, on the universality of reason judgments.

28. This can be hard to make out. After all, if the circumstance includes psychological facts about the agent in question, we are bound to want the same things when our circumstances are the same. This is, however, irrelevant to the advice model, which asks for the desires we would have, if we were fully rational, *about* our behavior in C, not what desires we would have in C itself. Suppose, for instance, that sound deliberation is narrowly instrumental, just a matter of putting means to ends; and suppose that A is altruistic, desiring happiness for all, while B is utterly selfish. If A were fully rational, what desires would he have about his behavior in

the unfortunate circumstance in which he becomes like B? To answer this question, imagine that A meets standards of sound instrumental reasoning but is otherwise unchanged. Being altruistic, he wishes even those without altruistic desires would act in ways that benefit others. That is what he wants himself to do in the circumstance described. In contrast, if B met standards of sound instrumental reasoning, he would want himself to act only to benefit himself. Smith predicts a similar divergence even on Williams's richer and more flexible account.

29. Pettit and Smith (2006, 147–148) defend this reading explicitly. For objections to this and other aspects of their approach, see McDowell 2006.

30. This is a simplified version of the principle called '*Reasons*' in Setiya 2007, 9–14. The idea of reasons as premises of sound deliberation is shared with Raz 1978, 5, 15, though he goes on to identify the conclusion of practical reasoning with a deontic proposition—that one ought to ϕ relative to these considerations, or that there is a reason to ϕ—not intention or desire.

31. Nagel's own remarks on this topic are flawed (see Wallace 1990, 362–363). Nagel implies that when a desire is motivated, it is "*arrived at* by decision and after deliberation," which suggests more reflection than is required in wanting something for a reason (this volume, 197). Nor should we assume, with Nagel, that unmotivated desires "simply assail us . . . like the appetites and in certain cases the emotions" (this volume, 197). Unmotivated desires need not be momentary passions. Despite these defects of exposition, Nagel is right to contrast desires that are had for reasons with those that are not.

32. See Wallace 1990, 373–374. Smith seems to argue for the more ambitious Humean theory (Smith 1987, 58–60), but in a later paper he clarifies his view. While he allows that "beliefs can rationally explain desires" without the help of prior desires, he denies that such beliefs are rightly called 'motives', because the explanations in which they figure are not teleological (Smith 1988, §III). For a recent attempt to rehabilitate ambitious Humeanism, see Lenman 1996.

33. Davidson 1980a,c.

34. For related claims about reasons-explanation, see McDowell 1998, 328; Korsgaard in this volume, 220–222; Raz 1999b: 22–24; Dancy 2000, 9–10, 95–97, 106; and for doubts about this principle, Setiya 2010.

35. It is a difficult question how this claim about M/E relates to the earlier phase of Dreier's argument (this volume, 138–140). He begins by noting a different property of M/E, that if one does not accept it, one cannot be brought to do so by the provision of new desires. This property is, he claims, unique. Even if we grant this, however, why infer that one must accept M/E in order to act for reasons at all? Dreier takes this up at the end of his essay, arguing on independent grounds that there is no adequate alternative to M/E (this volume, 143–144). Maybe so; but we

are left with doubts about the point of the earlier moves. These issues are addressed in unpublished work by Hille Paakkunainen.

36. As Troy Jollimore, in effect, complains (this volume, chap. 7).

37. See also Korsgaard (this volume, 230–231) on the interdependence of hypothetical and categorical imperatives. In later work, Nagel rejects or qualifies his early view (Nagel 1986, 1997). Even in *The Possibility of Altruism*, he is concerned with principles by which reasons generalize, less with the original source of reasons themselves. His theory may not be internalist through and through.

38. A partial exception is Korsgaard 2009, though she embraces more of the Aristotelian view than the argument strictly requires.

39. See Clark's objection to Velleman: even if Velleman is right about the constitutive aim of action, as autonomy, this aim cannot supply the standard of practical reason, since "every fully intentional action is autonomous," and we need to make sense of "intentional action [that] is contrary to the weight of reasons" (this volume, 287–289). Elsewhere, Velleman takes a different view, that intentional action aims at self-knowledge, of which one can have more or less (Velleman 1989, 2000b: 1–31). For objections, see Bratman 1991; Setiya 2007, 107–114.

40. For arguments against this claim, see *Reasons without Rationalism* (Setiya 2007).

41. See also Dreier in this volume, 135–137, 143–144.

42. For Smith, it is an open question whether there is more to practical reason, and to the functional roles of belief and desire, than instrumentalists suppose. In this respect, and in its teleological framework, Smith's argument can be compared with that of Mark van Roojen (1995).

43. Compare Davidson 1980b on the constitutive role of rationality in the mind.

44. This is the terminology of Setiya 2007.

45. For objections to instrumentalism and the Internal Reasons Theory, see Quinn 1992 and this volume, chap. 8; Korsgaard in this volume, chap. 10; and Setiya 2005.

46. See Railton 1997 on the "High Brow" view.

47. See Korsgaard 1996, lectures 3 and 4; Korsgaard 2009, chap. 9; and Velleman 2009.

48. There are steps toward epistemological rationalism in Velleman's theory of belief (this volume, 257–262; see also Railton 1997, §1). Since belief aims at truth, he argues, reasons for belief are "indicators of truth": the "constitutive aim" approach can be applied. The problem is that, while this theory may exclude some forms of belief revision as irrational, it cannot explain the detailed standards of "indication" or epistemic probability.

49. See, for instance, Smith in this volume, 309–311.

50. Foot 2001, drawing on the metaphysics of Thompson 1995. See also Hursthouse 1999; Quinn 1992 and in this volume, chap. 8, esp. §IV.

51. Quinn is also an externalist; see this volume, 186.

52. A similar demand is placed on practical justification in Korsgaard's book, *The Sources of Normativity* (1996).

53. Velleman would not agree; see this volume, 265.

54. This is in the spirit of McDowell (chap. 3, §6) and Jollimore (chap. 7, §III) in the present volume.

55. See Wedgwood 2007, chap. 10.

References

Bird, A. 1998. Dispositions and antidotes. *Philosophical Quarterly* 48:227–234.

Bond, E. J. 1983. *Reason and Value*. Cambridge: Cambridge University Press.

Bratman, M. 1991. Cognitivism about practical reason. *Ethics* 102:117–128.

Broome, J. 1997. Reasons and motivation. *Proceedings of the Aristotelian Society, Supplementary Volume* 71:131–146.

Cooper, J. 1997. *Plato: Complete Works*. Indianapolis: Hackett Publishing.

Dancy, J. 2000. *Practical Reality*. Oxford: Oxford University Press.

Darwall, S. 1983. *Impartial Reason*. Ithaca, NY: Cornell University Press.

Davidson, D. 1980a. Actions, reasons, and causes. In D. Davidson, *Essays on Actions and Events*. Oxford: Oxford University Press. Originally published 1963.

Davidson, D. 1980b. Mental events. In D. Davidson, *Essays on Actions and Events*. Oxford: Oxford University Press. Originally published 1970.

Davidson, D. 1980c. Freedom to act. In D. Davidson, *Essays on Actions and Events*. Oxford: Oxford University Press. Originally published 1973.

Fara, M. 2005. Dispositions and habituals. *Noûs* 38:43–82.

Foot, P. 2001. *Natural Goodness*. Oxford: Oxford University Press.

Foot, P. 2002. Reasons for action and desires. Reprinted with postscript in P. Foot, *Virtues and Vices*. Oxford: Oxford University Press. Originally published 1972.

Hooker, B. 1987. Williams' argument against external reasons. *Analysis* 47:42–44.

Hubin, D. C. 1996. Hypothetical motivation. *Noûs* 30:31–54.

Hursthouse, R. 1999. *On Virtue Ethics*. Oxford: Oxford University Press.

Johnson, R. 1999. Internal reasons and the conditional fallacy. *Philosophical Quarterly* 49:53–71.

Johnston, M. 1992. How to speak of the colors. *Philosophical Studies* 68:221–263.

Korsgaard, C. 1996. *The Sources of Normativity*. Cambridge: Cambridge University Press.

Korsgaard, C. 2009. *Self-Constitution*. Oxford: Oxford University Press.

Lenman, J. 1996. Belief, desire and motivation: an essay in quasi-hydraulics. *American Philosophical Quarterly* 33:291–301.

Lewis, D. K. 1997. Finkish dispositions. *Philosophical Quarterly* 47:143–158.

McDowell, J. 1998. Functionalism and anomalous monism. Reprinted in J. McDowell, *Mind, Value, and Reality*. Cambridge, MA: Harvard University Press. Originally published 1985.

McDowell, J. 2006. Response to Pettit and Smith. In *McDowell and His Critics*, ed. C. Macdonald and G. Macdonald. Oxford: Blackwell.

Nagel, T. 1970. *The Possibility of Altruism*. Princeton: Princeton University Press.

Nagel, T. 1986. *The View from Nowhere*. Oxford: Oxford University Press.

Nagel, T. 1997. *The Last Word*. Oxford: Oxford University Press.

Pettit, P., and M. Smith. 2006. External reasons. In *McDowell and His Critics*, ed. C. Macdonald and G. Macdonald. Oxford: Blackwell.

Quinn, W. 1992. Rationality and the human good. In W. Quinn, *Morality and Action*. Cambridge: Cambridge University Press.

Railton, P. 1997. On the hypothetical and non-hypothetical in reasoning about belief and action. In *Ethics and Practical Reason*, ed. G. Cullity and B. Gaut. Oxford: Oxford University Press.

Raz, J. 1978. Introduction. In *Practical Reasoning*, ed. J. Raz. Oxford: Oxford University Press.

Raz, J. 1999a. When we are ourselves: the active and the passive. In J. Raz, *Engaging Reason*. Oxford: Oxford University Press.

Raz, J. 1999b. Agency, reason, and the good. In J. Raz, *Engaging Reason*. Oxford: Oxford University Press.

Scanlon, T. M. 1998. *What We Owe to Each Other*. Cambridge, MA: Harvard University Press.

Setiya, K. 2004. Against internalism. *Noûs* 38:266–298.

Setiya, K. 2005. Is efficiency a vice? *American Philosophical Quarterly* 42:333–339.

Setiya, K. 2007. *Reasons without Rationalism*. Princeton: Princeton University Press.

Setiya, K. 2010. Sympathy for the devil. In *Desire, Practical Reason, and the Good*, ed. S. Tenenbaum. Oxford: Oxford University Press.

Shope, R. K. 1978. The conditional fallacy in contemporary philosophy. *Journal of Philosophy* 75:397–413.

Smith, M. 1987. The Humean theory of motivation. *Mind* 96:36–61.

Smith, M. 1988. Reason and desire. *Proceedings of the Aristotelian Society* 88:243–258.

Smith, M. 2009. The explanatory role of being rational. In *Reasons for Action*, ed. D. Sobel and S. Wall. Cambridge: Cambridge University Press.

Sobel, D. 2001. Explanation, internalism, and reasons for action. *Social Philosophy & Policy* 18:218–235.

Svavarsdóttir, S. 2006. Evaluations of rationality. In *Metaethics after Moore*, ed. T. Horgan and M. Timmons. Oxford: Oxford University Press.

Thompson, M. 1995. The representation of life. In *Virtues and Reasons*, ed. R. Hursthouse, G. Lawrence, and W. Quinn. Oxford: Oxford University Press.

van Roojen, M. 1995. Humean motivation and Humean rationality. *Philosophical Studies* 79:37–57.

Velleman, J. D. 1989. *Practical Reflection*. Princeton: Princeton University Press.

Velleman, J. D. 2000a. What happens when someone acts? In J. D. Velleman, *The Possibility of Practical Reason*. Oxford: Oxford University Press. Originally published 1992.

Velleman, J. D. 2000b. *The Possibility of Practical Reason*. Oxford: Oxford University Press.

Velleman, J. D. 2009. *How We Get Along*. Cambridge: Cambridge University Press.

Wallace, R. J. 1990. How to argue about practical reason. *Mind* 99:355–385.

Wedgwood, R. 2003. Choosing rationally and choosing correctly. In *Weakness of Will and Practical Irrationality*, ed. S. Stroud and C. Tappolet. Oxford: Oxford University Press.

Wedgwood, R. 2007. *The Nature of Normativity*. Oxford: Oxford University Press.

White, S. 1990. Rationality, responsibility and pathological indifference. In *Identity, Character, and Morality*, ed. O. Flanagan and A. Rorty. Cambridge, MA: MIT Press.

Williams, B. 1995. Internal reasons and the obscurity of blame. Reprinted in B. Williams, *Making Sense of Humanity*. Cambridge: Cambridge University Press. Originally published 1989.

I Williams and His Critics

1 Internal and External Reasons

Bernard Williams

Sentences of the forms 'A has a reason to φ' or 'There is a reason for A to φ' (where 'φ' stands in for some verb of action) seem on the face of it to have two different sorts of interpretation. On the first, the truth of the sentence implies, very roughly, that A has some motive which will be served or furthered by his φ-ing, and if this turns out not to be so the sentence is false: there is a condition relating to the agent's aims, and if this is not satisfied it is not true to say, on this interpretation, that he has a reason to φ. On the second interpretation, there is no such condition, and the reason-sentence will not be falsified by the absence of an appropriate motive. I shall call the first the 'internal', the second the 'external', interpretation. (Given two such interpretations, and the two forms of sentence quoted, it is reasonable to suppose that the first sentence more naturally collects the internal interpretation, and the second the external, but it would be wrong to suggest that either form of words admits only one of the interpretations.)

I shall also for convenience refer sometimes to 'internal reasons' and 'external reasons', as I do in the title, but this is to be taken only as a convenience. It is a matter for investigation whether there are two sorts of reasons for action, as opposed to two sorts of statements about people's reasons for action. Indeed, as we shall eventually see, even the interpretation in one of the cases is problematical.

I shall consider first the internal interpretation, and how far it can be taken. I shall then consider, more sceptically, what might be involved in an external interpretation. I shall end with some very brief remarks connecting all this with the issue of public goods and free-riders.

The simplest model for the internal interpretation would be this: A has a reason to φ iff A has some desire the satisfaction of which will be served by his φ-ing. Alternatively, we might say . . . some desire, the satisfaction of which A believes will be served by his φ-ing; this difference will concern us later. Such a model is sometimes ascribed to Hume, but since in fact Hume's own views are more complex than this, we might call it *the sub-Humean model*. The sub-Humean model is certainly too simple. My aim will be, by addition and revision, to work it up into something more adequate. In the course of trying to do this, I shall assemble four propositions which seem to me to be true of internal reason statements.

Basically, and by definition, any model for the internal interpretation must display a relativity of the reason statement to the agent's *subjective motivational set*, which I shall call the agent's S. The contents of S we shall come to, but we can say:

(i) An internal reason statement is falsified by the absence of some appropriate element from S.

The simplest sub-Humean model claims that any element in S gives rise to an internal reason. But there are grounds for denying this, not because of regrettable, imprudent, or deviant elements in S—they raise different sorts of issues—but because of elements in S based on false belief.

The agent believes that this stuff is gin, when it is in fact petrol. He wants a gin and tonic. Has he reason, or a reason, to mix this stuff with tonic and drink it? There are two ways here (as suggested already by the two alternatives for formulating the sub-Humean model). On the one hand, it is just very odd to say that he has a reason to drink this stuff, and natural to say that he has no reason to drink it, although he thinks that he has. On the other hand, if he does drink it, we not only have an explanation of his doing so (a reason why he did it), but we have such an explanation which is of the reason-for-action form. This explanatory dimension is very important, and we shall come back to it more than once. If there are reasons for action, it must be that people sometimes act for those reasons, and if they do, their reasons must figure in some correct explanation of their action (it does not follow that they must figure in all correct explanations of their action). The difference between false and true beliefs on the agent's part cannot alter the *form* of the explanation which will be appropriate to his action. This consideration might move us to ignore the intuition which we noticed before, and lead us just to legislate that in the case of the agent who wants gin, he has a reason to drink this stuff which is petrol.

I do not think, however, that we should do this. It looks in the wrong direction, by implying in effect that the internal reason conception is only concerned with explanation, and not at all with the agent's rationality, and this may help to motivate a search for other sorts of reason which are connected with his rationality. But the internal reasons conception is concerned with the agent's rationality. What we can correctly ascribe to him in a third-personal internal reason statement is also what he can ascribe to himself as a result of deliberation, as we shall see. So I think that we should rather say:

(ii) A member of S, D, will not give A a reason for φ-ing if either the existence of D is dependent on false belief, or A's belief in the relevance of φ-ing to the satisfaction of D is false.

(This double formulation can be illustrated from the gin/petrol case: D can be taken in the first way as the desire to drink what is in this bottle, and in the second way as the desire to drink gin.) It will, all the same, be true that if he does φ in these circumstances, there was not only a reason why he φ-ed, but also that that displays him as, relative to his false belief, acting rationally.

We can note the epistemic consequence:

(iii) (a) *A* may falsely believe an internal reason statement about himself, and (we can add)

(b) *A* may not know some true internal reason statement about himself.

(b) comes from two different sources. One is that *A* may be ignorant of some fact such that if he did know it he would, in virtue of some element in S, be disposed to φ: we can say that he has a reason to φ, though he does not know it. For it to be the case that he actually has such a reason, however, it seems that the relevance of the unknown fact to his actions has to be fairly close and immediate; otherwise one merely says that *A* would have a reason to φ if he knew the fact. I shall not pursue the question of the conditions for saying the one thing or the other, but it must be closely connected with the question of when the ignorance forms part of the explanation of what *A* actually does.

The second source of (b) is that *A* may be ignorant of some element in S. But we should notice that an unknown element in S, D, will provide a reason for *A* to φ only if φ-ing is rationally related to D; that is to say, roughly, a project to φ could be the answer to a deliberative question formed in part by D. If D is unknown to *A* because it is in the unconscious, it may well not satisfy this condition, although of course it may provide the reason why he φ's, that is, may explain or help to explain his φ-ing. In such cases, the φ-ing may be related to D only symbolically.

I have already said that

(iv) internal reason statements can be discovered in deliberative reasoning.

It is worth remarking the point, already implicit, that an internal reason statement does not apply only to that action which is the uniquely preferred result of the deliberation. '*A* has reason to ɸ' does not mean 'the action which *A* has overall, all-in, reason to do is ɸ-ing'. He can have reason to do a lot of things which he has other and stronger reasons not to do.

The sub-Humean model supposes that ɸ-ing has to be related to some element in *S* as causal means to end (unless, perhaps, it is straightforwardly the carrying out of a desire which is itself that element in *S*). But this is only one case: indeed, the mere discovery that some course of action is the causal means to an end is not in itself a piece of practical reasoning.[1] A clear example of practical reasoning is that leading to the conclusion that one has reason to ɸ because ɸ-ing would be the most convenient, economical, pleasant etc. way of satisfying some element in *S*, and this of course is controlled by other elements in *S*, if not necessarily in a very clear or determinate way. But there are much wider possibilities for deliberation, such as: thinking how the satisfaction of elements in *S* can be combined, e.g. by time-ordering; where there is some irresoluble conflict among the elements of *S*, considering which one attaches most weight to (which, importantly, does not imply that there is some one commodity of which they provide varying amounts); or, again, finding constitutive solutions, such as deciding what would make for an entertaining evening, granted that one wants entertainment.

As a result of such processes an agent can come to see that he has reason to do something which he did not see he had reason to do at all. In this way, the deliberative process can add new actions for which there are internal reasons, just as it can also add new internal reasons for given actions. The deliberative process can also subtract elements from *S*. Reflection may lead the agent to see that some belief is false, and hence to realise that he has in fact no reason to do something he thought he had reason to do. More subtly, he may think he has reason to promote some development because he has not exercised his imagination enough about what it would be like if it came about. In his unaided deliberative reason, or encouraged by the persuasions of others, he may come to have some more concrete sense of what would be involved, and lose his desire for it, just as, positively, the imagination can create new possibilities and new desires.

(These are important possibilities for politics as well as for individual action.)

We should not, then, think of S as statically given. The processes of deliberation can have all sorts of effect on S, and this is a fact which a theory of internal reasons should be very happy to accommodate. So also it should be more liberal than some theorists have been about the possible elements in S. I have discussed S primarily in terms of desires, and this term can be used, formally, for all elements in S. But this terminology may make one forget that S can contain such things as dispositions of evaluation, patterns of emotional reaction, personal loyalties, and various projects, as they may be abstractly called, embodying commitments of the agent. Above all, there is of course no supposition that the desires or projects of an agent have to be egoistic; he will, one hopes, have non-egoistic projects of various kinds, and these equally can provide internal reasons for action.

There is a further question, however, about the contents of S: whether it should be taken, consistently with the general idea of internal reasons, as containing *needs*. It is certainly quite natural to say that A has a reason to pursue X, just on the ground that he needs X, but will this naturally follow in a theory of internal reasons? There is a special problem about this only if it is possible for the agent to be unmotivated to pursue what he needs. I shall not try to discuss here the nature of needs, but I take it that insofar as there are determinately recognisable needs, there can be an agent who lacks any interest in getting what he indeed needs. I take it, further, that that lack of interest can remain after deliberation, and also that it would be wrong to say that such a lack of interest must always rest on false belief. (Insofar as it does rest on false belief, then we can accommodate it under (ii), in the way already discussed.)

If an agent really is uninterested in pursuing what he needs; and this is not the product of false belief; and he could not reach any such motive from motives he has by the kind of deliberative processes we have discussed; then I think we do have to say that in the internal sense he indeed has no reason to pursue these things. In saying this, however, we have to bear in mind how strong these assumptions are, and how seldom we are likely to think that we know them to be true. When we say that a person has reason to take medicine which he needs, although he consistently and persuasively denies any interest in preserving his health, we may well still be speaking in the internal sense, with the thought that really at some level he *must* want to be well.

However, if we become clear that we have no such thought, and persist in saying that the person has this reason, then we must be speaking in another sense, and this is the external sense. People do say things that ask to be taken in the external interpretation. In James' story of Owen Wingrave, from which Britten made an opera, Owen's father urges on him the necessity and importance of his joining the army, since all his male ancestors were soldiers, and family pride requires him to do the same. Owen Wingrave has no motivation to join the army at all, and all his desires lead in another direction: he hates everything about military life and what it means. His father might have expressed himself by saying that *there was a reason for Owen to join the army*. Knowing that there was nothing in Owen's S which would lead, through deliberative reasoning, to his doing this would not make him withdraw the claim or admit that he made it under a misapprehension. He means it in an external sense. What is that sense?

A preliminary point is that this is not the same question as that of the status of a supposed categorical imperative, in the Kantian sense of an 'ought' which applies to an agent independently of what the agent happens to want: or rather, it is not undoubtedly the same question. First, a categorical imperative has often been taken, as by Kant, to be necessarily an imperative of morality, but external reason statements do not necessarily relate to morality. Second, it remains an obscure issue what the relation is between 'there is a reason for A to . . .' and 'A ought to . . .' Some philosophers take them to be equivalent, and under that view the question of external reasons of course comes much closer to the question of a categorical imperative. However, I shall not make any assumption about such an equivalence, and shall not further discuss 'ought'.[2]

In considering what an external reason statement might mean, we have to remember again the dimension of possible explanation, a consideration which applies to any reason for action. If something can be a reason for action, then it could be someone's reason for acting on a particular occasion, and it would then figure in an explanation of that action. Now no external reason statement could *by itself* offer an explanation of anyone's action. Even if it were true (whatever that might turn out to mean) that there was a reason for Owen to join the army, that fact by itself would never explain anything that Owen did, not even his joining the army. For if it was true at all, it was true when Owen was not motivated to join the army. The whole point of external reason statements is that they can be true independently of the agent's motivations. But nothing can explain an agent's (intentional) actions except something that motivates him so to act. So something else is needed besides the truth of the external reason statement to explain action, some psychological link; and that psychological link would seem to be belief. *A*'s believing an external reason statement about himself may help to explain his action.

External reason statements have been introduced merely in the general form 'there is a reason for *A* to . . .', but we now need to go beyond that form, to specific statements of reasons. No doubt there are some cases of an agent's ϕ-ing because he believes that there is a reason for him to ϕ, while he does not have any belief about what that reason is. They would be cases of his relying on some authority whom he trusts, or, again, of his recalling that he did know of some reason for his ϕ-ing, but his not being able to remember what it was. In these respects, reasons for action are like reasons for belief. But, as with reasons for belief, they are evidently secondary cases. The basic case must be that in which *A* ϕ's, not because he believes only that there is some reason or other for him to ϕ, but because he believes of some determinate consideration that it constitutes a reason for him to ϕ. Thus Owen Wingrave might come to join the army because (now) he believes that it is a reason for him to do so that his family has a tradition of military honour.

Does believing that a particular consideration is a reason to act in a particular way provide, or indeed constitute, a motivation to act? If it does not, then we are no further on. Let us grant that it does—this claim indeed seems plausible, so long at least as the connexion between such beliefs and the disposition to act is not tightened to that unnecessary degree which excludes *akrasia*. The claim is in fact *so* plausible, that this agent, with this belief, appears to be one about whom, now, an *internal* reason statement could truly be made: he is one with an appropriate motivation in his *S*. A man who does believe that considerations of family honour constitute reasons for action is a man with a certain disposition to action, and also dispositions of approval, sentiment, emotional reaction, and so forth.

Now it does not follow from this that there is nothing in external reason statements. What does follow is that their content is not going to be revealed by considering merely the state of one who believes such a statement, nor how that state explains action, for that state is merely the state with regard to which an internal reason statement could truly be made. Rather, the content of the external type of statement will have to be revealed by considering what it is to *come to believe* such a statement—it is there, if at all, that their peculiarity will have to emerge.

We will take the case (we have implicitly been doing so already) in which an external reason statement is made about someone who, like

Owen Wingrave, is not already motivated in the required way, and so is someone about whom an internal statement could not also be truly made. (Since the difference between external and internal statements turns on the implications accepted by the speaker, external statements can of course be made about agents who are already motivated; but that is not the interesting case.) The agent does not presently believe the external statement. If he comes to believe it, he will be motivated to act; so coming to believe it must, essentially, involve acquiring a new motivation. How can that be?

This is closely related to an old question, of how "reason can give rise to a motivation," a question which has famously received from Hume a negative answer. But in that form, the question is itself unclear, and is unclearly related to the argument—for of course reason, that is to say, rational processes, can give rise to new motivations, as we have seen in the account of deliberation. Moreover, the traditional way of putting the issue also (I shall suggest) picks up an onus of proof about what is to count as a "purely rational process" which not only should it not pick up, but which properly belongs with the critic who wants to oppose Hume's general conclusion and to make a lot out of external reason statements—someone I shall call the 'external reasons theorist'.

The basic point lies in recognising that the external reasons theorist must conceive *in a special way* the connexion between acquiring a motivation and coming to believe the reason statement. For of course there are various means by which the agent could come to have the motivation and also to believe the reason statement, but which are the wrong kind of means to interest the external reasons theorist. Owen might be so persuaded by his father's moving rhetoric that he acquired both the motivation and the belief. But this excludes an element which the external reasons theorist essentially wants, that the agent should acquire the motivation *because* he comes to believe the reason statement, and that he should do the latter, moreover, because, in some way, he is considering the matter aright. If the theorist is to hold on to these conditions, he will, I think, have to make the condition under which the agent appropriately comes to have the motivation something like this, that he should deliberate correctly; and the external reasons statement itself will have to be taken as roughly equivalent to, or at least as entailing, the claim that if the agent rationally deliberated, then, whatever motivations he originally had, he would come to be motivated to φ.

But if this is correct, there does indeed seem great force in Hume's basic point, and it is very plausible to suppose that all external reason statements are false. For, *ex hypothesi*, there is no motivation for the agent to deliberate *from*, to reach this new motivation. Given the agent's earlier existing motivations, and this new motivation, what has to hold for external reason statements to be true, on this line of interpretation, is that the new motivation could be in some way rationally arrived at, granted the earlier motivations. Yet at the same time it must not bear to the earlier motivations the kind of rational relation which we considered in the earlier discussion of deliberation—for in that case an internal reason statement would have been true in the first place. I see no reason to suppose that these conditions could possibly be met.

It might be said that the force of an external reason statement can be explained in the following way. Such a statement implies that a rational agent would be motivated to act appropriately, and it can carry this implication, because a rational agent is precisely one who has a general disposition in his S to do what (he believes) there is reason for him to do. So when he comes to believe that there is reason for him to φ, he is motivated to φ, even though, before, he neither had a motive to φ, nor any motive related to φ-ing in one of the ways considered in the account of deliberation.

But this reply merely puts off the problem. It reapplies the desire and belief model (roughly speaking) of explanation to the actions in question, but using a desire and a belief the content of which are in question. *What is it that one comes to believe when he comes to believe that there is reason for him to φ, if it is not the proposition, or something that entails the proposition, that if he deliberated rationally, he would be motivated to act appropriately?* We were asking how any true proposition could have that content; it cannot help, in answering that, to appeal to a supposed desire which is activated by a belief which has that very content.

These arguments about what it is to accept an external reason statement involve some idea of what is possible under the account of deliberation already given, and what is excluded by that account. But here it may be objected that the account of deliberation is very vague, and has for instance allowed the use of the imagination to extend or restrict the contents of the agent's S. But if that is so, then it is unclear what the limits are to what an agent might arrive at by rational deliberation from his existing S.

It *is* unclear, and I regard it as a basically desirable feature of a theory of practical reasoning that it should preserve and account for that unclarity. There is an essential indeterminacy in what can be counted a rational deliberative process. Practical reasoning is a heuristic process, and an imaginative one, and there are no fixed boundaries on the continuum from rational thought to inspiration and conversion. To someone who thinks that reasons for action are basically to be understood in terms of the internal reasons model, this is not a difficulty. There is indeed a vagueness about '*A* has reason to ϕ', in the internal sense, insofar as the deliberative processes which could lead from *A*'s present *S* to his being motivated to ϕ may be more or less ambitiously conceived. But this is no embarrassment to those who take as basic the internal conception of reasons for action. It merely shows that there is a wider range of states, and a less determinate one, than one might have supposed, which can be counted as *A*'s having a reason to ϕ.

It is the external reasons theorist who faces a problem at this point. There are of course many things that a speaker may say to one who is not disposed to ϕ when the speaker thinks that he should be, as that he is inconsiderate, or cruel, or selfish, or imprudent; or that things, and he, would be a lot nicer if he were so motivated. Any of these can be sensible things to say. But one who makes a great deal out of putting the criticism in the form of an external reason statement seems concerned to say that what is particularly wrong with the agent is that he is *irrational*. It is this theorist who particularly needs to make this charge precise: in particular, because he wants any rational agent, as such, to acknowledge the requirement to do the thing in question.

Owen Wingrave's father indeed expressed himself in terms other than 'a reason', but, as we imagined, he could have used the external reasons formulation. This fact itself provides some difficulty for the external reasons theorist. This theorist, who sees the truth of an external reason statement as potentially grounding a charge of irrationality against the agent who ignores it, might well want to say that if Wingrave *père* put his complaints against Owen in this form, he would very probably be claiming something which, in this particular case, was false. What the theorist would have a harder time showing would be that the words *meant* something different as used by Wingrave from what they mean when they are, as he supposes, truly uttered. But what they mean when uttered by Wingrave is almost certainly *not* that rational deliberation would get Owen to be motivated to join the army—which is (very roughly) the meaning or implication we have found for them, if they are to bear the kind of weight such theorists wish to give them.

The sort of considerations offered here strongly suggest to me that external reason statements, when definitely isolated as such, are false, or incoherent, or really something else misleadingly expressed. It is in fact harder to isolate them in people's speech than the introduction of them

Internal and External Reasons

at the beginning of this chapter suggested. Those who use these words often seem, rather, to be entertaining an optimistic internal reason claim, but sometimes the statement is indeed offered as standing definitely outside the agent's S and what he might derive from it in rational deliberation, and then there is, I suggest, a great unclarity about what is meant. Sometimes it is little more than that things would be better if the agent so acted. But the formulation in terms of reasons does have an effect, particularly in its suggestion that the agent is being irrational, and this suggestion, once the basis of an internal reason claim has been clearly laid aside, is bluff. If this is so, the only real claims about reasons for action will be internal claims.

A problem which has been thought to lie very close to the present subject is that of public goods and free riders, which concerns the situation (very roughly) in which each person has egoistic reason to want a certain good provided, but at the same time each has egoistic reason not to take part in providing it. I shall not attempt any discussion of this problem, but it may be helpful, simply in order to make clear my own view of reasons for action and to bring out contrasts with some other views, if I end by setting out a list of questions which bear on the problem, together with the answers that would be given to them by one who thinks (to put it cursorily) that the only rationality of action is the rationality of internal reasons.

1. Can we define notions of rationality which are not purely egoistic?
   Yes.

2. Can we define notions of rationality which are not purely means–end?
   Yes.

3. Can we define a notion of rationality where the action rational for A is in no way relative to A's existing motivations?
   No.

4. Can we show that a person who only has egoistic motivations is irrational in not pursuing non-egoistic ends?
   Not necessarily, though we may be able to in special cases. (The trouble with the egoistic person is not characteristically irrationality.)

Let there be some good, G, and a set of persons, P, such that each member of P has egoistic reason to want G provided, but delivering G requires action C, which involves costs, by each of some proper sub-set of P; and let A be a member of P: then

5. Has A egoistic reason to do C if he is reasonably sure either that too few members of P will do C for G to be provided, or that enough other members of P will do C, so that G will be provided?
   No.

6. Are there any circumstances of this kind in which *A* can have egoistic reason to do *C*?
   Yes, in those cases in which reaching the critical number of those doing *C* is sensitive to his doing *C*, or he has reason to think this.

7. Are there any motivations which would make it rational for A to do C, even though not in the situation just referred to?
   Yes, if he is not purely egoistic: many. For instance, there are expressive motivations—appropriate e.g. in the celebrated voting case.3 There are also motivations which derive from the sense of fairness. This can precisely transcend the dilemma of "either useless or unnecessary," by the form of argument "somebody, but no reason to omit any particular body, so everybody."

8. It is irrational for an agent to have such motivations?
   In any sense in which the question is intelligible, no.

9. Is it rational for society to bring people up with these sorts of motivations?
   Insofar as the question is intelligible, yes. And certainly we have reason to encourage people to have these dispositions—e.g. in virtue of possessing them ourselves.

I confess that I cannot see any other major questions which, at this level of generality, bear on these issues. All these questions have clear answers which are entirely compatible with a conception of practical rationality in terms of internal reasons for action, and are also, it seems to me, entirely reasonable answers.

Notes

1. A point made by Aurel Kolnai: see his "Deliberation is of Ends," in *Ethics, Value and Reality* (London and Indianapolis, 1978). See also David Wiggins, "Deliberation and Practical Reason," *Proceedings of the Aristotelian Society*, New Series 76 (1975–6); reprinted in part in *Practical Reasoning*, ed. J. Raz (Oxford, 1978).

2. It is discussed in Bernard Williams, "*Ought* and Moral Obligation," reprinted in Williams, *Moral Luck* (Cambridge, 1981).

3. A well-known treatment is by M. Olson, Jr., *The Logic of Collective Action* (Cambridge, Mass., 1965). On expressive motivations in this connexion, see S. I. Benn, "Rationality and Political Behaviour," in S. I. Benn and G. W. Mortimore, eds., *Rationality and the Social Sciences* (London, 1976). On the point about fairness, which follows in the text, there is of course a very great deal more to be said: for instance, about how members of a group can, compatibly with fairness, converge on strategies more efficient than everyone's doing C (such as people taking turns).

2 Skepticism about Practical Reason

Christine Korsgaard

The Kantian approach to moral philosophy is to try to show that ethics is based on practical reason: that is, that our ethical judgments can be explained in terms of rational standards that apply directly to conduct or to deliberation. Part of the appeal of this approach lies in the way that it avoids certain sources of skepticism that some other approaches meet with inevitably. If ethically good action is simply rational action, we do not need to postulate special ethical properties in the world or faculties in the mind, in order to provide ethics with a foundation. But the Kantian approach gives rise to its own specific form of skepticism, skepticism about practical reason.

By *skepticism about practical reason*, I mean doubts about the extent to which human action is or could possibly be directed by reason. One form that such skepticism takes is doubt about the bearing of rational considerations on the activities of deliberation and choice; doubts, that is to say, about whether "formal" principles have any content and can give substantive guidance to choice and action. An example of this would be the common doubt about whether the contradiction tests associated with the first formulation of the categorical imperative succeed in ruling out anything. I will refer to this as *content skepticism*. A second form taken by skepticism about practical reason is doubt about the scope of reason as a motive. I will call this *motivational skepticism*. In this paper my main concern is with motivational skepticism and with the question whether it is justified. Some people think that motivational considerations alone provide grounds for skepticism about the project of founding ethics on practical reason. I will argue, against this view, that motivational skepticism must always be based on content skepticism. I will not address the question of whether or not content skepticism is justified. I want only to establish the fact that motivational skepticism has no independent force.

I

Skepticism about practical reason gets its classical formulation in the well-known passages in the *Treatise of Human Nature* that lead Hume to the conclusion that

> Reason is, and ought only to be the slave of the passions, and can never pretend to any other office than to serve and obey them.[1]

According to these passages, as they are usually understood, the role of reason in action is limited to the discernment of the means to our ends. Reason can teach us how to satisfy our desires or passions, but it cannot tell us whether those desires or passions are themselves "rational"; that is, there is no sense in which desires or passions are rational or irrational. Our ends are picked out, so to speak, by our desires, and these ultimately determine what we do. Normative standards applying to conduct may come from other sources (such as a moral sense), but the only standard that comes from reason is that of effectiveness in the choice of means.

The limitation of practical reason to an instrumental role does not only prevent reason from determining ends; it even prevents reason from ranking them, except with respect to their conduciveness to some other end. Even the view that those choices and actions which are conducive to our over-all self-interest are rationally to be preferred to self-destructive ones is undermined by the instrumental limitation. Self-interest itself has no rational *authority* over even the most whimsical desires. As Hume says:

> 'Tis not contrary to reason to prefer the destruction of the whole world to the scratching of my finger. 'Tis not contrary to reason for me to chuse my total ruin, to prevent the least uneasiness of an *Indian* or person wholly unknown to me. 'Tis as little contrary to reason to prefer even my own acknowledg'd lesser good to my greater, and have a more ardent affection for the former than the latter. (*Treatise* 416)

Under the influence of self-interest [or of "a general appetite to good, and aversion to evil, consider'd merely as such" (417)] we may rank our ends, according to the amount of good that each represents for us, and determine which are, as Hume puts it, our "greatest and most valuable enjoyments" (416). But the self-interest that would make us favor the greater good need not itself be a stronger desire, or a stronger reason, than the desire for the lesser good, or than any of our more particular desires. Reason by itself neither selects nor ranks our ends.

Hume poses his argument as an argument against "the greatest part of moral philosophy, ancient and modern" (413). Moral philosophers, Hume says, have claimed that we ought to regulate our conduct by reason, and either suppress our passions or bring them into conformity with it; but he is going to show the fallacy of all this by showing, first, that reason alone can never provide a motive to any action, and, second, that reason can never oppose passion in the direction of the will. His argument for the first point goes this way: all reasoning is concerned either with abstract relations of ideas or with relations of objects, especially causal relations, which we learn about from experience. Abstract relations of ideas are the subject of logic and mathematics, and no one supposes that those by themselves give rise to any motives. They yield no conclusions about action. We are sometimes moved by the perception of causal relations, but only when there is a pre-existing motive in the case. As Hume puts it, if there is "the prospect of pleasure or pain from some object," we are concerned with its causes and effects. The argument that reason cannot oppose a passion in the direction of the will depends on, and in fact springs directly from, the argument that reason by itself cannot give rise to a motive. It is simply that reason *could* oppose a passion only if it could give rise to an *opposing motive*.

What is important to notice in this discussion is the relation between Hume's views about the possible content of principles of reason bearing on action and the scope of its motivational efficacy. The answer to the question what sorts of operation, procedure, or judgment of reason exist is presupposed in these passages. In the first part of the argument Hume goes through what by this point in the *Treatise* is a *settled* list of the types of rational judgment. The argument is a sort of process of elimination: there are rational judgments concerning logical and mathematical relations; there are empirical connections such as cause and effect: Hume looks at each of these in turn in order to see under what circumstances it might be thought to have a bearing on decision and action. In other words, Hume's arguments against a more extensive practical employment of reason depend upon Hume's own views about what reason is—that is, about what sorts of operation and judgment are "rational." His motivational skepticism (skepticism about the scope of reason as a motive) is entirely dependent upon his content skepticism (skepticism about what reason has to *say* about choice and action).

Yet Hume's arguments may give the impression of doing something much stronger: of placing independent constraints, based solely on motivational considerations, on what might count as a principle of practical reason. Hume seems to say simply that all reasoning that has a motivational influence must start from a passion, that being the only possible source of motivation, and must proceed to the means to satisfy that passion, that being the only operation of reason that transmits motivational force. Yet these are separate points: they can be doubted, and challenged, separately. One could disagree with Hume about his list of the types of rational judgment, operation, or possible deliberation, and yet still agree with the basic point about the source of motivation: that all rational motivation must ultimately spring from some nonrational source, such as passion. At least one contemporary philosopher, Bernard Williams, has taken something like Hume's argument to have this kind of independent force, and has so argued in his essay "Internal and External Reasons,"[2] which I will take up later in this paper.

The Kantian must go further, and disagree with Hume on both counts, since the Kantian supposes that there are operations of practical reason which yield conclusions about actions and which do not involve discerning relations between passions (or any pre-existing sources of motivation) and those actions. What gives rise to the difficulty about this further possibility is the question of how such operations could yield conclusions that can motivate us.

II

The problem can best be stated in some terms provided by certain recent discussions in moral philosophy. W. D. Falk, William Frankena, and Thomas Nagel, among others, have distinguished between two kinds of moral theories, which are called 'internalist' and 'externalist'.[3] An *internalist* theory is a theory according to which the knowledge (or the truth or the acceptance) of a moral judgment implies the existence of a motive (not necessarily overriding) for acting on that judgment. If I judge that some action is right, it is implied that I have, and acknowledge, some motive or reason for performing that action. It is part of the sense of the judgment that a motive is present: if someone agrees that an action is right, but cannot see any motive or reason for doing it, we must suppose, according to these views, that she does not quite know what she means when she agrees that the action is right. On an *externalist* theory, by contrast, such a conjunction of moral comprehension and total unmotivatedness is perfectly possible: knowledge is one thing and motivation another.

Examples of unquestionably external theories are not easy to find. As Falk points out (125/6), the simplest example would be a view according to which the motives for moral action come from something wholly separate from a grasp of the correctness of the judgments—say, an interest in obeying divine commands. In philosophical ethics the best example is John Stuart Mill (see Nagel 8/9), who firmly separates the question of the proof of the principle of utility from the question of its "sanctions." The reason why the principle of utility is true and the motive we might have for acting on it are not the same: the theoretical proof of its truth is contained in chapter IV of *Utilitarianism*, but the motives must be acquired in a utilitarian upbringing. It is Mill's view that *any* moral principle would have to be motivated by education and training and that "there is hardly anything so absurd or so mischievous" that it cannot be so motivated.[4] The "ultimate sanction" of the principle of utility is *not* that it can be proved, but that it is in accordance with our natural social feelings. Even to some who, like Mill himself, realize that the motives are acquired, "It does not present itself . . . as a superstition of education, or a law despotically imposed by the power of society, but as an attribute which it would not be well for them to be without" (Mill 36). The modern intuitionists, such as W. D. Ross and H. A. Prichard, seem also to have been externalists, but of a rather minimal kind. They believed that there was a distinctively moral motive, a sense of right or desire to do one's duty. This motive is triggered by the news that something is your duty, and only by that news, but it is still separate from the rational intuition that constitutes the understanding of your duty. It would be possible to have that intuition and not be motivated by it.[5] The reason why the act is right and the motive you have for doing it are separate items, although it is nevertheless the case that the motive for doing it is "because it is right." This falls just short of the internalist position, which is that the reason why the act is right is the reason, and the motive, for doing it: it is a practical reason. Intuitionism is a form of rationalist ethics, but intuitionists do not believe in practical reason, properly speaking. They believe there is a branch of theoretical reason that is specifically concerned with morals, by which human beings can be motivated because of a special psychological mechanism: a desire to do one's duty. One can see the oddity of this if one considers what the analogue would be in the case of theoretical reasoning. It is as if human beings could not be convinced by arguments acknowledged to be sound without the intervention of a special psychological mechanism: a belief that the conclusions of sound arguments are true.

By contrast, an internalist believes that the reasons why an action is right and the reasons why you do it are the same. The reason that the action is right is both the reason and the motive for doing it. Nagel gives as one example of this the theory of Hobbes: the reason for the action's rightness and your motive for doing it are both that it is in your interest. The literature on this subject splits, however, on the question of whether the Kantian position is internalist or not. Falk, for instance, characterizes the difference between internalism and externalism as one of whether the moral command arises from a source outside the agent (like God or society) or from within. If the difference is described this way, Kant's attempt to derive morality from autonomy makes him a paradigmatic internalist (see Falk 125, 129). On the other hand, some have believed that Kant's view that the moral command is indifferent to our desires, needs, and interests—that it is categorical—makes him a paradigmatic externalist.[6] Since Kant himself took the categorical character of the imperative and autonomy of the moral motive to be necessarily connected, this is a surprising difference of opinion. I will come back to Kant in section VII.

This kind of reflection about the motivational force of ethical judgments has been brought to bear by Bernard Williams on the motivational force of reason claims generally. In "Internal and External Reasons" [this volume, chap.1] Williams argues that there are two kinds of reason claims, or two ways of making reason claims. Suppose I say that some person P has a reason to do action A. If I intend this to imply that the person P has a motive to do the action A, the claim is of an internal reason; if not, the claim is of an external reason. Williams is concerned to argue that only internal reasons really exist. He points out (106/7 [this volume, 42–43]) that, since an external-reason claim does not imply the existence of a motive, it cannot be used to explain anyone's action: that is, we cannot say that the person P did the action A because of reason R; for R does not provide P with a motive for doing A, and *that* is what we need to explain P's doing A: a motive. Nagel points out that if acknowledgment of a reason claim did not include acknowledgment of a motive, someone presented with a reason for action could ask: Why do what I have a reason to do? (9; see also Falk 121/2). Nagel's argument makes from the agent's perspective the same point that Williams makes from the explainer's perspective, namely, that unless reasons are motives, they cannot prompt or explain actions. And, unless reasons are motives, we cannot be said to be practically rational.

Thus, it seems to be a requirement on practical reasons, that they be capable of motivating us. This is where the difficulty arises about reasons that do not, like means/end reasons, draw on an obvious motivational source. So long as there is doubt about whether a given consideration is able to motivate a rational person, there is doubt about whether that consideration has the force of a practical *reason*. The consideration that such and such action is a means to getting what you want has a clear motiva-

Skepticism about Practical Reason

tional source; so no one doubts that this is a reason. Practical-reason claims, if they are really to present us with reasons for action, must be capable of motivating rational persons. I will call this the *internalism requirement*.

III

In this section I want to talk about how the internalism requirement functions—or, more precisely, malfunctions—in skeptical arguments. Hume winds up his argument by putting the whole thing in a quite general form. Reason is the faculty that judges of truth and falsehood, and it can judge our ideas to be true or false because they represent other things. But a passion is an original existence or modification of existence, not a copy of anything: it cannot be true or false, and therefore it cannot in itself be reasonable or unreasonable. Passions can be unreasonable, then, only if they are accompanied by judgments, and there are two cases of this kind. One is when the passion is founded on the supposition of the existence of objects that do not exist. You are outraged at the mocking things you heard me say about you, but I was talking about somebody else. You are terrified by the burglars you hear whispering in the living room, but in fact you left the radio on. It is of course only in an extended sense that Hume can think of these as cases where a passion is irrational. Judgments of irrationality, whether of belief or action, are, strictly speaking, relative to the subject's beliefs. Conclusions drawn from mistaken premises are not *irrational*.[7] The case of passions based on false beliefs seems to be of this sort.

The second kind of case in which Hume says that the passion might be called unreasonable is

> ... when, in exerting any passion in action, we chuse means insufficient for the design'd end, and deceive ourselves in our judgment of causes and effects. (*Treatise* 416)

This is in itself an ambiguous remark. Hume might, and in fact does, mean simply that we base our action on a false belief about causal relations. So this is no more genuinely a case of irrationality than the other. Relative to the (false) causal belief, the action is not irrational. But it is important that there is something else one might mean in this case, which is that, knowing the truth about the relevant causal relations in the case, we might nevertheless choose means insufficient to our end or fail to choose obviously sufficient and readily available means to the end. This would be what I will call *true irrationality*, by which I mean a failure to respond appropriately to an available reason.

If the only possibility Hume means to be putting forward here is the possibility of action based on false belief about causes and effects, we get a curious result. Neither of the cases that Hume considers is a case of true irrationality: relative to their beliefs, people *never* act irrationally. Hume indeed says this:

> ... the moment we perceive the falsehood of any supposition, or the insufficiency of any means, our passions yield to our reason without any opposition. (*Treatise* 416)

But it looks as if a theory of means/end rationality ought to allow for at least one form of true irrationality, namely, failure to be motivated by the consideration that the action is the means to your end. Even the skeptic about practical reason admits that human beings can be motivated by the consideration that a given action is a means to a desired end. But it is not enough, to explain this fact, that human beings can engage in causal reasoning. It is perfectly possible to imagine a sort of being who could engage in causal reasoning and who could, therefore, engage in reasoning that would point out the means to her ends, but who was not motivated by it.

Kant, in a passage early in the *Foundations*, imagines a human being in just such a condition of being able to reason, so to speak, theoretically but not practically. He is talking about what the world would have been like if nature had had our happiness as her end. Our actions would have been controlled entirely by instincts designed to secure our happiness, and:

> ... if, over and above this, reason should have been granted to the favored creature, it would have served only to let it contemplate the happy constitution of its nature.[8]

The favored creature is portrayed as able to see that his actions are rational in the sense that they promote the means to his end (happiness); but he is not motivated by their reasonableness; he acts from instinct. Reason allows him to admire the rational appropriateness of what he does, but this is not what gets him to do it—he has the sort of attitude toward all his behavior that we in fact might have toward the involuntary well-functioning of our bodies.

Being motivated by the consideration that an action is a means to a desirable end is something beyond merely reflecting on that fact. The motive force attached to the end must be transmitted to the means in order for this to be a consideration that sets the human body in motion—and only if this is a consideration that sets the human body in motion can we say that reason has an influence on action. A practically rational person is not merely capable of performing certain rational mental operations, but capable also of transmitting motive force, so to speak, along the paths laid out by those operations. Otherwise even means/end reasoning will not meet the internalism requirement.

But the internalism requirement does not imply that nothing can interfere with this motivational transmission. And generally, this is something there seems to be no reason to believe: there seem to be plenty of things that could interfere with the motivational influence of a given rational consideration. Rage, passion, depression, distraction, grief, physical or mental illness: all these things could cause us to act irrationally, that is, to fail to be motivationally responsive to the rational considerations available to us.[9] The necessity, or the compellingness, of rational considerations lies in those considerations themselves, not in us: that is, we will not necessarily be motivated by them. Or rather, to put the point more properly and not to foreclose any metaphysical possibilities, their necessity may lie in the fact that, when they do move us—either in the realm of conviction or in that of motivation—they move us with the force of necessity. But it will still not be the case that they necessarily move us. So a person may be irrational, not merely by failing to observe rational connections—say, failing to see that the sufficient means are at hand—but also by being "willfully" blind to them, or even by being indifferent to them when they are pointed out.[10]

In this respect practical reason is no different from theoretical reason. Many things might cause me to fail to be convinced by a good argument. For me to be a theoretically rational person is not merely for me to be capable of performing logical and inductive operations, but for me to be appropriately *convinced* by them: my conviction in the premises must carry through, so to speak, to a conviction in the conclusion. Thus, the internalism requirement for theoretical reasons is that they be capable of convincing us—insofar as we are rational. It is quite possible for me to be able to perform these operations without generating any conviction, as a sort of game, say, and then I would not be a rational person.

Aristotle describes the novice in scientific studies as being able to repeat the argument, but without the sort of conviction that it will have for him later, when he fully understands it. In order for a theoretical argument or a practical deliberation to have the status of reason, it must of course be capable of motivating or convincing a rational person, but it does not follow that it must at all times be capable of motivating or convincing any given individual. It may follow from the supposition that we are rational persons and the supposition that a given argument or deliberation is rational that, if we are not convinced or motivated, there must be some explanation of that failure. But there is no reason at all to believe that such an explanation will always show that we had mistaken reasons, which, if true, would have been good reasons. Many things can interfere with the functioning of the rational operations in a human body. Thus there is no reason to deny that human beings might be practically irrational in the sense that Hume considers impossible: that, even with the truth at our disposal, we might from one cause or another fail to be interested in the means to our ends.

IV

My speculation is that skepticism about practical reason is sometimes based on a false impression of what the internalism requirement requires. It does not require that rational considerations always succeed in motivating us. All it requires is that rational considerations succeed in motivating us insofar as we are rational. One can admit the possibility of true irrationality and yet still believe that all practical reasoning is instrumental. But once this kind of irrationality is allowed in the means/end case, some of the grounds for skepticism about more ambitious forms of practical reasoning will seem less compelling. The case of prudence or self-interest will show what I have in mind. I have already mentioned Hume's account of this matter: he thinks that there is "a general appetite to good, and aversion to evil" and that a person will act prudently insofar as this calm and general passion remains dominant over particular passions. It is under the influence of this end that we weigh one possible satisfaction against another, trying to determine which conduces to our greater good. But if this general desire for the good does not remain predominant, not only the motive, but the reason, for doing what will conduce to one's greater good, disappears. For Hume says it is not contrary to reason to prefer an acknowledged lesser good to a greater.

Suppose, then, that you are confronted with a choice and, though informed that one option will lead to your greater good, you take the other. If true irrationality is excluded, and you fail to take the means to some end, this is evidence either that you don't really have this end or that it is not the most important thing to you. Thus, in this imagined case, where you do not choose your greater good, this is evidence either that you do not care about your greater good or that you do not care about it as much as you do about this particular lesser good. On the other hand, if you do respond to the news that one option leads to your greater good, then we have evidence that you do care about your greater good. This makes it seem as if your greater good is an end you might care about or not, and rationality is relative to what you care about. But, once we admit that one might from some other cause fail to be responsive to a rational consideration, there is no special reason to accept this analysis of the case. I do not mean that there is a reason to reject it, either, of course; my point is that whether you accept it depends on whether you *already* accept the limitation to means/end rationality. If you do, you will say that the case where the lesser good was chosen was a case where there was a stronger desire for it, and so a stronger reason; if you do not, and you think it *is* reasonable to choose the greater good (because prudence has rational authority), you will say that this is a case of true irrationality. The point is that the motivational analysis of the case *depends* upon your views of the content of rational principles of action, not the reverse. The fact that one might or might not be motivated to choose a certain course of action by the consideration that it leads to the greater good does not by itself show that the greater good is just one end among others, without special rational authority, something that some people care about and some people do not. Take the parallel case. The fact that one might or might not be motivated to choose a certain course of action by the consideration that it is the best available means to one's end does not show that taking the means to one's ends is just one end among others, an end some people care about and some people do not. In both cases, what we have is the fact that people are sometimes motivated by considerations of this sort, and that we all think in the latter case and some think in the former case that it is rational to be so motivated.

The argument about whether prudence or the greater good has any special rational authority—about whether it is a rational consideration—will have to be carried out on another plane: it will have to be made in terms of a more metaphysical argument about just what reason does, what its scope is, and what sorts of operation, procedure, and judgment are rational. This argument will usually consist in an attempt to arrive at a general notion of reason by discovering features or characteristics that theoretical and practical reason share; such characteristic features as universality, sufficiency, timelessness, impersonality, or authority will be appealed to.[11] What the argument in favor of prudence would be will vary from theory to theory; here, the point is this: the fact that someone might fail to be motivated by the consideration that something will serve her greater good cannot by itself throw any doubt on the argument, whatever it is, that preferring the greater good is rational. If someone were not convinced by the logical operation of conjunction, and so could not reason with conviction from "*A*" and from "*B*" to "*A* and *B*," we would not be eager to conclude that conjunction was just a theory that some people believe and some people do not. Conjunction is not a theory to believe or disbelieve, but a principle of reasoning. Not everything that drives us to conclusions is a theory. Not everything that drives us to action need be a desired end (see Nagel 20–22).

V

An interesting result of admitting the possibility of true irrationality is that it follows that it will not always be possible to argue someone into rational behavior. If people are acting irrationally only because they do not know about the relevant means/end connection, they may respond properly to argument: point the connection out to them, and their behavior will be modified accordingly. In such a person the motivational path, so to speak, from end to means is open. A person in whom this path is, from some cause, blocked or nonfunctioning may not respond to argument, even if this person understands the argument in a theoretical way. Aristotle thinks of the incontinent person as being in a condition of this sort: this happens to people in fits of passion or rage, and the condition is actually physiological.[12] Now this is important; for it is sometimes thought, on the basis of the internalism requirement, that if there is a reason to do something it must be possible to argue someone into doing it: anyone who understands the argument will straightaway act. (The conclusion of a practical syllogism is an action.) Frankena, for example, argues against an internalist construal of the moral 'ought' on the grounds that even after full reflection we do not always do what is right (71). But if there is a gap between understanding a reason and being motivated by it, then internalism does not imply that people can always be argued into reasonable conduct. The reason motivates someone who is capable of being motivated by the perception of a rational connection. Rationality is a condition that human beings are capable of, but it is not a condition that we are always in.

It is for this reason that some ethical theories centered on the idea of practical reason are best thought of as establishing ideals of character. A person with a good character will be, on such a view, one who responds to the available reasons in an appropriate way, one whose motivational structure is organized for rational receptivity, so that reasons motivate in accord with their proper force and necessity. It is not an accident that the two major philosophers in our tradition who thought of ethics in terms of practical reason—Aristotle and Kant—were also the two most concerned with the methods of moral education. Human beings must be taught, or habituated, to listen to reason: we are, as Kant says, imperfectly rational.

In fact, the argument of the last section can be recast in terms of virtues. Suppose that it *is* irrational not to prefer the greater good: this need have nothing at all to do with having the greater good *among* your desired ends. It is of course true that some people are more steadily motivated by considerations of what conduces to their greater good than others: call such a person *the prudent person*. The fact that the prudent is more strongly motivated by reasons of greater good need not be taken to show that he has stronger reasons for attending to his greater good. (People have varying theoretical virtues too.[13]) We may indeed say that the prudent person "cares more" about his greater good, but that is just another way of saying that he responds more strongly to these kinds of consideration, that he has the virtue of prudence. It need not be taken to imply that his greater good is a more heavily weighted end with him and that, therefore, it really does matter more to him that he achieve his greater good than it does to another person, an imprudent person, that he achieve his. It makes more sense to say that this other person ignores reasons that he has. Again, take the parallel: some people respond much more readily and definitely to the consideration that something is an effective means to their end. We might call such a person a *determined* or *resolute* person. Presumably no one feels like saying that the determined or resolute person has a stronger reason for taking the means to her ends than anyone else does. We all have just the same reason for taking the means to our ends. The fact that people are motivated differently by the reasons they have does not show that they have different reasons. It may show that some have virtues that others lack. On a practical-reason theory, the possibility of rationality sets a standard for character; but that standard will not always be met. But this is not by itself a reason for skepticism about the scope of the deliberative guidance that reason *can* provide. This is a reason for skepticism only about the extent to which that guidance will ever be taken advantage of.

VI

Nevertheless, the fact that a practical reason must be capable of motivating us might still seem to put a limitation on the scope of practical reason: it might be thought that it is a subjective matter which considerations can motivate a given individual and that, therefore, all judgments of practical reason must be conditional in form. In Hume's argument, this kind of limitation is captured in the claim that motivation must originate in a passion. In the means/end case, we are able to be motivated by the consideration that action *A* will promote purpose *P* because, and only if, we have a pre-existing motivational impulse (a passion) attached to purpose *P*. As Hume says, a relation between two things will not have any motivational impact on us unless one of the two things has such impact. This does not limit practical reason to the means/end variety, but it might seem to impose a limitation of this sort: practical-reason claims must be reached by something that is recognizably a rational deliberative process from interests and motives one already has. This position is advocated by Bernard Williams in "Internal and External Reasons." Williams, as I have mentioned, argues that only internal reasons exist; but he takes this to have a strong Humean implication. Williams takes it that internal reasons are by definition relative to something that he calls the agent's 'subjective motivational set': this follows from the fact that they can motivate. The contents of this set are left open, but one kind of thing it will obviously contain is the agent's desires and passions. Internal reasons are reasons reached by deliberation from the subjective motivational set: they can motivate us because of their connection to that set. Means/end deliberation, where the end is in the set and the means are what we arrive at by the motivating deliberation, is the most characteristic, but not the only, source of reasons for action. Williams calls the means/end view the 'sub-Humean model', and he says this:

> The sub-Humean model supposes that φ-ing [where φ-ing is some action we have a reason for doing] has to be related to some element in [the subjective motivational set] as causal means to end (unless perhaps it is straightforwardly the carrying out of a desire which is itself that element in [the subjective motivational set]). But this is only one case. . . . there are much wider possibilities for deliberation, such as: thinking how the satisfaction of elements in [the subjective motivational set] can be combined, e.g. by time-ordering; where there is some irresoluble conflict among the elements of [the subjective motivational set] considering which one attaches most weight to . . . or again, finding constitutive solutions, such as deciding what would make for an entertaining evening, granted that one wants entertainment.[14] (104/5) [This volume, 40]

Anything reached by a process of deliberation from the subjective motivational set may be something for which there is an internal reason, one that can motivate. External reasons, by contrast, exist regardless of what is in one's subjective motivational set. In this case, Williams points out, there

Skepticism about Practical Reason

must be some rational process, not springing from the subjective motivational set and therefore not relative to it, which could bring you to acknowledge something to be a reason and at the same time to be motivated by it. Reason must be able to produce an entirely new motive, the thing that Hume said could not be done.

Thus, Williams takes up one part of the skeptic's argument: that a piece of practical reasoning must start from something that is capable of motivating you; and drops the other, that the only kind of reasoning is means/end. One might suppose that this limits the operations or judgments of practical reason to those functions which are natural extensions or expansions of the means/end variety, and the things Williams mentions in this passage, such as making a plan to satisfy the various elements in the set, or constitutive reasoning, are generally thought to be of that sort. But in fact this is not Williams' view, nor is it necessitated by his argument, as he points out.

> The processes of deliberation can have all sorts of effect on [the subjective motivational set], and this is a fact which a theory of internal reasons should be very happy to accommodate. So also it should be more liberal than some theorists have been about the possible elements in the [subjective motivational set]. I have discussed [the subjective motivational set] primarily in terms of desires, and this term can be used, formally, for all elements in [the subjective motivational set]. But this terminology may make one forget that [the subjective motivational set] can contain such things as dispositions of evaluation, patterns of emotional reaction, personal loyalties, and various projects, as they may abstractly be called, embodying commitments of the agent. (105) [This volume, 41]

Williams can accommodate the case of someone's acting for reasons of principle, and in this case the form the deliberation will take is that of applying the principle or of seeing that the principle applies to the case at hand. The advocate of the view that all deliberation is strictly of the means/end variety may claim to assimilate this case by the formal device of saying that the agent must have a desire to act on this principle, but this will not change the important fact, which is that the reasoning in this case will involve the application of the principle, which is not the same as means/end reasoning.[15]

In this kind of case, Williams' point will be that in order for the principle to provide reasons for a given agent, acceptance of the principle must constitute part of the agent's subjective motivational set. If the principle is not accepted by the agent, its dictates are not reasons for her. Reasons are relativized to the set. If this is true, it looks at first as if all practical reasons will be relative to the individual, because they are conditioned by what is in the subjective motivational set. Reasons that apply to you regardless of what is in your subjective motivational set will not exist.

This argument, however, having been cut loose from Hume's very definite ideas about what sort of rational operations and processes exist, has a very unclear bearing on claims about pure practical reason. If one accepts the internalism requirement, it follows that pure practical reason will exist if and only if we are capable of being motivated by the conclusions of the operations of pure practical reason as such. Something in us must make us capable of being motivated by them, and this something will be part of the subjective motivational set. Williams seems to think that this is a reason for doubting that pure practical reasons exist, whereas what seems to follow from the internalism requirement is this: if we can be motivated by considerations stemming from pure practical reason, then that capacity belongs to the subjective motivational set of every rational being. One cannot argue that the subjective motivational set contains only ends or desires; for that would be true only if all reasoning were of the means/end variety or its natural extensions. What sorts of items can be found in the set does not limit, but rather depends on, what kinds of reasoning are possible. Nor can one assume that the subjective motivational set consists only of individual or idiosyncratic elements; for that is to close off without argument the possibility that reason could yield conclusions that every rational being must acknowledge and be capable of being motivated by. As long as it is left open what kinds of rational operations yield conclusions about what to do and what to pursue, it must be left open whether we are capable of being motivated by them.

Consider the question of how an agent comes to accept a principle: to have it in her subjective motivational set. If we say that the agent comes to accept the principle through reasoning—through having been convinced that the principle admits of some ultimate justification—then there are grounds for saying that this principle is in the subjective motivational set of every rational person: for all rational persons could be brought to see that they have reason to act in the way required by the principle, and this is all that the internalism requirement requires. Now this is of course not Williams' view: he believes that the principles are acquired by education, training, and so forth, and that they do not admit of any ultimate justification.[16] There are two important points to make about this.

First, consider the case of the reflective agent who, after being raised to live by a certain principle, comes to question it. Some doubt, temptation, or argument has made her consider eliminating the principle from her subjective motivational set. Now what will she think? The principle does not, we are supposing, admit of an ultimate justification, so she will not find that. But this does not necessarily mean that she will reject the principle. She may, on reflection, find that she thinks it better (where this will be relative to what other things are in her motivational set) that people should have and act on such a principle, that it is in some rough way a good idea—perhaps not the only but an excellent basis for community living, etc.—and so she may retain it and even proceed to educate those under her influence to adopt it. The odd thing to notice is that this is almost exactly the sort of description Mill gives of the reflective utilitarian who, on realizing that his capacity to be motivated by the principle of utility is an acquirement of education, is not sorry. But Mill's position, as I mentioned earlier, is often taken to be the best example of an *externalist* ethical position.

More immediately to the point, what this kind of case shows is that for Williams, as for Hume, the motivational skepticism depends on what I have called the 'content skepticism'. Williams' argument does not show that if there were unconditional principles of reason applying to action we could not be motivated by them. He only thinks that there are none. But Williams' argument, like Hume's, gives the appearance of going the other way around: it looks as if the motivational point—the internalism requirement—is supposed to have some force in limiting what might count as a principle of practical reason. Whereas in fact, the real source of the skepticism is a doubt about the existence of principles of action whose content shows them to be ultimately justified.

VII

The internalism requirement is correct, but there is probably no moral theory that it excludes. I do not think that it even excludes utilitarianism or intuitionism, although it calls for a reformulation of the associated views about the influence of ethical reasoning or motivation. The force of the internalism requirement is psychological: what it does is not to refute ethical theories, but to make a psychological demand on them.

This is in fact how philosophers advocating a connection between morality and practical reason have thought of the matter. From considerations concerning the necessity that reasons be internal and capable of motivating us which are almost identical to Williams', Nagel, in the opening sections of *The Possibility of Altruism*, argues that investigations into practical reason will yield discoveries about our motivational capacities. Granting that reasons must be capable of motivating us, he thinks that if we then are able to show the existence of reasons, we will have shown something capable of motivating us. In Nagel's eyes, the internalism requirement leads not to a limitation on practical reason, but to a rather surprising increase in the power of moral philosophy: it can teach us about human motivational capacities; it can teach us psychology.[17]

As Nagel points out, this approach also characterizes the moral philosophy of Kant. By the end of the second section of the *Foundations*, there is in *one* sense no doubt that Kant has done what he set out to do: he has shown us what sort of demand pure reason would make on action. Working from the ideas that reasons in general (either theoretical or practical) must be universal, that reason seeks the unconditioned, and that its binding force must derive from autonomy, he has shown us what a law of pure reason applying to action would look like. But until it has been shown that we can be motivated to act according to the categorical imperative, it has not been completely shown that the categorical imperative really exists—that there really is a law of pure practical reason. And this is because of the internalism requirement. The question how the imperative is possible is equated to that of "how the constraint of the will, which the imperative expresses in the problem, can be conceived" (Beck 34; Acad. 417). Thus, what remains for proof by a "deduction" is that we are capable of being motivated by this law of reason: that we have an autonomous will. In the third section of the *Foundations*, Kant does try to argue that we can be motivated by the categorical imperative, appealing to the pure spontaneity of reason as evidence for our intelligible nature and so for an autonomous will (Beck 70/1; Acad. 452). In the *Critique of Practical Reason*,[18] however, Kant turns his strategy around. He argues that we know that we are capable of being motivated by the categorical imperative and therefore that we know (in a practical sense) that we have an autonomous will. Again, explorations into practical reason reveal our nature. It is important, however, that although in the *Critique of Practical Reason* Kant does not try to argue *that* pure reason can be a motive, he has detailed things to say about *how* it can be a motive—about how it functions as an incentive in combatting other incentives.[19] Something is still owed to the internalism requirement: namely, to show what psychological conclusions the moral theory implies.

It may be that we are immune to motivation by pure practical reason. But, for that matter, it may be that we are immune to motivation by means/ends connections. Perhaps our awareness of these in cases where we seem to act on them is epiphenomenal. In fact we are quite sure that we are not immune to the reasons springing from means/ends connections; and Kant maintained that, if we thought about it, we would see that we are not immune to the laws of pure practical reason: that we know we can do what we ought. But there is no guarantee of this; for our knowledge of our motives is limited. The conclusion is that, if we are rational, we will act as the categorical imperative directs. But we are not necessarily rational.

VIII

I have not attempted to show in this paper that there is such a thing as pure practical reason, or that reason has in any way a more extensive bearing on conduct than empiricism has standardly credited it with. What I have attempted to show is that this question is open in a particular way: that motivational considerations do not provide any reason, in advance of specific proposals, for skepticism about practical reason. If a philosopher can show us that something that is recognizably a law of reason has bearing on conduct, there is no special reason to doubt that human beings might be motivated by that consideration. The fact that the law might not govern conduct, even when someone understood it, is no reason for skepticism: the necessity is in the law, and not in us.

To the extent that skepticism about pure practical reason is based on the strange idea that an acknowledged reason can never fail to motivate, there is no reason to accept it. It is based on some sort of a misunderstanding, and I have suggested a misunderstanding of the internalism requirement as a possible account. To the extent that skepticism about pure practical reason is based on the idea that no process or operation of reason yielding unconditional conclusions about action can be found, it depends on—and is not a reason for believing—the thesis that no process or operation of reason yielding unconditional conclusions about action can be found. To the extent that skepticism about pure practical reason is based on the requirement that reasons be capable of motivating us, the correct response is that if someone discovers what are recognizably reasons bearing on conduct and those reasons fail to motivate us, that only shows the limits of our rationality. Motivational skepticism about practical reason depends on, and cannot be the basis for, skepticism about the possible content of rational requirements. The extent to which people are actually moved by rational considerations, either in their conduct or in their credence, is beyond the purview of philosophy. Philosophy can at most tell us what it would be like to be rational.

Acknowledgments

I would like to thank Timothy Gould, Charlotte Brown, and audiences of an earlier version of this paper at Columbia and the University of Chicago, for comments on and discussions of the issues of this paper, from which I have learned a great deal.

Notes

1. David Hume, *Treatise of Human Nature*, L. A. Selby-Bigge, ed. (London: Oxford, 1888), p. 415. Page references to the *Treatise* will be to this edition.

2. This paper was originally published in Ross Harrison, ed., *Rational Action* (New York: Cambridge, 1979), and is reprinted in Williams, *Moral Luck* (New York: Cambridge, 1981), pp. 101–113 [this volume, chap. 1]. Page references to Williams are to this article, as it appears in *Moral Luck*.

3. Actually, Falk and Frankena speak of internalist and externalist senses of 'ought'. See Falk, "'Ought' and Motivation," *Proceedings of the Aristotelian Society*, 1947/1948. Frankena's discussion, "Obligation and Motivation in Recent Moral Philosophy," was originally published in A. I. Melden, ed., *Essays in Moral Philosophy* (Seattle: University of Washington Press, 1958) and is reprinted in *Perspectives on Morality: Essays of William K. Frankena*, Kenneth E. Goodpaster, ed. (Notre Dame, Ind.: University Press, 1976), pp. 49–73 (page references are to the reprint). Nagel's discussion is in *The Possibility of Altruism* (Princeton: Princeton University Press, 1970), Part I.

4. *Utilitarianism*, in Samuel Gorovitz, ed., *Utilitarianism with Critical Essays* (Indianapolis: Bobbs-Merrill, 1971), p. 34.

5. See Prichard, "Duty and Interest," in *Duty and Interest* (London: Oxford, 1928). Falk's original use of the distinction between internal and external senses of 'ought' in "'Ought' and Motivation" is in an argument responding to Prichard's paper.

6. See Frankena, "Obligation and Motivation," p. 63, for a discussion of this surprising view.

7. I am ignoring here the more complicated case in which the passion in question is parent to the false beliefs. In my examples, for instance, there might be cases such as these: irritation at me predisposes you to think my insults are aimed at you; terror of being alone in the house makes you more likely to mistake the radio for a burglar. Hume does discuss this phenomenon (*Treatise* 120). Here, we might say that the judgment is irrational, not merely false, and that its irrationality infects the passions and actions based on the judgment. If Hume's theory allows him to say that the judgment is irrational, he will be able to say that some passions and actions are truly irrational, and not merely mistaken, although he does not do this.

8. Immanuel Kant, *Foundations of the Metaphysics of Morals*, Lewis White Beck, trans. (New York: Library of Liberal Arts, 1959), p. 11. Prussian Academy Edition, p. 395.

9. 'Available to us' is vague, for there is a range of cases in which one might be uncertain whether or not to say that a reason was available to us. For instance there are (1) cases in which we don't know about the reason, (2) cases in which we couldn't possibly know about the reason, (3) cases in which we deceive ourselves about the reason, (4) cases in which some physical or psychological condition makes us unable to see the reason; and (5) cases in which some physical or psychological condition makes us fail to respond to the reason, even though in some sense we look it right in the eye. Now no one will want to say that reason claims involving reasons people do not know about are therefore external, but as we move down the list there will be a progressive uneasiness about whether the claim is becoming external. For toward the end of the list we will come to claim that someone is psychologically incapable of responding to the reason, and yet that it is internal: capable of motivating a rational person. I do not think there is a problem about any of these cases; for all that is necessary for the reason claim to be internal is that we can say that, if a person did know and *if nothing were interfering with her rationality*, she would respond accordingly. This does not trivialize the limitation to internal reasons as long as the notion of a psychological condition that interferes with rationality is not trivially defined.

10. I have in mind such phenomena as self-deception, rationalization, and the various forms of weakness of will. Some of these apply to theoretical as well as practical reason, and for the former we can add the various forms of intellectual resistance or ideology (though 'willful' is not a good way to characterize these). For some reason, people find the second thing that I mention—being indifferent to a reason that is pointed out to you—harder to imagine in a theoretical than in a practical case. To simply shrug in the face of the acknowledged reason seems to some to be possible in practice in a way that it is not in theory. I think part of the problem is that we can push what the practically paralyzed person accepts over into the realm of theory: he *believes* "that he ought to do such-and-such," although he is not moved to; whereas there seems to be nowhere further back (except maybe to a suspense of judgment) to push what the theoretically paralyzed person accepts. It may also be that the problem arises because we do not give enough weight to the difference between being convinced by an argument and being left without anything to say by it, or it may be just that what paralysis *is* is less visible in the case of belief than in the case of action.

11. Universality and sufficiency are appealed to by Kant; timelessness and impersonality by Nagel, and authority by Joseph Butler.

12. *Nicomachean Ethics*, VII.3, 1147b5–10.

13. The comparisons I have been drawing between theoretical and practical reason now suggest that there should also be something like an ideal of good theoretical

character: a receptivity to theoretical reasons. The vision of someone free of all ideology and intellectual resistance might be such an ideal.

14. Williams uses the designation 'S' for 'subjective motivational set', but I have put back the original phrase wherever it occurs; hence the brackets.

15. It is true that the application of a principle may be so simple or immediate that it will be a matter of judgment or perception rather than deliberation. In such a case there will be some who want to deny that practical reason has been used. On the other hand, the reasoning involved in applying a principle may be quite complicated (as in the case of the contradiction tests under the categorical imperative), and so be such that anyone should be willing to call it reasoning. If the fact that you hold the principle gives motivational force to either the insight or the deliberative argument to the effect that this case falls under the principle, then the result is a practical reason.

16. Williams himself remarks that the "onus of proof about what is to count as a 'purely rational process' . . . properly belongs with the critic who wants to oppose Hume's general conclusion and to make a lot out of external reason statements" (p. 108) [this volume, 44]. Although I think he is quite right in saying that the burden of proof about what is to count as a purely rational process—about *content*—belongs to Hume's opponents, I am arguing that there is no reason to suppose that if this burden is successfully picked up the reasons will be external.

17. *Op. cit.*, p. 13. Nagel calls this a "rebellion against the priority of psychology" (p. 11) and accordingly distinguishes two kinds of internalism: one that takes the psychological facts as given and supposes that we must somehow derive ethics from them in order to achieve an internalist theory, and one that supposes that metaphysical investigations into what it is to be a rational person will have psychological conclusions. Hobbes would be an example of the first kind and Kant of the second.

18. See especially pp. 30 and 43–51 in the translation by Lewis White Beck (New York: Library of Liberal Arts, 1956) and pp. 30 and 41–50 in the Prussian Academy Edition.

19. In chapter III of the Analytic of the *Critique of Practical Reason*, where Kant's project is "not . . . to show a priori why the moral law supplies an incentive but rather what it effects (or better, must effect) in the mind, in so far as it is an incentive" (Beck 17; Acad. 72).

3 Might There Be External Reasons?

John McDowell

1. This paper is directed to a question that has been posed by Bernard Williams, in his interesting and insufficiently discussed article "Internal and External Reasons" [this volume, chap. 1]. Statements to the effect that someone has reason to act in a specified way (say to ϕ), or that there is reason for someone to ϕ, are apparently susceptible of two sorts of interpretation. The first is the internal interpretation, on which the statement is falsified by the agent's lack of any "motive which will be served or furthered by his ϕ-ing" (p. 101) [this volume, 37].[1] The second is the external interpretation, on which that is not so. This is how things seem at first blush, but Williams argues for a scepticism about whether reason statements are ever true on the external interpretation.[2] That is the question I want to consider. The question is quite abstract and general, but it is obvious that it bears on a familiar problem that arises about ethical reasons in particular, in view of the evident possibility of being left cold by them. The implication of Williams's scepticism is that ethical reasons are reasons only for those for whom they are internal reasons: only for those who have motivations to which ethical considerations speak, or can be made to speak.

2. It is a strength of Williams's argument that he bases it on a subtle and flexible conception of the materials available to the internal interpretation. On the crudest understanding of that interpretation, an agent would have a reason to ϕ only by virtue of having a desire such that ϕ-ing either is its satisfaction or is conducive to its satisfaction as means to end. I shall note two main ways in which Williams refines this.

First, about the role of desire. What is required if there is to be an internal reason is that the action in question is suitably related to an element in the agent's "subjective motivational set" (p. 102) [this volume, 38]; and if the term 'desire' is used for all such elements, we must be clear that this is only a "formal" (or, as one might say, philosopher's) usage. Subjective motivational sets are not restricted to what would ordinarily be called 'desires'; they "can contain such things as dispositions of evaluation, patterns of emotional reaction, personal loyalties, and various projects, as they may be abstractly called, embodying commitments of the agent" (p.105) [this volume, 41].

Second, about what it is for an action to be suitably related to an element in the agent's subjective motivational set. The crude view already allows that an agent can have a reason to ϕ without being actually motivated to ϕ, if he does not realize that ϕ-ing is a means to something he desires. The general idea is that one has reason to do what practical reasoning, starting from one's existing motivations, would reveal that one has reason to do—even if one has not realized that one has reason to do it. But the effect of the crude view is to limit the way in which practical reasoning can expand one's awareness of one's internal reasons; the expansion is restricted to cases where practical reasoning brings to light matters whose bearing on one's practical situation is, roughly speaking, technical.[3] Williams's refinement drops this exclusive concentration on means and ends. The conception of practical reasoning or deliberation involved in his version of the general idea is much less restricted; he sketches it only by means of examples. (Such a procedure is unavoidable, he suggests, since "there is an essential indeterminacy in what can be counted a rational deliberative process" [p. 110] [this volume, 45].) He writes (p. 104 [this volume, 40]):

A clear example of practical reasoning is that leading to the conclusion that one has reason to ϕ because ϕ-ing would be the most convenient, economical, pleasant etc. way of satisfying some element in S [the agent's subjective motivational set], and this of course is controlled by other elements in S, if not necessarily in a very clear or determinate way. But there are much wider possibilities for deliberation, such as: thinking how the satisfaction of elements in S can be combined, e.g. by time-ordering; where there is some irresoluble conflict among the elements of S, considering which one attaches most weight to (which, importantly, does not imply that there is some one commodity of which they provide varying amounts); or, again, finding constitutive solutions, such as deciding what would make for an entertaining evening, granted that one wants entertainment.

One important ingredient in this freeing of the idea of practical rationality from restriction to satisfactions, and means to satisfactions, of given desires is that Williams is able to insist on the relevance of imagination to deliberation. By letting his imagination play on an outcome which he supposes he has reason to promote, an agent "may come to have some more concrete sense of what would be involved, and lose his desire for it"; conversely, "the imagination can create new possibilities and new desires" (p. 105) [this volume, 40].

So the idea is this: what one has reason to do, on the internal interpretation, is whatever one can conclude that one has reason to do by an exercise of practical reasoning, conceived on these unrestrictive lines. Practical reasoning is "a heuristic process, and an imaginative one" (p. 110) [this volume, 45]. The significance of elements in one's subjective motivational set is not that one has reason to do only what is conducive to, or constitutes, their satisfaction, but that they "control" the thinking by which one determines what one has reason to do, in ways like those exemplified in the long quotation above: ways that it is impossible to codify in some simple theory.

3. Does this leave any room for the external interpretation? Williams argues, on the following lines, that it does not.

Any reason for action must be something that *could* explain someone's acting in the way for which it is a reason. If a reason did explain an action, the agent *would* have a motivation towards acting in the way in question—a motivation that the reason-giving explanation would spell out. But *ex hypothesi* an external reason statement can be true of someone without his actually having any motive that would be "served or furthered" by his doing what he is said to have a reason to do—not even one whose relevance to his doing that would need to be uncovered by deliberation. (This simply spells out the idea of the external interpretation.) We can reconcile this with the point that any reason, even an external one, must be potentially explanatory of action, on these lines. Consider an agent who is not motivated by an external reason. It must nevertheless be true that some consideration constitutes a reason for him to act in a certain way; his not being motivated by it is a matter of his not *believing*, of the consideration, that it is a reason to act in that way.[4] If he came to believe that, he would come to be motivated. That is, certainly, he would come to have an internal reason statement true of him. But this hypothetical internal reason need not pre-empt all the space an external reason might occupy: we can preserve the external reason if we can make sense of something that would be true throughout such a transition, and which is such that we can see how coming to believe it would be coming to have the motivation that makes the internal reason statement true.

So we need to consider the transition from not being motivated by a putatively external reason to being motivated by it. The question is whether we can make sense of this as coming to believe something that was true already in advance of the agent's being motivated. What "the external reasons theorist" needs, Williams says, is "that the agent should acquire the motivation *because* he comes to believe the reason statement, and that he should do the latter, moreover, because, in some way, he is considering the matter aright" (pp. 108–109) [this volume, 44].

At this point Williams makes a claim that is crucial for his argument (p. 109) [this volume, 44]:

If the theorist is to hold on to these conditions, he will, I think, have to make the condition under which the agent appropriately comes to have the motivation something like this, that he should deliberate correctly; and the external reasons statement itself will have to be taken as roughly equivalent to, or at least as entailing, the claim that if the agent rationally deliberated, then, whatever motivations he originally had, he would come to be motivated to ϕ.

The effect of this is to represent the external reasons theorist as committed to returning an affirmative answer to Hume's question, whether reason alone can give rise to a motivation. The predicament itself determines an interpretation for 'alone' here. As Williams describes his position, the external reasons theorist must envisage a procedure of correct deliberation or reasoning that gives rise to a motivation, but is not "controlled" by existing motivations, in the way that figures in the account of internal reasons; for, if the deliberation were thus "controlled" by existing motivations, the reason it brought to light would simply be an internal reason. So the external reasons theorist has to envisage the generation of a new motivation by reason, in an exercise in which the directions it can take are not determined by the shape of the agent's prior motivations—an exercise that would be rationally compelling whatever motivations one started from. As Williams says (p. 109) [this volume, 44–45], it is very hard to believe there could be a kind of reasoning that was pure in this sense—owing none of its cogency to the specific shape of pre-existing motivations—but nevertheless motivationally efficacious. If the rational cogency of a piece of deliberation is in no way dependent on prior motivations, how can we comprehend its giving rise to a new motivation?

4. But need the external reasons theorist fight on this ground?

Let us retrace our steps. We have to consider the transition from not being motivated by a supposedly external reason to being motivated by it. The external reasons theorist must suppose the agent acquires the new motivation by coming to believe the external reason statement. To be an external reason statement, that statement must have been true all along; in coming to believe it, the agent must be coming to consider the matter aright. The crucial question is this: why must the external reasons theorist envisage this transition to considering the matter aright as being effected by *correct deliberation*? He cannot make sense of the motivational effect of the transition by crediting it to deliberation "controlled" by prior motivations, since that would merely reveal the reason to be internal. So, if there must be deliberation—reasoning—that could bring about the transition, he needs to invent an application of reason in which it can impel people to action without owing its cogency to the specific shape of their prior motivations; and this is what Williams rightly says it is hard to believe in. The argument debars the external reasons theorist from supposing that there is no way to effect the transition except one that would not count as being swayed by reasons: for instance (p. 108) [this volume, 44], being persuaded by moving rhetoric, and, by implication (p. 110) [this volume, 46], inspiration and conversion. But what is the ground for this exclusion?

Williams's wording may seem to answer this question. To repeat a passage I have already quoted, he says that what the external reasons theorist needs is "that the agent should acquire the motivation *because* he comes to believe the reason statement, and that he should do the latter, moreover, because, in some way, he is considering the matter aright" (pp. 108–109) [this volume, 44]. If "considering the matter aright" figures, as this suggests, in an *explanation* of the agent's coming to believe the reason statement, suited to reveal the transition as one to a *true* belief, it may seem that the phrase must single out and endorse something like a procedure of argument or reasoning. But in fact all that the external reasons theorist needs at that point in the argument—this is quite clear from the rephrasing of it in my last paragraph—is that *in* coming to believe the reason statement, the agent is coming to consider the matter aright. This leaves it quite open how the transition is effected.

It is worth emphasizing that there need be nothing philosophically mysterious about the notion of considering matters aright in this kind of context: no implication of a weird metaphysic, for instance, in which values or obligations are set over against our subjectivity, as independent of it as the shapes and sizes of things.[5] If we think of ethical upbringing in a roughly Aristotelian way, as a process of habituation into suitable modes of behaviour, inextricably bound up with the inculcation of suitably related modes of thought, there is no mystery about how the process can be the acquisition, simultaneously, of a way of seeing things and of a collection of motivational directions or practical concerns, focused and activated in particular cases by exercises of the way of seeing things.[6] And if the upbringing has gone as it should, we shall want to say that the way of seeing things—the upshot, if you like, of a moulding of the agent's subjectivity—involves considering them aright, that is, having a correct conception of their actual layout. Here talking of having been properly brought up and talking of considering things aright are two ways of giving expression to the same assessment, one that would be up for justification by ethical argument.

Let me emphasize what is implicit in this last sentence: I am using the notion of proper upbringing only to defuse the threat of metaphysical peculiarity, not as a foundational element in some sort of ethical theory—as if we had independent access to what counts as a good ethical upbringing, and could use that to explain ethical truth as a property enjoyed by the judgements that a properly brought up person would make.

What if someone has not been properly brought up? In order to take seriously the idea that someone who has been properly brought up tends to consider matters aright in the relevant area, we surely do not need to embrace the massively implausible implication that someone who has not been properly brought up—someone who has slipped through the net, so to speak—can be induced into seeing things straight by directing some piece of *reasoning* at him. On the contrary, reasoning aimed at generating new motivations will surely stand a chance of working only if it appeals to something in the audience's existing motivational make-up, in something like the way exploited in Williams's account of the internal interpretation; and the trouble with someone who has in some radical way slipped through the net is that there may be no such point of leverage for reasoning aimed at generating the motivations that are characteristic of someone who has been properly brought up. What it would take to get such a person to consider the relevant matters aright, we might plausibly suppose, is exactly the sort of thing that, according to Williams's argument, the external reasons theorist may not appeal to: something like conversion. Admittedly, it is not straightforwardly obvious how we should think of this, or some better substitute, as operating; the bare idea of conversion points at best to a schema for explanations of shifts of character, and the weight of the explanation in any real case would rest on our comprehension of the psychic efficacy of the specific converting factor (a religious experience, say). But it does not seem hopeless to suppose that at least sometimes we really might be able to understand on these lines how someone who had slipped through the net might suddenly or gradually become as if he had been properly brought up, with the interlocking collection of concerns and way of seeing things that he failed to acquire earlier. The idea of conversion would function here as the idea of an intelligible shift in motivational orientation that is exactly *not* effected by inducing a person to discover, by practical reasoning controlled by existing motivations, some internal reasons that he did not previously realize he had. But if its upshot *is* a case of considering matters aright, why should such a process not count as someone's being made aware of some *external* reasons, reasons that he had all along, for acting in the relevant ways?

It is plausible, then, that from certain starting-points there is no rational route—no process of being swayed by reasons—that would take someone to being as if he had been properly brought up. (Being properly brought up is not itself a rational route into being that way.) But this has no evident tendency to disrupt the natural connection between being that way and considering matters aright. So why not suppose that the kind of conversion I have envisaged might be a case of what the external reasons theorist needed: acquisition of a new motivation by way of acquiring correct beliefs?

5. Williams simply assumes what rules this out, that the external reasons theorist must envisage a transition to considering matters aright that would be effected by reasoning. This assumption is held in place by what Williams takes to be the only point of believing in external reasons. According to Williams, the external reasons theorist wants to be able to bring a charge of *irrationality* against anyone who is not motivated in some direction that the theorist thinks he should be motivated in; "he wants any rational agent, as such, to acknowledge the requirement to do the thing in question" (p. 110) [this volume, 46].

There is certainly a recognizable temptation hereabouts. Moralists in particular are prone to suppose that there must be a knockdown argument, an appeal to unaided reason, which, if one could only find it and get people to listen, would force anyone capable of being influenced by reasons at all into caring about the sorts of things one ought to care about. In itself this might be no more than a harmless fantasy (although when the expectation of finding such an argument is disappointed, this can lead to morality's seeming problematic in ways that it should not).[7] What is in question at present, however, is a related temptation, which one can see that one should avoid however optimistic one is about the prospects for the knockdown argument: the temptation, lacking the knockdown argument as we all do, to talk as if the argument is out in the open and people who do not care about the sorts of things they ought to care about are flying in the face of it. Williams's excellent point is that an accusation of irrationality that is supposed to convey something on those lines is nothing but "bluff" (p. 111) [this volume, 47].[8]

As Williams notes, there are plenty of things that the internal reasons approach allows one to say against someone who is not motivated by the considerations one thinks he should be motivated by: for instance, "that he is inconsiderate, or cruel, or selfish, or imprudent; or that things, and he, would be a lot nicer if he were so motivated" (p. 110) [this volume, 46]. (We can add: that the shape of his motivations reveals that he has not been properly brought up.) So what is the point of holding out for the right to make an accusation of irrationality as well, if it is not to bluff the person into mending his ways by means of a fraudulent suggestion that he is flouting considerations that anyone susceptible to reasons at all would be moved by? Perhaps the answer is "None"; it may be that calling a person 'irrational' carries, beyond the possibility of cancellation, the illicit implication that he is unmoved by something that would move anyone capable of being moved by reasons at all. (I shall come back to this later.) But even if we renounce any right to direct an accusation of irrationality against a *person* when he is unmoved by considerations we think he should be moved by, that does not quite settle the question whether, as Williams puts it at one point (p. 111) [this volume, 47], "the only rationality of action is the rationality of internal reasons."

What is at issue here is the relation between the *explanatory* role of the concept of reason and a *critical* or *normative* dimension that it must have. Williams is considering this issue when he raises the question (pp. 102–103) [this volume, 38] whether someone who believes of some petrol that it is gin, and wants a gin and tonic, should be said to have a reason to mix the petrol with tonic and drink it. If he does that, we shall have an explanation, of the reason-giving kind, for his doing what he does. But Williams suggests that an internal reasons theorist should not say, on those grounds, that the person does have a reason to drink the stuff which is in fact petrol:

It looks in the wrong direction, by implying in effect that the internal reason conception is only concerned with explanation, and not at all with the agent's rationality, and this may help to motivate a search for other sorts of reason which are connected with his rationality. But the internal reason conception is concerned with the agent's rationality. What we can correctly ascribe to him in a third-personal internal reason statement is also what he can ascribe to himself as a result of deliberation . . . [This volume, 38–39]

Here Williams is making room for a thought on these lines: the explanatory power of reason-giving explanations depends on there being a critical dimension to the concept of rationality. These explanations do not merely reveal actions as the outcome of some way—to whose detail we can be indifferent—in which the agent happens to be internally organized; that the operations of an internal organization from which an action is represented as flowing are recognizably the right kind of operations for the explanation to be of the reason-giving sort requires that they approximate sufficiently closely to something in the nature of an ideal.[9] Reason-giving explanations require a conception of how things ideally would be, sufficiently independent of how any actual individual's psychological economy operates to serve as the basis for critical assessment of it. In particular, there must be a potential gap between the ideal and the specific directions in which a given agent's motivations push him.

Williams secures an independence that conforms to this abstract description, in the passage I have quoted, by his appeal to deliberation: what practical rationality requires of an agent is not simply read off from his specific motivations just as they stand (including, in Williams's example, a wish to drink some stuff that is in fact petrol), but is determined, from those motivations, by deliberation, whose capacity to correct and enrich the specific motivations one starts with is supposed to open up the necessary gap between actual and ideal.

But it is open to question whether this puts the *right* distance between the basis for criticism of the way an agent's actions flow from his psychological states, on the one hand, and the way his psychology happens to be, on the other.[10] Certainly the appeal to deliberation interposes some space between these things, but the standard is still, albeit with the indirection that that imposes, fixed by the agent's motivations as they stand. There is thus a sense in which it can be claimed that the resulting picture of the critical dimension of the concept of practical rationality is *psychologistic*. That term has become attached[11] to Frege's reproach against positions that treated the principles of logic, which we can think of as delineating an important part of the structure of theoretical rationality, as "laws of thought" rather than "laws of truth."[12] Frege's point was, in effect, that if logic is to be able to stand in judgement over the workings of minds, it cannot be constructed out of mere facts about how psychological transitions take place. One reason, then, for doubting that "the only rationality of action is the rationality of internal reasons," quite distinct from the wish to browbeat people into (for instance, and especially) morality by a fraudulent accusation of irrationality, might be the idea that the critical dimension of the notion of practical rationality requires an analogous transcendence of the mere facts of individual psychology—even as corrected by the sort of deliberation that the internal reasons conception allows.

Beliefs are not rationally self-contained psychic phenomena, which could be aggregated just anyhow, with no restrictions on their interrelations and their relations to the subject's world, and still add up to a state of mind. Theoretical reason, both formal and substantive, puts limits on the attributions of belief that so much as make sense. It would get things back to front to think that an adequate conception of theoretical reason could be derivative from a set of supposedly independent data about the workings of minds. Now a point of this sort should be applicable to practical no less than to theoretical reason. Desires, in the broad "formal" sense of ingredients in subjective motivational sets, are similarly not rationally self-contained psychic phenomena, which can be unproblematically conceived as determinants, from the outside, of the shape that practical reason takes, for the individual agent whose desires they are.[13] But the idea that "the only rationality of action is the rationality of internal reasons" seems to involve thinking of the desires (in that sense) from which an individual agent starts in just this way.

In the context of this kind of refusal to find "the rationality of internal reasons" sufficient, the idea of not reasoning correctly might be glossed in terms of not giving a consideration the right weight in deliberation. On these lines, deliberating correctly would be giving all relevant considerations the force they are credited with in a correct picture of one's practical predicament. This yields a sense in which to believe an external reason statement is, as Williams indeed suggests it must be (p. 109) [this volume, 44], to believe that if the agent deliberated correctly he would be motivated (of course not necessarily conclusively) in the direction in which the reason points.[14] But there is no implication, as in Williams's argument, that there must be a deliberative or rational procedure that would lead anyone from not being so motivated to being so motivated. On the contrary, the transition to being so motivated is a transition *to* deliberating correctly, not one effected *by* deliberating correctly; effecting the transition may need some non-rational alteration such as conversion.

Perhaps we can even give a sense to the accusation of irrationality within this framework. There would now be no question of a bluff, any more than one need be bluffing if one says, to someone who cannot find anything to appreciate in, say, twelve-tone music, "You are missing the reasons there are for seeking out opportunities to hear this music." (It might take something like a conversion to bring the reasons within the person's notice; there is no suggestion that he is failing to be swayed by something that would sway anyone capable of being influenced by reasons at all.) However, it is (at least) difficult to separate calling someone 'irrational' from the suggestion that he is missing the force of something in the nature of an argument. (It would be odd to say that a person who finds no reasons to listen to twelve-tone music is irrational, even though one thinks that the reasons are there.) So far as I can see, scepticism about the adequacy of the internal reason conception has no need to insist on classifying people in these terms, and it is probably safest for it not to do so.

6. There is no question of my trying to establish the tenability of a position on these lines in this paper: my main point is only that, though Williams is surely right about the bluff he attacks, that does not show that the internal conception of practical reason gives us everything we want. In this section, I shall very briefly mention some possible different lines on which a scepticism about external reasons might be defended, and suggest responses to them.

On the internal conception, practical reason can be, in a sense, content-neutral: deliberation is indifferent to the nature of the motivations that constitute input to it, and might be conceived as a procedure for imposing coherence and practical determinacy on whatever collection of prior motivations one presents it with. On an external conception, by contrast, practical reason is not something that can be equally well exemplified whatever the content of the motivations one begins with. If one is tempted to think that the content-neutrality of deductive rationality ought to generalize over all applications of reason, one will be inclined to see an argument for the internal conception here. But the argument would be no stronger than the case for generalizing that feature of deductive logic. And surely it is no more obvious that we should expect practical reason to be content-neutral than it is that we should expect, for instance, scientific reason to be so.[15]

Reasons must be capable of explaining actions; and it can seem that if we are to find that intelligible, we must conceive practical reason as directing the action-generating efficacy of a collection of motivations that are prior to it, and, as far as rational explanation goes, simply given. This idea is clearly congenial to the internal conception. But it rests on what looks like a misconception of the way actions are explained by reasons, one that assimilates that to the way events are explained by mechanical forces such as the tension in a tightly wound spring. One can be suspicious of this assimilation without threat to the thesis that reason-giving explanations are causal.[16] To respect the truism that reason-giving explanations work by revealing how actions are motivated, it is not necessary to picture motivations as antecedent quasi-mechanical sources of energy: in explaining an action, a reason-giving explanation can equally make the motivation of the action rationally intelligible, and there is no basis for insisting that this must be by way of representing that motivation as the upshot of reason's channelling a pre-rational motivational force in a certain direction.[17]

The opposition to psychologism I have described pictures practical predicaments as structured by collections of values that are independent of any individual's motivational make-up, and this may seem to reintroduce the threat of a weird metaphysic which I discounted earlier. But this is a mistake. One way to avoid such a metaphysic is to regard values as reflections or projections of psychological facts involving affect or sentiment, and such a position might indeed have difficulties in accepting the kind of transcendence I have envisaged. But in order to acknowledge the constitutive connection of values to human subjectivity, it is not obligatory to suppose the genealogy of value can be unravelled, retrospectively, in such a way as to permit factoring out a contribution made by isolable facts about our individual psychology to the evaluative contours of our world. A sane subjectivism can allow that value transcends independently describable psychological fact.[18]

There may seem to be something suspect about the way I have exploited Williams's phrase 'considering the matter aright'. I suggested that when the supposed external reasons in question are ethical ones, the assessment expressed in 'aright' would be grounded in ethical argument; and I meant argument internal to some specific ethical outlook, not argument that would somehow win over someone unmoved by what one wants to represent as external reasons. There is an intelligible temptation to suppose that such a use of 'aright' cannot be more than bluster. That is indeed what it would be if it were meant somehow to impress outsiders, even in the absence of any ability to persuade them; that is Williams's point about bluff. But I have disavowed any aim of manipulating the notion like this. Nothing more would be in question, in any particular appeal to a determinate conception of how the relevant matters are rightly considered, than confidence in some part of an ethical outlook. (Ethical external reasons are not external to ethics.) This can seem a second-grade application of the concept of correctness, but it is open to question whether we can do better in any region of our thinking.[19] We do not conceive our values as owing their authenticity, and their relevance to what we do, to our motivational make-up or to anything in the psychological genesis of our coming to have them; and that, together with our managing to sustain confidence in them through reflection, is all it takes for us to suppose they yield reasons that are not internal in the sense Williams explains. This sustaining of confidence is fraught with difficulties; but it is a mistake to let a supposed metaphysical insight, expressed in depreciating the sense of 'aright' available in appraisal of ethical thinking, seem to add to them.

I began this section as if it were going to be something of a digression, but in fact I believe the last couple of paragraphs have touched on what is in one sense the heart of the matter. Williams's explicit argument has no deeper foundation than the assumption that the external reasons theorist wants to be entitled to find irrationality when someone is insensitive to the force of a supposed external reason; and in its naked form, the assumption seems too transparently flimsy to be the real basis for his conclusion. It is too easy to drive a wedge between irrationality and insensitivity to reasons that are nevertheless there: recall the case of not appreciating twelve-tone music. But perhaps we can begin to find it intelligible that this simple point goes missing if we locate the real foundation of the argument deeper down, in an idea on these lines: the notion of truth or objectivity, implicit in the appeal to "considering the matter aright" that the external reasons theorist needs, requires beliefs to be capable of being formed either under the causal control of the circumstances that render them true or as a result of exercising rationality conceived in purely procedural terms, as something that can be compelling without need of substantive presuppositions. Beliefs about values or obligations had better not fall under the first of these disjuncts, on pain of a weird metaphysic; so, according to this line of thought, they would have to fall under the second. I do not mean to suggest that starting here would make the argument against external reasons any stronger; on the contrary, we might just as well argue by *modus tollens* from the continued ease of driving the wedge to the conclusion that there must be something wrong with the disjunction. But there are familiar philosophical concerns about truth and objectivity whose operation, in some such form as this, might make it seem that Williams's starting assumption would have to be common ground.[20] All this, however, is off stage so far as Williams's article is concerned, and in another sense this section remains simply a digression.

7. Williams's argument depends crucially on the basic premise that a transition to a correct view of the reasons for acting that apply to an agent—to considering these matters aright—must be capable of being effected, for the agent, by reasoning. The internal reasons approach gives an account of such transitions that represents the possibilities for making them, and therefore the content of a correct view of reasons, as determined by the motivational orientation from which the agent in question begins. If one is suspicious of this account of how a correct view of reasons is determined,

one's only recourse, given the basic premise, is to postulate a kind of reasoning that is practical but not shaped by the motivations of those who engage in it; this then looks like a supposed exercise of that bloodless or dispassionate Reason that stands opposed to Passion in a familiar and unprepossessing genre of moral psychology, one that Hume made it difficult to take seriously.

What I have been suggesting is that the basic premise distorts the issue. In order to urge that there is more substance to practical *reason* than the internal reasons conception allows, one need not seek to supplement the internal reasons picture of practical *reasoning*. This distinction enables us to decline the choice between, on the one hand, taking a correct view of an agent's reasons for acting to be determined (indirectly, via deliberation) by his "passions" as they stand—Williams's internal approach—and, on the other, taking it to be determined by dispassionate Reason—in effect, the only alternative Williams allows. We do not need to choose between conceiving practical reason psychologistically and conceiving it as an autonomous source of motivational energy over and above the "passions." This should begin to suggest a proper location for an investigation of practical reason that can accommodate the surely indubitable relevance of human psychology to what human beings have reason to do; the right way to think about this topic belongs between the individualistic psychologism of the internal reasons approach and the apsychologism, so to speak, of the only alternative that Williams's argumentative structure allows.[21]

Notes

1. As will become clear immediately, this can be understood so as not to require that the agent is actually motivated towards φ-ing.

2. One might say: about whether there are any external reasons. Williams allows this sort of formulation (for instance in his title; I have followed suit in mine). But I shall follow him in treating this only as a convenience; nothing turns on whether we are looking for a classification of sorts of reasons for action or merely a classification of sorts of things that can be said.

3. Williams even suggests, on the basis of the fact that "the mere discovery that some course of action is the causal means to an end is not in itself a piece of practical reasoning" (p. 104) [this volume, 40], that the effect is to obliterate practical *reasoning* from the picture altogether.

4. There are two possible cases here: one in which the consideration is in view, but not believed to constitute a reason, and one in which the consideration is not even in view, or, if in view, not in clear focus.

5. Here I am in agreement with Simon Blackburn (see, e g., chaps. 5 and 6 of *Spreading the Word* [Oxford: Clarendon Press, 1984]); although I do not think it is felicitous to represent the metaphysically undemanding notion of correctness or truth that is in question as a construction on an *anti*-realistic base, as in Blackburn's projectivism.

6. See *Nicomachean Ethics*, book 2; but no specific Aristotelian detail matters to the point I am making—what is in question is barely more than common sense. The terminology I have used to describe what I allege to be unmysterious in the light of Aristotelian common sense comes from David Wiggins: see "Deliberation and Practical Reason" (reprinted in his *Needs, Values, Truth* [Oxford: Blackwell, 1987]).

7. I use 'morality' here as a mere variant on 'ethics'; the point is not one about the special topic that Williams discusses in chap. 10 of *Ethics and the Limits of Philosophy* (Cambridge, Mass.: Harvard University Press, 1985).

8. A similar point is made by Philippa Foot, in "Morality as a System of Hypothetical Imperatives" (reprinted in her *Virtues and Vices* [Oxford: Blackwell, 1978]). In "Are Moral Requirements Hypothetical Imperatives?" (*Proceedings of the Aristotelian Society, Supplementary Volume* 52 [1978]: 13–29), I try to defend a version of the idea of the categorical imperative whose point would not lie in this kind of intellectual dishonesty.

9. Donald Davidson has written in this connection of the constitutive role of the concept of rationality (in its normative or critical application) in organizing our understanding of the concepts of common-sense psychology. See *Essays on Actions and Events* (Oxford: Clarendon Press, 1980), especially essays 11 and 12. (The point comes out in the plausibility of saying that it would make no sense to suppose that an explanation was of the reason-giving sort while disallowing the question how *good* the reason is for which the agent is said to have acted. This suggests that Williams did not need to deny that the agent has a reason, in the case he describes: he could have made the essential point about the importance of the critical dimension of the concept of rationality by allowing that the agent has a reason, but insisting that the reason is open to objection.)

10. Of course it is not only (or even, perhaps, primarily) actions that can be criticized on the basis of a conception of rationality; but the topic of this paper is reasons for action in particular.

11. See Michael Dummett, *Frege: Philosophy of Language* (London: Duckworth, 1973).

12. See the opening of "Thoughts" (in *Frege: Logical Investigations*, trans. P. T. Geach and R. H. Stoothoff [Oxford: Blackwell, 1977]).

13. See, again, Davidson, *Essays on Actions and Events*, especially essays 11 and 12. Against the idea of desire as a self-standing phenomenon, so that particular desires stand in no need of a conception of rationality to underwrite their intelligibility,

see G. E. M. Anscombe's well-known remarks about wanting a saucer of mud, in *Intention* (Oxford: Blackwell, 1957), pp. 70–71.

14. This is essentially the point made by Brad Hooker, "Williams' Argument Against External Reasons" *Analysis* 44 (1987): 42–44; he credits it to Robert Gay. Hooker does not question Williams's claim that the transition to being moved by an allegedly external reason would have to be effected by reasoning.

15. Williams himself would clearly have no sympathy with the idea of a purely *formal* account of practical reason.

16. For which see Davidson, "Actions, Reasons, and Causes" (reprinted in his *Essays on Actions and Events*).

17. See chap. 5 of Thomas Nagel, *The Possibility of Altruism* (Princeton: Princeton University Press, 1970) [this volume, chap. 9].

18. See David Wiggins, "A Sensible Subjectivism?" reprinted in *Needs, Values, Truth*. It was the possibility of a subjectivism of this kind that I had in mind in my remark about projectivism in n. 5 above.

19. Against Williams's suggestion, in *Ethics and the Limits of Philosophy*, that natural science is in a relevantly different position, see my "Critical Notice," *Mind* 95 (1986): 377–386.

20. The assumption seems to be conceded without question in Christine M. Korsgaard's acute discussion of Williams, in "Skepticism about Practical Reason," *Journal of Philosophy* 83 (1986): 5–25 [this volume, chap. 2].

21. I am grateful to Annette Baier and Paul Hurley for helpful comments on an earlier draft. T. M. Scanlon responded to a version of this paper that I delivered to the Eastern Division of the American Philosophical Association in December 1987, and his remarks have been very useful (though I have by no means met all his points). More recently, I have been greatly helped by comments from Jonathan Dancy.

4 Reply to McDowell

Bernard Williams

The first matter I should like to take up is my view about internal and external reasons,[1] and John McDowell's criticism of it [this volume, chap. 3]. McDowell has set out the main argument, and I shall not repeat it in detail. The central idea is that if B can say truly of A that A has a reason to ϕ, then (leaving aside the qualifications needed because it may not be his strongest reason) there must be a sound deliberative route to ϕ-ing which starts from A's existing motivations. It follows that what an agent has a reason to do will be a function of what I called his 'S'—that is to say, the existing set of his motivational states—or, alternatively, ϕ-ing will have to be an action that an agent could rationally decide to do as a result of deliberation *whatever* his S might be. The latter alternative McDowell agrees with me in finding unattractive. The former alternative represents what I called 'internalism' about practical reason, which, equally, McDowell does not want to accept. His aim is to leave room for an intelligible account of "external" reasons for action: that is to say, to give a sense to 'A has a reason to ϕ' that does not necessarily ground ϕ-ing in A's existing S.[2]

McDowell's strategy is to question an assumption that he finds lying behind the two alternatives (and which, he remarks, is also made by some writers who have criticized the argument). The assumption, he claims, is that the external reasons theorist must take a certain view of the transition from the state in which A is not motivated by the alleged reason to a state in which he is motivated by it. The assumption is said to be that an external reasons theorist must see this transition as being effected by *correct deliberation*. It is this assumption, McDowell argues, that permits me to force a choice between two alternatives: between a deliberation that is a function of A's existing S, and a deliberation that will arrive at the desired conclusion whatever A's S may be. But, if the external reasons theorist need not assume that A would arrive at the right conclusion by deliberation, then I cannot force this choice.

Now McDowell does agree that there is a sense in which

> to believe an external reason statement is . . . to believe that if the agent deliberated correctly he would be motivated (of course not necessarily conclusively) in the direction in which the reason points. But there is no implication, as in Williams's argument, that there must be a deliberative or rational procedure that would lead anyone from not being so motivated to being so motivated. On the contrary, the transition to being so motivated is by transition *to* deliberating correctly, not one effected *by* deliberating correctly; effecting the transition may need some non-rational alteration like conversion. (p. 78, his emphases) [this volume, 82]

I do not think that my argument presupposes quite what McDowell says that it presupposes, and, before moving to some more basic issues, I shall try to say where, as it seems to me, a misunderstanding has arisen. Consider the statements

(R) A has a reason to φ.

(D) If A deliberated correctly, he would be motivated to φ.

McDowell agrees that to believe (R) is in some sense to believe (D). It seems to follow that, if someone (for instance A) is presented with the statement (R), he must understand it as claiming (roughly) (D). But I certainly did not want to say that A would have to come to believe *the statement (D)* through deliberation. That would be a very implausible idea. There is a point that may confuse the issue here, and make it look as though this implausible idea were at work. If A were to deliberate in the manner that the commentator regards as correct, he would arrive at a conclusion which he himself could express as a first-personal version of (R). In this sense, (R) is something that can be, and if all is going correctly will be, arrived at by deliberation. This shows that, despite the close relations between (R) and (D), they cannot be equivalent: if they were, then (D) itself could be arrived at, in first-personal form, by correct deliberation. My argument does involve a connection between (R) and (D), and it also uses the idea of A's arriving at a first-personal form of (R) by deliberation, but I do not think that it relies on the assumption which McDowell is questioning.

My argument can be best approached through the converse question: can every occurrence of (D) be replaced by (R)? Given a reasonable construction of the hypothetical itself,[3] the internalist can give an account of (D) in which it may be replaced by (R). This is because he can impose, as he supposes, some constraints on what counts as deliberating correctly. Those constraints, as I emphasized, are by no means fully determinate, and they are certainly not "formal." They allow for such things as the exercise of the imagination. Nevertheless, the internalist's idea is that there are some processes that would count, and others that would not count, as deliberatively arriving, from one's existing S, at the project of φ-ing. Granted this, the internalist can give a constrained sense to (D), one which—he claims—matches it to (R). But this does not imply, as McDowell's objection suggests, that the agent should be able to conduct the relevant deliberation in fact. Perhaps some unconscious obstacle, for instance, would have to be removed before he could arrive at the motivation to φ. Someone who claimed something of this sort would have to make good on the claim; he would have to be able to make some distinction between, for instance, removing blocks to the expression of A's existing S, and adding to A's S. This may not be easy to do, but the fact that there is an onus to be discharged here just marks the point, on the internalist's view, that (R) has a content which distinguishes it from other things that might be said about A.

How does it stand with the externalist's view? He agrees that there is a close relation between (R) and (D), and, since he does not want the internalist's constraints on (R), he does not want them on (D), either. Then it seems that (D)—the claim that if A deliberated correctly, he would be motivated to φ—means only this:

(C) if A were a correct deliberator, A would be motivated in these circumstances to φ,

where 'a correct deliberator' means someone who deliberates as a well-informed and well-disposed person would deliberate: and, in McDowell's account, this seems to be someone like Aristotle's *phronimos*, or, as McDowell puts it, someone who has been properly brought up.

If we take (C) in this way, we face questions about such Aristotelian conceptions, and how stable, objective, and so on they are. . . . But it is important that this is not the only question we face when we take (C) in this way; this is one reason why the issue of external reasons, though it is closely connected with other matters, remains a special question. Let us grant for the moment that it is known, more or less, what the *phronimos* would be motivated to do in certain circumstances, and that it is a good thing, all round, to be a *phronimos*. We agree, that is to say, that we can know things of the form

(G) A correct deliberator (i.e., a *phronimos*) would be motivated in these circumstances to φ.

In virtue of what the external reasons theorist has given us so far, (C) gets its content from (G). (C) merely says (G) with reference to A, where 'with reference to' means only that (G) is applied to A—A is mentioned, and is the occasion of a reiteration of (G). (G) can be applied in this way, it seems, to anybody. Given (G), the sentence form

If x were a correct deliberator, x would be motivated in these circumstances to φ

will yield a truth under any substitution for x, granted only that the substitution in the antecedent yields an intelligible possibility (a point I shall come back to). It follows that on this account (R) does not make a statement distinctively about A at all. The reference to A may, in a familiar way, serve to pick out some circumstances that form part of the reason and would be specified if the reason were fully spelled out, but that is the most that it can do. On the externalist account, so construed, statements of the type (R) do not relate actions to persons, but types of action to types of circumstances, and they are most revealingly expressed in the form 'in circumstances X, there is reason to φ'.

This last formula does not have to be taken in a formalistic or rule-based spirit. The formula is perhaps most familiarly invoked in connection with Kantian or prescriptivist moral theories, but it is not essentially tied to such theories. On the contrary, the externalist account I am considering gives an explanation of such formulae not in terms of rules or principles, but in terms of what a *phronimos* would do. But the *phronimos* is an ideal type, and the fact that he is invoked does not make the formula any less impersonal, relative to particular agents. On this account, (R) invokes the person A, but none of its content is distinctively about A.

This immediately raises a problem, which is as much ethical as analytical. If (R) gets its content from (C), and (C) gets its content from (G), then what A has reason to do in certain circumstances is what the *phronimos* would have reason to do in those circumstances. But, in considering what he has reason to do, one thing that A should take into account, if he is grown up and has some sense, are the ways in which he relevantly fails to be a *phronimos*. Aristotle's *phronimos* (to stay with that model) was, for instance, supposed to display temperance, a moderate equilibrium of the passions which did not even require the emergency semi-virtue of self-control.[4] But, if I know that I fall short of temperance and am unreliable with respect even to some kinds of self-control, I shall have good reason not to do some things that a temperate person could properly and safely do. The homiletic tradition, not only within Christianity, is full of sensible warnings against moral weight-lifting.

It will be no good trying to accommodate this difficulty, of squeezing the good into the right through the tubes of imperfection, by putting all A's limitations into the account of the circumstances. If the circumstances are defined partly in terms of the agent's ethical imperfection, then the *phronimos* cannot be in *those* circumstances, and (G) cannot apply at all. Rather, we shall have to modify the interpretation of (C), away from (G) and in the direction of accommodating it more closely to the actual nature of A. The question then becomes, how we can do that without ending up with internalism.

It is not clear to me what exactly McDowell's view is on the question that I have expressed in terms of the relations between (R), (C), and (G). On the one hand, what he says seems not to offer any content for external reason statements except considerations about what the *phronimos* (the person who has been "properly brought up") would do. On the other hand, he introduces, towards the end of his paper, the example of what one might say to "someone who cannot find anything to appreciate in, say, twelve-tone music." I doubt that 'someone' here means 'anyone'. The fact that listening to twelve-tone music can be a worthwhile activity surely does not give everyone a reason to engage in it. If not, then 'A has a reason to try twelve-tone music' must have a content that goes beyond 'listening to this music is a worthwhile activity'—a content, one might suppose, that has something to do with A's S, such as his present taste in music. However, it may be that this example, on McDowell's view, brings in further considerations: he may not take it to be unqualifiedly part of what it is to be "properly brought up" that one has a taste for music, or at least for twelve-tone music.

I insisted in my writings about this question that no account of 'A has reason to ϕ' can be adequate unless it has normative force, and I tried to explain how the internalist account (with the indeterminacies that any realistic account demands) meets this requirement. McDowell acknowledges that this is my aim, but he claims that I have not left enough, or the right-shaped, space for normativity; that my account is too "psychologistic." I accept that the account is psychologistic, in the sense that on my view a statement about A's reasons is partly a statement about A's psychology. I do not see this as an objection, as it is (I agree) an objection to say that a theory of arithmetic is psychologistic. McDowell may think that I have drawn the line in the wrong place, and have relied on too "procedural" a conception of the relation between the hypothetical deliberation and A's S. But *some* constraints on the idea of deliberating correctly, as it appears in (C) above, are needed if statements about people's reasons, on the model of (R), are to say anything distinctive. I said earlier that it was a problem, so far, with an externalist account that (R) does not emerge as a statement distinctively about the person A. It is also, and relatedly, true that, if (R) does say anything about A, this externalist account does not sufficiently distinguish what (R) says about him from other things that might be said about him. I agree with McDowell that it was a mistake to pick out 'irrational' as a crucial term in this connection. But I want still to press the point that I made originally, that from both an ethical and a psychological point of view it is important that (R) and its relatives should say something special about A, and not merely invoke in connection with him some general normative judgment. An externalist account that simply bases (R) on (G) cannot satisfy that condition.

The difficulty we have just encountered, about temperance and the relations between the good and the right, represents just one aspect of a wider question: granted (G), what does that mean for a particular person A? Here it is very important to distinguish two different positions. One is the externalist position I have been discussing, which bases (R) simply on (G). This treats the person A merely as a point of reference or occasion for the general judgment (G). The other position also bases (R) on (G), *but in association with an internalist account of (R)*. This invokes a substantive account of a human S, and claims that the best life, relative to such an S, is that of the *phronimos*. This latter is the position which, in *Ethics and the Limits of Philosophy*, I ascribed, with some qualifications, to Aristotle. It may be that the qualifications I made there were not strong enough.[5] It was not Aristotle's view that a human being, as such, is capable of the good life. He thought that women and natural slaves lacked distinctive capacities which enable someone to become a *phronimos*, and, further, that even a male who was not a natural slave, but who had not been properly brought up, could not become a *phronimos*: earlier it would have been possible for him to become one, but later he could not do so. The fact that these various things are not possible, or no longer possible, does not affect judgments of *the good*. The good life is what it is, the life of the *phronimos*, and the fact that it is inaccessible to women and to (natural) slaves and to the now irreversibly corrupted is, roughly speaking,[6] their bad luck. But the incapacities from which these people suffer do affect what they have reason to try to do. In terms of Aristotle's own outlook, these people have no reason to try to be like a *phronimos*, to the extent that such a life lies beyond their competence, their understanding, and their possible motivations.[7] Aristotle's own way of focusing considerations of the good life on to the individual was, if I understand him, internalist.

However, there might be a different way of focusing on to the individual agent general Aristotelian considerations about the good life, which did not adopt the relativity to that agent's S which is the mark of the internalist view. This method would lie in taking very seriously a question that I mentioned earlier, whether the supposition of the agent's being a correct deliberator (that is to say, a *phronimos*) represents a real possibility. If we could make something of this, we might be able to say that (G), by itself, does not support (R); rather, it supports (R) only in conjunction with the premise that there is a real possibility that A should be a *phronimos*. Such an account would represent (R) as being, in a more substantive sense, a statement about A than it is if it is simply an instantiation of (G), but (at least at first sight) it avoids the path of internalism.

Externalists who feel, as they should, a need for some constraints on the route from the good to the right, from (G) to (R), may want to explore this area. They will have to start from the consideration that the real possibility they need must take the form of 'A could be a *phronimos*' and not merely 'A could have been a *phronimos*'; if the latter were enough for this purpose, we would be left with the sad mockery that a person who has been born defective as a result of *in utero* damage has reason to act as the *phronimos* acts. In trying to locate the kinds of people for whom it is a real possibility that they should be a *phronimos*, such theorists will have in mind the sobering reflection that Aristotle himself on this matter was in effect an actualist. For him, the only grown-up people who can (now) be *phronimoi* are actually *phronimoi*, and this leaves the class of those who have reason to act in the approved ways smaller than it may be for a non-Aristotelian internalist. To avoid this conclusion, neo-Aristotelians who take this path will presumably want to reject Aristotle's own harsh opinions about what is possible for one who has been brought up badly. But can they run far with this without finding themselves, with the Kantians, in an area which they strongly and very reasonably wanted to avoid—the deep swamp of questions about free will and determination by character? Moreover, if one considers what might be involved in the kind of possibility that is at issue, it is reasonable to expect that it will revolve round the potential expressions or developments of the agent's S—that is to say, the materials of internalism. The more one considers the problems that lie in this direction, the more discouraging they seem. There are no doubt many undiscussed considerations to be pursued here. I confess, though, that nothing yet has persuaded me to give up the opinion that internalism in some form is the only view that plausibly represents a statement about A's reasons as a distinctive kind of statement about, distinctively, A.

Notes

1. See "Internal and external reasons," in *Moral Luck* (Cambridge: Cambridge University Press, 1981) [this volume, chap. 1], and "Internal Reasons and the Obscurity of Blame," *Logos* (USA) 10 (1989): 1–11, which offers some clarifications to the earlier piece. There are connections between this view and other aspects of my work, as Herbert Hart pointed out in a review of *Ethics and the Limits of Philosophy* [Cambridge, Mass.: Harvard University Press, 1985] in *The New York Review of Books*, 17 July 1986. . . .

2. For the purpose of the present discussion, I shall accept McDowell's formulation, under which internalism requires an agent's reason to depend on the contents of his S. Matters are more complicated than this implies, above all because of the case of Kant. Martin Hollis, in "The Shape of a Life" (essay 9 in *World, Mind, and Ethics*, J. E. J. Altham and R. Harrison, eds. [Cambridge: Cambridge University Press, 1995]), takes it as evident that Kant is, in my sense, an externalist, because an agent, for Kant, can have a reason to do a certain thing "regardless of [his] present motives." But I do not agree that this in itself is enough to make Kant an externalist (cf. "Internal Reasons and the Obscurity of Blame," and my reference there to the paper by Christine Korsgaard to which McDowell refers [this volume, chap. 2]). The issue is difficult, in ways which relate to the discussion that follows here. Kant thought that a person would recognize the demands of morality if he or she deliberated correctly from his or her existing S, whatever that S might be, but he thought this because he took those demands to be implicit in a conception of practical reason which he could show to apply to *any rational deliberator as such*. I think that it best preserves the point of the internalism/externalism distinction to see this as a limiting case of internalism.

3. In particular to exclude boring counter-examples in which the motivation to φ is merely a causal consequence of the activity of deliberating.

4. Neo-Aristotelians will want to consider whether temperance is an item that they want to transport unchanged from the fourth century to the present time. They should ask how much of Aristotle's apparatus can really have applied to people (who? how many?) in his own time. It is hard to believe that Athens can have changed quite so dramatically from the world known to Sophocles and Euripides, Thucydides and Plato, as Aristotle's restful *endoxa* about virtue seem to imply. It is important, on the other hand, that Aristotle himself did not believe that everyone had reason to act as the *phronimos* would: see below.

5. If not, I have righted the balance (neo-Aristotelians will probably think, tipped it in the wrong direction) in chapter 5 of *Shame and Necessity* (Berkeley: University of California Press, 1993).

6. Only roughly speaking: while it is my bad luck if I have been badly brought up, it is not, on Aristotle's views, X's bad luck that X is a woman, or (I take it) a natural slave—though he leaves it, unsurprisingly, vague what we are supposed to think about the latter case. I take up such issues in chapter 5 of *Shame and Necessity*.

7. This is why I said in *Ethics and the Limits of Philosophy* that Aristotle's theory did not offer a reason *to* each person. The question does not present itself to Aristotle in exactly this form. In part, this is connected with the complex question of the supposed audience of his treatises on ethics; as Martha Nussbaum points out in "Aristotle on Human Nature and the Foundations of Ethics" (essay 6 in *World, Mind, and Ethics*), it is important to remember the role of these books as guides to rulers or educators rather than to the ethically perplexed.

5 Internal Reasons

Michael Smith

Introduction

According to one popular version of the dispositional theory of value, the version I favour, there is an analytic connection between the desirability of an agent's acting in a certain way in certain circumstances and her having a desire to act in that way in those circumstances if she were fully rational (Rawls 1971: chap. 7; Brandt 1979: chap. 1; Smith 1989, 1992, 1994).[1] If claims about what we have reason to do are equivalent to, or are in some way entailed by, claims about what it is desirable for us to do—if our reasons follow in the wake of our values—then it follows that there is a plausible analytic connection between what we have reason to do in certain circumstances and what we would desire to do in those circumstances if we were fully rational.

The idea that there is such an analytic connection will hardly come as news. It amounts to no more and no less than an endorsement of the claim that all reasons are "internal," as opposed to "external," to use Bernard Williams's terms (Williams 1981) [this volume, chap. 1]. Or, to put things in the way Christine Korsgaard favours, it amounts to an endorsement of the "internalism requirement" on reasons (Korsgaard 1986) [this volume, chap. 2]. But how exactly is the internalism requirement to be understood? What does it tell us about the nature of reasons? And wherein lies its appeal? My aim in this paper is to answer these questions.

The paper divides into three main sections. In the first I distinguish between two different models of the internalism requirement—the "advice" model and the "example" model—and I say why the requirement should be understood in terms of the advice model. In the second and longest section I spell out the requirement in some detail and I explain why, contrary to Bernard Williams, it is not especially allied to a relativistic conception of reasons—indeed I say why those of us who embrace the requirement should endorse a non-relative conception. And in the third section I use the advice model, understood in the way explained in the second section, to explain the appeal of the internalism requirement. As we will see, the internalism requirement helps us solve an otherwise troubling problem about the effectiveness of deliberation.

1 The Advice Model versus the Example Model

The internalism requirement tells us that the desirability of an agent's φ-ing in certain circumstances C depends on whether she would desire that she φs in C if she were fully rational. This idea can be made more precise as follows.

We are to imagine two possible worlds: the *evaluated* world in which we find the agent in the circumstances she faces, and the *evaluating* world in which we find the agent's fully rational self. In these terms, the internalism requirement tells us that the desirability of the agent's φ-ing in the evaluated world depends on whether her fully rational self in the evaluating world would desire that she φs in the evaluated world. Note what I have just said, for the precise formulation is important. The idea is that we are to imagine the agent's fully rational self in the evaluating world looking across at herself in the evaluated world (so to speak) and forming a desire about what her less than fully rational self is to do in the circumstances she faces in that evaluated world. We might imagine that the self in the evaluating world is giving the self in the evaluated world advice about what to do. Accordingly, this is what I call the 'advice' model of the requirement.

The advice model of the requirement contrasts with the example model. On this alternative way of thinking about the requirement, the idea is that the desirability of an agent's φ-ing in the evaluated world depends on whether her fully rational self in the evaluating world would desire to φ *in the evaluating world*. We are not to suppose that the agent's fully rational self is giving advice to herself in the evaluated world, but rather that the agent's fully rational self is setting up her own behaviour in her own world, the evaluating world, as an example to be followed by the self in the evaluated world. The issue of interpretation, then, turns on whether the internalism requirement tells us that in acting on reasons we follow the *advice*, or the *example*, of our fully rational selves.

I said that the details of the formulation are important, and the reason why is because the details are something about which those who accept the requirement may yet disagree. Consider, for example, Christine

Korsgaard's own official formulation of the requirement. According to Korsgaard the internalism requirement is the claim that the considerations that constitute reasons must "succeed in *motivating* us insofar as we are rational" (1986: 15, emphasis is mine) [this volume, NN]. But on the plausible assumption that a fully rational agent's desires will only succeed in motivating *her* if they are desires that concern the circumstances in which *she* finds *herself*, the idea, in our terms, must be that a consideration constitutes a reason in the evaluated world just in case, in the evaluating world, the agent's fully rational self would desire that she acts on that consideration *in the evaluating world*. Korsgaard thus seems to have in mind the example model of the internalism requirement, not the advice model.[2]

But the example model is plainly wrong. In order to see why consider the following case, a variation on an example of Gary Watson's (1975). Suppose I have just been defeated in a game of squash. The defeat has been so humiliating that, out of anger and frustration, I am consumed with a desire to smash my opponent in the face with my racket. But if I were fully rational, we will suppose, I wouldn't have any such desire at all. My desire to smash him in the face is wholly and solely the product of anger and frustration, something we can rightly imagine away when we imagine me in my cool and calm fully rational state. The consideration that would motivate me if I were fully rational is rather that I could show good sportsmanship by striding right over and shaking my opponent by the hand. In that case, does it follow that what I have reason to do *in my uncalm and uncool state* is stride right over and shake him by the hand?

In essence, this is what Korsgaard's formulation of the internalism requirement tells us, for she supposes that a consideration constitutes a reason just in case it would motivate the fully rational person, and this is what my fully rational self would be motivated to do. And yet this is surely quite wrong. Striding right over and shaking my opponent by the hand might be the last thing I have reason to do, especially if being in such close proximity to him, given my anger and frustration, is the sort of thing that would cause me to smash him in the face. Rather, we might plausibly suppose, what I have reason to do in my uncalm and uncool state is to smile politely and leave the scene as soon as possible. For this is something that I can get myself to do and it will allow me to control my feelings. Moreover—and importantly for the advice model—*this is exactly what my fully rational self would want my less than fully rational self to do in the circumstances that my less than fully rational self finds himself*. But, to repeat, it is not something I would be motivated to do if I were fully rational because it is not something that I would have any *need* to be motivated to do if I were fully rational.

The example model of the internalism requirement thus gives us the wrong answer in cases in which what we have reason to do is in part determined by the fact that we are irrational. For what an agent's fully rational self is motivated to do will depend on the circumstances in which she finds herself, and, by definition, these circumstances will never include her own irrationality. It therefore seems to me that we should reject the example model of the internalism requirement in favour of the advice model. What we have reason to do in the circumstances in which we find ourselves is fixed by the advice our fully rational selves would give us about what to do in these circumstances that we face.

2 The Internalism Requirement and the Idea of Being Fully Rational

The internalism requirement tells us that it is desirable for an agent to φ in certain circumstances C, and so she has a reason to φ in C, if and only if, if she were fully rational, she would desire that she φs in C. The content of our reasons is thus fixed by the advice we would give ourselves if we were fully rational. However, note that I haven't yet said anything about what being "fully rational" means, and that we must do so if we are to understand what the internalism requirement tells us, substantively, about the reasons we have.

In his own similar analysis of internal reasons Bernard Williams suggests, in effect, that to be fully rational in the practical sphere an agent must satisfy the following three conditions:

(i) the agent must have no false beliefs
(ii) the agent must have all relevant true beliefs
(iii) the agent must deliberate correctly

His reason for insisting on the first two conditions is straightforward enough.

If our desire to do something is wholly dependent on false beliefs, then we ordinarily suppose that it isn't really desirable to do that thing. Suppose, for example, I desire to drink from a particular glass, but that my desire to do so depends on my belief that the glass contains gin and tonic when in fact it contains gin and petrol. Then we would ordinarily say that though I might think that it is desirable to drink from the glass, it isn't really desirable to do so. Why not? Because I would not desire that I do so if I were fully rational: that is, if, *inter alia*, I had no false beliefs—thus condition (i).

Similarly, in the case of condition (ii), if we fail to desire something, and if our failure to do so is wholly dependent on our failure to believe something that is true, then we ordinarily suppose that that thing may yet be desirable. Suppose, for example, that I do not desire to drink from a particular glass, but that my failure to do so is to be explained by the fact that I am ignorant of the contents of the glass. In fact it contains the most delicious drink imaginable. Then we would ordinarily say that despite the fact that I do not desire to drink from the glass, doing so may yet be desirable. Why? Because I may well desire that I do so if I were fully rational: that is, if, *inter alia*, I had all relevant true beliefs.

But what about condition (iii)? Williams's idea here is that even if we fail to desire that we ϕ, ϕ-ing may still be desirable because we would desire that we ϕ if our other beliefs and desires interacted in the ways appropriate for the generation of new desires: that is, if we deliberated and did so correctly. For example, the means to an end is desirable, but we will in fact desire the means to our ends only if we reason in accordance with the means-ends principle, for only so does a desire for an end turn into a desire for the means.

Moreover, as Williams points out, means-ends reasoning is only one mode of rational deliberation among many. Another example is

. . . practical reasoning . . . leading to the conclusion that one has reason to ϕ because ϕ-ing would be the most convenient, economical, pleasant etc. way of satisfying some element in . . . [one's set of desires] . . . and this of course is controlled by other elements in . . . [one's set of desires] . . . if not necessarily in a very clear or determinate way. . . . [And] . . . there are much wider possibilities for deliberation, such as: thinking how the satisfaction of elements in . . . [one's set of desires] . . . can be combined: e.g. by time-ordering; where there is some irresoluble conflict among the elements of . . . [one's set of desires] . . . considering which one attaches most weight to . . . ; or, again, finding constitutive solutions, such as deciding what would make for an entertaining evening, granted that one wants entertainment. (1981: 104) [this volume, 40]

And he thinks that there are other, more radical, possibilities for deliberation as well.

More subtly, . . . [an agent] . . . may think he has reason to promote some development because he has not exercised his imagination enough about what it would be like if it came about. In his unaided deliberative reason, or encouraged by the persuasions of others, he may come to have some more concrete sense of what would be involved, and lose his desire for it, just as, positively, the imagination can create new possibilities and new desires. (1981: 104–105) [this volume, 40]

Thus, according to Williams, we must include the operation of the imagination in an account of what is involved in deliberating correctly as well.

Williams's conditions (i) through (iii) seem to me to constitute a fairly accurate spelling out of our idea of what it means to be practically rational. An agent who has defective beliefs or who deliberates badly is indeed the sort of agent we tend to think of as being practically irrational in some way. It seems to me that Williams's conditions do require supplementation and amendment, however. For one thing, I see no way in which the effects of anger and frustration could be precluded by conditions (i) through (iii)—unless some such constraint is supposed to be presupposed by condition (iii), the condition of correct deliberation. Yet, as we have seen, emotions can cause us to desire to do what we have no reason to do (remember the effects of that humiliating defeat I suffered in squash). Here, then, there is need for supplementation. And for another—and this is the point on which I wish to focus—it seems to me that Williams omits from his discussion of condition (iii) an account of perhaps the most important form of deliberation. The omission is serious as it leads him to overstate the role of the imagination in deliberation. Here, then, as we will see, there is need for both supplementation and amendment.

Williams admits that deliberation can produce new and destroy old underived desires. As he puts it, an agent "may think he has reason to promote some development because he has not exercised his imagination enough about what it would be like if it came about," just as, more "positively, the imagination can create new possibilities and new desires." When the imagination does create and destroy desires in these ways Williams tells us that we take its operations to be sanctioned by reason.

Williams is right, I think, that deliberation can both produce new and destroy old underived desires. But he is wrong that the only, or even the most important, way in which this happens is via the exercise of the imagination. By far the most important way in which we create new and destroy old underived desires when we deliberate is by trying to find out whether our desires are, as a whole, *systematically justifiable*. And, if this is right, then that in turn requires a significant qualification of Williams's claim that reason sanctions the operation of the imagination.

What do I mean when I say that we sometimes deliberate by trying to find out whether our desires, as a whole, are systematically justifiable? I mean just that we can try to decide whether or not some particular underived desire that we have or might have is a desire to do something that is itself non-derivatively desirable, and that we do this in a certain characteristic way: namely, by trying to integrate the object of that desire into a more *coherent* and *unified* desiderative profile and evaluative outlook. Rawls describes the basics of this procedure of systematic justification in his discussion of how we attempt to find a "reflective equilibrium" among our specific and general evaluative beliefs (Rawls 1951; Daniels 1979). I will restrict myself to saying a little about the way in which achieving reflective equilibrium may also be a goal in the formation of underived desires.

Suppose we take a whole host of desires we have for specific and general things, desires which are not in fact derived from any desire we have for something more general. We can ask ourselves whether we wouldn't get a more systematically justifiable set of desires by adding to this whole host of specific and general desires another general desire, or a more general desire still, a desire that, in turn, justifies and explains the more specific desires that we have. And the answer might be that we would. If the new set of desires—the set we imagine ourselves having if we add a more general desire to the more specific desires we in fact have—exhibits more in the way of coherence and unity, then we may properly think that the new imaginary set of desires is rationally preferable to the old. For the coherence and unity of a set of desires is a virtue, a virtue that in turn makes for the rationality of the set as a whole. This is because exhibiting coherence and unity is partially constitutive of having a systematically justified, and so rationally preferable, set of desires, just as exhibiting coherence and unity is partially constitutive of having a systematically justified, and so rationally preferable, set of beliefs.

The idea here is straightforwardly analogous to what Rawls has to say about the conditions under which we might come to think that we should acquire a new belief in a general principle given our stock of rather specific evaluative beliefs. The thought there is that we might find that our specific value judgements would be more satisfyingly justified and explained by seeing them as all falling under a more general principle. The imaginary set of beliefs we get by adding the belief in the more general principle may exhibit more in the way of coherence and unity than our current stock of beliefs. Likewise, the idea here is that our imaginary set of desires may exhibit more in the way of coherence and unity than our current set of desires.

If we do come to believe that our more specific desires are better justified, and so explained, in this way, then note that that belief may itself cause us to have a new, underived, desire for that more general thing. And, if it does, then it seems entirely right and proper to suppose that this new desire has been arrived at by a rational method. Indeed, the acquisition of the new more general desire will seem rationally required in exactly the same way that the acquisition of the new belief that the object of the desire is desirable will seem rationally required. In fact, if the internalism requirement is right, the acquisition of a new evaluative belief will be the cognitive counterpart of the acquisition of the new desire. For, according to the requirement, an evaluative belief is simply a belief about what would be desired if we were fully rational, and the new desire is acquired precisely because it is believed to be required for us to be more rational.

Moreover, if this is agreed, then note that we can not only explain how we might come to have new underived desires as the result of such reflection, but that we can also explain how we might come to lose old underived desires as well. For, given the goal of having a systematically justifiable set of desires, it may well turn out that, as the attempt at systematic justification proceeds, certain desires that seemed otherwise unassailable have to be given up. Perhaps because we can see no way of integrating those desires into the set as a whole they will come to seem *ad hoc* and so unjustifiable to us. Our belief that such desires are *ad hoc* may then cause us to lose them. And, if so, then it will seem sensible to describe this as a loss that is itself mandated by reason; as again straightforwardly analogous to the loss of an unjustifiable, because *ad hoc*, belief.

As this procedure of systematic justification continues we can therefore well imagine wholesale shifts in our desiderative profile. Systematic reasoning creates new underived desires and destroys old. Since each such change seems rationally required, the new desiderative profile will seem not just different from the old, but better; more rational. Indeed, it will seem better and more rational in exactly the same way, and for the same reasons, that our new corresponding evaluative beliefs will seem better and more rational than our old ones.

To a first approximation, then, this is what I mean by saying that we can create new and destroy old underived desires by trying to come up with a set of desires that is systematically justifiable. But even this first approximation is enough to see why Williams's claims about the role of the imagination in deliberation requires significant qualification. For true though it is that the imagination can produce new and destroy old underived desires via vivid presentations of the facts, its operations are not guaranteed to produce and destroy desires that would themselves be sanctioned in an attempt at systematic justification of the kind just described. In fact quite the opposite is the case. For the imagination is liable to all sorts of distorting influences, influences that it is the role of systematic reasoning to sort out. Consider an example. Vividly imagining what it would be like to kill someone, I might find myself thoroughly averse to the prospect no matter what the imagined outcome. But, for all that, I might well find that the desire to kill someone, given certain outcomes, is one element in a systematically justifiable set of desires. Merely imagining a killing, no matter what the imagined circumstances, may cause in me a thoroughgoing aversion, but it will not justify such an aversion if considerations of overall coherence and unity demand that I have a desire to kill in certain sorts of circumstances, and such considerations may themselves override the effects of the imagination and cause me to have the desire I am justified in having.[3] The role played by attempts at systematic justification is thus what is crucially required for an understanding of how deliberation creates new and destroys old underived desires, not the role played by the imagination.

Let's recap. According to the internalism requirement, the desirability of an agent's φ-ing in certain circumstances C is fixed by whether or not she would desire that she φs in C if she were fully rational. The aim in this section is to spell out the idea of being fully rational. Taking our lead from Bernard Williams the suggestion so far is that an agent is fully rational just in case she has no false beliefs and all relevant true beliefs, and just in case she deliberates correctly in the light of these beliefs, and an agent is in turn understood to have deliberated correctly just in case her underived desires are systematically justifiable: that is, to a first approximation, just in case her underived desires form a maximally coherent and unified desire set. Do we need to say more? Indeed we do, something we see clearly once we focus on a consequence Williams wants us to draw from his own similar analysis of reasons.

According to Williams, the internalism requirement supports a *relative* conception of reasons. He puts the point this way.

[T]he truth of the sentence . . . ['A has a reason to φ'] . . . implies, very roughly, that A has some motive which will be served or furthered by his φ-ing, and if this turns out not to be so the sentence is false: there is a condition relating to the agent's aims, and if this is not satisfied it is not true to say . . . that he has a reason to φ. (1981: 101) [this volume, 37]

And again later:

Basically, and by definition, . . . [an analysis of reasons] . . . must display a relativity of . . . [a] . . . reason statement to the agent's *subjective motivational set* . . . (1981: 102) [this volume, 38]

Now in fact it is initially quite difficult to see why Williams says any of this at all. For, as we have seen, what the internalism requirement suggests is that claims about an agent's reasons are claims about her *hypothetical* desires, not claims about her *actual* desires. The truth of the sentence 'A has a reason to φ' thus does not imply, not even "very roughly," that A *has* some motive which will be served by his φ-ing; indeed A's *motives* are beside the point—that was the difference between the advice model and the example model. What the internalism requirement implies is rather that A has a reason to φ in certain circumstances C just in case he *would* desire that he φs in those circumstances if he were fully rational.

Williams might concede this. But, he might say, it doesn't show that he is wrong when he says that the requirement supports the relativity of an agent's reasons to her actual desires, it simply shows that the relativity of reasons requires more careful formulation. The crucial point, he might insist, is that the desires an agent would have if she were fully rational are themselves simply functions from her actual desires, where the relevant functions are those described in conditions (i) through (iii). An agent's reasons are thus relative to her actual desires, he might say, because under conditions of full rationality agents would all have different desires about what is to be done in the various circumstances they might face. Even if it is rational for each of us to change our actual desires by trying to come up with a set of desires that can be systematically justified, in the manner captured by conditions (i) through (iii), such changes will always fall short of making us have the same desires as our fellows; they will always reflect the antecedent fact that we have the actual desires that we have. The content of the maximally coherent and unified desire set any particular agent could have will always reflect the content of that agent's actual desires.

As I see it, this is what Williams has in mind when he says that our reasons are all relative.[4] It explains why he rightly insists that he is defending a "Humean" conception of reasons (1981: 102) [this volume, 38]. For his conception of reasons, like Hume's own, is predicated on skepticism about the scope for reasoned change in our desires (Korsgaard 1986) [this volume, chap. 2]; predicated on denying that, through a process of rational deliberation—through attempting to give a systematic justification of our desires, for example—we could ever come to discover reasons that we all share. For what we have reason to do is given by the content of the desires we would have if we were fully rational, and these may differ in content from agent to agent.

Williams claims to derive this relative conception of reasons from the internalism requirement. But as a *derivation* this is hardly compelling. It goes through only if we assume that it is no part of our task, in trying to come up with a systematically justifiable set of desires, to come up with the same set of desires as our fellow rational creatures would come up with if they set themselves the same task. And this suggests, in turn, that there are therefore two quite distinct conceptions of *internal* reasons. There is a relativistic, Humean, conception of internal reasons—the conception embraced by Williams—and there is also a non-relativistic, anti-Humean or Kantian conception according to which, if we were to engage in a process of systematically justifying our desires we would all eventually reason ourselves towards the same conclusions as regards what is to be done. That is, according to the opposing conception, all possible rational creatures would desire alike as regards what is to be done in the various circumstances they might face because this is, *inter alia*, what defines them to be "rational." Part of the task of coming up with a maximally coherent and unified set of desires is coming up with a set that would be converged upon by other rational creatures who too are trying to come up with a maximally coherent and unified set of desires; each rational creature is to keep an eye out to her fellows, and to treat as an aberration to be explained any divergence between the sets of desires they come up with through the process of systematic justifications.[5,6]

The final question to ask, then, in spelling out our idea of full rationality, is whether Williams is right that our ordinary concept of a reason is Humean or anti-Humean. Does our ordinary concept of a reason presuppose skepticism about the scope for reasoned change in our desires? In other words, does it presuppose that there will, or alternatively that there will not, be a convergence in the desires that we would have under conditions of full rationality? If it presupposes that there will not be such a convergence then our concept of a reason is indeed relative, just as Williams says. If it presupposes instead that there will be such a convergence then our concept of a reason is, by contrast, non-relative.

Let me emphasise that we are asking a conceptual question, not a substantive question. We are asking what we mean when we talk of people being fully rational; whether it is part of what we mean by 'rational' that fully rational people converge in their desires, or whether this is no part of what we mean by 'rational'. And note as well that no matter how we answer this question, we do not thereby beg any substantive questions. For example, even if our concept of a reason is itself non-relative—even if our concept optimistically presupposes that we would all converge on the same desires under conditions of full rationality—the world might disappoint us. Entrenched and apparently rationally inexplicable differences in what we desire might make it impossible to believe, substantively, that there are any such non-relative reasons (Smith 1991, 1993, 1994).

Let's, then, confront the conceptual question head on. Is our ordinary concept of a reason relative or non-relative? The relativity of a claim should manifest itself in the way we talk. Consider, for example, the schematic claim 'It is desirable that p in circumstances C'. On the non-relative conception of internal reasons—at least if we abstract away from some complications to be dealt with presently—this claim has a straightforward truth condition: it is desirable that p in C just in case we would all desire that p in C if we were fully rational. There is, then, a sense in which we can talk about rational justification or desirability *simpliciter*. When you and I talk about the reasons that there are for acting, we are therefore talking about the same thing. We are talking about reasons *period*; about the common set of reasons that are appreciable by each of us.

On the relative conception, however, matters are quite different. For in order to give the truth condition of the schematic claim 'It is desirable that p in C' we need first to know from whose perspective the truth of the claim is to be assessed. For while 'It is desirable that p in C' as assessed from A's perspective is true if and only if A would desire that p in C if A were fully rational, 'It is desirable that p in C' as assessed from B's perspective is true if and only if B would desire that p in C if B were fully rational, and so on and so forth. There is thus no such thing as desirability or the considerations that rationally justify *simpliciter*, but only desirability$_A$, desirability$_B$, . . . ; considerations that rationally-justify-from-A's-perspective, rationally-justify-from-B's-perspective, . . . and so on. If I say to you "There is a reason for φ-ing," and you deny this, we are therefore potentially talking about quite different things: reasons$_{me}$ and reasons$_{you}$. The question to ask is therefore whether the way in which we talk about reasons for action and the considerations that rationally justify our actions reflects a relative or a non-relative conception of the truth conditions of reason claims.

One reason for thinking that it reflects the non-relative conception comes from the broader context in which the question is being asked. For it is important to remember that we have a whole range of normative concepts: truth, meaning, support, entailment, desirability, and so on. Between them these concepts allow us to ask all sorts of normative questions, questions about what we should and should not believe, say and do. But how many of these other normative concepts are plausibly thought to give rise to claims having relativised truth conditions? As I understand it, none of them do.

Consider our concept of support, by way of example. It seems quite implausible to suppose that the truth of claims about which propositions support which others is implicitly relative to the individual; that when A says "p supports q" and B says "p does not support q" they are potentially talking about quite different things: that A is talking about what supports$_A$ q and B is talking about what supports$_B$ q, for instance. For if this were the case then we should expect to find that we are sometimes able to dissolve apparent disagreements by finding that both parties are speaking truly. It should be permissible for B to say "A said 'p supports q' and what she said is true, but p does not support q." However it is a striking feature of our talk about which propositions support which others that we *never* dissolve apparent disagreements in this way. Propositions have normative force *simpliciter*, not just normative-force-relative-to-this-individual or relative-to-that. When one individual says "p supports q" and the other says "p does not support q" they thus express their disagreement about whether p supports q in a *non-relative* sense.

If our concept of desirability were implicitly relativised, then, it seems that this would mark a significant difference between this concept and our other normative concepts. We should expect to find that with claims about what is desirable, unlike claims about which propositions support which, we *are* able to dissolve apparent disagreements in the way just described. But do we find this?

It might be thought that we do. After all, aren't there all sorts of familiar cases in which we say things like "That may be a reason for you, but it isn't for me," "Desirable for you maybe, but not desirable for me," and the like? But though there are indeed such cases, it is important to note that the sort of relativity we signal when we say such things is quite different from the kind just described; quite different from the kind of relativity Williams has in mind. For, in the familiar cases, "That may be a reason for you, but it isn't for me" signals the fact that there is a relativity built in to the *considerations* that we use to rationally justify our choices. It does not signal the fact that *our concept of a reason* is itself relative to the individual; that there is no such thing as which considerations, relative or not, rationally justify our choices, but only which considerations rationally-justify-relative-to-this-person or rationally-justify-relative-to-that-person. Here, then, we come to the complications abstracted away from earlier.

Sometimes what we have in mind when we say "That may be a reason for you, but it isn't for me" is that the considerations that rationally justify our choices are, to use Parfit's terms, *agent-relative*, rather than *agent-neutral* (Parfit 1984). Suppose you are standing on a beach. Two people are drowning to your left and one is drowning to your right. You can either swim left and save two, in which case the one on the right will drown, or you can swim right and save one, in which case the two on the left will drown. You decide to swim right and save the one and you justify your choice by saying "The one on the right is my child, whereas the two on the left are perfect strangers to me."

In one sense, of course, I may well say "That may be a reason for you, but it isn't for me." For if the three people drowning are all perfect strangers to me then, had I been standing on the beach instead of you, I would not have been able to justify the choice of swimming right and saving the one. But in another sense it seems that what is a reason for you may indeed be a reason for me. For if I had been standing on the beach instead of you, and if the one on the right had been my child—that is, if my circumstances had been in all crucial respects *the same* as yours—then surely I too would have been able to justify the choice of swimming right and saving the one by saying "The one on the right is my child." Indeed, if we think that a parent who fails to save her child in such circumstances fails to act on a reason available to her—as it seems to me that we do—then we are in fact obliged to say this; obliged to assume the non-relative conception of internal reasons.

What this sort of example shows is therefore that, even if reasons are non-relative in the crucial sense at issue here, among the considerations that may rationally justify our choices are both considerations that are properly given a *de dicto* formulation and considerations that are properly given a *de se* formulation (see also Lewis 1989). That is, there are both *de dicto* and *de se* internal reasons. We can each express the content of the *de dicto* reason relevant in this case by using the words 'There is a reason to save people quite generally'. And we can each express the content of the *de se* reason by using the words 'There is a reason to save my child in particular'. In these terms what is a reason for you, in this case, is not a reason for me in the sense that, if it had been me standing on the beach rather than you, and if the same people had been drowning, then the only consideration that would have been relevant to my choice is the *de dicto* reason. The *de se* reason would not have been relevant to my choice because the people who are in fact drowning are all perfect strangers to me. But in another sense what is a reason for you is indeed a reason for me. For if I had been standing on the beach and the one person on the right had been my child, as the one on the right is your child, then both the *de se* and the *de dicto* reason would have been relevant to my choice in just the way they are both relevant to yours.

I said that this sort of relativity is entirely different from the kind that Williams has in mind and it should now be plain why this is so. For, in terms of the analysis, even if some of the considerations that rationally justify our choices are relative because *de se*, the existence of such *de se* reasons may still require a convergence in the desires that we would all have if we were fully rational. That is, the existence of reasons with *de se* contents may still require that, under conditions of full rationality, we would each have desires whose contents we would express by using words like 'to help my children', 'to promote my welfare', and the like. The mere existence of *de se* reasons is thus quite different from the relativity Williams has in mind. For his claim is that reasons are relative in the sense of requiring no such convergence; that the fact that my act helps my child may constitute a reason$_{me}$ even though the fact that your act helps your child does not constitute a reason$_{you}$.

There is another familiar sort of relativity in our claims about the reasons we have as well, a sort that derives from the fact that what we have reason to do is relative to our circumstances, where our circumstances may include aspects of our own psychology. Suppose, for example, that you and I differ in our preferences for wine over beer. Preferring wine, as you do, you may tell me that there is a reason to go to the local wine bar after work for a drink, for they sell very good wine. But then, preferring beer, as I do, I may quite rightly reply "That may be a reason for you to go to the wine bar, but it is not a reason for me."

Now while this might initially look like the claim that our reasons are relative to our desires in something like the sense Williams has in mind, it again isn't really. For the crucial point in this case is that a relevant feature of your circumstances is your preference for wine, whereas a relevant feature of my circumstances is my preference for beer. That this is a relevant feature of our circumstances is manifest from the fact that I can quite happily agree with you that if I were in your circumstances—if I preferred wine to beer—then the fact that the local wine bar sells very good wine would constitute a reason for me to go there as well, just as it constitutes a reason for you.

This sort of relativity is thus completely different from the kind that Williams has in mind as well. For, in terms of the analysis, even if an agent's preferences may enter into a specification of the circumstances that she faces it might still be the case that whether or not she is rationally justified in taking her own preferences into account, and the way in which she is justified in taking them into account, if she is, depends on whether fully rational agents would all converge on a desire which makes the preferences she in fact has relevant in that way to her choice. In this case, for example, it may be crucial that, under conditions of full rationality we would all converge on a desire to satisfy whatever preferences we might have (perhaps within limits) in deciding where to go for a drink after work.[7] The fact that in rationally justifying our choices our preferences may sometimes be a relevant feature of our circumstances thus does nothing to support Williams's view that our reasons are relative; does nothing to support the view that really there are only the considerations that rationally-justify-relative-to-this-person or rationally-justify-relative-to-that.

In order to find support for the sort of relativity Williams has in mind, we therefore need to look for cases in which it is permissible to make much more radically relativised claims about what there is reason to do. But in fact, as far as I can tell, we find no such claims. Suppose someone tells me that she has a reason to take a holiday and that I think I would have no reason to take a holiday in the circumstances she faces. Provided we have taken proper account of the *de se* considerations that might be relevant to her choice, and provided we have taken proper account of the way in which her preferences may constitute a relevant feature of her circumstances, it seems that I straightforwardly disagree with her about the rational justifiability of her taking a holiday in the circumstances she faces, a disagreement I can express by saying "She thinks that there is a reason to take a holiday in her circumstances, but there is no such reason." If she cites a consideration in support of her taking a holiday that I think fails to justify, then I do not conclude that it may justify-relative-to-her, though not justify-relative-to-me, I conclude that it fails to justify *simpliciter*.

The point is important, for it suggests that when we talk about reasons for action we quite generally take ourselves to be talking about a common subject matter: reasons *period*. We are thus potentially in agreement or disagreement with each other about what constitutes a reason and what doesn't. This is why, when we find ourselves in disagreement—as for example in the case of disagreement about whether or not there is a reason to take a holiday in certain circumstances—we always have the option of engaging in argument in the attempt to find out who is right and who is wrong. Other people's opinions about the reasons that there are thus constitute potential challenges to my own opinions. I have something to learn about myself and my own assessment of the reasons that there are by finding out about others and their assessment. This is why books and films are so engaging. All of this is flat out inconsistent with the claim that our concept of a reason for action is quite generally relative to the individual; that it typically means reason$_{me}$ out of my mouth, reason$_{you}$ out of yours, reason$_{her}$ out of hers and so on. It suggests rather that our concept of a reason is stubbornly non-relative.

Indeed, it seems to me that we have no choice but to think this. For if reasons were indeed relative then mere reflection on that fact would itself suffice to undermine their normative significance. In order to see why, remember that on the relative conception it turns out that, for example, the desirability$_{me}$ of some consideration, p, is entirely dependent on the fact that *my* actual desires are such that, if *I* were to engage in a process of systematically justifying *my* desires, weeding out those that aren't justified and acquiring those that are, a desire that p would be one of the desires *I* would end up having. But what my actual desires are to begin with is, on this relative conception of internal reasons, an entirely *arbitrary* matter, one without any normative significance of its own. I might have had any old set of desires to begin with, even a set that delivered up the desire that not p after a process of systematic justification! The desirability$_{me}$ of the fact that p thus turns out to be an entirely arbitrary fact about p. But this is surely a *reductio*, as *arbitrariness* is precisely a feature of a consideration that tends to undermine any normative significance it might initially appear to have. Internal reasons on the relative conception are thus without normative significance (Darwall 1983: 218–239; Smith 1989; Darwall, Gibbard and Railton 1992). And if this is right then it follows that *relative* internal reasons are not *reasons* at all.

On the non-relative conception, by contrast, reflection on our concept of desirability reveals no such arbitrariness. For on that conception everyone is supposed able to reason themselves towards the same desires if they engage in a process of systematic justification of their desires, and they are supposed able to do so precisely because the task of systematic justification is *inter alia* a matter of finding desires that can be shared by their fellow rational creatures. Which desires *I* would end up with, after engaging in such a process, thus in no way depends on what *my* actual desires are to begin with, because reason itself determines the content of our fully rational desires, not the arbitrary fact that we have the actual desires that we have. On the non-relative conception, reflection on the concept of desirability thus leaves the normative significance of facts about what is desirable and undesirable perfectly intact.

This, then, is the final element in our account of what it means when the internalism requirement tells us that the desirability of an agent's φ-ing in certain circumstances C depends on whether or not she would desire that she ϕs in C if she were "fully rational." Fully rational agents *converge* in their desires about what is to be done in the various circumstances they might face. Of course, the mere fact that a convergence in the hypothetical desires of fully rational creatures is required for the truth of internal reason claims does nothing to guarantee that such a convergence is forthcoming. In defending the non-relative *conception* of internal reasons we have said nothing to suggest that, *substantively*, there are any such reasons. But what we have said does suggest that, in order to discover whether there are any such reasons, and if so what they are, we have no alternative but to give the arguments and see where they lead. Substantive convergence is always assumed available, in so far as we converse and argue about the reasons that we have. But whether or not this assumption is true is always *sub judice*; something to be discovered by the outcome of those very conversations and arguments; something that will emerge when we see where our attempts to systematically justify our desires lead us.

3   The Advice Model and the Appeal of the Internalism Requirement

So far I have argued that the internalism requirement on reasons is best understood in terms of the advice model, rather than the example model, and I have argued that reasons, understood in terms of the advice model, are best thought of as being non-relative, rather than relative. The two points are related, of course. For I have argued that it is only if we think of reasons on the advice model, and it is only if we think of reasons as being non-relative, that we can properly account for the normative significance of reason claims. However, the most important question about the internalism requirement remains yet to be answered. Why exactly should we accept the internalism requirement in the first place? Why shouldn't we think, instead, that reasons have nothing to do, constitutively, with the desires of fully rational agents, as I have defined the idea of full rationality? The answer is that the internalism requirement on reasons enables us to solve an otherwise disturbing puzzle about the role of deliberation in the production of action. Let me begin by explaining the puzzle.

Hume taught us that desires and means-end beliefs each play an essential role in the explanation of action (Smith 1987). Suppose, for example, that all we know about someone is that she believes that if she flicks a particular switch the light will go on and that if she refrains the light will stay off. Then, so far, we have no more reason to suppose that she will flick the switch than refrain. Whether she will flick or refrain must therefore depend on something else about her beyond her beliefs about the way the world is. And indeed it does. It depends on what she happens to desire. Does she desire the causal upshot of flicking the switch, the light's being on, or the causal upshot of refraining from doing so, the light's being off? If the former, then she will flick the switch; if the latter, then she will refrain. Desires are thus essential for the explanation of action. But so are beliefs as well. For if all we know about someone is that she desires the light to be on then, again, so far we have no more reason to suppose that she will flick the switch than that she will refrain. For whether she will flick the switch or refrain depends on whether she believes the light's being on is the causal upshot of flicking or refraining. To sum up: beliefs alone are unable to motivate action, for beliefs can only motivate action in conjunction with a separate desire; but desires alone are also unable to motivate action, for desires can only motivate action in conjunction with a separate means-end belief.

Compelling though this Humean story of how we explain action is, it presents us with a disturbing puzzle about the role of deliberation in the production of action. For it seems undeniable that we sometimes deliberate in order to find out what we are rationally justified in doing: that is, we sometimes deliberate in order to form beliefs about what it is desirable to do. And it also seems undeniable that we sometimes act upon the outcome of those very deliberations: that is, we sometimes do what we do because we believe that doing so is desirable. But the Humean story about how we explain action seems to leave no room for these undeniable facts. For the belief that it is desirable to act in a certain way is not itself a desire, it is a belief, and so whether or not we happen to act in accordance with this belief, given the Humean story about how we explain actions, must depend entirely on whether we just so happen to have a desire to act in that way, or just so happen to have some other desire which can combine with this belief to yield a desire to act in that way.[8] On Hume's account of the matter it thus appears to be a massive fluke, an inexplicable miracle of nature, that our desires match our beliefs about what it is desirable to do to the extent that they do. For there is nothing in the nature of our evaluative beliefs to explain why this should be the case. What is needed is an extra desire, an extra desire we are not rationally required to have.

Here we see the real appeal of the internalism requirement. For it promises to explain how it can be that our beliefs about what we are rationally justified in doing play a proper causal role in the genesis of our actions, and it promises to do so while leaving Hume's story about the way in which actions are explained largely intact. In order to see why, consider again what the requirement tells us about the content of our evaluative beliefs, at least on the advice model.

When I believe that it would be desirable to φ in certain circumstances C, the internalism requirement tells us that my belief has the following content: that I would desire that I φ in C if I were fully rational. But now, if indeed I do believe this, and if I believe that I am in circumstances C, then surely the only rational thing for me to desire is to φ. For a psychology that includes both the belief that I would desire that I φ in C if I were fully rational—that is, the belief that I would have that desire if my desires formed a maximally coherent and unified set—*and* the desire that I φ in C is itself a more coherent and unified psychology than one that includes the belief that I would desire to φ in C if I were fully rational and yet *lacks* the desire to φ in C. Coherence and unity are thus on the side of a *match* between the content of our evaluative beliefs and our desires.

Here is another way of putting the same point. What would an agent's fully rational self want her less than fully rational self to desire in circumstances in which her less than fully rational self believes that she would desire to φ in C if she were fully rational? On the plausible assumption that the agent's fully rational self desires that the psychology of her less than fully rational self is as coherent as possible she will want her less than fully rational self to desire that she φs in C. It thus follows that it is desirable for an agent to desire that she φs in C in circumstances in which she believes that it is desirable that she φs in C. Agents thus quite generally have a reason to desire in accordance with their evaluative beliefs.[9]

But if this is right then it follows that in *rational* creatures at least—that is, in those who do not manifest the form of unreasonableness or irrationality just described, those who are sensitive to the facts about what they have reason to desire—we would therefore expect there to be a causal connection between believing that it is desirable to act in a certain way and desiring to act in that way. That is, given the internalist account of the content of our evaluative beliefs, we would expect a rational deliberator's evaluative beliefs to cause her to have matching desires in much the same way, and for much the same reason, as the rational thinker's beliefs that p and that p → q cause her to believe that q. For the psychological states of rational deliberators and thinkers connect with each other in just the way that they rationally should. In this way, then, the internalism requirement can thus underwrite not just the rationality of desiring in accordance with our evaluative beliefs, but also the effectiveness of our evaluative beliefs in bringing about these desires in those who are rational.[10]

Note that the explanation just given is simply unavailable if we reject the internalism requirement. For on an externalist conception of reasons, the reasons we have are not themselves defined in terms of what we would desire if our psychology exhibited maximal coherence and unity. Without inquiring further into what exactly the content of a reason claim on such a conception is we can therefore already see that there is no reason to expect that a psychology which pairs a belief that there is reason to φ in circumstances C with a desire to do something other than φ in C will exhibit less in the way of coherence and unity than a psychology that pairs that belief with the desire to φ in C. It thus appears that externalists will be unable to explain why it is rational to desire in accordance with our beliefs about the reasons that we have.

Note also that the explanation just given presupposes not just the internalism requirement, but the internalism requirement understood in terms of the advice model. For if we interpret the internalism requirement in terms of the example model, the argument just given simply fails to go through at the crucial point. Suppose, for instance, that you believe your fully rational self would desire to φ in the circumstances she faces; that this is the example she would set for you in her own world. Why should this have any effect at all on what you desire to do in the circumstances you face? If your circumstances are quite unlike hers, then you can quite rationally acknowledge her example, and be impressed by it, while still being left entirely unmoved. Coherence and unity do not argue in favour of acquiring a desire like hers because her example—marvelous though it is in the circumstances in which *she* finds *herself*—doesn't engage with the circumstances in which *you* find *yourself*. This is not the case if instead we interpret the requirement in terms of the advice model. For then what you have to believe is that your fully rational self would want your less than fully rational self to φ in the circumstances your less than fully rational self actually faces. Your fully rational self's advice engages with your predicament because it is precisely tailored to it. You may still say "So what?," of course, but if you do you simply reveal that you are unable to accept good advice; you reveal the extent to which your psychology fails in terms of norms of coherence and unity that define a systematically justified psychology. You thus simply betray your own irrationality.

Here, then, we see the real appeal of the internalism requirement. It offers us an explanation of how and why our evaluative beliefs come to play a proper causal role in the production of our desires, an explanation that leaves the Humean's claim that intentional actions are themselves the product of desires and means-end beliefs perfectly intact. The crucial idea, to repeat, is that given the content of an agent's evaluative beliefs—that is, given the internalism requirement—the desires that the Humean rightly supposes play a causal role in the genesis of intentional actions will themselves be caused by the agent's evaluative beliefs to the extent that she is a rational deliberator. The Humean's account has thus been supplemented, not replaced.

Conclusion

My aim in this paper has been to answer three questions. How exactly is the internalism requirement on reasons to be understood? What does it tell us about the nature of reasons? And wherein lies its appeal?

As regards the first question, I have argued that the content of the internalism requirement is best captured by what I have called the 'advice' model rather than the 'example' model. According to the advice model, the desirability of an agent's ϕ-ing in certain circumstances C is fixed by whether or not her fully rational self would advise her less than fully rational self to ϕ in the circumstances that she, the less than fully rational self, faces: that is, in circumstances C. The idea is not that the desirability of an agent's ϕ-ing in C is fixed by the example her fully rational self would set for her less than fully rational self by her own behaviour in her own world. Thus, even though the requirement is concerned with the *desires* of a fully rational agent, it is crucially not concerned with the *motivations* of a fully rational agent.

As regards the second question, I have argued that the substantive content of the internalism requirement depends on the way in which we understand the key idea of having certain desires under conditions of full rationality. My claim has been that it is part of our concept of full rationality that fully rational agents are those who have a systematically justifiable set of desires, where this idea is to be cashed out in terms of having a psychology that is maximally coherent and unified, and where it is presupposed that the maximally coherent and unified set of desires any one particular fully rational agent would come up with is exactly the same as the maximally coherent and unified set of desires any other rational agent would come up with. The internalism requirement is thus best understood as offering us a non-relativistic, rather than a relativistic, conception of reasons.

Finally, as regards the third question, I have argued that, given our answers to the earlier two questions, the appeal of the internalism requirement is easy to understand. For it allows us to see that though the Humean is right that all *actions* are caused by desires, in rational deliberators at least, the *desires* that cause an agent's actions may themselves be caused by her evaluative beliefs. The internalism requirement thus enables us to assign a proper causal role to an agent's beliefs about the rational justifiability of her actions when she deliberates.

For all I have said it of course remains an open possibility that there are no internal reasons—and hence that there are no reasons for action at all. After all, the mere fact that our concept of a reason presupposes that fully rational creatures would converge in their desires does nothing to show that such a convergence is forthcoming. But that is no objection to what has been said here. For my aim has not been to argue that there are any reasons, it has rather been to articulate the conceptual framework in which debates about what our reasons are, if there are any, can sensibly take place.[11]

Notes

1. Adherents of other versions of the dispositional theory may agree that desirability is a feature that elicits an appropriate response in subjects under conditions of full rationality, but disagree about whether that response is desire (Johnston 1989 appears to take this view), or they may instead agree that desirability is a feature that elicits desire in agents under the appropriate conditions, but disagree about whether those are conditions of full rationality (Lewis 1989 appears to take this view).

2. Rawls (1971) and Brandt (1979) seem to have had in mind the example model of the internalism requirement as well. Contrast Peter Railton's account of a person's own good (1986) which is formulated in terms in terms of the advice model precisely to avoid problems like those I go on to describe in the text. For criticisms of Rawls's and Brandt's example versions of the internalism requirement see Shope (1978) and Pettit and Smith (1993). (Here I am grateful to Stephen Darwall.)

3. Mark Johnston (1989) pursues a similar line in his criticism of David Lewis's account of the role of imaginative acquaintance in valuing (1989).

4. See especially Williams's discussion of the Owen Wingrave example (1981: 106–111) [this volume, 42–47].

5. Compare Philip Pettit on rule-following (1993: especially 96–97).

6. The claim is not that on the non-relative conception of reasons the existence of reasons-in-the-actual-world presupposes a convergence in the desires of fully rational creatures in the actual world. For this is itself a relative conception of reasons: reasons are *world*-relative. The non-relative conception really is *non*-relative. It claims

that there is a convergence in the desires that all possible creatures would have, so long as those creatures are fully rational, whether those creatures exist in the actual world or not. Angels, ourselves in other possible worlds, the inhabitants of Mars—on the non-relative conception we are all of us supposed to desire the very same thing for the various circumstances we might face, at least insofar as we are rational.

7. Note that the preferences we have are not always a relevant feature of our circumstances. If I just so happen to prefer kicking the cat to leaving it sleep in peace, my fully rational self might want that I do not kick the cat despite my preference. For relevant discussion of this point, and the relevance of actual desires to the desirability or justifiability of our actions generally, see Pettit and Smith 1990, 1993, 1997.

8. For example, it might be supposed that when we deliberate we *de facto* have a desire to do what we believe it is desirable to do. I will have more to say about this in note 10. The point here is simply that the Humean must regard it a happy accident that we all just so happen to have such a desire. For the Humean cannot agree that such a desire is itself required by reason.

9. It is, of course, consistent to claim both that: (i) it is desirable that an agent desires to ϕ in C *in circumstances in which she believes that it is desirable to ϕ in C*, and (ii) it is not desirable that an agent desires to ϕ *in circumstances C*. For whereas (i) tells us what an agent's fully rational self would want her less than fully rational self to desire in one set of circumstances, (ii) tells us what her fully rational self would want her less than fully rational self to desire in another, quite different, set of circumstances. The point is important, as it serves to explain why certain theories of reasons for action are properly thought to be *self-effacing* (Smith 1994: chap. 5, footnote 2).

10. Note that the externalist who tries to explain the effectiveness of deliberation by positing an extra desire to do what we believe desirable (see note 8) has an explanation that is inferior to the internalist's explanation just given in two respects. First, since the externalist claims that the extra desire to do what we believe desirable is itself rationally optional, he is committed not just to the view that it is a miracle of nature, a massive fluke, that so many of us just so happen to have such a desire, but also to the view that if someone just so happened to lack such a desire, that would not itself suffice to show that that person was irrational. By contrast the internalist has a principled reason for insisting that someone who lacks a desire to ϕ while believing that ϕ-ing is desirable is *as such* irrational. Second, the externalist who posits a quite general desire to do what is desirable must think that if we end up desiring to, say, ϕ in C, as a result of coming to believe that it is desirable to ϕ in C, then the desire to ϕ in C must itself, of necessity, be an *instrumental* desire. The externalist must therefore hold that deliberation never produces a non-instrumental desire to do what we believe desirable, where this is read *de re* rather than *de dicto*. The only thing we desire to do non-instrumentally, when we deliberate, is

what it is desirable to do, where this is read *de dicto* rather than *de re*. This seems to me to be an extremely implausible claim. Indeed, as I have argued elsewhere, it seems to constitute a *reductio* of externalism (1994: chap. 3). The internalist, by contrast, has an explanation of how the belief that it is desirable to ϕ in C generates a desire to ϕ in C that is perfectly consistent with the claim that the resulting desire to ϕ in C is *non-instrumental* in character.

11. An earlier version of this paper was presented at "Internal and External Reasons," a symposium held at the Pacific Division APA meetings in Los Angeles, April 1994. I would like to thank Stephen Darwall for the many useful suggestions and observations he made as commentator on that occasion, suggestions and observations that have helped me greatly improve the paper. I also received useful advice from John Broome, David Copp, Frank Jackson, Douglas MacLean, Kevin Mulligan, Philip Pettit, Denis Robinson, Holly Smith, Galen Strawson, Anita Superson, Sigrún Svavarsdóttir, David Velleman and Susan Wolf. The second section of the paper draws on material that appears in chapter 5 of *The Moral Problem* (Basil Blackwell, 1994).

References

Brandt, Richard. 1979. *A Theory of the Good and the Right*. Oxford: Oxford University Press.

Daniels, Norman. 1979. Wide reflective equilibrium and theory acceptance in ethics. *Journal of Philosophy* 76:256–282.

Darwall, Stephen. 1983. *Impartial Reason*. Ithaca, NY: Cornell University Press.

Darwall, Stephen, Allan Gibbard, and Peter Railton. 1992. Toward *fin de siècle* ethics: Some trends. *Philosophical Review* 101:115–189.

Johnston, Mark. 1989. Dispositional theories of value. *Proceedings of the Aristotelian Society, Supplementary Volume* 63:139–174.

Korsgaard, Christine. 1986. Skepticism about practical reason. *Journal of Philosophy* 83:5–25.

Lewis, David. 1989. Dispositional theories of value. *Proceedings of the Aristotelian Society, Supplementary Volume* 63:113–137.

Parfit, Derek. 1984. *Reasons and Persons*. Oxford: Oxford University Press.

Pettit, Philip. 1993. *The Common Mind*. Oxford: Oxford University Press.

Pettit, Philip, and Michael Smith. 1990. Backgrounding desire. *Philosophical Review* 99:565–592.

Pettit, Philip, and Michael Smith. 1993. Brandt on self-control. In B. Hooker, ed., *Rationality, Rules and Utility*. Boulder, CO: Westview Press.

Pettit, Philip, and Michael Smith. 1997. Parfit's P. In J. Dancy, ed., *Reading Parfit*. Oxford: Blackwell.

Railton, Peter. 1986. Moral realism. *Philosophical Review* 95:163–207.

Rawls, John. 1951. Outline of a decision procedure for ethics. *Philosophical Review* 60:177–197.

Rawls, John. 1971. *A Theory of Justice*. Cambridge, MA: Harvard University Press.

Shope, Robert K. 1978. Rawls, Brandt, and the definition of rational desires. *Canadian Journal of Philosophy* 8:329–340.

Smith, Michael. 1987. The Humean theory of motivation. *Mind* 96:36–61.

Smith, Michael. 1989. Dispositional theories of value. *Proceedings of the Aristotelian Society, Supplementary Volume* 63:89–111.

Smith, Michael. 1991. Realism. In Peter Singer, ed., *A Companion to Ethics*. Oxford: Basil Blackwell.

Smith, Michael. 1992. Valuing: Desiring or believing? In David Charles and Kathleen Lennon, eds., *Reduction, Explanation, Realism*. Oxford: Oxford University Press.

Smith, Michael. 1993. Objectivity and moral realism: On the phenomenology of moral experience. In John Haldane and Crispin Wright, eds., *Reality, Representation and Projection*. Oxford: Oxford University Press.

Smith, Michael. 1994. *The Moral Problem*. Oxford: Basil Blackwell.

Watson, Gary. 1975. Free agency. Reprinted in Gary Watson, ed., *Free Will*. Oxford: Oxford University Press, 1982.

Williams, Bernard. 1981. Internal and external reasons. Reprinted in Bernard Williams, *Moral Luck*. Cambridge: Cambridge University Press. Originally published in Ross Harrison, ed., *Rational Action*, Cambridge: Cambridge University Press, 1979.

II Instrumentalism

6 Humean Doubts about the Practical Justification of Morality

James Dreier

Humeans[1] doubt that there is any categorical justification of morality, in that they doubt that practical reason demands compliance with morality. In this essay I examine the grounds for their scepticism. One kind of ground is dubious. After exposing its flaws, I explain why there is a plausible ground for scepticism anyway.

1 The Justification of Morality

Why is there a problem about the justification of morality? This question is, admittedly, too vague to have any good answer. Let me formulate it better.

Morality consists of rules. So saying, I certainly beg some questions, especially against virtue ethics. But the questions so begged are not going to be in question here, so I will beg them unabashedly. Morality consists of rules, in that it is constituted by some rules, rules that tell us what we are to do. Here I might be thought to he begging questions in favour of deontological conceptions of morality, and against teleological conceptions, since according to teleological conceptions of morality, it tells us which things are of value. But I don't think that the claim that morality consists of rules that tell us what to do does beg any questions against teleological conceptions. Teleologists, after they have told us what is of value, go on to tell us what to do: we are to maximize (or satisfice, or otherwise advance) the realization of value in the world.[2]

Now suppose a moral theorist has proposed a certain set of rules, as the set of moral rules, the set that constitutes morality. We are bound to have some questions. We might question whether these rules really do constitute morality. This challenge is a kind of request for justification: what is the justification for the claim that these rules constitute morality? But we could also ask for another kind of justification. We could ask what reason we, or anyone, has to follow these rules. This would be a request for a practical justification.[3]

But why should we expect those rules to have any external justification? Why, for instance, could they not have a merely internal sort; they all hang together; or, perhaps they are simply very plausible, more so than any alternative; or they could just be *the rules of morality, by definition*, as the rules of chess are the rules of chess, by definition, with no justification necessary. Still, this last gambit would be a way of avoiding not the request for a practical justification, but the request for a theoretic justification. Presumably, if someone admitted that the rules of chess forbid castling when in check, but asked why this fact should have any grip on what he plans to do with the plastic pieces, we would either be prepared to give some reason or else to admit that the rules really don't have any justification.

We have strong feelings, and strong interests, that are served by the compliance of others with moral rules. So of course we do want others to follow moral rules, and we have that reason and other practical reasons to hope that we can give a justification.[4] This explains why we want there to be some justification for moral rules. And the model of the rules of games, and other various arbitrary collections of rules, explains the perfectly coherent worry that there might not be any such justification. I want to stress that such a worry is coherent. For sometimes it can seem as though the request for a justification of morality doesn't make sense at all. But we can see how an arbitrary set of rules might be justified. For example, if you want to play chess, then you must follow the game's rules. This is not exactly a practical justification, if all we mean is that these *are* the rules of chess, so that just by definition you can't play chess without following them. But consider instead some rules for playing chess well. For instance, you ought to try to control the centre of the board, you ought to castle early to get your king out of danger, and so on. There is a kind of practical justification for these rules, but it depends on your having a certain goal: to play chess well. That is typical of practical justifications of rules: their force for you depends on your having some relevant goal.

Now it looks as though an external justification of practical rules must have its ground in some other practical rules. At least this is ordinarily so. For example, a practical justification of laws would generally proceed by reference to moral considerations. It is a complication that there are also generally prudential reasons to follow laws. Independent of the prudential reasons, we often want some moral justification of legal obligations. And even if the justification offered were purely prudential, this would still be a justification by reference to other rules, namely, the rules of prudence. It is imprudent, extremely so, to take a significant chance of landing in prison.

We would not think of justifying morality by grounding it in just any old other system of rules. Of course, most systems of rules are obviously unable to provide anything like a justification for morality. For instance, when we want a justification for morality, it would be no help if we were shown that etiquette requires that we follow moral rules.[5] There are apparently only two systems of rules which look at all appropriate for providing some justification of morality, and they are the rules of prudence and the rules of rationality. And I think really, the rules of prudence have seemed appropriate *only* because they are sometimes taken to *be* rules of rationality, or to be derived from them.[6]

This is why the Kantian view of morality and its justification is so compelling. A justification of morality is a "deduction" of its principles from the principles of rationality. Or perhaps even better, it is a demonstration that moral rules *are* rules of rationality. Such a justification would satisfy the demand, in a way that no other justification could. Why are the rules of rationality the ones that have to lie at the bottom of a satisfactory justification of morality? A request for justification is a request for reasons. So much seems obvious. Indeed, it is exactly why the request for justification can be of two different sorts. We can ask for reasons to believe that some philosopher's account of morality is correct, or we can ask for reasons to follow those moral rules.

Now, a certain set of rules will, in one sense, provide its own set of reasons. The reason we can't bring in Martinez to pitch, is that we pinch hit for him last inning. That reason comes from the rules of baseball. The reason for sending a cheque to the American Philosophical Association, even though they have lost their records and don't know whether or not you've already paid your dues, is that it would be unfair not to send it. That reason comes from the rules of morality. But we can also wonder whether there is any reason to follow those rules. In this sense, there being a rule does not in itself count as a reason. There is a more fundamental sense of 'having a reason', and it is in this sense that we can wonder whether we have any reason to follow moral rules. But even in this more fundamental respect, I think, there is no sense at all to be made of the question whether we have a reason to follow the rules of rationality. To think that there might be reasons for following the rules of rationality, I would say, is to misunderstand what reasons are. Reasons are *in terms of* the rules of rationality. There is a reason to do something, just in case it is rational to do it. This is why there seems to be a pressing need for a justification of morality, but no similar need for a justification of rationality.[7] The contrast here seems to me to be important. I will argue below for my view that there is such a contrast, and try to explain why there is.

In what follows, I will examine the Humean attitude toward the issue of justifying morality. I would like to vindicate a central part of that attitude.

2 Categorical Imperatives

Humeans doubt that morality could be a set of categorical imperatives, and this doubt might even be thought of as a hallmark of Humeans. The question whether there are any categorical imperatives, and whether morality consists of categorical imperatives, is clearly related to the problem of the justification of morality. Before I explain what I think the relation between the questions is, I need to clarify what is meant by a categorical imperative. Following Foot,[8] we should really distinguish a couple of senses in which imperatives might be categorical. First, we might say that an imperative is categorical when our application of it to the behaviour (or deliberations) of someone does not depend on any aim, on any desire of that person. In this sense, the rule "Practice your scales daily" is not categorical, since we should withdraw it upon learning that the addressee had no interest in learning to play the piano. There is little question that moral imperatives are categorical in this sense. Informing your critic that you aren't interested in according respect to other persons isn't going to make him withdraw the imperative to keep your promises. We are interested rather in a second sense of categoricity. A rough try at expressing this sense is to say that a categorical imperative is one that each person has reason to follow, no matter what her desires. This is only a *rough* try because whether it succeeds in explaining the sense of 'categorical' in which Humeans deny that morality could be categorical, depends on how we fill in an explanation of what it is to have a reason. But it will do for a start.

Humeans sometimes say that *no* imperatives are categorical. I think they are mistaken to say so, for reasons that will emerge. But let's focus first on the special case of moral imperatives. Why couldn't they be categorical, according to the Humean view?

Suppose we want to explain why someone acted the way he did. Suppose he walked to the corner shortly before noon, and we want to explain why. Since he does it intentionally, we typically cite some mental states of the agent that rationalize the action. We could cite mental states of his that merely cause the behaviour, but that is a different kind of explanation.[9] The classic form of explanation is the citing of a belief/desire pair. He walked to the corner shortly before noon, because he wanted to eat a sandwich at noon and believed that by walking to the corner shortly before noon he could bring it about that he would eat a sandwich at noon. In this explanation we cite the agent's reason. His reason is a belief/desire pair. For short, we might say that his reason was that he wanted a sandwich, or, that he thought that walking to the corner was the only way he could get a sandwich. Which is the sensible thing to say depends on context, of course. But it doesn't follow that what his reason really was depends on context. I am denying that it does depend on context. There are only pragmatic grounds, not deep ones, for describing the person's reason one way rather than another.

As I just admitted, in ordinary talk we can give reason-for-action explanations that do not make explicit reference to any desire. Maybe he walked to the corner shortly before noon because he believed that this was the only way to save his life. We would not ordinarily add, "and he wanted to save his life." But this is a shallow feature of ordinary talk. It is unusual but conceivable *not* to desire to save one's own life, and if indeed our agent does not, then citing his belief that walking to the corner shortly before noon was the only way to save his life provides no explanation of his walking, and so doesn't count as a reason in the explanatory sense of 'reason'. But it's also true that we sometimes seem to cite reasons for action without citing desires, when we aren't just failing to mention a desire that we assume must be present. Maybe the agent walked to the corner shortly before noon because he remembered his promise to meet his sister on the corner at noon. Do we need to add, "and he wanted to keep his promise"? We might. But we might instead say, "he believed that he had an obligation to keep the promise." Then must we add, "and he wanted to discharge his obligation"?

I think we *do* need to add *something*. For after all, some people recognize their obligations and do not act on them. What we need to add is something to the effect that this is a sort of person whom the thought of obligation normally moves to action. The question I want to examine now is how that sort of thing, that sort of fact about a person, can sensibly and illuminatingly be described. Once that is done, we'll be in position to understand why Humeans think that moral imperatives couldn't be categorical.

3 Motivating Reasons

A motivating reason is a reason that someone has to do something, where his doing it (if he does it) is explained by his having that reason. Following Michael Smith, among others, we can contrast this sort of reason with a normative reason. A normative reason is, to put it somewhat loosely, a reason that a person *ought* to do something. If she then does it, this is explained not by the fact that she had the reason, but by the fact that she recognized this reason and was motivated by it. For example, I had a normative reason to wear a suit to my brother's wedding. And I did wear one. That I did is explained not by the fact that I had this reason, but by the fact that I "accepted" it, we might say, that I cared about that sort of reason and recognized that I had it.

Suppose a person has a belief, and that he performs some action, he ϕs. What must the belief be, and what do we need to add to the belief in order to explain the action by citing the agent's reason for performing it? The simplest Humean view would be that the belief must have a content of the form, By ϕ-ing I will ψ, and we must add that the agent has a desire to ψ. This is Michael Smith's account in *The Moral Problem*.[10] It requires a defence, a much longer one than I can give it here. But the main idea can be given fairly easily. The primary access that we have to the whole idea of a desire is that it is a state of mind characterized by its output in behaviour. Let's allow ourselves a little weaselling: a desire to ϕ is a mental state that *normally* motivates its bearer to ϕ. 'Normally' clauses are very suspicious, but for now at least we'll take it in a loose and intuitive way; we aren't offering an analysis or placing any great weight on the claim.

Putting the weasel aside, then, we have very good grounds to say that a person has a motivating reason to ϕ only when she has a desire to ψ, and a belief that by ϕ-ing she will ψ. For suppose she believed that by ϕ-ing she would ψ, and that this explains why she ϕs—that's what's necessary for her to have a motivating reason to ϕ. What do we have to add? We have to add that she had some motivation to do what she believed she would do by ϕ-ing. What state is that? A motivation to do what she believes she will do by ϕ-ing is a motivation to ψ (since that's what she believes she'll do by ϕ-ing). The state that explains this motivation is one which normally produces the motivation as its output. So it is a desire to ψ.

One might question whether this account of the desire to ψ is a correct analysis. I think this issue is probably a red herring. 'Desire' here is really a term of art. It covers what is covered in ordinary language by the notions of desire proper, wanting, valuing, having a goal, preferring, and probably many other things. What they have in common is precisely what the (weaselly) analysis says.

So much for the Humean view of motivating reasons. I intend it to convince only temporarily. With it in place, we return to the question of why Humeans say that moral imperatives couldn't be categorical.

A categorical imperative, I said, is one that each person has reason to follow, no matter what her desires. What kind of reason do we mean? Not a merely normative reason. Each person does have a normative reason to refrain from harming others, irrespective of what she wants. This is one sense of 'categorical', but not the one we want here. It seems that we want the sense of 'categorical' that results from plugging *motivating* reasons into the 'reason' slot of the formula. We can see now why anyone who accepts the Humean account of motivating reasons should think that what (motivating) reasons a person has is entirely dependent on what desires she has. For a person's having a motivating reason just is a matter of her having a belief and a desire. *That* reason, the one that she has, is a reason that she wouldn't have were she to lack *that* desire. This chunk of theory completes the simple Humean story. Let's recap.

Humeans doubt that morality could consist of categorical imperatives, because (i) a categorical imperative is one that you have reason to follow irrespective of your desires, and (ii) what you have motivating reason to do is not independent of your desires. Furthermore, morality can be justified only if someone can be given reasons to follow moral rules. If morality cannot consist of categorical imperatives, then a person can be given reasons to follow moral rules only if she has certain relevant desires. In particular, she must desire that she follow moral rules, or desire those things which the moral rules tell her to pursue, or the like. What desires we have is a contingent fact about us. So the justification of morality is a contingent matter. This is a disappointment, and falls short of the kind of justification we sometimes hope for. David Copp puts it this way: a justification for following moral rules that appeals to contingencies of the agent addressed is not a justification of morality *per se*, but only a justification of morality for someone.[11] Humeans think that it is a disappointment we will have to learn to live with.[12]

There is a major (glaring?) flaw in the reasoning of the last paragraph above. The conclusion, that the justification of morality is contingent, follows from the premiss (let's call it a 'lemma', since it was independently established), that morality does not consist of categorical imperatives, only if the kind of reason that fills out the content of the conclusion is the same as the kind of reason that gives content to the lemma. Are the kinds of reason the same? In the lemma, we are plugging motivating reasons into the slot. Is that the sort of reason we mean when we think about the justification of morality? This is still unsettled. We are thinking of reasons of rationality, which I argued are ultimate reasons in some sense. Motivating reasons are also ultimate, in a way. But it is not obvious that reasons of rationality and motivating reasons are the same thing. If they aren't, then it might be that morality can be justified to anyone, independent of her desires, because everyone has a reason of rationality to follow moral rules, even though whether a person has a motivating reason to follow moral rules is contingent.

Nearly all of the remainder of the essay is devoted to understanding the relation between motivating reasons and reasons of rationality. Only at the end will we return to the question of the justification of morality.

4 The Interpretation of Motivating Reasons

Are motivating reasons just the same as reasons of rationality? On the face of it, no. They do not seem to be the same *kind* of thing. Motivating reasons are psychologically real, since they are explanatory by nature. A motivating reason that you have is an empirical property that you bear, or how could it explain anything that you do? But a reason of rationality is something normative. For you to have a reason of rationality is for it to be the case that you *ought* to act in a certain way. As I said, citing a normative reason can be a kind of explanation, but it is only an explanation on the (tacit) assumption that the agent does, or at least is disposed to do, what she ought to do. As I have put it, citing a normative reason is explanatory only on the assumption that the agent *accepts* the norms in question. Here 'accepts' is really a term of art; there is a sense of 'accepting a reason', no doubt, according to which one may accept one and have not even the slightest tendency to act on it. But I am using 'accepts' for whatever it takes actually to be motivated by the kind of reason in question.

Since reasons of rationality are, after all, normative, they are not the same kind of thing as motivating reasons, so the Humean argument does not go through as sketched. I think this is an important fact, so let me support my claim. Someone might think that reasons of rationality are not really normative at all. Maybe standards of rationality are something like canons of interpretation, so that acting rationally is just a matter of being interpretable. To say that someone has a reason of rationality to φ, in that case, might just be to say that in case she does φ, her φ-ing is interpretable as intentional action. While I think there must be something to this idea, I also think it can't be correct as stated. For there is such a thing as irrational action. There is such a thing as fallacious reasoning. People do reason incorrectly, not merely from false premises, and when they do they are precisely reasoning as they *ought not* to reason. They have good reasons not to draw the conclusions they draw. What sorts of reasons could these be? Reasons of rationality. I will give examples below, but it seems to me that the point is clear enough in the abstract. Reasons of rationality are normative.

Here is a suggestion for why motivating reasons and normative reasons of rationality might be conflated. We are calling 'motivating reasons to φ' those belief–desire pairs of the following form: the desire to ψ, and the belief that by φ-ing I will ψ. So we have this claim:

(MR) A has a motivating reason to φ iff there is some ψ such that A desires to ψ and believes that by φ-ing, she will ψ.

Now in fact, I think this claim can be understood in two different ways. According to one reading, it really is a normative claim. It says, in effect, that you ought to perform the necessary and sufficient means to your desired ends. You might not do this. You might, at least on occasion, find yourself lacking the motivation to perform the necessary and sufficient means to some end you desire. This would be a fault of yours, a failure of rationality. Glossing over some distinctions, we might say that your failure would be a failure of instrumental reason. So this reading of (MR) takes it to be a statement of the norm of instrumental reason.

Second, the claim could be understood in a different way. It might be a partial analysis of desire and belief; it might be a purported analytic truth. A motivating reason, according to this reading, would be something that actually does motivate you. The claim would be that unless you are in fact motivated to φ, there is no ψ such that you desire to ψ and believe that by φ-ing you will ψ. According to the analysis, a crude functionalist analysis, it is of the very essence of the desire to ψ that, when combined with the belief that by φ-ing you will ψ, it produces a desire in you to φ; and it is of the very essence of the belief that by φ-ing you will ψ that, when combined with the desire to ψ, it produces in you the desire to φ. Let's call this the 'constitutive' reading. According to it, belief and desire are partly constituted by the stated role in the production of motivation.

I object to the second reading, for reasons I have just given. It implies that it is impossible to desire to ψ, believe that by φ-ing you will ψ, and yet fail to desire to ϕ. But this does not seem to be impossible, it seems to be irrational. When I say how it seems, admittedly, I am reporting my intuitions, and the very existence of seriously held philosophical views to the contrary of mine demonstrates that these intuitions aren't universally shared. Mine are hardly unique, though. Kant says,

> Whoever wills the end, wills (so far as reason has decisive influence on his actions) also the means that are indispensibly necessary and in his power. So far as willing is concerned, this proposition is analytic . . . (Ak 417)

> [I]t could alike be said "Who wills the end, wills also (necessarily, if he accords with reason) the sole means which are in his power." (Ak 417–418)

The parenthetic condition, in each case, is crucial. The crude functionalist reading of (MR) would in effect leave out that condition, and say that willing the end *is* willing the means.[13]

Not to leave the point resting on my intuitions and the authority of Kant's, let me give some theoretic backing to my objection. The desire to ψ and belief that by ϕ-ing I will ψ do, I admit, have conceptual connections to the desire to ϕ. Can we imagine someone who under no circumstances would come to have the latter desire on the basis of the former plus the belief? Perhaps not. Maybe this would be a case of someone so wildly irrational that we could not think of her as an agent at all. But it is a long jump to conclude that there is a universal necessary connection between beliefs and desires of the sort postulated by (the second reading of) (MR). For desire has other conceptual facets. For instance, in us sophisticated linguistic creatures, beliefs and desires are normally available to introspection. So I ought to know whether I desire a French fry, and whether I believe that the one and only way to get one is by ordering some. So my sincere report that I so believe and so desire might be enough to ground the attribution to me, even if I don't order some French fries (or even want to order any). Good functionalist analyses ought to respect the plurality of links that mental states have to other states and to actions and linguistic behaviour, and to perceptual inputs, and the like. That is why I called the second reading of (MR) "crude."

But finally, even if my objection is not convincing, I want to insist on a weaker claim. We cannot have both readings of (MR) at once. They are exclusive. If (as I deny) (MR) can be read as a kind of functionalist analysis of belief and desire, then it cannot also be normative, it cannot be an expression of an instrumentalist conception of rationality. For norms are things which it is possible to violate. The idea of a norm which it is logically impossible to violate makes no sense. So reasons of rationality, which are normative, cannot be the same sorts of things as motivating reasons, which are explanatory of action. (MR) defines motivating reasons only on the second, functionalist reading, and it defines a normative means/ends principle only on the first reading.

To conclude this section, let's recall why this distinction, between motivating reasons and normative reasons of rationality, is important.

(1) Morality can be justified only if it consists of categorical imperatives.
(2) An imperative is categorical if and only if a person has reason to follow it independent of what she desires.
(3) A person's having reason to φ depends on there being some ψ such that she desires to ψ and believes that by φ-ing she will ψ.
(4) So any reason a person might have depends on a desire of hers.
(5) So there are no categorical imperatives.
(6) So morality cannot be justified.

This argument goes through just in case 'reason' can be understood univocally in the premisses (1)–(3). (3) was offered and defended as a conception of motivating, explanatory reasons (though I cast some doubt on it even when construed that way). But (2) cannot be understood to be about motivating reasons, because if it is then the sense of 'categorical' it defines makes (1) terribly implausible. We don't deny that people sometimes behave immorally. If being able to justify morality meant being able to force people to behave morally by dint of argument, there would be no question of success.

The ground for scepticism about, and thus for scepticism about the justification of, morality, is very shaky. At least as I have presented it so far, it relies on a dubious conflation of two kinds of reasons. We may doubt that there are any motivating reasons to follow moral rules, that each person has necessarily and independent of what she happens to desire, but that doesn't in itself provide any ground for doubting that morality can be justified, since justification is a matter of normative reasons.

I think that scepticism is called for none the less. I will argue that there is something special about exactly the kind of norms of rationality that Humeans accept.[14] This special status confers a kind of necessity on the Humean norms which we may properly doubt can accrue to other sorts of norms. The request for justification, I will argue, is intelligible as a demand for reasons bearing just that kind of necessity. And we may properly doubt that the demand for moral justification can be satisfied.

5 Rules and Desires

Suppose we tell Ann that she ought to φ. She asks why. We cite some rules, R, that tell her to φ. She shrugs. These rules have no grip on her. She can see that the rules do tell her to φ, but she doesn't accept the rules, they don't motivate her. We might think she is missing something. What is she missing? What must be true of her, that isn't, in order for her to be motivated by our explanation? In so far as we think there is something wrong with Ann for failing to be motivated by the belief that she is required by R to φ, we will think that her missing this something is exactly what's wrong with her.

Schematic as this story is, there is an almost entirely general answer that we can give. Ann is missing a desire. How can we know this? How do we know that what she's missing isn't a capacity of some other sort, or a belief? Couldn't what's wrong with Ann be that she believes something false, or that she fails to believe some truth? We know that what's missing is a desire, because we have enough characterization of the missing state to see that it fits the bill to be a certain desire, a desire with a certain specifiable content. Since she believes that were she to φ, she would comply with R, and we want a state that gets her from that belief to the motivation to φ, we know that the state is the desire to comply with R. That's what the desire to comply with R *is*.

We have to be a bit careful here. We have already rejected the simple functionalist definition of desire, so we can't say that S is a desire to ψ iff S is a state producing a desire to φ upon input of a belief that by φ-ing one will ψ. The means/end principle is a normative principle of rationality. Given that Ann is means/ends rational, all we need to give her in order to get her to φ, is the desire to comply with R.

I said that the missing desire answer is an *almost* entirely general answer to the question raised in the schematic story. Why only almost? We're taking it as a kind of methodological axiom that whatever is missing when someone has a belief and lacks a certain motivation is a desire of some sort or other. There doesn't seem to be any room for exceptions.

Suppose Ann's case is like this. We tell her that she ought to take a prep course for the Law School Admissions Test. She asks why. We point out that she wants to raise her chances of getting into a competitive law school, and she can raise her chances by taking the prep course. She admits as much, but still isn't motivated to take the prep course. So we cite a rule, the means/ends rule:

M/E If you desire to ψ, and believe that by φ-ing you will ψ, then you ought to φ.

Now suppose that Ann agrees that this rule does indeed instruct her to take the prep course, given what she believes and desires, but she shrugs at the rule. She doesn't accept it.

We must now conclude that there is something wrong with Ann. She *ought* to take the prep course, given what she believes and wants, but she doesn't, and she has no motivation to take the course.[15] The story is an instance of the schematic story. We can ask ourselves what exactly Ann is missing. What state is it that she lacks, the absence of which explains what's wrong with her? Isn't it a desire of some sort? For we thought that any state that bridges the gap between a belief and a motivation must be a desire. But not this one. What Ann is missing can't be any desire.

The desire that is supposed to bridge the gap between believing that a rule requires her to φ, and being motivated to φ, is the desire to comply with the rule. But suppose Ann's mental inventory were supplemented with a desire to comply with the rule, in this case to comply with M/E. Could this complete the picture? Were she to desire to comply with M/E, would she then be motivated to take the LSAT prep course? By hypothesis, Ann suffers from this failure of practical reason: she fails to be motivated by the acknowledged means to her desired ends. So adding a desired end does not in her bring about the motivation to perform the acknowledged means to that end. We cannot bring about in Ann the motivation to perform an action acknowledged by her to be a means to a certain end, by getting her to desire that end. That is a good way to motivate normal, rational agents, but in Ann's case it is futile. But this futile attempt is exactly what we would be engaged in, if we were to try to bring Ann to desire to take the LSAT prep course by giving her a desired end (the end of complying with M/E) the means to which (she believes) is to take the prep course. So what Ann is missing cannot be a desire. Call this the Tortoise argument (for a reason I will explain shortly).

Maybe this argument looks too quick. We do agree that what's wrong with Ann is that she is missing some sort of state. And that state takes the input of belief (that taking the prep course is a necessary means to improving her chances of getting into a competitive law school) and desire (to get into a competitive law school) to the output of motivation, or action. And such states just *are* desires, one might say. After all, we are being broad in our classification of desires. What prevents us from counting this state, whatever its ordinary description, as a desire?[16] What prevents us is that desires are typed by their content. When asked which desire Ann needs, we have to be able to say something like, "The desire that p," or "The desire to ϕ." We can't just cite inputs and outputs. No doubt, what Ann is missing is very much like a desire in certain respects, but if it isn't a desire to . . . or a desire that . . . or even a desire for . . . , then it is no desire at all. But as soon as some content is given to this purported desire, the one that is supposed to be the missing state, then the Tortoise argument shows that it could not be what Ann is missing.

Compare Lewis Carroll's Tortoise.[17] His problem, his irrationality, was that he did not draw the logical conclusion of an argument whose premisses he accepted and whose reasoning was valid and simple. What state was he missing? He did not accept the inference rule, modus ponens. There is no temptation here to suppose that what the Tortoise was missing was a desire of any sort,[18] but there might be *some* temptation to think that his failure to accept the rule was a matter of his lacking a certain belief. At least, Achilles was so tempted. Achilles tried to get the Tortoise to believe that (an instance of) modus ponens is valid. And he succeeded! But futilely. For from this additional, otiose premiss, the Tortoise was still unable (or unwilling?) to draw the logically implied conclusion. I find this parallel striking.

Now we've singled out the means/ends rule as special. Once you have (accept) the means/ends rule, what you need to get you to acceptance of other rules is one or another desire. But no desire will get you to the means/ends rule itself. (Compare modus ponens. Once you have modus ponens, what you need to get you to acceptance of other rules is some conditional belief, the belief in some conditional. But a belief in a conditional won't get you modus ponens itself.) So means/ends rationality has a special status. But is this special status relevant to the question at hand?

When someone asks for a justification of practical rules, for example, morality, she is asking to be given a reason to follow them. The justification of morality is given by reasons, normative, practical reasons. Since they are normative reasons, they are grounded in some set of rules, some norms. When we give a justification we are either explicitly citing or adverting to some norms. But we can't just cite any old bunch of norms. Which norms count toward justification? The problem is that if we simply cite a bunch of rules, the agent may well ask, what are those rules to me? She may ask for a reason to follow them. And we can't just shrug this off. Suppose someone cited the laws of India in support of moral principles. We ourselves recognize that this sort of justification is useless. We have to say why the rules we cite are better.

If we cite the laws of India, and our subject asks what reason she has to follow them, we understand what she's asking. She's asking for reasons, again. She doesn't see any force in the rules we've cited. She's missing whatever it takes to be motivated by the belief we've instilled, namely, that the laws of India require her to abide by moral norms. That state is a desire. We can understand how someone might lack that desire. Asking for a reason, in this context, makes perfectly good sense.

If our subject were asking for some reason to follow M/E, the matter would be different. Suppose she isn't motivated to φ when she believes that by φ-ing she will ψ, and desires to ψ. So she asks what reason she has, and when we cite the M/E principle, she asks what reason she has to follow that. But now, I think, we are at a loss. Not merely at a loss to provide a compelling answer, but at a loss to know what to think of such a person. What would *count* as a reason, by her lights? As long as she accepts M/E, we know what would count as a reason: some belief that by following the rule to be justified she would achieve some end she desires.

Compare the theoretic case. Suppose someone asks for a theoretic justification of some proposition, *q*. We could try to get her to believe that *p*, and that if *p* then *q*. We know what's required; it's a matter of getting her to believe the right things, the propositions from which she can infer that *q*. But what about the Tortoise? We can't give him a justification to believe the conclusion, not one that he can see to be a justification. We can't give him a reason that he will see as a reason. That's because there doesn't seem to be anything that counts as a reason, for the Tortoise. Those conditionals we count on to give reasons have no effect on the Tortoise.

We give you reasons to believe something by finding things you believe and getting you to draw inferences. If you can't draw those inferences, then nothing counts as a reason for you. And similarly for practical reasons. We can give you practical reasons by finding things you want, and some things you believe, and getting you to draw practical inferences. If you can't draw the practical inference, not even the fundamental, M/E kind, then nothing counts as a reason for you. This is why M/E has a kind of ground-level normative status. I think it counts as a categorical imperative, too. Of course, the particular reasons that M/E generates are all hypothetical reasons. But M/E itself is not hypothetical. Its demands must be met by you, in so far as you are rational, no matter what desires you happen to have. That is why I said (in section 2) that I think Humeans are mistaken to say that there are no categorical imperatives at all.

We would like to be able to give a justification for morality, in the sense of being able to give someone reasons for abiding by moral rules. Some people already want to abide by moral rules. Those people have reasons already. But their reasons seem to depend on their contingent wants. A satisfying justification of morality would give reasons that are independent of contingent wants. Humeans doubt that there is any such justification, because they doubt that there are any such reasons. For suppose someone cited a reason for complying with moral rules. Citing a reason is referring or adverting to some norm. If the reason cited is grounded in an arbitrary norm, say, in the laws of India, then it can't count as a justification, precisely because we may perfectly sensibly ask what reason there is to comply with *that* norm. Nor is this a facile tactic of demanding that reasons be given *ad infinitum*. The laws of India clearly do not count as a reason to comply with moral rules, even if they entail that we ought to comply with moral rules. Admitted: reasons must end somewhere. But they may not end just anywhere. Humeans may plausibly claim that instrumental reasons are ground-level reasons. But instrumental reasons are never independent of our contingent desires. This is the ground for Humean scepticism about the justification of morality.

In closing, here are some prospects for combating the scepticism.

I have claimed a kind of *sine qua non* status for M/E. Giving an M/E reason counts as giving a reason if anything does; if it doesn't count, then the request for reasons is empty. But no principle other than M/E has this status. So the only ultimate sort of reasons are instrumental reasons. And this means that moral rules are not categorical, they depend for their compelling force on contingent desires. So I claimed. I can see two ways that an anti-Humean could resist.

First, she might claim that there are other sorts of practical principles with the same status as M/E. Maybe these other principles could yield enough content, independent of contingent aims, to provide justification for moral rules. I think this is one way of seeing "transcendental" Kantian arguments. One might think that something of this sort happens in the case of theoretic reason when we wonder about the justification of induction. On the one hand, the demand that we provide a reason to believe (that the future will resemble the past) does get some grip, since the sceptic is willing to count *deductive* reasons as reasons, and points out that all the deductive grounds for induction are question-begging. Inductive principles of reasoning are independent of deductive ones. On the other hand, arguably the willingness to infer future predications from past ones is as much embedded in the functional character of belief as modus ponens is embedded in the functional character of a conditional belief (by which I mean only, a belief whose content is a conditional). Are there practical principles apart from M/E that have a similar status?

Second, and to my mind more plausibly, she might claim that there are *alternatives* to M/E. Let me explain. The first line of resistance insists that M/E is only one of a set of principles, all of which must be accepted if the idea of a reason is to make sense at all. But instead it might be that M/E is only one of a set of principles, *one* of which must be accepted if the idea of a reason is to make sense at all. To illustrate, think again of the theoretic analogue. A person (or Tortoise) who doesn't accept modus ponens can't be brought to accept it by supplying him with some conditional premises. But modus ponens is not unique in this respect. He might accept disjunctive syllogism, for example. Then we could get him to believe that q, when he believes already that p and that if p then q, by adding the premiss,

$$\neg(p \to q) \vee (\neg p \vee q)$$

which is, after all, a tautology.

He could then reach $(\neg p \vee q)$ from $(p \to q)$, which he has, plus the second premiss; and q from the p, which he has, plus the intermediary conclusion. The point is that you need some inference rule or other, in addition to your beliefs, to draw inferences, but there isn't any particular inference rule you need. It is not obvious what practical rules one might use as a general alternative to M/E.[19] This strategy *might* yield a principle, one having a status at least equal to M/E, which itself has substantial moral content.

It might, but I doubt it. When we first looked at M/E, we noted that it can be thought of in two ways. The way I chose, with some argument, was as a desire. According to this, the constitutive reading, someone who desires an end and believes that some action is a necessary means to that end, cannot fail to desire the means. It would count decisively against the attribution of the instrument-belief and the end-desire, that the agent did not desire the means. I argued that the constitutive reading is false—as stated, it is too strong a condition. I also said, though, that something like the constitutive reading seems right, something suitably weakened. The output of the means-desire is *partly* constitutive of the combined functions of the end-desire and the instrument-belief. Bringing about the means-desire when in the presence of the end-desire is a part of the concept of an instrument-belief, but the connection may fail and the state still be attributable, as long as there are some other conceptual connections in place, and as long as there is some story surrounding the failure that makes it understandable.

We might say, failure of M/E rationality cannot be "global," an agent cannot be perfectly generally and always M/E irrational, or we could not see him as having those beliefs and those desires. It can be local, so long as the surrounding story gives us enough material to attribute the instrument-belief and the end-desire.

Other inferential principles do not seem to have this feature. If they don't, it's hard to see how an alternative to M/E could be established.

Let me forestall a possible misunderstanding of my argument. It is *not*: that you had better use M/E, or you will be unintelligible as having reasons. That, I think, is a dubious argument. It suggests that after all, everyone will want to be intelligible as having reasons, whatever else she wants.[20] Rather, the argument is that a request for reasons makes sense only if there is something that could count as a reason. Of course, in one sense the project of justifying morality straightforwardly fails if nothing counts as a reason at all. But, the reason there is a problem about the justification of morality is that there are (possible?) beings who can recognize reasons, who act on reasons, who are moved by reasons, but are not moved by moral considerations. A justification would show them what reason they have. So long as a person is M/E rational, there are reasons she can act on, that can motivate her, reasons that she accepts as reasons. If we cannot provide her with a reason to abide by moral rules, then we cannot justify morality. The problem of justifying morality stands in stark contrast to the problem of justifying the M/E principle itself. Someone who doesn't accept the M/E principle cannot be given reasons of any sort. That we cannot justify our principle to such a person is no more troubling than our inability to justify principles of deduction.

This argument has a transcendental feel about it quite alien to Humeanism. As a Humean myself, I think we should be up front about this. The special status of instrumental reason is due to its being the *sine qua non* of having reasons at all. We shouldn't be embarrassed to take the insights of Kantian philosophizing to heart. Certain aspects of the Humean position deserve to be abandoned. We should abandon a hardline metaphysical position according to which the very idea of practical reason is mysterious. Our scepticism should consist in doubts that the content of practical reason is anything like the content of morality.[21] We should be contesting the normative ground, not contesting its very existence.

Notes

1. 'Humean', as I use it, is the name of a kind of philosophical theory of practical reason. I do not address the historical question of whether Hume had a theory of this kind. Nor will I give any explicit definition of the kind.

2. This point is spelled out nicely in William Kymlicka, "Rawls on Teleology and Deontology," *Philosophy and Public Affairs* 17 (1988), 173–190.

3. See David Copp, "Moral Skepticism," *Philosophical Studies* 62 (1991), 203–233. Whether it really is another kind, or whether in fact a justification for the claim that certain rules constitute morality is really the same thing as a justification for following them, I will leave open. Personally, I suspect that they do amount to the same sort of justification. But on their face they at least appear to be distinct.

4. For example: it is very plausibly part of our ordinary moral view that we shouldn't coerce others unless we can justify our actions *to* them. If we can't justify morality to others who don't already accept our moral views, then we would often be unable to satisfy this ordinary moral requirement.

5. Well, it might, but only under very special circumstances. It would not answer the philosopher's question, if someone did manage to show that it was rude to act wrongly.

6. E.g. in Thomas Nagel, *The Possibility of Altruism* (Princeton: Princeton University Press, 1970).

7. So here I am disagreeing, I think, with some of Peter Railton's remarks in "On the Hypothetical and Non-Hypothetical in Reasoning about Belief and Action" (in G. Cullity and B. Gaut, eds., *Ethics and Practical Reason* [Oxford: Oxford University Press, 1997]). I am disagreeing more directly with his "Some Questions about the Justification of Morality," in J. Tomberlin, ed., *Philosophical Perspectives*, VI: *Ethics* (Atascadero, Calif.: Ridgeview, 1992), 27–53.

8. Philippa Foot, "Morality as a System of Hypothetical Imperatives," in her *Virtues and Vices* (Berkeley: University of California Press, 1978), 157–173.

9. Not to say that rationalizing explanations aren't also causal. I don't see how they could fail to be causal. I don't think this point matters to the main argument in the text.

10. Michael Smith, *The Moral Problem* (Oxford: Blackwell, 1994).

11. "Moral Skepticism."

12. There is a completely different sort of conclusion that one might draw, in fact, one which I have myself been inclined to draw. It is that the justification of morality is not contingent at all, but rather that the content of morality is relative to agents. The content of morality relative to an agent is always something that can be justified to that agent. In this essay I am ignoring this move, even though in fact I think it is very promising as a move in a different context. Here I am assuming that a proper justification, in the sense that's usually meant, must be a justification of the same content to each person, or more simply, a justification of a certain content of morality. In Kant's terms, I am interested in what must be the case "if morality is

to be something real" (Ak 445). The Humean view is that the necessary condition is not met, that morality is not "something real," though we Humeans prefer not to put it in those terms.

My sense is that there is a lot of in-fighting among Humeans that is quite interesting to us Humeans. I include David Brink, a moral realist, who certainly would reject Kant's criteria for whether morality is something real; John Mackie, who accepts Kant's criteria and concludes straightforwardly that morality is nothing real at all; all expressivists, including quasi-realists who believe that morality is something quasi-real (and that quasi-real is good enough), but not R. M. Hare, whom I take to be a Kantian in the relevant sense. I find this in-fighting very interesting, but the present essay is about the grander dispute, in which all Humeans are on the same side.

13. Quite possibly the distinction between desiring and willing is important here.

14. See Elijah Millgram, "Was Hume a Humean?," *Hume Studies* 21 (1995), 75–93, on whether Hume is a Humean in this sense.

15. This point is made by Jean Hampton in her "Hobbes and Ethical Naturalism," in J. Tomberlin, ed.: 333–353.

16. Simon Blackburn put this objection to me.

17. Lewis Carroll, "What the Tortoise said to Achilles," *Mind* 4 (1895), 278–280.

18. But see Railton, "Some Questions about the Justification of Morality." Railton's use of the Tortoise in "On the Hypothetical and Non-Hypothetical in Reasoning about Belief and Action" is for a different end, though a related one. See also my "Perspectives on the Normativity of Ethics," *Noûs* 28 (1994), 514–525, for the relevance of the Tortoise to the views presented by Railton in "Some Questions."

19. But see Elijah Millgram and Paul Thagard, "Inference to the Best Plan: A Coherence Theory of Decision," in D. Leake and A. Ram, eds., *Goal-Driven Learning* (Cambridge, Mass.: MIT Press, 1996), 439–454.

20. See Peter Railton, "On the Hypothetical and Non-Hypothetical in Reasoning about Belief and Action." Also relevant is Simon Blackburn, "Practical Tortoise Raising," *Mind* 104 (1995), 695–711.

21. The kind of scepticism mentioned and distinguished, but *not* discussed, in Christine Korsgaard, "Skepticism about Practical Reason," *Journal of Philosophy* 83 (1986), 5–25 [this volume, chap. 2].

7 Why Is Instrumental Rationality Rational?

Troy Jollimore

I

It is relatively common for philosophers to doubt whether we have any reason to act as morality requires. But it is very difficult to find philosophers who are willing to doubt, in a similar way, the idea that we have reason to act as instrumental rationality requires; reason, that is, to take effective steps toward attaining the ends we have accepted as our own. The inference from the fact that a certain action is an effective means of satisfying an agent's ends to the conclusion that that agent has reason to perform that action is held by almost everyone to be, as it is sometimes said, *automatic*: once it is determined that the action in question bears the specified relation to one's goals, nothing more needs to be shown.[1] But fewer philosophers are willing to grant that morality possesses this sort of automatic reason-giving force. Rather, it is quite commonly held that some additional consideration needs to be cited in order to show that an agent has reason to act as she is morally required. The fact that an action is morally required, claim those who adhere to this type of position, is not enough in itself.

The point is not to claim that we never have reason to act morally. After all, even those who claim that moral considerations in themselves can never give rise to reasons for action will acknowledge that morality and instrumental rationality may sometimes happen to require the same thing. One might refrain from cruelty or injustice in order to avoid the opprobrium of one's neighbors, out of fear of legal penalties, or even because one simply desires not to be cruel or unjust. But if this sort of position is right, then one's reason for acting will not ultimately be a moral reason; rather, an instrumental reason is required to make the action rational. One might say that on such a position, morality loses its authority; the only truly authoritative source of reasons for action is instrumental rationality, and all real reasons must ultimately stem from this source. Reasons of instrumental rationality are thus seen as *foundational*; whereas other sorts of practical reasons, particularly moral reasons, must, if they are to exist at all, ultimately reduce to a reason of the foundational sort. In this paper I will use the term *instrumental foundationalism* to refer to this view of practical reason.

In arguing for their position, instrumental foundationalists often cite certain facts about irrationality. It is widely acknowledged that one can act immorally without acting irrationally. By contrast, failing to act as instrumental rationality requires is often taken as a paradigm of (if not definitive of) irrationality. Thus, there seems to be a significant sense of the term 'rationally required' in which acting on one's instrumental reasons is rationally required, whereas acting as morality requires is not; and it is in this sense, I take it, that instrumental rationality is thought to be an automatic reason-generator, in a way that morality is not.

Having admitted the existence of this asymmetry, it would perhaps be easy to think that we have already admitted the truth of instrumental foundationalism: for is it not to be expected that the proper explanation of the asymmetry is precisely that moral considerations, unlike instrumental considerations, need to be "backed up" by some other, non-moral sort of consideration in order to provide a reason for action? And that really, it is the consideration that does the backing up—an instrumental consideration, presumably—that is the true source of the reason? But although this line of thought is attractive, it moves too quickly, and we should resist it. For while the view of the instrumental foundationalist does indeed provide one sort of explanation of the asymmetry, it is, as I will argue, not the only explanation available.

My argument for this conclusion will proceed by stages. In section II, I assess the plausibility of the premises of what I take to be the main argument for instrumental foundationalist. In section III, I develop an analogous argument in the realm of theoretical reason, and argue that it fails. Section IV applies this lesson to the realm of practical reason, arguing that despite surface appearances, the practical argument is no more convincing than its theoretical counterpart. Finally, in section V, I entertain the suggestion that my account fails to take irrationality sufficiently seriously, and suggest, perhaps somewhat heretically, that the significance of irrationality has in fact been overestimated, or at any rate misunderstood, by a large number of philosophers working in this area.

II

I will refer to the main argument for instrumental foundationalism as the Asymmetry Argument. The premises of this argument can be stated as follows:[2]

(1) It is necessarily irrational to acknowledge that an action will contribute to the achievement of one's goals, and yet fail to recognize a reason to perform it.
(2) It is not necessarily irrational to acknowledge that an action is morally required, and yet fail to recognize a reason to perform it.
(3) Therefore, one may rationally doubt whether one has reason to do what morality requires, but may not rationally doubt whether one has reason to do what instrumental rationality requires.

From (3), it is generally taken to follow that moral reasons are in some sense weaker than instrumental reasons; they are, at any rate, more dubious—and from this it is taken to follow that some version of instrumental foundationalism ought to be accepted. If a person may doubt that she has reason to act morally, but not that she has reason to act on her instrumental reasons, then surely, it might be claimed, in order to convincingly show that a person has reason to be moral we must show that instrumental rationality requires it. For the moment I will not attempt a more precise formulation of the conclusion than this. My ultimate purpose will be to try to cast doubt on the idea that anything resembling instrumental foundationalism follows from the premises; first, though, we must ask whether the premises themselves ought to be accepted.

Of the two independent premises (for (3) is thought to follow from (1) and (2)), (2) seems reasonably unproblematic: whatever it is, exactly, that is wrong with the amoralist, it is not that she is *irrational*. Of course some philosophers, following Kant's lead, have tried to show otherwise. If (2) is false, then what I take to be the best argument for instrumental foundationalism fails. Unfortunately, however, I do not believe that anyone has yet convincingly demonstrated the falsehood of (2), and I am not optimistic as to the prospects of anyone's doing so. (One reason for my pessimism about this project will become clear by the end of this section.) For the sake of the argument, then, I will grant (2); at any rate, I hope to demonstrate that the foundationalist argument can be defeated, and the authority of morality defended, even if (2) is true.

Surprisingly, perhaps, I am also willing to grant the truth of (1). What matters here, however, is not simply whether (1) is true, but also what it means for (1) to be true. And this is a matter that will take some investigation to illuminate.

If (1) is true, it is presumably because the following claim, which I will refer to as the *Instrumental Principle of Practical Reason* (IP for short), is not only true, but in some sense fundamental for rational agents:

(IP) The fact that an agent endorses *e* as one of her ends guarantees that she has (at least some) reason to pursue *e*.[3]

Like (1), (IP) might seem so obvious that it does not need any defense. But is this so? As I have said, to support (1) we need to show not only that (IP) is true, but also that its truth is in some way a fundamental element of rationality. (If it were true but unimportant, or true but unobvious, then a failure to recognize it might not constitute irrationality.) And it might be wondered whether we even know that (IP) is true. There are after all, at least two ways in which its apparent plausibility might be explained away.

First, suppose our belief in (IP) were based on a kind of widespread, albeit perhaps largely unconscious, inference to the best explanation, where what needs to be explained is the fact that human beings so often seem to have reason to pursue their ends. The truth of (IP) would, of course, explain this phenomenon: indeed if (IP) is true, then human beings *always* have reason to pursue their ends, for the fact that something is one of my ends *guarantees* that there is reason for me to pursue it. The problem is that we can easily imagine another possible explanation, and one of a very different sort: perhaps human beings are simply very good at identifying ends which there is reason for them to pursue. If this were true, then there might be a very tight connection between *e*'s being an end of *P*'s and *P*'s having reason to pursue *e*, whether or not (IP) was true. To the extent that the widespread belief in (IP) could be explained as the result of this kind of potentially faulty inference, our commitment to (IP) would be undermined.

Another possible explanation for the widespread acceptance and apparent plausibility of (IP) posits a confusion between the explanatory and the normative senses of the word 'reason'. A person who desires an end *e*, and who pursues *e*, has a reason for what she does in the explanatory sense of the word 'reason': that is, we can explain her action, and so make sense of it. She is not simply acting randomly; rather, we can understand what she is doing. However, what is claimed by (IP) is that such an agent must have a *normative* reason for trying to bring about *e*; thus (IP)'s claim is not that there is something to be said that can *explain* her action, but rather that there is something to be said *in favor of* her action. Again, to the extent that our acceptance of (IP) can be shown to be based on such a confusion, our reasons for believing (IP) can be held to have been undermined.

What is needed is a *normative* argument to establish (IP) as both true and fundamental. As it happens, a version of the argument we need, which I will refer to as the Practical Regress Argument, has recently been proposed and defended by James Dreier.[4] The Practical Regress Argument asks us to consider whether an agent might reasonably reject (IP). Consider, then, an agent (Dreier calls her Ann) who desires an end e; and suppose that as a matter of fact, there is a certain action, a, that would be, of the available alternatives, the most effective means to Ann's achieving e. We will assume, too, that achieving e is compatible with, and indeed required by, the general achievement of Ann's ends, and that Ann's performing e is thus required by instrumental rationality. Now imagine that we are attempting to convince Ann that she ought to do a, and that we have reached the following impasse: Ann has been convinced by our evidence that a is indeed the best means to e, but she claims not to see why that gives her any reason to perform a.

What are we to say to Ann? Obviously it will not help to cite further evidence for the claim that a will help her achieve e: she already accepts that claim. Nor will it help to cite further ends to which a might contribute. For Ann's problem is precisely that she does not take the fact that an action will contribute to the achievement of her ends as giving rise to a reason for performing that action. One might say, then, that Ann's problem is that she does not *want* to do what is necessary to bring about her ends. Perhaps, then, what Ann lacks is the desire to conform with (IP). Suppose that we could somehow bring about that desire in Ann, so that Ann explicitly made conformance with (IP) one of her ends. Would this help? In fact there is no reason to expect this to help.

For again, Ann's problem is that she cannot see how the fact that something is one of her ends gives her reason to pursue the necessary steps to attaining it. In other words, given that Ann's desire for e does not move Ann to do what she acknowledges is necessary to bring e about, it is entirely unclear that a *further* desire (here, the desire to act as (IP) requires) would be any more successful in moving her. A desire to behave in accordance with (IP), then, would presumably be practically impotent; as would a desire to desire to behave in accordance with (IP), and so on *ad infinitum*.

It is rapidly becoming obvious that there is nothing whatsoever that is guaranteed to help Ann; nothing, that is, that is guaranteed to move her from where she is (her acknowledged end plus her acknowledgment that a certain action will achieve that end) to where she clearly ought to be (her acknowledgment that she ought to perform that action).[5] And this is so despite the fact that a perfectly compelling case exists for Ann's performing that action. Ann is simply not in a position to appreciate the strength of this case, for she is lacking something—one might call it a fundamental practical disposition, in this case a disposition to act as (IP) recommends—without which effective practical reasoning appears quite impossible. Thus, in order to be considered even minimally practically rational, an agent needs to be committed to (IP) in a fundamental, and non-derivative, way. (IP), then, seems to be nothing less than a fundamental *a priori* requirement of practical rationality.[6]

The Practical Regress Argument, then, establishes not only that (IP) is true, but that it is a fundamental principle of practical rationality; and it thus seems to show that premise (1) of the Asymmetry Argument is true. At the same time, the argument also lends some support to (2). For there is no comparable case for establishing any *moral* principle as an *a priori* principle of practical rationality. An agent who accepts (IP) but refuses to acknowledge that she has reason to act as moral considerations suggest might be obstinate, coldhearted, or lacking in empathy or imagination, but she does not seem to be irrational in the way in which Ann is irrational. Such an agent is receptive to practical arguments, in the sense that she is capable of being swayed by them—so long as they refer to those ends which she herself recognizes as worthy. To view one's ends as giving rise to reasons for taking the means to them is, then, a necessary requirement of practical rationality. But to view *moral* ends as giving rise to reasons for taking the means to those ends is not. The asymmetry exploited by the Asymmetry Argument is both real and deep.

III

The premises of the Asymmetry Argument, then, seem to be defensible. And this will be taken by the instrumental foundationalist as evidence that instrumental rationality is indeed foundational in the relevant sense. As suggested previously, the inference may strike us as obvious. For if one can always doubt the reasons allegedly provided by morality, but may never doubt the reasons provided by instrumental rationality, does this not at least strongly suggest that moral requirements are valid precisely where, and only where, they are backed up by instrumental considerations?

I now want to argue, however, that the argument does not in fact provide any significant support for instrumental foundationalism. I think we should accept both (1) and (2), and thus acknowledge, as stated by (3), that there is an asymmetry, in terms of rational doubt, between morality and instrumental rationality. Still, I will argue, the explanation of this asymmetry need not appeal in any way to the truth of instrumental foundationalism.

To see this, it will help to make use of an analogy from the realm of theoretical reason. Suppose we are attempting to convince a recalcitrant friend, Simon, that he ought to accept a given belief, *b*. Simon accepts belief *e*, and he accepts the claim that *b* follows logically from *e*; he denies, however, that he has any reason to accept beliefs that follow logically from beliefs he accepts. Simon, then, fails to accept the following principle, which I will call *The Inferential Principle of Theoretical Reason*, or IT:

(IT) An agent has (at least some) reason to accept those claims that follow logically from beliefs he accepts.

Our position with respect to Simon is as hopeless as was our position with respect to Ann. For there is very little reason to suspect that any argument, no matter how convincing, could bring him to accept either *b* or (IT). Even supposing that we somehow managed to come up with a conclusive argument for (IT), and that Simon accepted both the premises of this argument and the claim that (IT) followed logically from these premises, there would still be no reason to expect Simon to accept (IT) itself. For he may well ask again, "Why should I accept claims that follow from claims I accept?" That is, he may well happily accept the premises, and acknowledge that they do indeed logically imply (IT), while nevertheless continuing to reject (IT) itself.[7]

Thus, we can construct an analogue of the Practical Regress Argument as applied to theoretical, rather than practical, reason. What the Theoretical Regress Argument suggests is that just as (IP) should be viewed as an *a priori* principle of practical reasoning, (IT) should be viewed as an *a priori* principle of theoretical reasoning. And this seems quite right: an agent who does not accept that there is reason to believe claims that follow logically from claims he already accepts is in no position to engage in theoretical reasoning at all. But this suggests that it may be possible to find in the realm of theoretical reason asymmetries analogous to the one exploited by the Asymmetry Argument, and thus to construct an equally compelling argument for the theoretical counterpart of Instrumental Foundationalism.

In the practical realm, the target of our attack was taken to be morality. Let us take, as the target of our theoretical analogue, scientific evidence (broadly understood as whatever evidence is regarded as convincing in current scientific practice). The argument, then, will look something like this:

(1_t) It is necessarily irrational to acknowledge that a claim is logically implied by one's current beliefs, and yet fail to recognize a reason to believe it.

(2_t) It is not necessarily irrational to acknowledge that a claim is supported by the best currently available scientific evidence, and yet fail to recognize a reason to believe it.[8]

(3_t) Therefore, one may rationally doubt whether one has reason to believe what is supported by scientific evidence, but may not rationally doubt whether one has reason to believe what is implied by one's current beliefs.

But if a person may doubt that she has reason to believe what is supported by scientific evidence, but not that she has reason to believe what follows from her current beliefs, then surely, it might be claimed (in parallel to our argument for Instrumental Foundationalism), in order to convincingly show that a person has reason to believe what is supported by scientific evidence we must show that this does follow from her current beliefs. Thus the argument, if successful, establishes what we can call Deductive Foundationalism (DF), which claims that an agent only has reason to accept those beliefs that follow from what she already believes, and thus that scientific evidence *in itself* never provides reason for belief.

The argument for skepticism about science is formally analogous to its practical counterpart. Nevertheless, it is clear that the argument is flawed in some way, for its conclusion is unacceptable. That conclusion, (DF), seems to imply that in cases of conflict between one's current beliefs and scientific evidence, the latter should always give way to the former, for one will necessarily have reason to accept what follows from one's current beliefs, but will not necessarily have reason to accept what is supported by scientific evidence. Moreover, this is true *regardless* of the nature of one's current beliefs. Thus, consider a person brought up in an anti-scientific environment, who has accepted an internally consistent but ludicrous belief set (astrology, if that example works for you). This person, whom I will call Andy, does not much trouble himself with the question of whether he has good *evidence* for his beliefs: "They just feel like they *must* be true," he says, whenever anyone asks him to defend them. Andy, then, no longer bothers to subject his initial beliefs to rational criticism; instead he spends his time deriving logical implications of the beliefs he already has, and incorporating those implications into his belief set. According to (DF), Andy's method of forming new beliefs is a good one. Indeed, the argument as a whole seems to imply that Andy's method of belief formation is more reasonable, and presumably more reliable, than that of his friend Rajini, a physics student who likes to keep up with current scientific research. For Andy possesses an ironclad *guarantee* that every new belief he forms will be supported by a reason; whereas poor Rajini possesses no such guarantee. Indeed, Andy can go further, pointing out that the acceptance of these beliefs was rationally required; he would have been irrational, in any given case, *not to* have accepted the beliefs that followed from the beliefs he had already accepted. Whereas poor Rajini, again, can say no such thing.

And yet poor Rajini, quite obviously, is not really so poor; it is Andy who is at an epistemological disadvantage here. If this is not already apparent, consider the fact that Andy's claims apply equally well regardless of the content of the particular beliefs with which he is starting; equally well, that is, whether he happens to be an astrologer, a Flat Earther, or an acolyte of L. Ron Hubbard. Consider, too, the fact that Andy's skeptical argument need not take science as its target; an analogous argument could have been constructed to motivate skepticism with respect to *any* substantive method for forming beliefs. This skeptical argument, then, can be deployed against any target whatsoever, in order to defend any position whatsoever. As such, it seems to be a recipe for an extremely radical subjectivism.

In seeing where the argument for (DF) goes wrong, start with the following observation: conducting oneself as required by (IT) is a reasonable thing to do. And to say that something is reasonable might be thought to imply that one has a good reason for doing it. But this is true in one sense, false in another. It is reasonable for an agent who cannot tell poisonous mushrooms from edible mushrooms to avoid eating all wild mushrooms, and in a very straightforward sense she has good reason to do so. But there is also a sense in which what she *really* has reason to do is only to avoid the *poisonous* ones; it is in this sense that, with respect to any mushroom that happens (unbeknownst to her) to be safe to eat, we could truly say, "She has no reason to avoid *that* one." The second sense is what we might call the objective sense: it concerns, let us say, the reasons our agent would see herself as having if she had all the relevant information. Correspondingly, the first sense can be termed the subjective sense. An agent has a subjective reason to do (or believe) *x* if and only if the evidence she currently possesses reasonably leads her to believe that doing (or believing) *x* is reasonable.⁹ (I leave to the side the difficult question of whether an agent who unreasonably judges herself to have reason to *x* can be said to have subjective reason to *x*.)

We should note two things that we do not want to say here. First, we do not (quite) want to say that an agent has a subjective reason to do (or believe) *x* if and only if it is reasonable for her to believe that she has an *objective* reason to do (or believe) *x*. For consider our mushroom avoider. Faced with an unknown mushroom, our agent has a perfectly good subjective reason not to eat it. But she does not have the evidence to conclude, even provisionally, that she has an objective reason not to eat it. The point is that she *might* have an objective reason not to eat it, and that the chance that this reason obtains is sufficiently high to make it reasonable not to eat it.

The second thing we do not want to say is that the person who has only a *subjective* reason in favor of doing *x* does not really have any sort of reason at all, although she quite reasonably thinks that she does (or, as in the mushroom case, thinks that she might). Subjective reasons are reasons, and indeed quite good reasons. For the fact that a person thinks that a certain action is supported by compelling objective reasons (or, as in the mushroom case, that it is sufficiently likely that it is so supported) can itself constitute a good reason for performing that action, whether or not the objective reasons do in fact obtain; and it would be quite wrong to accuse a person who acted on such a reason of having no reason on which to act.¹⁰

At the same time we should keep in mind that the objective sense is the more fundamental of the two senses of the word 'reason'. After all, when an agent finds out that her subjective reason is *only* a subjective reason, she is generally prepared, and quite properly so, to give it up altogether. To have a subjective reason is to think that one has (or is sufficiently likely to have) an objective reason; thus, to be convinced that one's reason for *x*-ing is *only* subjective is to believe that one in fact has no reason for *x*-ing at all. The ultimate goal of the agent who has adopted the mushroom avoidance policy is not to act always in a manner that is reasonable by her own lights; rather, so acting is an intermediate strategy for achieving her ultimate goal, which is to avoid being poisoned.¹¹

The so-called "guarantee" provided by (IT) is not, then, as interesting or valuable as might have been thought. For while the status of (IT) as an *a priori* principle of theoretical reasoning does indeed guarantee that an agent will have at least some reason to accept every claim that meets the conditions set forth in that principle, it does *not* guarantee that these reasons will not be merely subjective reasons. Just as the fact that it is generally reasonable for our mushroom eater to avoid wild mushrooms does not guarantee that, in any particular case, the mushroom she avoids is one she was better off avoiding, the fact that it is generally reasonable to accept claims that follow logically from the claims one already believes does not guarantee that any particular claim meeting this condition will be true. The reason why, in the theoretical case, is straightforward: it is that the things one already believes, which constitute the starting points of this belief expansion process, might themselves be false.

The flaw in our argument for Deductive Foundationalism should be clear. (1_t), (2_t), and (3_t) should all be acknowledged to be true, with the proviso that the reasons for belief mentioned in (3_t) are understood to be subjective rather than objective reasons. But this proviso gives the game away; for the fact that (IT) consistently provides subjective reasons in favor of certain beliefs hardly justifies us in holding the reasons provided by the considerations it deems relevant (i.e. one's current beliefs) to be on firmer ground than reasons provided by scientific evidence. Indeed, the two can hardly be compared; their roles are deeply different. A principle such as (IT) is purely formal: it tells us how to add additional beliefs to the set with which we start. Such a principle presupposes that we have some method of deciding which beliefs to start with; and it is as a contender for this position that the methods of science will enter the arena.[12] The argument errs, then, in regarding deductive reasoning and inductive reasoning as competitors. (IT), like other formal principles of reasoning, is at best only a secondary principle. It tells us nothing more than how to proceed once an initial set of accepted beliefs is on hand, and leaves entirely unanswered the crucial question of how that initial set is to be arrived at and evaluated. For the latter is a question to which a substantive rather than merely formal answer is required.

IV

Few, if any, philosophers, of course, are tempted to endorse the anti-science argument we have just finished examining. Its flaws are all too obvious. Its interest for us lies not in itself, but in its application to the argument for instrumental foundationalism we developed in section II. For (IP), like (IT), is merely a formal principle; and this suggests that the argument for instrumental foundationalism, like the argument for the superiority of one's current beliefs over scientific evidence, is ultimately quite weak. It is this suggestion that I would now like to pursue.

Suppose for the moment that desires are like beliefs, in that they can be, and need to be, supported by reasons, and are thus subject to rational criticism. (Humeans will protest this assumption, of course; we will return to their protest in a moment.) I will refer to this as the *objective desirability* view. On this view, practical rationality is not just the business of deciding how to satisfy our desires, but also, and more fundamentally, the business of deciding which desires ought to be satisfied; the business, that is, of deciding which things are genuinely *desirable*. On such a view the guaranteed irrationality noted in (1) (like that noted in (1_t)) merely reflects the necessity of a rational agent's acting (or forming beliefs) on the basis of what she takes to be the best reasons available to her. It is, after all, a good general policy to endorse the means to the outcomes one has judged desirable. What alternatives are there, other than simply to act at random, or to refrain from acting at all? (Note, however, that this is not to deny that there are some means that ought not to be endorsed. Better, in such cases, to revise one's ends. But [1] will still be true with respect to whatever ends one ends up with when deliberation is done, just as it was true with respect to the ends with which one began—*up to the point where one ceased to acknowledge them as one's ends*.)

This, then, is the source of our feeling that there is something wrong with an agent such as Ann, who desires e but sees no reason to take the means to e. What makes instrumental rationality rational, on this sort of view, is simply the fact that it is a good policy for the practical agent: indeed, no better alternative policy is available. And we can say the same with respect to (IT) and its necessity for the theoretical agent. But it must be emphasized that to say that these are good policies is not to say that an agent who adopts them will be guaranteed to succeed, though it is to say that an agent who rejects them will almost inevitably fail.

But if this is so, then the Asymmetry Argument does no better than the anti-science argument. For the fact that instrumental rationality reliably provides subjective reasons can no more establish its practical superiority over morality than can the fact that inferential rationality reliably provides subjective reasons establish its theoretical superiority over the methods of the sciences. In neither case is the fact that a certain method of reasoning is a good (indeed, *necessary*) policy sufficient to establish that the results of that method of reasoning will automatically be valid or correct. And in neither case is it correct to treat whatever substantive reasoning methods are being employed as being in competition with the formal methods that supplement them. On the objective desirability view, there are facts about which outcomes are desirable, and these facts are at least somewhat independent of the facts regarding what we do in fact happen to desire.[13] On this view, morality, in picking out certain outcomes as worth bringing about, either does or does not get it right: that is, it either does or does not identify as worth pursuing outcomes that are objectively desirable, and thus, genuinely worth pursuing. If, contrary to the claims of many moral skeptics, morality's identifications are generally correct, so that there is generally something to be said in favor of the outcomes it identifies as worth pursuing, then there will generally be something to be said in favor of taking the means to these outcomes as well. If, on the other hand, morality's claims are generally incorrect, as many moral skeptics tend to believe, then there might be no real reason for pursuing the ends it identifies, and so no real reason for taking the means to these ends. In this eventuality the application of instrumental rationality to the ends determined by morality will turn out to be no more reliable than the results of the moral judgments themselves. But of course this is the case with respect to *any* substantive method of distinguishing desirable from undesirable ends. The important thing is to see that, on the supposition that desires are like beliefs in the respect specified, moral reasoning (or whatever substantive method of end identification is in question) is not only not in competition with instrumental reasoning, it is prior to it. The latter is merely a formal device to be applied to the results of the former (or of other substantive methods of desire formation), in order to expand the set of desires and, in doing so, avoid the practical paralysis that afflicts agents such as Ann.

If something like the objective desirability view of desire is correct, then the answer to the question, "What makes instrumental rationality rational?" is simply that the practice of taking the means to the ends we have adopted is the best policy available to agents such as ourselves. Again, in saying this, we are not saying that it is a policy whose results are guaranteed to be correct. This will only tend to be the case where instrumental reasoning is applied to a set of goals and desires that have themselves been formed through some fairly reliable process (or, in isolated cases of sheer good luck, where the results happen to be largely correct *despite* the unreliability of the processes through which they were formed). So long as this condition is met, however, proper instrumental reasoning will tend to result in valid judgments, just as proper inferential reasoning, applied to true claims, will preserve their truth. Moreover, if the condition is not met, and one happens to be an agent who is incapable of reliably determining which goals are worth pursuing, then one is in essence already lost. An agent who begins with defective practical judgments will be almost guaranteed to meet with disaster, no matter how well developed his capacity for instrumental reasoning might be; and there is simply no alternative reasoning method that would allow such an agent to do any better.

Moreover, one's choice from among substantive methods of goal selection will be crucial in resolving an issue I have, for the most part, sidestepped: how agents ought to determine when it is more reasonable to revise one's ends rather than endorse a goal recommended by a valid pattern of instrumental reasoning beginning from that set of ends. In terms of their judgments as to what types of actions are off limits or inherently undesirable, the judgments of an agent who accepts the general validity of morality's claims as to what is generally desirable will differ greatly from one who claims, say, that all and only things which promote her own self-interest are desirable. Indeed the self-interested agent, who accepts a theory of value that is both consequentialist (albeit strictly first-personal) and monistic, might only rarely think it reasonable to reject a suggested means to her acknowledged ends. Even here, however, we should say "only rarely" rather than "never," for there is at least the possibility that some instrumentally recommended means may have to be rejected, if only due to the fact that mistakes will inevitably be committed in the judgment of what really is in one's interest. A more complex situation is that of the agent who accepts a pluralistic theory of value; here the revision of ends will almost certainly be mandatory on at least some occasions. The most complex situation, however, is very likely to be that of an agent whose behavior is largely governed by a deontological or otherwise non-consequentialist moral view, and who perhaps combines this with a pluralistic theory of value. Such agents will inevitably find themselves faced not only with conflicting and perhaps incommensurable values, but with situations in which the most effective means to an end that is judged to be highly valuable is an action that is itself forbidden by deontological morality.[14] Depending on the nature of the circumstances and of the agent, an unanticipated or apparently irreconcilable conflict of this nature may on any given occasion lead either to a more or less drastic revision of one's ends, or to a further reconceptualization of the relationship between one's ends and one's means.

Of course, this entire line of reasoning is based on the possibility of what I am calling the objective desirability view; and most Humeans will object to that view of practical reasoning. They will claim that desires are immune to rational criticism and are therefore *not* like beliefs, that practical reasoning is thus *not* analogous to theoretical reasoning, and that this is the explanation of why the skeptical argument based on (IP) is powerful whereas the one based on (IT) is ultimately unconvincing. They are correct, of course, that if we follow the Humean tradition of thinking desires to be immune to rational criticism, then we cannot counter the skeptical argument in the way I have suggested. For if we suppose that a desire is not the sort of thing that needs a reason of some sort to support it, but rather that a desire possesses a kind of intrinsic normative validity merely by virtue of the fact that it exists, then it is very natural if not inevitable to see desires as automatically giving rise to reasons for action. Such a view will almost certainly end up viewing morality and instrumental rationality as competitors, simply because the set of goals identified as desirable by the two perspectives will almost certainly fail at some point to coincide. There are few if any people whose desires coincide perfectly with what morality requires. Moreover this does at least suggest that where morality *can* be justified, it is only with a justification that terminates in (one or more of) an agent's desires. The problem, though, is that the Asymmetry Argument was supposed to be an argument *for* a Humean view of this sort; that is, the argument was supposed to *demonstrate* that we needed to see desires as automatically giving rise to substantial reasons for action (in a way that moral considerations do not), by demonstrating that (IP) was an a priori principle of practical reason. But what is now in question is precisely whether this fact about (IP) must lead to the conclusion that desires do in fact automatically give rise to reasons for action of the appropriate sort. It would be flagrantly circular to call in a Humean view in order to defend *this* claim, and then use the claim, in turn, to defend the Humean view.

The Practical Regress Argument, then, seems to be neutral between the objective desirability view and the Humean view of desire. Given certain Humean presuppositions, the Practical Regress Argument's account of what makes instrumental rationality rational (its account, that is, of the truth of the premises of the Asymmetry Argument) does indeed lead to the conclusion desired by the instrumental foundationalist: that instrumental requirements are more fundamental than moral requirements, that they tend to compete with moral requirements, and that they are guaranteed to win when they do.

But these Humean presuppositions must themselves be defended in order to arrive at this result. For, as I have argued, an alternative account of the reason-giving force of instrumental rationality is available: one that sees allegiance to the principles of instrumental rationality as nothing more than a (practically necessary) good policy. Admittedly, this account, by holding that the justification of instrumental rationality is essentially a pragmatic one, diverges radically from more traditional accounts; but this in itself seems no reason to reject it. Further argument, of course, would be required to conclusively settle the question of which of these alternative accounts ought to be preferred.[15] My intent has been only to undermine the Asymmetry Argument by pointing out the existence of an alternative, not to prove that this alternative is indeed the correct one.

V

One important objection to my account remains to be considered. It might be suggested that the view I have outlined fails to account for the significance of irrationality, and for the force that can be carried by an accusation of irrationality. The whole point of the original skeptical argument was that irrationality was clearly a weighty and indeed decisive charge, so that the advantage of instrumental rationality over morality, as a source of reasons for action, was precisely that the former and not the latter could properly employ the charge of irrationality as a penalty. But this kind of view, it seems to me, misunderstands what makes the accusation of irrationality so compelling. The special virtue of a well-grounded charge of irrationality is not that it implies anything with respect to the strength of the reasons in question, but rather that it is, in an important sense, inescapable.[16] Consider once again the case of theoretical reason. To criticize an agent on the basis that she has endorsed inconsistent beliefs is to level an extremely effective charge: once such a contradiction has been acknowledged, an agent has essentially no choice but to admit the existence of a problem, and drop one of the offending beliefs. In criticizing such an agent, we are in effect saying to her, "What you are now saying cannot be true, *given what you yourself have already admitted is the case.*" This is often far more effective, of course, than saying, "What you are now saying cannot be true, given what I believe and think you ought to accept as well." But there is no guarantee that the inconsistency is of any great consequence; it is as easy to have inconsistent trivial beliefs as to have inconsistent weighty beliefs. So in the theoretical realm, the special effectiveness of the charge of irrationality stems not from the fact that the rational failure in question is necessarily highly significant, but merely from the fact that it is extremely difficult if not impossible for a person manifesting such a contradiction to deny that a rational failure has indeed taken place. Moreover, there is no guarantee that after having removed the grounds for the accusation, the agent's beliefs will be true; she might remove the inconsistency by abandoning a true belief and holding on to a false one, or she might even have started out with two conflicting beliefs both of which happened to be false.

The same is true in the practical realm. It is especially effective, and especially satisfying, to be able to accuse an agent of failing to act rationally *by her own lights*—by the lights, that is, of the values she accepts and the ends she has endorsed—precisely because such a charge is difficult to escape or shrug off. One cannot simply deny the standard by which one's action is being judged, since it is a standard whose legitimacy one has already endorsed. On the other hand, an agent who is told that she ought to accept different standards, values, or ends than the ones she does in fact accept can always, it seems, simply shake her head and reply, "I don't think so." This is what explains the fact, which plays such a large role in the arguments we have considered, that an agent may reasonably challenge the reason-giving force of morality's verdicts, but may not in the same way challenge the verdicts of instrumental rationality. For instrumental rationality simply tells her to do what she has, in effect, already acknowledged herself to have reason to do, and to contradict its requirements is thus to contradict oneself.

It is presumably this fact which has led to what I consider to be an inordinate philosophical fascination with inconsistency and irrationality, and has led so many defenders of morality, for instance, to hope that it could somehow be demonstrated that the immoralist, or the amoralist, must be held to possess inconsistent beliefs or commitments, or that it could be shown in some other way that such characters turn out to be irrational by their own lights. I myself think it highly doubtful that such a thing can be shown; but I also doubt that it matters much. The closed-minded astrologist need not be guilty of any inconsistency when he expresses his skepticism toward science. What he is guilty of is poor judgment, and of having false, and indeed unreasonable, beliefs. Similarly, the deeply immoral person does not manifest inconsistency or irrationality in shrugging off our attempts to persuade her to adopt moral standards and ends. But she, too, is guilty of poor judgment; and when we say to her, unsuccessfully, such things as "You should not take unfair advantage of people," what we say is quite true and she is in fact wrong (though not irrational) to ignore it. To place the entire hope for a possible justification of morality on the possibility of locating, in immorality, some sort of formal irrationality, is a serious mistake. For in doing so, we not only cut ourselves off from a range of possible suggestion and criticism that is often more pertinent, and at least sometimes more effective, than a charge of irrationality; we also commit ourselves to abstaining from useful comment in cases in which there is no formal inconsistency to be found, but in which agents are nevertheless acting badly, and have reason to act differently.[17]

Notes

1. The use of the word 'automatic' in this context is first found, so far as I am aware, in Philippa Foot, "Morality as a System of Hypothetical Imperatives," *Philosophical Review* 81 (1972), 305–316.

2. Versions of this argument can be found in Philippa Foot, "Hypothetical Imperatives"; Bernard Williams, "Internal and External Reasons," in his *Moral Luck* (Cambridge: Cambridge University Press, 1981) [this volume, chap. 1]; and James Dreier, "Humean Doubts about the Practical Justification of Morality," in *Ethics and Practical Reason*, G. Cullity and B. Gaut, eds. (Oxford: Oxford University Press, 1997) [this volume, chap. 6].

3. Note that (IP) is very close, but not equivalent, to the principle Dreier calls M/E, or the 'means/ends rule'. According to Dreier, M/E states that "if you desire to ψ, and believe that by φ-ing you will ψ, then you ought to φ" (Dreier, "Humean Doubts," 93) [this volume, 139]. Whereas M/E is stated in terms of desires, (IP) is stated in terms of goals. Given the broad Humean conception of desire, the difference in terminology seems to me insignificant.

4. Dreier, "Humean Doubts" [this volume, chap. 6]. See also Peter Railton, "On the Hypothetical and Non-Hypothetical in Reasoning About Belief and Action," also in Cullity and Gaut, eds.; and Donald C. Hubin, "What's Special About Humeanism," *Noûs* 33 (1999), 30–45. Dreier calls his version the Tortoise argument, after Lewis Carroll's famous argument in "What the Tortoise said to Achilles," *Mind* 4 (1895), 278–280. The Theoretical Regress Argument, which is described in section III, is essentially identical to Carroll's argument.

5. Of course, the commitment need not be explicit. What is necessary is not that Ann must *acknowledge* (IP), but that she must be motivated to act as it requires.

6. Dreier does not use this terminology in describing M/E (see n. 3). But it seems to me to capture the status he wants to grant to this principle, on the basis of the argument described.

7. This is, of course, the famous Tortoise argument presented by Lewis Carroll. See n. 4.

8. Perhaps (2_t) will strike some as implausible. Isn't it, it might be urged, really *irrational* in some strong sense to refuse to believe what science tells us there is good

evidence for? So long, however, as 'scientific evidence' is not defined so broadly as to make this a tautology, the answer to this question must be no: it must be possible, at least in principle, rationally to doubt whether the sciences do in fact provide us with compelling evidence. One might, of course, regard the sciences as so convincing, and so well established, that it would be pure foolhardiness to refuse to accept their conclusions. But one might well regard the practical reasons provided by morality in just the same way. In either case, while the refusal to accept reasons of the designated sort might quite reasonably be considered *unreasonable*, it seems a stretch to judge such a refusal to be *irrational*.

9. John Broome ("Are Intentions Reasons?" in C. Morris and A. Ripstein, eds., *Practical Rationality and Preference: Essays for David Gauthier* [Cambridge: Cambridge University Press, 2001]) draws a related distinction; but rather than distinguish between subjective and objective reasons, he distinguishes between reasons and normative requirements. On his view, a person is normatively required to believe those claims that logically follow from claims she believes; but this does not necessarily mean that she has any actual reason to believe them (though he acknowledges that there is a misleading sense of the word 'reason' in which she may be said to have such reason).

10. *Contra* Broome (see n. 9).

11. Cf. Williams, "Internal and External Reasons," 102–103 [this volume, 38–39].

12. I would not want my reference to the beliefs "with which we start" to suggest an overly simplistic picture of the process of belief formation. Belief formation is presumably best viewed not as a two-step process, but as one in which beliefs evolve over time, being subjected to successive applications of both deductive and inductive methods. The fundamental point is simply that purely formal methods can only work once they are given something to work on, and that some other sort of method is required to do this. (My thanks to the anonymous commentator who pointed out the need for this note.)

13. "At least somewhat" because the fact that I desire something can itself be relevant to the question of whether I have objective reason to pursue it. An objective desirability view can recognize three types of objects: those that there is reason to pursue whether I desire them or not, those that there is no reason to pursue whether I desire them or not, and those that there is reason to pursue (and thus, to desire) only if I do in fact desire them.

14. For a good discussion of many of the issues connected with moral conflicts and moral pluralism see Michael Stocker, *Plural and Conflicting Values* (Oxford: Clarendon Press, 1990).

15. Some powerful arguments against the traditional Humean view of desires as providers of reasons can be found in Joseph Raz, "Incommensurability and Agency,"

in his *Engaging Reason: On the Theory of Value and Action* (Oxford: Oxford University Press, 1999).

16. Hubin acknowledges this ("What's Special About Humanism," 39). He does not, however, draw from this any skeptical conclusions about the force of the irrationality charge.

17. I would like to thank Talbot Brewer, Christian Coons, Elijah Millgram and three anonymous referees for comments and discussion that helped shape this paper.

8 Putting Rationality in Its Place

Warren Quinn

One kind of metaethical debate between realists and antirealists is about the character of ethical truth, with realists asserting and antirealists denying that truth in moral thought transcends our capacity to find reasons in support of our moral judgments. The antirealist in this kind of debate, no less than the realist, thinks that there is objective moral truth and knowledge. And the truth in question is not merely disquotational. Both parties think that a true moral claim corresponds, in some way or other, to the way the world is. Their disagreement, like that of their counterparts in mathematics, is about the nature of this correspondence. The antirealist sees it as a relation between the claim and the publicly available facts that could be adduced as good reasons to accept it, while the realist sees it as a relation to what he thinks of as the truth condition of the claim—a state of the world that may transcend our ability to detect its presence by way of reasoned argument. This issue is surely an important one, but it is posterior to the more fundamental question that has dominated metaethics in the last half-century. This is the question whether what lies at the heart of moral thought are beliefs capable of genuine truth or noncognitive attitudes that cannot be so assessed: feelings, emotions, desires, preferences, prescriptions, decisions, and the like.

Let's use J. L. Mackie's terms 'subjectivism' and 'objectivism' to name the opposing camps in this older debate.[1] In this essay (in section II) I will argue against a certain common and influential version of subjectivism as it bears on the nature of reasons for action and practical rationality, and then (in sections III and IV) try to sketch out part of the defense of a vaguely neo-Aristotelian version of objectivism. But first I will try to bring out some important features of the contrasting conceptions.

I

The earlier subjectivists, notably Charles Stevenson and R. M. Hare, argued that the primary function of ethical thought and language is emotive or prescriptive rather than descriptive. Stevenson thought that the job of ethical language is to express moral feeling and so to influence the feelings and behavior of others.[2] Hare thought that a person's morality consists in the universalized principles he decides to try to live by and therefore prescribes to himself and others.[3] These authors were, in short, noncognitivists about ethical judgment. To say or think that an act is good or bad might, in a secondary way, imply certain facts about it, but its goodness or badness could never consist in such facts. Ethical concepts and judgments are on this view quite special. The concepts do not have the function of picking out properties or relations, and the judgments do not have the function of ascribing them. Their job is rather to enable us to express to ourselves or others the noncognitive attitudes mentioned above.

J. L. Mackie himself rejects this noncognitivist version of subjectivism in favor of an "error theory."[4] According to him, our ethical concepts and judgments have the same descriptive function as their empirical counterparts. The trouble is that there are no moral properties or relations answering to the concepts and no moral truths answering to the judgments.[5] For such properties and truths would be unacceptably "queer." They seem real only because we mistakenly project our own attitudes onto the world. But Mackie wishes not simply to do away with morality, but to reconstruct it. And if this reconstruction is to be done along metaphysically respectable lines, it will have to avoid the vulgar projective error. This is what he must have in mind when, speaking of the honest ethics that is "not to be discovered but to be made," he says that "the morality to which someone subscribed would be whatever body of principles he *allowed* ultimately to guide or determine his choice of action."[6] So Mackie's reconstructed morality looks something like Hare's version of noncognitivism.

This is not surprising. The subjectivists I want to consider are not, in Mackie's terms, "first order" moral skeptics.[7] They want to be able to make and "defend" moral claims. So given that the point of *belief* has so much to do with the acquisition of truth, morality—conceived as a set of false beliefs, or beliefs that can be neither true nor false—seems needlessly defective. The natural remedy is to reconceive, or remake it along expressivist lines. So, following this line of thought, I will treat all error theorists who think, like Mackie, that what lies behind and animates each sincere moral belief is a corresponding noncognitive attitude as potential noncognitivists.

But there is another aspect to typical subjectivist thought that is as essential as its noncognitivism. *It is the idea that an agent's moral judgments can and must, despite their noncognitive character, rationalize the moral choices that he makes in accordance with them.*[8] The objectivist agrees, at least when the moral judgments are reasonable. But the agreement is superficial. For we find two very different conceptions of how the rationalization comes about. The subjectivist of the kind I am imagining adopts a broadly instrumentalist (or derivitivist) theory of practical rationality that includes finding suitable means to one's determinate ends, suitable determinations of one's indeterminate ends, and suitable applications of one's chosen principles.[9] If, for example, an agent has a moral pro-attitude toward helping the poor and believes that something he can now do will relieve someone's poverty, he then has a perfectly objective instrumental *prima facie* reason to do it. And if he subscribes to the principle of keeping his promises, then he has a perfectly objective *prima facie* reason to keep this particular promise.[10]

Moral pro- and con-attitudes, whether directed to goals or to principles, thus have the power to rationalize choice. And this power is essential. For it is extremely uninviting to suppose that an agent's moral judgments—or on cognitivist accounts, an agent's reasonably correct moral judgments—could fail to provide reasons for action. For subjectivists, these reasons are provided only with the help of the noncognitive attitudes that moral judgments express. In this respect modern subjectivists have extended Hume's idea that morality produces motives only through its noncognitive content to the idea that it produces reasons only in the same way.[11]

This shows up in Bernard Williams' "Internal and External Reasons," where he includes *"dispositions of evaluation"* in an agent's "subjective motivational set" (*S*-set), the set from which all the agent's reasons for action derive through various acts of deliberating.[12] The evaluations that an agent's *S*-set disposes him to make presumably include the moral evaluations that he has internalized and made part of his way of life. But the practical reasons afforded by these moral evaluations do not derive from his recognizing them to be true. Even if he could come to see that they were false and others not flowing from his *S*-set true, he would not, on Williams' view, have any reason to follow the latter. For he would have no rational method of transferring the motivation present in his existing dispositions to the better ones.[13] Indeed he would be caught in such a bizarre dilemma (forced to accept his self-acknowledged false evaluations as reasons and unable to act on their true alternatives) that the overall position can be saved, I think, only by denying that the evaluations that flow from his motivational set can be rationally assessed as true or false. And, by our criterion, this not only makes Williams, at least in "Internal and External Reasons," a subjectivist about what must be an important class of moral evaluations, but also one who thinks that reasons follow from their noncognitive force.

Objectivists—at least of the kind I am considering—see things very differently. They agree that moral thought, at least when it is correct, provides reasons for action. But they think it does so only because of its cognitive content. What rationalizes or makes sense of the pursuit of a goal, they assert, is some way in which the goal in question seems *good*. And what rationalizes or makes sense of strict conformity to a principle is some way in which it seems that one can act *well* only by following it.

According to this kind of objectivism, practical rationality is not as different from theoretical rationality as the subjectivist supposes. Practical thought, like any other kind of thought, requires a subject matter. And for human beings the subject matter that distinguishes thought as practical is, in the first instance, human ends and action insofar as they are good or bad in themselves. The branch of practical thought that is usually called practical reasoning is the determination of how something desired as good can be obtained. In practical reasoning, thus defined, one does not critically examine the desired good to see if it is genuine or, if it is, to question whether something in the special circumstances forbids its pursuit.

These important questions belong to a more fundamental kind of practical thought that might be called ethical. Here one tries to determine what, given the circumstances, it would be good or bad in itself to do or to aim at. These questions are referred to larger ones: what kind of life it would be best to lead and what kind of person it would be best to be. The sense of 'good' and 'best' presupposed in this noncalculative form of practical thought is very general. In an Aristotelian version of objectivism these notions attach to actions, lives, and individuals as belonging to our biological species.

The object of this kind of thought is not in the first instance morality or prudence as these are commonly understood. For most people think that a human being may be prudent without being good, and many think that there is room for Nietzschean or Thrasymachean skepticism, according to which the best kind of human life might be immoral in one or another way. An objectivist of the kind I wish to defend sees practical thought as deploying a master set of noninstrumental evaluative notions: that of a good or bad human end, a good or bad human life, a good or bad human agent, and a good or bad human action. Practical reason is, on this view, the faculty that applies these fundamental evaluative concepts. If there is no truth to be found in their application, then there is no point to practical reason and no such thing as practical rationality.

I have already indicated a way in which subjectivists who hold an instrumentalist conception of practical rationality can be objectivists about practical reason and rationality. While they deny that ends, principles, and actions are objectively good or bad in themselves, they hold that a person acts rationally in trying to realize his own ends or maximize conformity to his own principles. On the plausible assumption that acting rationally is a natural and not merely conventional form of acting well (and acting irrationally a natural form of acting badly), and in the apparent absence of grounds for other not merely conventional forms, instrumental rationality thus becomes the one objective virtue and instrumental irrationality the one objective vice.[14] In contrast, my objectivist regards instrumental rationality, in this sense, as mere cleverness—something that may or may not be a good to its possessor or make her a better agent. If, on the other hand, someone's practical reasoning is necessarily constrained by appropriate ends and principles, and a sense of the fine and the shameful, then his cleverness constitutes a real virtue—part of his overall practical rationality.[15]

According to the objectivism I will defend, the primary job of practical reason is the correct evaluation of ends, actions, and qualities as good and bad in themselves. And what it is for something to be a reason for action follows from this. *On this view, a reason to act in a certain way is nothing more than something good in itself that it realizes or serves, or, short of that, something bad in itself that it avoids.* To the extent that one realizes or serves some such good one acts well. To the extent that one realizes or serves some such bad one acts badly. An objectivist therefore sees moral obligation as giving an agent reason to act only because, and only to the extent that, the agent will act well in discharging it or badly in neglecting it. Moral skepticism therefore comes to nothing more than the doubt that acting morally is a genuine form of acting well.[16] This is the kind of doubt with which moral philosophy began. And, on this view, it is the most important doubt for moral philosophy to resolve.

The subjectivist has a very different account of how moral judgment provides reasons for action. He obviously wishes to avoid bringing in any of these allegedly grounding concepts of actions, lives, ends, and agents as good or bad in themselves. He proposes instead an appeal to basic and therefore cognitively uncriticizable *attitudes*. And this is what, as I shall now try to argue, he cannot do. As unpromising (or even "queer") as the objectivist picture may seem (and I shall be examining some objections to it later), I wonder if it is not our only hope of retaining the idea of practical rationality that we want.

II

The problem lies, I think, in what the subjectivist must take these noncognitive pro- and con-attitudes—these emotions, desires, aversions, preferences, approvals, disapprovals, decisions of principle, and so on—to be.[17] So far as I can see, a reasonably up-to-date subjectivist would present them as functional states that, *inter alia*, tend to move an agent in various practical directions and therefore help explain why his having certain beliefs and perceptions makes him choose, or feel inclined to choose, one course rather than another. They underlie his *tendencies* or *dispositions* to form and express feelings and to choose certain practical actions in the presence of various perceptions and beliefs. To say in the intended sense that someone has a pro-attitude toward world peace is to say, among other things, that his psychological setup disposes him to do that which he believes will make world peace more likely. And to say that keeping his promises is one of his principles is to say that, among other things, he is set up to do that which he sees as required by the promises he has made.

But how can a noncognitive functional state whose central significance in this context is to help explain our tendency to act toward a certain end, or in accordance with a certain principle, *rationalize* our pursuit of the end or our deference to the principle? How can the fact that we are set up to go in a certain direction make it (even *prima facie*) rational to decide to go in that direction? How can it even contribute to its rationality? Even if a past decision is part of the cause of the psychological setup, there still remains the question whether to continue to abide by it. It is not, according to the view we are considering, the specifically moral aspect of the noncognitive attitude that gives *it* the power to rationalize. Moral attitudes, whatever their special moral earmarks, rationalize because they are dispositive functional states and not because they are moral. The underlying neo-Humean theory of rationalization is completely general. So in testing its plausibility we are free to turn to nonmoral examples. Such examples also free us from the distracting worry whether a given functional-dispositional state rationalizes in a distinctively moral way. *The basic issue here* is more fundamental: whether pro- and con-attitudes conceived as functional states that dispose us to act have any power to rationalize those acts.[18]

Suppose I am in a strange functional state that disposes me to turn on radios that I see to be turned off. Given the perception that a radio in my vicinity is off, I try, all other things being equal, to get it turned on. Does this state rationalize my choices? Told nothing more than this, one may certainly doubt that it does. But in the case I am imagining, this is all there is to the state. I do not turn the radios on in order to hear music or get news. It is not that I have an inordinate appetite for entertainment or information. Indeed, I do not turn them on in order to *hear* anything.[19] My disposition is, I am supposing, basic rather than instrumental. In this respect it is like the much more familiar basic dispositions to do philosophy or listen to music.

I cannot see how this bizarre functional state in itself gives me even a *prima facie* reason to turn on radios, even those I can see to be available for cost-free on-turning. It may help explain, causally, why I turn on a particular radio, but it does not make the act sensible, except insofar as resisting the attendant disposition is painful and giving in pleasant. But in that case it is not the present state that is the reason but the future prospect of relief.[20] Now at this point someone might object that the instrumentalist subjectivist does not or need not regard basic noncognitive pro-attitudes as rationalizing their *objects*, but rather as rationalizing actions that are the *means* to them. So, of course, my odd pro-attitude gives me no reason to turn on radios.

The picture here is of practical reason as a cognitively criticizable mechanism for transferring motivation from the objects of attitudes to that which is "toward" them.[21] Since the ultimate objects are rationally uncriticizable, no reasons are produced for them—no reasons to have those ends or principles or to do those things that are wanted or chosen for their own sakes. But since it is possible to reason well or badly about what will enable one to have or do those objects, reasons are produced for ancillary actions. So if, for example, one loves to listen to music—a contingent taste unassessable by reason—one's attitude does not give a reason actually to listen, but only, in the context of further intentions, to get a record down from the shelf and put it on the turntable.

I find this construction of instrumentalism, while possible, unattractive. If my basic love of listening to music doesn't give me a reason to listen, then it doesn't, I think, give me a reason to take the record down. The appeal of the view, apart from suggesting a line of escape from my argument, may come from conflating two distinct points: (a) that, on an instrumentalist view, a person's ultimate preferences are uncriticizable (except by reference to their compatibility), and (b) that a person's ultimate preferences do not mark off their objects as, given that he has those preferences, rationally appropriate for him. The first point is essential to instrumentalism, but the second does not follow from it. Nor is it a particularly plausible part of that view. But even if it were, my counterexample still works. For my basic noncognitive pro-attitude (conceived as a dispositive functional state) toward turning on radios seems not only to give me no reason to turn on radios but also no reason to take the necessary steps, such as plugging them in. Both seem equally senseless.[22]

But surely my disposition must strike me as odd, if only because it must strike others as odd. Perhaps then I regard it as an embarrassment and wish to be rid of it. And this might seem to make a difference that the subjectivist can exploit. It is not any old functional-dispositional state that rationalizes action, but only one that an agent is ready to stand behind or is at least not alienated from. A second-order endorsement (or the absence of a second-order rejection) is the missing ingredient.

It will be admitted, of course, that an unwelcome first-order attitude can provide the actual point of someone's doing something. A pyromaniac may hate it that he takes pleasure in setting fires, yet set another fire for that very pleasure. But perhaps the subjectivist will say that in such a case the pyromaniac's pleasure fails to give him a genuine reason to set the fire. For that he would need to approve it, or at least not disapprove it, at some higher level.

Now I think it very doubtful that a subjectivist can legitimately attach this significance to the existence or nonexistence of opposing higher-level attitudes. Here, as elsewhere, he is presupposing a significance that depends not on level but on content. An objectivist would take the pyromaniac's higher-level disapproval seriously because he would see in it an evaluation of the pleasure as bad—for example, perverse or shameful. And this would be relevant simply because someone who thinks that an attraction is bad in some such way can scarcely think that he will act well by giving in to it. So the higher-level disapproval shows that the *positive evaluation* that would normally attach to an action as pleasure-producing is canceled. The self-disapproving pyromaniac would not see the prospective pleasure as something that tends to make the torching choice-worthy. But the subjectivist, in rejecting the idea of choice-worthiness as the subject matter of practical reason, can see nothing in the higher-level disapproval except more complexly structured psychological *opposition*, and such opposition would seem to leave the lower-level attitude securely in place with its own proper force.

This point is perhaps worth emphasis. Higher-order attitudes pro and con lower-order attitudes will presumably be treated by the subjectivist as further noncognitive states of the same generic functional type—states grounding, among other things, dispositions to choose one thing rather than another in the face of certain percepts and beliefs. Rather than grounding dispositions to seek certain first-order ends such as pleasure or health, they ground dispositions to seek to be or not to be a person who has or acts toward those ends. What this picture does not explain, however, is the *authority* of the higher-level attitudes.

If the pyromaniac regards his fascination as sick and reprehensible, then he will not see it as giving him a reason to set fires. He may succumb to it as a temptation, but as he looks back on his choice he will not regard the pleasure he took as at least something positive to be credited to his choice. But on the subjectivist's view, it is hard to see why he shouldn't be consoled in just this way. For the subjectivist sees the pyromaniac as having two practical attitudes at odds with each other. His lower-level attraction moves him toward the act of pouring the kerosene, and his higher-level aversion moves him away from it. If he goes ahead he satisfies one of these attitudes, if he refrains he satisfies the other. There is therefore something to be said for and against each alternative. Without the thought that the appetite for fires is bad and therefore *without power to rationalize choice*, there seems no way to keep it from counting.[23]

Even setting this point aside, I cannot see how the subjectivist can insist that I *must* have some higher-level disapproval of my odd disposition to turn on radios. Perhaps, upbeat person that I am, I positively like my first-order attitude. But even if I do, this still doesn't seem to help rationalize my behavior. Turning on radios still seems perfectly senseless.

Perhaps a subjectivist should simply reject the example as too bizarre. According to this objection, we can make sense of someone's behavior as revealing pro- and con-attitudes only if the attitudes are ones we share to some considerable extent. So if my allegedly basic pro-attitude toward turning on radios is not rendered in one way or other familiar, it may have to be rejected. Attempts to undermine the neo-Humean theory by way of outlandish examples are thus doomed to failure.

Subjectivists may hope by means of some such argument to bring the actual implications of their theory of rational action more in line with those of objectivists who think that we make sense of an action only when we find something that seems good about it—some advantage, pleasure, boost to the ego, or the like. For the objectivist, the state disposing me to turn on radios fails for want of a point. Neither acts of turning on radios nor the state of affairs in which radios are on can intelligibly be seen as goods in themselves. But since the pro-attitude is stipulated to be basic, it cannot be rationalized by being referred to any further good, such as entertainment or knowledge.

Perhaps subjectivists can rule out motivational interpretations that are very strange. But it is difficult to see how. For I do not see how they could rule it out that I might actually engage in the odd behavior in question and that the best functional explanation would be that I had a correspondingly odd pro-attitude understood in their favorite functionalist terms. Indeed, I do not see how they could rule it out that someone might have basic pro-attitudes (conceived as such favored functional states) toward very many bizarre things (disease, pain, poverty, or the like). This is easiest to imagine in someone who desires to communicate reasonably truthfully,[24] is aware of her own eccentricity, has a reasonably accurate picture of the world, deliberates well about means toward and constituents of her largely bizarre ends, and acts accordingly. Such a person would be intelligible as desiring these strange things *if* desires were the things subjectivists took them to be.[25] And she would not be incapable of recognizing her odd ends and counterends for what they were, and for their oddity. A person does not have to be set up to strive for health to know what health is, a gloomy ascetic temperament does not rule out the knowledge of pleasure, perverse drives frequently recognize (indeed revel in) their own perversity, and so on. Such odd psychologies might, of course, be determined by an anomalous brain state. We might even come to recognize the neurological causal factors. But then the rest of us could imagine that we too might (unhappily) come to have these attitudes.

So I do not think that subjectivists can rule out the possibility of my radio case. Nor can they rule it out that, if I perform my odd routine cheerfully and without regret, my first-order attitude is unopposed by higher-order attitudes of disapproval. So they ought to see it as having the power to rationalize. But that is exactly what it seems to me not to have. It may in some way explain the fact that I turn on another radio, but it does not, in my view, go one step toward showing it to be sensible.

I have chosen a bizarre example to make my point as sharply as possible. But the argument applies, I think, with complete generality. No noncognitive, dispositive functional state of the kind under consideration can, by itself, make the contribution to rationalizing action that subjectivist instrumentalists suppose it to make. This is true even if the state points toward something good like pleasure or health. For pleasure or health provide a point to their pursuit that does not consist in the fact that they are pursued. A noncognitive pro-attitude, conceived as a psychological state whose salient function is to dispose an agent to act, is just not the kind of thing that can rationalize. That I am psychologically set up to head in a certain way, cannot by itself rationalize my will's going along with the setup. For that I need the *thought* that the direction in which I am psychologically pointed leads to something good (either in act or result) or takes me away from something bad.

Someone might object that I am imputing to the subjectivist too narrow a conception of desire, aversion, preference, approval, disapproval, commitment, and the like—that I am focusing too exclusively on their role in explaining tendencies to *act*. These states may have other characteristic noncognitive features that better account for their rational force. Chief among these would be the pleasing light that positive attitudes, and the unflattering light that negative attitudes, cast on their objects.[26] These hedonic colors may also be lent to the idea of doing that which will make the pleasant or painful prospect more likely. And perhaps it is here that we find the rationalizing force of pro- and con-attitudes.

But how is this to be spelled out? It might be said that pleasure or pain in the prospect of having or doing something makes pleasure or pain in the reality more likely. So a person with a basic pro-attitude can expect pleasure in achieving his object and frustration in failing to achieve it, just as someone with a basic con-attitude can expect unpleasantness in getting his. And it is this that rationalizes pursuit or avoidance.

There are at least two problems that stand in the way of this solution. To the extent that a present basic pro-attitude rationalizes by virtue of a promised pleasure, then rationalization should also be present—and just as strong—in the case where the agent expects the pleasure but oddly lacks the present motivation. If I believe that I will get just as much pleasure from this piece of candy, which tempts me, as from that piece, which oddly does not, then it is hard to see, at least as far as gustatory pleasure is concerned (the typical reason for buying candy), how I could have more reason to choose the first. That I now find pleasure in the *thought* of eating or buying the first piece but not the second seems irrelevant. Or if I believe that I will feel as much psychic pain in violating a rule (in the sense of a possible rule) that I have deliberately not subscribed to (perhaps because I feel its pull on me is irrational) as in violating a rule that I have adopted, it is hard to see how the prospect of pain can give me more reason to observe the second than the first.

But there is an even more serious problem with supposing that a basic pro-attitude rationalizes by reference to the pleasure its fulfillment promises or the pain its frustration threatens. For the objects of many basic desires do not include the subject's pleasure or pain at all. Suppose, for example, I want to see famine ended in Ethiopia. I therefore take pleasure in the very idea of famine relief (and perhaps also in the idea of working toward it) and feel pained when politics stands in the way. But if I attach basic value to the end to famine, then it is the thought that doing such and such will help feed people that gives me my basic reason to do it—not the thought that doing it will bring me pleasure or save me pain. These might give me *additional* reasons, but they cannot be my basic ones.

It seems, moreover, that the pleasure one expects in getting (or working toward) what one basically wants and the displeasure in failing to get it are themselves rationally assessable. It generally *makes sense* to be pleased or frustrated in these circumstances. What more sensible thing to be pleased or displeased about? But surely the subjectivist will want to say that this good sense depends entirely on the attitude. It is rationally appropriate to be pleased at getting what one wants or displeased at failing to get it *because* one wants it. So, again, the pleasure or displeasure cannot provide the basic reason to pursue the object.

In any case, it seems to me a mistake to think of the concepts of pleasure and displeasure as purely descriptive, psychological concepts. To call an experience pleasant or unpleasant is already to bring it under an evaluative concept.[27] That is why purely psychological accounts of pleasure seem to leave it utterly mysterious *why* we should pursue the pleasant and shun the unpleasant. On one such account, a pleasant experience is, roughly speaking, one whose intrinsic character makes an agent want to prolong it. When we combine this with a subjectivist account of wanting, we conclude that a pleasant experience is one whose intrinsic character creates a functional state grounding, among other things, the disposition to prolong it. But why should anybody want to be in such a state? Suppose I tell you that if you start scratching your ear the experience will strongly dispose you to keep on scratching. Does this by itself give you reason to want to scratch? Conceived as a kind of psychological inertial force, pleasure takes on a somewhat sinister aspect. This is because the account leaves out the salient thing: that an agent wants to prolong a pleasant experience precisely because it is pleasant—because it feels good. Pleasantness is not merely that which brings about a prolonging disposition, it is what makes sense of it.

So far, I have urged that neither the dispositional nor the hedonic aspect of pro-attitudes can provide what we want in the way of reasons for action. The subjectivist might respond by taking a somewhat different tack. He might claim that noncognitive attitudes may be formed in a rational or irrational way, and that *rationally formed* attitudes can provide reasons. This might, of course, mark a considerable retreat from the familiar subjectivist position that *any* pro- or con-attitude can give a reason for action. But if the requirements of rational attitude formation turn out to be weak, the retreat may be limited. If the requirement were merely one of reasonably adequate information, then many noncognitive attitudes would provide reasons. If, on the other hand, the requirement were as demanding as Kant's generalization test, far fewer would qualify.

My response to this strategy is to deny that the kinds of non-cognitive states the subjectivist means to be talking about can be made rational or irrational by the way in which they are formed. This is because I cannot see how, in the absence of objective prior standards for evaluating ends or actions as good or bad in themselves, a state disposing one to act can be any more rationally criticizable than a state disposing one to sneeze. Any factor (like having a perfectly regular character or being caused by true rather than false beliefs or valid rather than invalid reasoning) could be just as true of sneezing as acting. It's true that the disposition to sneeze can be irresistible, while dispositions to turn on radios or read philosophy papers typically are not. But space for the voluntary seems to me in itself devoid of rational significance unless it is in the service of an agent's values.

It is often said that an attitude formed in light of true beliefs has more power to rationalize than one formed in error. And while there is something right about this, it is not something that the subjectivist can obviously make use of. Suppose, liking canned chop suey and believing it to be a typical Chinese dish, I am moved to seek more Chinese food, and in particular to try out my local Szechwan restaurant (where my bland tastes are likely to be shocked). Such examples are often taken to show the need for some informational constraint on rational desire and preference.

But surely what is ultimately bad about my motivation here is not that it is based on false belief, but that it is a very uncertain guide to food that I will find good tasting. To the objectivist, information is relevant because without it I won't be pointed in the direction of good things, like innocent pleasure. But the subjectivist must reject the cognitive claim that pleasure is a good. For him, liking something is just another noncognitive pro-attitude. And his account of pleasure, in omitting the idea that what is liked is found experientially good, removes the sting from the criticism of my motivation to patronize the Szechwan restaurant. For if we ask the subjectivist why it's too bad that my desire for Chinese food was rooted in error, he can say only that it is because the functional state in which my desire consists will probably extinguish itself once I get real Chinese food. But this seems to miss the point. Why should cultivating a functional state that will extinguish itself be less rational than cultivating one that won't? What is so important about resistance to extinguishability?

One might agree that an informational constraint is not enough, but think that adding some other conditions will do the trick. Hare, for example, has argued that if we are going to give ourself certain kinds of prescriptions, we must give ourselves perfectly universal ones.[28] (He thinks that moral language is analytically cut out to express just such universal commands or norms.) Yet why should someone who sees himself as choosing in a cognitive void where there is no prior truth about good or bad action, insist on giving himself universal commands? Of course *we* wish to give ourselves such commands, because we think there is a subject matter of good and bad action that, like all genuine subject matters, is to some considerable extent regular. Since we think that certain *kinds* of actions are bad—for example, sticking one's hand in a fire—we tell ourselves not to do actions of *that kind*.[29] But if we thought there were no such knowledge of good and bad action to be had, I do not see why we should want our self-prescriptions, or some set of them, to be universal. And it would make no difference if there were, which I think there is not, some special vocabulary exclusively dedicated to making such commands. Why should we use this vocabulary? Or why shouldn't we subvert it?

Of course it may be said, plausibly, that we need to cooperate and coordinate, and so need to find common norms.[30] But I do not see it as a point of subjectivists. For on their reading, this need must consist in something like the fact that with the cooperation bred of common norms we will get more of what our pro-attitudes—either independent, norm-permitted ones (for example, my morally innocuous pro-attitude toward turning on radios) or new, norm-generated ones—point us toward. And if the preceding argument is correct, we have no reason to care about *this*. I suspect that the theoretical appeal to the importance of coordination works because we think that without common norms (or serviceable and just common norms) life with each other would be pretty bad—indecent, painful, suspiciously on guard, and too short to be meaningful. We need good common norms to live well together. If human beings didn't need to be thus coordinated, the selection of such norms would be pointless. Since they do need it, norms that make it possible, especially those that help us make the most of our human potential, have something objective in their favor.

III

But am I really claiming that desire and preference can't rationalize choice? Not at all. I am claiming instead that the subjectivist's account of desire is impoverished, leaving out precisely that element of desire that does the rationalizing. I have been careful not to raise the question whether my odd functional state is in fact a basic desire to turn on radios. That is, I have been careful not to raise the question whether the existence of a noncognitive dispositive functional state of the kind subjectivists would take desire to be is sufficient for desire. I have not raised it because I am not at all sure of the answer. What I feel sure of, and what I have argued, is that, whether or not the mere functional state is sufficient, it cannot ground reasons for action. What does that is another element (of necessity) typically present in basic desire, namely, some kind of evaluation of the desired object as good—for example, pleasant, interesting, advantageous, stature-enhancing, or decent. I am not saying, however, that desire is in general nothing more than positive evaluation. In some cases we would not speak of desire if the implicit positive evaluation did not provoke or were not accompanied by some kind of appetite that prods the will toward the object for the good that it seems to offer.[31] What seems amiss in standard neo-Humean subjectivism is the way it runs together the ideas of explanation and rationalization. The noncognitive attitude present in many cases of desire may sometimes be part of the causal account of why the desired object is pursued, but the pursuit is rationalized not by the attitude but by the apparent value that attaches to its object or to the pursuit of it. Without the appearance of the value, the attraction would be empty, as it is in my counterexample.

It might seem, however, that the view that desires and preferences rationalize only because of the value judgments they involve can scarcely be correct. Aren't there rationalizing desires and preferences that point to no real or apparent good? To answer this question I need to make some distinctions between different types of goods to be attained in action and the different types of rationalization that they involve. First and most obviously, an action may promote goods that speak in its favor *as a good action* and therefore one that ought to be done. It is in this way that considerations of health and pleasure typically support visits to the supermarket and doctor. A good such as this—one that in the circumstances tends to make its pursuit good—may be called *choice-worthy*. Some choice-worthy goods are in particular circumstances *conclusive*—they provide decisive reasons for acts that would bring them about—while others are *contributory*, providing reasons that may be overruled. Choice-worthy goods give full-fledged reasons for action. So here we may speak of rationalization in the fullest sense.

But we must also consider goods that are *not* choice-worthy. These are goods that do not ever, or at least in some particular circumstances, speak in favor of their pursuit. A plausible example is the pyromaniac's pleasure in watching a building burn. The pleasure of parent-child incest is another. No right-minded person who is capable of these pleasures would suppose that he had good reason to seek them. They are clearly not goods in the full-fledged sense, for they do not contribute to the goodness of action or life. Yet, contra Plato and Aristotle, these pleasures do seem genuine. We can imagine a prospect that has nothing in it to attract us but that, oddly, sets up in us a strong impulse to seek it. But the prospect of these pleasures, to one who can experience them, is not like that. They present such a person with a real temptation. It therefore seems plausible to regard them as some kind of experiential good. We might say that they *make intelligible*, but do not rationalize, a choice to pursue them.

Perhaps we should also briefly consider goods that are *merely apparent*. These are objects that appear good in some choice-worthy or nonchoice-worthy way, but are not. Some present simple illusions, like vanilla, which smells delicious but tastes bad. Some involve symbolic connections with real goods, as in the case of someone who anxiously avoids stepping on cracks. Other cases are less psychiatric. At some emotional level all of us invest certain minor successes and failures with a significance they really lack. Such "goods" and "evils" cannot, when they fail to take us in, rationalize pursuit or avoidance. Nor can they make pursuit or avoidance intelligible, at least not in the way in which the special class of goods and evils just considered can. Yet to the extent that we are taken in, they can, in a sense, do both.

With these distinctions in mind, we may consider cases in which an inclination unadorned by any prospect of objective value might seem to rationalize or make sense of action. What about whims, for example? Can't people have whims to do that which serves not even an apparent value?

I think we should not assume that they can. Philosophers' examples might, in this regard, be misleading. What we would do on whim is usually something whose value (or apparent value) can either be discerned or made the object of intelligent speculation. In some cases only the timing or means is capricious. One flies off to London for a haircut. One gets up at midnight, dresses, and goes out to seek pie à la mode. Anscombe's example of wanting to touch a spot on the wall or Davidson's example of wanting to drink a can of paint may not, I think, be all that typical. But they do count, so what can I say about them?

It seems to me a mistake to say that your wanting to drink paint counts as a whim only if there is no answer to the question what you see in it. We often, of course, put off that question by saying that it's just a whim. But putting off the question and there being no answer are different. The smooth and creamy paint might, after all, look delicious. And the allure of this appearance might be reinforced by a perverse curiosity. You might wonder what the paint tastes like.[32] The whim might have other explanations. It might be an odd desire to do something really, if trivially, original—to break the fetters of convention if only in some silly way. Adolescents are famous for this kind of desire, and there are outbreaks of adolescence even in the apparently mature. It might have a related but even more primitive significance. Children are continually performing actions that might at first glance seem pointless but that may well aim at the demonstration, however symbolically, of what they wish to be unlimited powers of independent agency in the physical world. They empty out drawers, pick up sticks and run them along fences, skim stones on the water, and so forth. Given the vicissitudes of the human predicament, all this makes a certain sense. And adult whims might sometimes be like this. They might reflect a curiously displaced need to demonstrate the power to act outside our rutted ways.

There are other diagnoses of very odd whims that have a more exclusively psychiatric significance. The odd desire to drink the paint might focus some unconscious need of rebellion. Perhaps you drank some paint as a child and were severely reprimanded by your frightened parents. Or perhaps the drinking has a hidden sexual significance. Doesn't everything?

I think we are very reluctant to rest content with the whim as a state that merely disposes you to drink the paint. This is because we wish to treat the whimsical urge as at least marginally intelligible. And to do this we need to see the whim as pointing to something that might be or at least seem attractive from your point of view. If we can find no such value—if there is nothing that you see or seem to see, consciously or unconsciously, in drinking the paint—then however effective its causal influence, the dispositive state gives no support to your choice to drink the paint.[33] Perhaps we should treat such a disposition as a limiting and degenerate case of desire. Or perhaps we should treat it as merely resembling genuine desire and preference. But on either view, I am inclined to see whims as no exception to the general rule that desires can rationalize only by reference to the conscious or unconscious evaluation that is (typically) at their core.

But here another, perhaps more difficult, objection arises. Even if some kind of value judgment is always, or almost always, present in desire and preference, a desire or preference is often, as I have indicated, more than a value judgment. We may see the availability of certain good things but be unmoved by them, and if we are unmoved then surely we may lack at least a certain kind of reason to seek them. Some good things that leave us cold (for example, our future health) still give us strong reasons for action, but in other cases an absence of felt attraction may affect our reasons. Both X and Y may offer the prospect of equally witty and intelligent conversation, but you may be much more attracted to the kind offered by X than to the kind offered by Y. Surely then you have much better reason to spend time with X.

According to this objection, at least some good things are rationally pursued only to the extent that they attract us. But then contrary to what I have been urging, our being moved must itself be part of our reason for pursuing them. If mere pro-attitudes are not sufficient to rationalize, they are in some cases necessary. But if so, then surely some doubt is thrown on the claim that they lack any kind of rationalizing force.

I cannot here try to consider all the kinds of cases in which reasons might seem to depend partly on attraction as well as on expected value. In cases that involve personal taste, such as taste in company, the significance of attraction might lie in its containing a foretaste of pleasure or satisfaction. Attraction to people, or for that matter to novels and paintings, promises a kind of personal pleasure in our future interactions with them. And that anticipated pleasure can give a perfectly respectable reason to seek them out.

Someone might object that such pleasure is nothing more than the consciousness of having gotten that to which one's noncognitive pro-attitude propelled one. If so, the pleasure would be a mere logical reflection of the earlier pro-attitude. But this picture seems wrong to me, although it may be encouraged by an easily missed ambiguity. An inclination might, in one sense, be said to be satisfied when its object is obtained. But it is a sad truth that this kind of technical satisfaction may lack any element of real pleasure or fulfillment. The anticipated pleasure that is part of ordinary attractions to people or art is, however, real pleasure. It might, as a matter of empirical fact, be pleasure partly caused by the previous inclination. And if it were, the existence of the inclination could be evidence for it. But even so, it is only the pleasure itself that makes sense of acting on the inclination.

There are many other cases in which we would have to look closely to see whether noncognitive attitudes were themselves providing reasons. Let me just mention one of the most puzzling. Two people may be equally supportive, kind, admirable, beautiful, pleasant to be with, and so on, but we may, because of some other difference of quality that in no way reflects well or badly on either, be fonder of the first than of the second. And when this happens most of us suppose, at least in practice, that we have greater reason to pursue the good of the first. Why? Someone might say that the greater fondness is simply constituted by a stronger altruistic disposition. But I think the answer must be more complicated. Human beings can thrive only in various private connections of concern and identification—as with family, friends, colleagues, or acquaintances. Some of these connections are thrust upon us, but many are not. And some people simply fit better than others into the highly personal sympathetic world we have already created for ourselves. These people belong in our story and so their good is especially important to us. I cannot claim to fully understand the nature and operation of such judgments of importance. But I feel it would be a travesty to interpret them as nothing more than functionally grounded tendencies to go for some people's good over that of others.

IV

My claim has been that noncognitive analyses of desire, preference, commitment, and the like cannot capture their reason-giving force. In depriving pro-attitudes of any evaluative thought, noncognitivism reduces them to functional states that, upon reflection, may show what we will do under certain conditions but not what we should do. Practical rationality, I have argued, requires a subject matter of the values to be achieved or realized in human action—a subject matter that only cognitivism can provide.

Even if I am right about this, there remains room for evaluative skepticism, which if correct, might remove actions altogether from the authority of reason. As noted earlier, Mackie and others have argued that certain evaluative judgments, while genuinely cognitive, cannot be true. There are in evaluative thought the concepts appropriate to a genuine subject matter, but the world does not, indeed cannot, furnish the corresponding properties and relations. Evaluative facts would be unacceptably queer in two ways: first, in providing motivation—in effect exercising a power over the will—and second, in providing reasons for action that do not depend on subjective inclinations. Mackie objects to the idea of motivation or rationalization (he speaks of the latter as prescriptive authority) that is not wholly explained in a neo-Humean manner. Like Hume, he thinks that genuine thought is by itself powerless to cause or make good sense of action.

Now I think an objectivist should be more or less unperturbed by the part of the argument that concerns motivation. To say that someone recognizes a value (say a moral value) that can be achieved in action is not to say that the recognition must be a spur to his will. To recognize that justice or decency requires us to do something is, in my view, to recognize that we shall act badly if we do not do it. The connection with motivation is indirect and conditional. To be unresponsive to the genuine badness of an action is to have a will that is unmoved by a conclusive reason for not doing something—a will that is, to that extent, irrational or unreasonable. If we were more reasonable, we would care more about the quality of our actions. And since most of us are not wholly unreasonable, we do to some extent care. That, I think, is what the motivational force of unconditioned value comes to. And that does not require value facts to have any "queer" power over the will. It requires instead a conception of the will as the part of human reason whose function is to choose for the best.

The other skeptical argument questions whether objective value could have rational authority. Let's begin with the objective value of ends. Why, it will be asked, should we care whether or not our ends have objective value? Why is such a concern rational? If, as I think, practical rationality chiefly consists in correctness of thought about human good and evil, a concern is rational just in case reason determines that it is a good concern for us to have. And if a concern belongs to real human virtue—the qualities that make us and our actions good—then it can hardly be denied that it is a good concern. So, on this conception of rationality, to show that we have reason to be concerned with the objective goodness of our ends it is enough to show that such concern is essential to human excellence. And while showing this may present many difficulties, it does not seem to be ruled out in advance as an unacceptably "queer" task. Something similar can be said about reasons given by the objective goodness of action itself. If, as I think, the reasons for doing an action just *are* the good-making features that it has either in itself[34] or that it derives from the good ends it serves, then the mystery of how the goodness of action can provide reasons seems to disappear. Mackie's problem depends on supposing that we start with an idea of practical rationalization or prescriptive authority that is prior to our idea of good and bad action. If that were true, and if goodness weren't in some way reducible to rationality, then we could raise the question, and so make it seem mysterious, how the mere recognition of something good about an action could give us a reason to do it. But I am skeptical of this prior conception of reasons, and therefore suspect that the real mystery that Mackie and others are circling around is how actions can have objective goodness in the first place. They suggest that the problem is how, if there were such a thing, it could give reasons. But, if I am right, the problem must be more fundamental.

In much of contemporary moral thought, rationality seems to be regarded as the basic virtue of action or motivation, one that grounds all the other virtues. This, I have been arguing, is a mistake. Practical rationality is a virtue of a very special kind. But it is not special in being the most fundamental merit of action or motivation. It is special by being the virtue *of* reason as it thinks about human good. A virtue isn't a virtue because it's rational to have it. A good action isn't good because it's rational to do. On my view, the only proper ground for claiming that a quality is rational to have or an action rational to do is that the quality or action is, on the whole, good. It is human good and bad that stand at the center of practical thought and not any independent ideas of rationality or reasons for action. Indeed, even in its proper place as a quality of practical reason, rationality is validated only by the fact that it is the *excellence*, that is, the *good* condition of practical thought. Even here the notion of good has the primary say.

But note that I have not here argued against the possibility that practical rationality makes demands on practical thought that should be understood antirealistically as requirements on the *construction* of a picture of human good and bad.[35] On such a constructivist view, we might have to begin practical philosophy with a critique of practical reason as it thinks about human good. Here I have been arguing only that the primary questions are not what it is rational or irrational, but what it is good or bad to be, seek, or do—that is, protesting the confusion that arises when the notions of rationality escape their proper place and become themselves the primary objects of practical thought.

Acknowledgments

This essay was written during 1987 and delivered in the fall of that year at the University of Washington and the University of Rochester. It was revised in 1988 with the very helpful comments of Tyler Burge, Bob Adams, and Philippa Foot. It was delivered in that form to the conference at Bowling Green State University. It benefited later from elaborate comments by Joseph Raz and interesting criticisms from Chris Morris, Mark Greenberg, and Ruth Chang.

Notes

1. J. L. Mackie, *Ethics: Inventing Right and Wrong* (Harmondsworth, England: Penguin Books, 1977), chap. 1. Mackie's introduction of "objectivism" (p. 15) as the view asserting that (intrinsic or categorical) moral values are "part of the fabric of the world" could at first suggest evaluative realism. And if so, subjectivism, which is introduced as the denial of objectivism, would be compatible with moral antirealism of the truth-admitting kind. But as Mackie gives content to the notions in the following discussion, it turns out that his subjectivism denies that moral evaluations of the relevant kind *can* be true. So the salient contrast turns out, after all, to be over truth.

2. The nub of the theory is clearly presented in Charles Stevenson, "The Emotive Meaning of Ethical Terms," reprinted in *Facts and Values* (New Haven: Yale University Press, 1963), pp. 10–31.

3. R. M. Hare, *The Language of Morals* (Oxford: Clarendon Press, 1952), pp. 69ff.

4. Mackie, *Ethics*, p. 35.

5. Mackie admits that certain claims of instrumental value can be true, but only because those claims are naturalistically reducible (ibid., pp. 50–59). Judgments of instrumental value that presuppose judgments of intrinsic value must be just as badly off as the judgments of intrinsic value they presuppose.

6. Ibid., p. 106. The emphasis of 'allowed' is mine.

7. Ibid., p. 16.

8. This use of 'rationalize' is an old one that completely lacks the modern psychoanalytical idea of finding false but self-comforting reasons for what one does or feels.

9. For an example of a very broad conception of instrumental rationality see Bernard Williams' "sub-Humean model" in "Internal and External Reasons," *Moral Luck* (Cambridge: Cambridge University Press, 1981), p. 102 [this volume, 38].

10. David Gauthier, who certainly holds that moral preferences and self-prescriptions give instrumental reasons, also accepts a kind of reason applying to certain important moral situations that cannot be counted as instrumental. On his view, if it is instrumentally rational for me to be disposed to honor personally advantageous agreements (as it might be if enough people could see through any insincerity) then I thereby have a special moral reason to comply with the terms of one that I made with the honorable intention to comply. See *Morals by Agreement* (Oxford: Clarendon Press, 1988), chap. 6. Of course, if I retain my earlier honorable disposition then I have, in my broad sense, an instrumental reason that flows simply from that. For complying instantiates a pattern of behavior that I personally value. This is a typical subjectivist reason that presumably remains present in Gauthier's system. But, given the other parts of his complex view, I would still have a reason even if I had lost the disposition. This latter reason does not fall under the present discussion of subjectivism.

11. Stevenson was, admittedly, strangely silent about reasons for action. But Hare makes it clear that moral reasons come from preferences, which he certainly regards as noncognitive dispositions to choose, exposed to facts and logic. See, for example, R. M. Hare, "Another's Sorrow," in *Moral Thinking: Its Levels, Methods and Points* (Oxford: Clarendon Press, 1981), pp. 104–105. Something similar holds, I believe, for Mackie, although his discussion of reasons in chap. 3 of *Ethics* makes things a bit tricky. He there distinguishes three categories of reasons or requirements: merely external and conventional ones (like the rules of a game or social practice seen from the outside), those that spuriously purport to bind categorically and intrinsically, and those that, depending on an agent's own attitudes, bind hypothetically. The latter might be called natural reasons. And it is these that, on his account, a properly "made" morality would give the agent whose morality it was.

12. Williams, *Moral Luck*, pp. 101–113 [this volume, chap. 1].

13. According to Williams, deliberation is always *from* existing motivations, bringing *them* to bear on the possibilities of action. See *Moral Luck*, p. 109 [this volume, 45].

14. Note, however, that some subjectivists have backed away from this theoretically odd hybrid—either, like Richard Brandt (in *A Theory of the Good and the Right* [Oxford: Clarendon Press, 1979], pp. 10–16) by adopting a descriptive account of practical rationality that does not require it to be regarded as an objective excellence or, like Allan Gibbard (in *Wise Choices, Apt Feelings: A Theory of Normative Judgment* [Cambridge, Mass.: Harvard University Press, 1990], for example, pp. 45–46) by applying an expressivist-prescriptivist account of rationality itself. For Gibbard there is no fact of the matter whether maximizing the satisfaction of one's preferences is rational, and argument can break down about fundamental questions of rationality in much the way Stevenson thought it could about fundamental questions of goodness. That such argument breaks down as rarely as it does (that there is mutual

argumentative influence over even such basic matters) is a result of the fact that we have been biologically selected to be conversationally cooperative creatures. While I suspect that the substance of my antisubjectivist argument could be applied to these authors, I must postpone the complexities of that discussion for another occasion.

15. A review and minor elaboration of this quasi-Aristotelian vocabulary might be helpful. *Practical reason* is the generic faculty of which *practical thought* is the characteristic generic activity and practical rationality the generic virtue. *Practical reasoning* (that is, *instrumental reasoning* in my broad sense) and *ethical thought* are the two main species of practical thought. If practical reasoning does not presuppose a correct evaluation of the ultimate suitability, whether in general or in the circumstances, of the desired goal or chosen principle, then its virtue is *cleverness*. For the neo-Humean, cleverness exhausts the virtue of practical rationality. If practical reasoning does rest on a correct assessment of the present suitability of the goal or principle, its virtue is, let us say, *real instrumental rationality*. And *wisdom* is the virtue of ethical thought. *Prudence* and so-called *moral goodness* are conspicuous but controversial candidate characteristics that wise ethical thought may deem the chief virtues of action.

16. Alternatively, that the so-called moral virtues are real human virtues.

17. I use the term 'noncognitive attitude' here broadly to cover all of these mental states. A decision of principle includes a pro-attitude toward the standard of behavior one has chosen and a con-attitude toward behavior that violates the standard.

18. My skepticism about this and related matters is shared by others in recent ethics, perhaps most thoroughly by E. J. Bond in *Reason and Value* (Cambridge: Cambridge University Press, 1983), esp. p. 56.

19. There are several variations on what the object of my pro-attitude might be: (a) the *act* of my turning on radios, (b) the *state of affairs* in which I turn them on, (c) the state of affairs in which they are turned on (by anyone), and so forth. For my purposes it doesn't matter how my state is conceived, although I will tend to use (a) for simplicity. Note that on all three interpretations, hearing something coming from a radio may be evidence that the object of my pro-attitude has been achieved, even though hearing something is not in itself the object of that attitude.

20. We will be coming back to the question of rationalization by the prospect of pleasure or pain.

21. This possible objection, to whose subtleties I may not be doing complete justice in the following remarks, was raised by Joseph Raz.

22. Since turning on radios and taking the steps thereto (for example, plugging them in) seem to me to stand or fall together, I will continue, for reasons of

economy, to apply the question of rationalization to the former. If the reader disagrees, he may, whenever I speak of turning radios on, substitute some mere means to that end.

23. In case one is tempted to think that the force of the higher-order attitude derives from its taking account of the lower-order attitude, note that in typical cases the lower-order attitude also takes account of the higher. That is, it remains in existence despite its recognition of opposition from above. Even though the pyromaniac may hate himself, he still wants to set fires.

24. That and other familiar pro-attitudes (about communication and learning) are certainly necessary when so many others are lacking.

25. It is sometimes said that some interpretations of preferences, conceived along subjectivist lines, will simply be ineligible on the ground that neither we nor the subject will be able to justify the interpretation. For example, that while the subject might, on perhaps frivolous aesthetic grounds, prefer normal oranges to red apples but green apples to normal oranges, she could not, for example, be understood to prefer normal oranges to red apples on high shelves but red apples on low shelves to normal oranges (at least not unless there was something more to the story—highness and lowness of shelf could simply not be an ultimate object of attachment). But again this seems to confuse the question of causation and justification. If preference is conceived along subjectivist lines as a preevaluative functional state causing one to feel and act in various ways under various conditions of belief and recognition, then there is no reason why this odd "preference" could not emerge. Indeed, the person might be bemused by her own highly unusual internal psychological economy. And to say this in no way implies that either the subject or anyone else is infallible about her "preferences"—we might come to see that it was something other than shelf height after all.

26. Here I return to a point that I explicitly put aside earlier. It may be more plausible with respect to desire and aversion than to commitment to principle. But it might also be thought that commitments (whether moral or personal) lend the prospect of their fulfillment a pleasing aspect of self-consistency and personal integrity, and their violation a disturbing aspect of incoherence and failure.

27. In *The Varieties of Goodness* (London: Routledge and Kegan Paul, 1963), pp. 63-85, Georg Henrik von Wright argued that pleasure is not merely good but is itself a kind of goodness.

28. Hare, *Moral Thinking*, pp. 1-24.

29. With perhaps an escape clause for very unusual situations.

30. A point stressed by Gibbard, *Wise Choices*; see, for example, pp. 26-27.

31. This kind of motivating state—one that has influence *on* the will—must be distinguished from dispositive states *of* the will, forms of executive rationality

(steadfastness, courage, prudence, and the like) or irrationality (distraction, cowardice, weakness, and the like) that enable or disable the will in its natural pursuit of the best course of action. On my anti-Humean conception, which has been greatly influenced by discussion with Philippa Foot and by Thomas Nagel's *The Possibility of Altruism* (Princeton: Princeton University Press, 1970), chap. 5 [this volume, chap. 9], much rational human action comes about without the influence of motivational pushes and pulls. I see that it is a convenient time to get needed service for my car and I simply proceed to do it. All that is required is the perception of overall advantage (the safety and comfort of having a well running car and the convenience of present service) and a reasonable degree of executive rationality. In such a case we may also speak of my desire for the advantage, but this desire is nothing more than my will's healthy recognition of its availability. Such a desire is not something the will *takes account of* in determining a rational choice.

32. When one is curious about something, the knowledge one seeks seems interesting and perhaps even important, even if at some level one knows that it is not. And it is this impression of significance (or urgency) that makes the curious behavior intelligible.

33. Unless of course it is unpleasant to resist.

34. Either directly (for example, its pleasantness) or because of the virtue or right principles to which it conforms (for example, its fidelity).

35. The evaluative realist thinks that every constraint on practical reason has the function of maximizing the likelihood of correspondence to a transcendent, and therefore possibly unapproachable, reality. The constructivist, in the perhaps special sense I have in mind, thinks that there are constraints that, coming from the nature of practical thought itself, must set limits on where the truth can lie and how much truth there can be. The method of reflective equilibrium as discussed by John Rawls in *A Theory of Justice* (Cambridge, Mass.: Harvard University Press, 1971) can be given a constructivist interpretation not as the best method for descrying an external or internal moral reality, but as the only systematically acceptable method of moral thought, the applications of which determine, insofar as such determination is possible, where the moral truth is to lie. Such constructivism might come, however, in two varieties. In one, the rational constraints would lead first to the identification of actions and ends as rational and therefore good. In the other, the constraints would be from the very start constraints on rational thought about the good. It is only the first kind of constructivism that I have been attacking.

III Kantian Conceptions

9 Selections from *The Possibility of Altruism*

Thomas Nagel

V Desires

1. Beginning with relatively uncontroversial cases, we must try to arrive at general conclusions about the sources of reasons and their mode of operation. Eventually we shall deal with prudence as a model for the treatment of altruism: the difficulties which arise in the two cases depend on similar arguments and fallacies. Most important, the interpretation of that feature of reasons on which prudence depends provides a model for the parallel enterprise in the case of altruism.

I shall argue that the superficially plausible method of accounting for all motivations in terms of the agent's desires will not work, and that the truth is considerably less obvious and more significant. It is therefore necessary to begin with an investigation of the role of desires in rational motivation generally, in order to demonstrate that what they can explain is limited, and that even in simple cases they produce action by a mechanism which is not itself explicable in terms of desires.

The attempt to derive all reasons from desires stems from the acknowledgment that reasons must be capable of motivating, together with an assumption which I shall attack—that all motivation has desire at its source. The natural position to be opposed is this: since all motivated action must result from the operation of some motivating factor within the agent, and since belief cannot by itself produce action, it follows that a desire of the agent must always be operative if the action is to be genuinely his. Anything else, any external factor or belief adduced in explanation of the action, must on this view be connected with it through some desire which the agent has at the time, a desire which can take the action or its goal as object. So any apparently prudential or altruistic act must be explained by the connection between its goal—the agent's future interest or the interest of another—and a desire which activates him now.

Essentially this view denies the possibility of motivational action at a distance, whether over time or between persons. It bridges any apparent gaps with desires of the agent, which are thought to supply the necessary links to the future and to external situations.

Prudence cannot on this view be explained merely by the perception that something is in one's future interest; there must be a desire to further one's future interests if the perception is to have an effect. What follows about altruism is similar: I cannot be motivated simply by the knowledge that an act of mine will have certain consequences for the interests of others; I must care what happens to them if this knowledge is to be effective. There seems little doubt that most people have the desire that makes prudence possible, though it is sometimes overcome by other, more immediate impulses. Altruistic or benevolent desires on the other hand seem less common. In neither case are we in any sense required to possess the desires in question: consequently we are not required to act on the specified considerations. If one lacks the relevant desire, there is nothing more to be said.

The consequence of this view, for a system of normative reasons, is that the interests of others, or his own future interests, cannot themselves provide a person with reasons for action unless we are prepared to admit also that reasons by themselves, or conditions sufficient for their presence, may provide us with no motivation for action whatever. The separation of normative from motivational discourse has of course been attempted. But if one finds that move implausible, and wishes some guarantee that reasons will provide a motive, then one is left with no alternative, on the motivational premises already laid out, but to include a present desire of the agent, one with appropriate scope, among the conditions for the presence of any reason for action whatever. Therefore another's interest, or my own future interest, can provide me with a reason—a reason capable of motivating—only if a desire for that object is present in me at the time.

The consequences for any other-regarding morality are extreme, for if one wishes to guarantee its universal application, one must make the presence of reasons for altruistic behaviour depend on a desire present in all men. (No wonder self-interest has so often been preferred to altruism as the foundation for justice and the other social virtues.) This view eliminates the possibility of construing ethical principles so based as requirements on action, unless one can somehow show that the appropriate underlying *desires* are required of us.

2. The assumption that a motivating desire underlies every intentional act depends, I believe, on a confusion between two sorts of desires, motivated

Selections from *The Possibility of Altruism*

and unmotivated. It has been pointed out before[1] that many desires, like many beliefs, are *arrived at* by decision and after deliberation. They need not simply assail us, though there are certain desires that do, like the appetites and in certain cases the emotions. The same is true of beliefs, for often, as when we simply perceive something, we acquire a belief without arriving at it by decision. The desires which simply come to us are unmotivated though they can be explained. Hunger is produced by lack of food, but is not motivated thereby. A desire to shop for groceries, after discovering nothing appetizing in the refrigerator, is on the other hand motivated by hunger. Rational or motivational explanation is just as much in order for that desire as for the action itself.

The claim that a desire underlies every act is true only if desires are taken to include motivated as well as unmotivated desires, and it is true only in the sense that *whatever* may be the motivation for someone's intentional pursuit of a goal, it becomes in virtue of his pursuit *ipso facto* appropriate to ascribe to him a desire for that goal. But if the desire is a motivated one, the explanation of it will be the same as the explanation of his pursuit, and it is by no means obvious that a desire must enter into this further explanation. Although it will no doubt be generally admitted that some desires are motivated, the issue is whether another desire always lies behind the motivated one, or whether sometimes the motivation of the initial desire involves no reference to another, unmotivated desire.

Therefore it may be admitted as trivial that, for example, considerations about my future welfare or about the interests of others cannot motivate me to act without a desire being present at the time of action. That I have the appropriate desire simply follows from the fact that these considerations motivate me; if the likelihood that an act will promote my future happiness motivates me to perform it now, then it is appropriate to ascribe to me a desire for my own future happiness. But nothing follows about the role of the desire as a condition contributing to the motivational efficacy of those considerations. It is a necessary condition of their efficacy to be sure, but only a logically necessary condition. It is not necessary either as a contributing influence, or as a causal condition.

In fact, if the desire is itself motivated, it and the corresponding motivation will presumably be possible for the same reasons. Thus it remains an open question whether an additional, unmotivated desire must always be found among the conditions of motivation by any other factor whatever. If considerations of future happiness can motivate by themselves, then they can explain and render intelligible the desire for future happiness which is ascribable to anyone whom they do motivate. Alternatively, there may be another factor operating in such cases, one which explains both the motivational influence of considerations about the future and the motivated desire which embodies that influence. But if a further, unmotivated desire is always among those further conditions, it has yet to be proved.

If we bring these observations to bear on the question whether desires are always among the necessary conditions of *reasons* for action, it becomes obvious that there is no reason to believe that they are. Often the desires which an agent necessarily experiences in acting will be motivated exactly as the action is. If the act is motivated by reasons stemming from certain external factors, and the desire to perform it is motivated by those same reasons, the desire obviously cannot be among the conditions for the presence of those reasons. This will be true of any motivated desire which is ascribable to someone simply in virtue of his intentional pursuit of a goal. The fact that the presence of a desire is a logically necessary condition (because it is a logical consequence) of a reason's motivating, does not entail that it is a necessary condition of the *presence* of the reason; and if it is motivated by that reason it *cannot* be among the reason's conditions.

VI Prudential Motives and the Present

1. Structural influences are apparent even when an unmotivated present desire motivates action. It will be useful to consider such a case before dealing with the more complex example of prudence.

If I am thirsty and a soft-drink machine is available, I shall feed it a dime, open the resulting bottle, and drink. In such a case desire, belief, and rudimentary theoretical reasoning evidently combine somehow to produce action. We should ordinarily say, moreover, that the circumstances provide at least prima facie reason for the act. So two questions must be answered: how does the motivation operate; and what provides the conditions for the presence of a reason?

I shall propose a single answer to both questions: Reasons are transmitted across the relation between ends and means, and that is also the commonest and simplest way that motivational influence is transmitted. No further desires are needed to explain this phenomenon, and moreover, attempts to explain it in such terms are bound to fail.

It must be realized that the case does require an explanation. Upon reflection, it can seem mysterious that *thirst* should be capable of motivating someone not just to drink, but to put a dime in a slot. Thirst by itself does not motivate such technical undertakings; an understanding of currency and the protocol of vending machines is essential. But when these factors have been added to the explanation, we still lack an account of how they combine with the thirst to produce action.

I think it is very important to resist the temptation to close this gap by expanding the original desire for drink, or by adding another desire. It is of course true that when one sees that the only way to get a drink is to put a dime in the slot, one then wants to put a dime in the slot. But that is what requires explanation: it is a desire *motivated* by thirst plus certain information. If we simply add it on as a further motive, we shall not do justice to its peculiar appropriateness; for *any arbitrary* desire might be added on in *that* capacity.

For example, it is imaginable that thirst should cause me to want to put a dime in my pencil sharpener, but this would be an obscure compulsion or the product of malicious conditioning, rather than a rational motivation. We should not say that thirst provided me with a *reason* to do such a thing, or even that thirst had motivated me to do it.

A theory of motivation is defective if it renders intelligible behaviour which is not intelligible. If we explain the ordinary case of adopting means to a desired end in terms of an additional desire or an extension of the original one, then we must allow a similar explanation for counter-rational cases.

But the fact is that such devices do not produce adequate motivational explanations of deranged behaviour. And if they do not yield adequate explanations in the peculiar case, there is reason to believe that their analogues are not the basis of intelligibility in the normal case. The analogous hypotheses seem to fill the motivational gap in the normal case only because they are not actually *needed* to make the behaviour intelligible, whereas in the abnormal case, where something more obviously is needed, they do not succeed. This leaves us, if we do not wish to be arbitrary, with the task of dividing the intelligible connections from the unintelligible ones and explaining why the former work and the latter do not.

2. The solution is to confer a privileged status on the relation between ends and means. This is easily incorporated into the definition of a reason. We may say that if being thirsty provides a reason to drink, then it also provides a reason for what enables one to drink. That can be regarded as the consequence of a perfectly general property of reasons for action: that they transmit their influence over the relation between ends and means. An exact statement of the thesis would have to include an analysis of that relation (or another better suited to the present purpose) as well as an

account of what reasons are. Both of these questions will be treated at greater length eventually, but the position is clear enough in outline: All reasons are in some respect general, and this is merely part of the specification of how far their generality extends.

If there is a reason to do something on a particular occasion, it must be specifiable in general terms which allow that same reason to be present on different occasions, perhaps as a reason for doing other things. All such general specifications, whatever else may be true of them, will share a certain formal feature. They will never limit the application of the reason to acts of one sort only, but will always include other acts which promote those of the original kind. And in some cases the general specification will simply assign the reason to all acts that promote some end which is not itself an act. Intuitively, this means that when a person accepts a reason for doing something he attaches value to its occurrence, a value which is either intrinsic or instrumental. In either case the relation of means to ends is involved in the evaluative conception: if the value is intrinsic it attaches derivatively to what will promote the likelihood of the act; if instrumental, the act is valuable as a means to something else, and the same value attaches to other means as well.

In the case with which we began, a desire was among the antecedent conditions of a rational motivation, and the problem was to explain how that desire could extend its motivational influence beyond the scope of its immediate, spontaneous manifestations, through connection with certain beliefs. The system which accounts for this case is operative not only for reasons stemming from desires but for all other reasons as well. Hence it cannot be embodied merely in a constraint on the scope of desires—e.g. an insistence that to desire the end is always to desire the means. Any acceptance of a reason for action must conform to the general principle concerning means and ends. The full influence of desires and of other types of motivation is explained by their interaction with the system. Consequently desires cannot account for its operation.

Note

1. For example by Aristotle: *Nicomachean Ethics*, book III, chap. 3.

10 The Normativity of Instrumental Reason

Christine Korsgaard

1 The Problem

Most philosophers think it is both uncontroversial and unproblematic that practical reason requires us to take the means to our ends. If doing a certain action is necessary for or even just promotes a person's aims, the person obviously has at least a prima facie reason to do it. Just as obviously, this reason is what we nowadays call an 'internal' reason, one that is capable of motivating the person to whom it applies. So those who hold that practical reasons *must* be internal point to the instrumental principle as a clear case of a source of reasons that pass that test.[1] But philosophers have, for the most part, been silent on the question of the normative foundation of this requirement. The interesting question, almost everyone agrees, is whether practical reason requires anything *more* of us than this.

In fact, in the philosophical tradition, three kinds of principles have been proposed as requirements of practical reason. First, there is the instrumental principle itself. Kant, one of the few philosophers who does discuss its foundation, identifies the instrumental principle as a kind of hypothetical imperative, a technical (*technisch*) imperative. But the instrumental principle is nowadays widely taken to extend to ways of realizing ends that are not in the technical sense "means," for instance to what is sometimes called "constitutive" reasoning. Say that my end is outdoor exercise; here is an opportunity to go hiking, which is outdoor exercise; therefore I have reason to take this opportunity, not strictly speaking as a means to my end, but as a way of realizing it. This is a helpful suggestion, but it should be handled with care. Taken to extremes, it makes it seem as if any case in which your action is guided by the application of a name or a concept to a particular is an instance of instrumental reasoning. Compare, for example: I need a hammer; *this* is a hammer; therefore I shall take *this*, not as a means to my end but as a way of realizing it. In this way the instrumental principle may be extended to cover *any* case of action that is self-conscious, in the sense that the agent is guided by a conception of what she is doing.[2] Now I do think that this is a natural way to extend the instrumental principle, and later I will suggest that this fact throws light on its foundation. But there is also a danger that such extensions will conceal important differences among the distinctive forms of reasoning by which human beings can be motivated.[3]

Second, there is what I will call the principle of prudence, which is sometimes identified with self-interest.[4] This principle concerns the ways in which we harmonize the pursuit of our various ends. Its correct formulation or extension is a matter of controversy. Some philosophers think it requires us to maximize the sum total of our satisfactions or pleasures over the course of our whole lives; others, that it requires us merely to give some weight, possibly discounted, to the ends and reasons we will have in the future as well as the ones we have now. What Derek Parfit calls 'present aim' theory requires only that we try to satisfy our "present" desires, projects, and aims to as great an extent as possible.[5] The common element in all of these formulations is that they serve to remind us that we characteristically have more than one aim, and that rationality requires us to take this into account when we deliberate. We should deliberate not only about how to realize the aim that occupies us right now, but also about how doing so will affect the possibility of realizing our other aims. The principle of prudence is often understood as a requirement that we should deliberate in light of what is best for us on the whole, or of what I will call our 'overall good', where that is conceived as a special sort of higher-order *end* to which more particular ends serve, in an extended sense, as means. Partly because he has something like this in mind, Kant supposes that the principle of prudence is also a hypothetical imperative.[6]

Finally, of course, many philosophers have claimed that moral principles, which Kant identifies as categorical imperatives, represent requirements of practical reason. If all of these claims are true, we exhibit practical irrationality in failing to take the means to our ends; in pursuing local satisfactions at the expense of our overall good; and in acting immorally.

In the *Groundwork of the Metaphysics of Morals*, Kant asks "how are all these imperatives possible?" What he wants to know, he explains, is "how the necessitation of the will, which the imperative expresses in the problem, can be thought" (*Groundwork* 4:417). In other words, Kant seeks an explanation of the normative force of all *three* kinds of imperatives. But this approach has not usually been followed in the Anglo-American tradition. Empiricist moral philosophers, as well as the social scientists who have followed in their footsteps, have characteristically assumed that hypothetical imperatives do not require any philosophical justification, while categorical imperatives are mysterious and apparently external constraints on our conduct. Moral requirements, they think, must therefore be given a foundation in one of two ways. Either we must show that they are based on the supposedly uncontroversial hypothetical imperatives—say, by showing that moral conduct is in our interest and so is required by the principle of prudence—or we must give them some sort of ontological foundation, by positing the existence of certain normative facts or entities to which moral requirements somehow refer.[7] The first option is the empiricist's own preferred method; while the second, moral realist option, represents the road taken by the dogmatic rationalists of the eighteenth century, as well as by many contemporary philosophers. Some philosophers with sympathies to the rationalist tradition—most notably Butler in the eighteenth century and Nagel in the twentieth—have pointed out that prudence, no less than morality, needs a normative foundation, and have proposed to throw light on the foundation of morality by investigating that of prudence. Parallel accounts of these two forms of normativity, they suggest, may be constructed.[8] But the instrumental principle has received very little attention from anyone.

One of the things I wish to do in this essay is to offer a diagnosis of this situation. Part of the problem is that empiricist philosophers and their social scientific followers have obscured the difference between the instrumental principle and the principle of prudence by making the handy but unwarranted assumption that a person's overall good is what he "really" wants. Prudent action is then just a matter of taking the means to your *true* end; and the instrumental principle is the only non-moral imperative we need. I will say more about this in section 2. More importantly, both empiricists and rationalists have supposed that the instrumental principle itself either needs no justification or has an essentially trivial one. Specifically, they have thought that the "necessitation of the will" to which Kant refers can be conceived either as a form of causal necessity or as a response to logical necessity. Empiricists who conceive it as a form of causal necessity suppose that the instrumental principle is either obviously normative or does not need to be normative because we are reliably motivated to take the means to our ends. Instrumental thoughts cause motives. Rationalists who conceive it as a response to logical necessity suppose that conformity to the instrumental principle is normative because "whoever wills the end also wills the means" is an analytic or logical truth, to which a rational agent as such conforms his will.

Behind these two accounts of instrumental reason lie two implicitly held conceptions of what it means for a person to be practically rational in general. On an empiricist view, to be practically rational is to be caused to act in a certain way—specifically, to have motives which are caused by the recognition of certain truths which are made relevant to action by one's pre-existing motives.[9] On a rationalist view, by contrast, to be rational is to deliberately conform one's will to certain rational truths, or truths about reasons, which exist independently of the will. In this essay, I will argue that neither of these general conceptions of practical rationality yields an adequate account of instrumental rationality. A practical reason must function both as a motive and as a guide, or a requirement. I will show that the empiricist account explains how instrumental reasons can motivate us, but at the price of making it impossible to see how they could function as requirements or guides. The rationalist account, on the other hand, allows instrumental reasons to function as guides, but at the price of making it impossible for us to see any special reason why we should be motivated to follow these guides.[10]

Kant is usually thought of as a rationalist, but the Kantian conception of practical rationality represents a third and distinct alternative. According to the Kantian conception, to be rational *just is* to be autonomous. That is: to be governed by reason, and to govern yourself, are one and the same thing. The principles of practical reason are *constitutive* of autonomous action: they do not represent external *restrictions* on our actions, whose power to motivate us is therefore inexplicable, but instead *describe* the procedures involved in autonomous willing. But they also function as normative or guiding principles, because in following these procedures we are guiding ourselves.

The course of my argument requires an explanation. In section 2, I argue against the empiricist view, focusing on the Humean texts that are usually taken to be its *locus classicus*. In section 3, I argue both *against* the dogmatic rationalist view, and *for* the Kantian view, through a discussion of Kant's own remarks about instrumental rationality in the second section of the *Groundwork*. This structure is dictated in part by a fact about Kant's own development.[11] At the time he wrote the *Groundwork*, Kant's views were in a transitional stage, and traces of the dogmatic rationalist view can be found in what he says, especially in this part of the text. By seeing what goes wrong with his early presentation of the instrumental principle, we are led to the mature Kantian view, which traces both instrumental reason and moral reason to a common normative source: the autonomy or self-government of the rational agent.[12]

My arguments for these points have another implication which I will be concerned to bring out in the course of the essay, namely, that the instrumental principle cannot stand alone. Unless there are normative principles directing us to the adoption of certain ends, there can be no requirement to take the means to our ends. The familiar view that the instrumental principle is the *only* requirement of practical reason is incoherent.

2 Hume and the Empiricist Account

It is common among empiricists to equate the question whether pure reason can be practical with the question whether we are ever motivated by belief alone. The impetus for this view comes from the so-called 'belief/desire' model of rational action. When we act in accordance with hypothetical imperatives, it is alleged, motivation is provided by the combination of a belief and a desire: say, I desire to avert the toothache foreseen, I believe that a trip to the dentist will enable me to do so, so I am motivated to go to the dentist. Since categorical imperatives are by definition not based on the presupposition of an existing desire, we must in following them be motivated by belief alone: perhaps simply the belief that a certain action is right or wrong, or, in a more complicated story, a belief, say, that someone else is in need.[13] Since the idea of being motivated by belief alone seems mysterious, the suspicion arises that categorical imperatives cannot meet the internalism requirement, and they are therefore supposed to be especially problematic.

But as Nagel points out in *The Possibility of Altruism*, the specifically rational character of going to the dentist to avert an unwanted toothache depends on *how* the belief and the desire are "combined." It is certainly not enough to say that they jointly *cause* the action, or that their bare co-presence effects a motive, for a person might be conditioned so that he responds in totally crazy ways to the co-presence of certain beliefs and desires. In Nagel's own example, a person has been conditioned so that whenever he wants a drink and believes the object before him is a pencil sharpener, he wants to put a coin into the pencil sharpener.[14] Here the co-presence of belief and desire reliably lead to a certain action, but the action is a mad one. What is the difference between this person and one who, rationally, wants to put a coin in a soda machine when she wants a drink? One may be tempted to say that a soda machine, unlike a pencil sharpener, is the source of a drink, so that the right kind of conceptual connection between the desire and the belief obtains. But so far that is only to note a fact about the relationship between the belief and the desire themselves, and that says nothing about the rationality of the *person* who is influenced by them. If the belief and desire still operate on that person merely by having a certain causal efficacy when co-present, the rational action is only accidentally or externally different from the mad one. After all, a person may be conditioned to do the correct thing as well as the incorrect thing; but the correctness of what she is conditioned to do does not make *her* any more rational. So neither the joint causal efficacy of the belief and the desire, nor the existence of an appropriate conceptual connection between them, nor the bare conjunction of these two facts, enables us to judge that a person acts rationally. For the person to act rationally, she must be motivated by her own *recognition* of the appropriate conceptual connection between the belief and the desire. We may say that she *herself* must combine the belief and the desire in the right way. A person acts rationally, then, only when her action is the expression of her own mental activity, and not merely the result of the operation of beliefs and desires *in* her.[15]

As a preliminary formulation of this point, let us say that a rational agent is one who is motivated by what I will call the *rational necessity* of doing something, say, of taking the means to an end, and who acts accordingly. Such an agent is *guided* by reason, and in particular, guided by what reason presents as necessary.[16] A comparison will help to illustrate the point. If all women are mortal, and I am a woman, then it necessarily follows that I am mortal. That is logical necessity. But if I *believe* that all women are mortal, and I *believe* that I am a woman, then I *ought* to conclude that I am mortal. The necessity embodied in that use of 'ought' is rational necessity. If I am guided by reason, then I will conclude that I am mortal.[17] But of course it is not logically necessary that I accept this conclusion, for, if it were, it would be impossible for me to fail to accept it. And it is perfectly possible for someone to fail to accept the logical implications of her own beliefs, even when those are pointed out to her. A rational believer is *guided* by reason in the determination of her beliefs. A rational agent would be *guided* by reason in the choice of her actions.[18]

But reason, in turn, is often thought to be guided by the passions; indeed, according to Hume, to be the slave of the passions. And empiricists who endorse the view that reason plays only an instrumental role in action commonly claim Hume as the founding father of their view (*A Treatise of Human Nature* 2.3.3,415). Hume's view, however, seems to have a much more radical implication than that. The rationality of an action, I have just suggested, depends upon the agent's being motivated by her own recognition of the rational necessity of doing the action. But Hume repeatedly asserts that there is only one coherent sense to be given to the idea of necessity (*Treatise* 1.3.14,171; 2.3.1,400). All necessity is causal necessity, in Hume's somewhat special sense: the necessity with which observers draw the conclusion that the effect will follow from the cause (*Treatise* 1.3.14,171). Accordingly, it looks as if all Hume can say is that the person is in fact caused to act by the recognition that an action will promote her end. And all that in turn means is that observers who know what the person's ends are may predict that certain conduct will follow. The person herself, the one whose behavior is in this way predicted, is not *guided* by any dictate of reason. This suggests that Hume's view is that there is no such thing as practical reason at all.[19]

And in fact there is another problem with supposing that Hume could have believed in instrumental reason. The instrumental principle, because it tells us only to take the means to our ends, cannot by itself give us a reason to *do* anything. It can operate only in conjunction with some view about how our ends are determined, about what they are. It is routinely assumed, by empiricists who see themselves as followers of Hume, that, absent any other contenders, our ends will be determined by what we desire. But if you hold that the instrumental principle is the *only* principle of practical rationality, you cannot also hold that desiring something is a *reason* for pursuing it. The principle, "take as your end that which you desire," is neither the instrumental principle itself nor an application of it. If the instrumental principle is the only principle of practical reason, then to say that something is your end is not to say that you have a reason to pursue it, but at most to say that you are *going* to pursue it (perhaps inspired by desire). And this shows that the instrumental principle will be formulated in different ways, depending on whether our theory of practical reason includes principles which determine ends or not. If we allow reason a role in determining ends, then the instrumental principle will be formulated this way: "if you have a *reason* to pursue an end then you have a reason to take the means to that end." But if we do not allow reason a role in determining ends, then the instrumental principle has to go like this: "if you are *going* to pursue an end, then you have a reason to take the means to that end." Now that first formulation—if you have a *reason* to pursue an end then you have a reason to take the means to that end—derives a reason from a reason, something normative from something normative. But the second formulation—if you are *going* to pursue an end then you have a reason to take the means to that end—derives, or attempts to derive, a reason from a fact. Now if Hume believed in instrumental reason, he would have to accept the second formulation, since it is perfectly clear that he thinks that reason does not play a role in the determination of ends. He would have to believe that the instrumental principle instructs us to derive a reason from what we are *going* to do. But Hume, after all, is famous for arguing that you cannot derive an *Ought* from an *Is*. And in the argument that follows, I will show why he is right. This seems to me to be grounds for doubting that Hume himself could have believed in instrumental reason.

Let's take as a point of comparison Hume's attitude towards the other (supposedly) hypothetical imperative, the principle of prudence. Hume clearly denies that prudence is a rational requirement. In a very famous passage, he says:

'Tis not contrary to reason for me to prefer the destruction of the whole world to the scratching of my finger. 'Tis not contrary to reason for me to chuse my total ruin, to prevent the least uneasiness of an *Indian* or person wholly unknown to me. 'Tis as little contrary to reason to prefer even *my own acknowledg'd lesser good* to my greater, and have a more ardent affection for the former than the latter. (*Treatise* 2.3.3, 416, second emphasis mine)

But Hume does not claim that we in fact live for the moment, like the grasshopper in the fable, and never take the future into account. He offers us an alternative explanation of what is going on when we take our future interests into account. Three passages are relevant.

First of all, there is a discussion in book 1, in the section entitled "Of the Influence of Belief." Flatly contradicting the belief/desire model of action, Hume argues here that beliefs operate on us in the same way that present impressions do. Hume offers this argument as evidence for his view that what distinguishes a belief from a mere idea is the fact that it is forceful and vivacious in nearly the same way that an impression is. When you are convinced, by causal reasoning, that a certain painful effect will occur, you recoil from the causes of that effect in much the same way that you would recoil from the effect itself, from present pain. You draw back from putting your hand *into* the flame with the same automatic character with which you would draw your hand *out of* the flame if it were already in. And if the painful effect would be caused by an action you propose to yourself, you recoil in just this way from performing the action. This is how the future consequences of our actions motivate us.[20] Hume describes this as a kind of middle way which nature has taken in the construction of animals. He points out that if we could be motivated only by present impressions, we would always be getting into trouble, and foresight could not help us to avoid it. On the other hand, if we were motivated indiscriminately by all of our ideas, we would never enjoy a moment's peace and tranquility. The bare idea of fear would fill us with fear. Hume says:

> Nature has, therefore, chosen a medium, and has neither bestow'd on every idea of good and evil the power of actuating the will, nor yet has entirely excluded this influence. Tho' an idle fiction has no efficacy, yet we find by experience, that the ideas of those objects, which we believe either are or will be existent, produce in a lesser degree the same effect with those impressions, which are immediately present to the senses and perception. (*Treatise* 1.3.10, 119)

What is most notable about this passage is what Hume does *not* say. He does not say that it is rational to be motivated by a belief, because you think that the object of a belief exists and therefore really is apt to affect you, while the object of a mere idea need not exist, and so there is no reason to think that it will affect you.[21] He merely says that we are in fact so constructed.

This thought is picked up later in the introduction to the discussion of the direct passions. Hume says:

> The mind by an *original instinct* tends to unite itself with the good, and to avoid the evil, tho' they be conceived merely in idea, and be consider'd as to exist in any future period of time. (*Treatise* 2.3.9, 438; my emphasis)

An 'original instinct' in Hume's terminology, is a psychological tendency that admits of no further explanation. In both passages, then, Hume asserts that our tendency to act prudently is not the result of our rational nature but rather of the original instincts which nature has implanted in us.

The third passage is in the section "On the Influencing Motives of the Will." Here we learn that the most general form of this tendency to desire the good—"the general appetite to good, and aversion to evil, consider'd merely as such"—is a calm passion, that is, one we know more from its effects than from its emotional turbulence (*Treatise* 2.3.3, 417). When we are under the influence of this calm passion we do prudent things, say, we pursue our overall good at the expense of present pleasure. Hume thinks that we tend to confuse the operation of the calm passions with the operations of reason because those are also calm. This is why we imagine that prudent conduct is a form of rational conduct: when we act under the influence of the general desire for good, our minds are calculating and cool. Nevertheless, when we are not under the influence of this calm passion, and pursue present pleasure at the expense of our overall good, there is no irrationality in the case.

From all of this it is clear that Hume thinks that it is a not requirement of reason that we should have concern for our future, but that it is natural to have such a concern. By the *original* arrangements of human nature, we have the capacity to be motivated, at least sometimes, by our beliefs about what will happen in the future. Of course a *rational* requirement of prudence, if it existed, would demand much more than this. A rational requirement of prudence would not demand merely that we give some weight, some of the time, to considerations of our overall good. It would demand that we *do* what conduces to our overall good.[22] By contrast, the calm passion that Hume calls 'the general appetite to good' is just one desire among others, which occasionally takes precedence.

But why does Hume believe this? A moment ago I quoted the famous passage in which Hume rejects the rational requirement of prudence. It continues this way:

> 'Tis not contrary to reason to prefer even my own acknowledg'd lesser good to my greater, and have a more ardent affection for the former than the latter. A trivial good may, from certain circumstances, produce a desire superior to what arises from the greatest and most valuable enjoyment; nor is there anything more extraordinary in this, than in mechanics to see one pound weight raise up a hundred by the advantage of its situation. (*Treatise* 2.3.3, 416)

Hume here appeals to the fact that a desire for present pleasure may get the better of prudence, having been rendered stronger by "the advantage of its situation." But how is that fact supposed to show us that prudence is not rationally required? We might take this passage to be an argument, based on the internalism requirement. Hume could be thinking that since prudence sometimes fails to motivate us, the principle of prudence fails to meet the internalism requirement, and so cannot count as a rational principle.[23] As I have argued elsewhere, however, such an argument would have to be based on a *misunderstanding* of the internalism requirement.[24] The internalism requirement can only specify that practical reasons must motivate us *insofar as* we are susceptible to the influence of reason. The requirement cannot be that a consideration must *in fact* motivate a person in order to *count* as a reason, for, in that case, we could never judge that a person has acted irrationally; if the person were not moved by the consideration, we would have to say that it was not a reason for him. In any case, whether we do judge that an instance of imprudent conduct is irrational *depends* upon our views about whether prudence is a rational requirement, and not the reverse.

To see this, consider the case of Howard. Howard, who is in his thirties, needs medical treatment: specifically, he must have a course of injections, now, if he is going to live past fifty. But Howard declines to have this treatment, because he has a horror of injections. Let me just stipulate that, were it not for his horror of injections, Howard would have the treatment. It's not that he really secretly wants to die young anyway, or anything fancy like that. Howard's horror of injections is really what is motivating him. Notice that there are three different ways in which we may explain his conduct.

First, we may suppose that Howard *is* governed by what Hume calls the general appetite to good (or by prudence), but that he is miscalculating. He thinks that having a course of injections will be so dreadful that it is worth dying young to avoid it, even though he believes that if he had the treatments, a long and happy life would await him at the other end. While it might be interesting to know how someone could make this particular mistake, the possibility of mistake is not in general very interesting. In any case, I want to leave this interpretation aside, so let's again stipulate that he has not miscalculated or made a mistake. He sees that, if he were governed by considerations of prudence, he would have the injections: he agrees that a long and happy life is a greater good than avoiding the injections. But he still declines to have them: he chooses "his own acknowledg'd lesser good."

What we say next depends on whether or not we think that the principle of prudence is a rational requirement. If we think that it is, we will regard Howard's dread of the injections as something that interferes with his rationality, as a source of weakness of the will. But if we reject the idea that prudence is rationally required, we may say simply that, because Howard so dreads the needle, avoiding the injections is what he wants most. His decision to decline the needed medical treatment is then not irrational. Absent a principle determining which ends we should prefer, such as the principle of prudence, a person will follow his stronger desire and will not be irrational for doing so. The point is not that it is *rational* for him to follow his stronger desire because it is stronger. The point is that he is rational in the only remaining sense—he is (apparently) following the instrumental principle. Refusing to take the injections is the means to his end, in the sense that it is the means to the end he is *going* to pursue: namely, a life free from injections.

So what we say about this case depends on our attitude about the principle of prudence. If we suppose prudence is a rational requirement, we will say: fear prevents Howard from pursuing the end he *ought* to prefer, his overall good, and therefore he is acting irrationally. But if we reject the claim that prudence is a rational requirement, we will say: fear determines what Howard's preferred end is, but there is no irrationality in the case, for reason has nothing to say about which ends we should prefer.

Does Hume think that the instrumental principle, unlike the principle of prudence, is a rational requirement? If he does, then as the argument above shows, there should be cases in which Hume would be prepared to identify someone's conduct as instrumentally irrational, that is, cases in which, without miscalculating or making a mistake, people fail or decline to take the means to their own "acknowledg'd" ends. Now Hume does not discuss this kind of case, but he does explicitly allow that actions can be irrational in two *derivative* ways: we act irrationally when our passions are provoked by non-existent objects, or when we act on the basis of false causal judgments (*Treatise* 2.3.3, 416). Both of these are cases of mistake; the actions that result are not, strictly speaking, irrational. And after discussing them, Hume asserts:

The moment we perceive the falsehood of any supposition, or the insufficiency of any means our passions yield to our reason without any opposition. (*Treatise* 2.3.3, 416)

This suggests that Hume thinks no one is ever guilty of violating the instrumental principle. Making a mistake, after all, is not a way of being irrational, and Hume thinks we do take the means to our ends as soon as mistakes are out of the way. But this is worrisome. How can there be rational action, in any sense, if there is no irrational action? How can there be an imperative that no one ever actually violates?

The problem is exacerbated when we see that Hume's view is not just that people don't *in fact* ever violate the instrumental principle. He is actually committed to the view that people *cannot* violate it. To see this, we need only consider why Hume might be led to deny that people are ever instrumentally irrational. Offhand, that denial doesn't seem very plausible. People fail to take the means to what they *say* are their ends all the time. And this does not happen only when those ends are demanded by abstract or distant considerations of what will conduce to the person's overall good. It happens in the case of more local ends that are expressly and directly wanted or chosen for their own sakes. You want to ride on this immense roller coaster but you are prevented by terror. Every night of the carnival you go and look at it, get in line for a ticket, and then lose your nerve and shuffle meekly away. You don't think riding the roller coaster is essential to your overall good. Maybe you even think it's risky and a little foolish. But you've made up your mind to do it. And all you have to do is buy a ticket and get on—only you can't bring yourself to. You want to see the movie but you are too idle to go downtown; you want to go out with him but you are too shy to call and ask him for a date; you want to work but depression holds you in its smothering embrace.

If we believe that the instrumental principle is a rational requirement, we will say that these people's terror, idleness, shyness, or depression is making them irrational and weak-willed, and so that they are failing to do what is necessary to promote their own ends. We will see these things as forces that block their susceptibility to the influence of reason. Now in the case of prudence, the other option was to reject the principle and say that Howard simply prefers to avoid the injections at any cost, and that he is not irrational for doing so. In this case, what is the other option? Could we *reject* the instrumental principle and say that the people in these examples simply *prefer* to indulge their terror, idleness, shyness, or depression, and that they are not irrational for doing so?

Well, notice that if we do say that, then it turns out that these people are *not* after all violating the instrumental principle, at least as Hume would have to formulate it. They are taking the means to the ends they are *going* to pursue, so we would not have rejected the instrumental principle after all. Now one thing that this means is that Hume cannot talk about the instrumental principle in the same way he talks about the principle of prudence. That is, if he *did* want to deny that the instrumental principle is a rational requirement, he could not do it by dramatically announcing: "It is not contrary to reason to refuse to take the means to my end . . ." because according to Hume *that cannot happen*. Whatever you do is the means to the end that you are *going* to pursue. But how then can we claim that the instrumental principle is a principle of reason? Hume's view seems to exclude the possibility that we could be *guided* by the instrumental principle. For how can you be guided by a principle when anything you do counts as following it? In fact, this argument shows that Hume's famous dictum is correct: you cannot derive an *ought* from an *is*. In this case, we cannot derive the *requirement* of taking the means from *facts* about which end an agent is actually going to pursue.[25]

Now it is clear enough where the problem here is coming from. The problem is coming from the fact that Hume identifies a person's *end* as what he *wants most*, and the criterion of what the person wants most appears to be what he actually *does*. The person's ends are taken to be revealed in his conduct. If we don't make a distinction between what a person's end is and what he actually pursues, it will be impossible to find a case in which he violates the instrumental principle. So the problem would be solved if we could make a distinction between a person's ends and what he actually pursues. Two ways suggest themselves: we could make a distinction between actual desire and rational desire, and say that a person's ends are not merely what he wants, but what he has reason to want. Or, we could make a more psychological distinction between what a person thinks he wants or locally wants and what he "really wants." After all, it does seem odd to say of the people in my examples that what they "really want" are ends which are shaped by their terror, idleness, shyness or depression. We know that these people would wish these conditions away if only they could. So perhaps it is plausible to say that these people do not do what they really want to do, and that therefore they are irrational.

But in order to distinguish rational desire from actual desire, it looks as if we need to have some rational principles determining which ends are worthy of preference or pursuit. So the first option takes us beyond instrumental rationality. The instrumental principle then tells us to promote those ends we have reason to want. But really the second option—the claim that these people are irrational because they do not promote the ends that they "really want"—also takes us beyond instrumental rationality, although this may not be immediately obvious. If we are going to appeal to "real" desires as a basis for making claims about whether people are acting rationally or not, we will have to argue that a person *ought* to pursue what he *really* wants rather than what he is in fact *going* to pursue. That is, we will have to accord these "real" desires some normative force. It must be something like a requirement of reason that you should do what you "really want," even when you are tempted not to. And then, again, we will have gone beyond instrumental rationality after all.

Let me now pay off a promissory note. According to a theory very fashionable in the social scientific and economic literature, sometimes called the self-interest or economic theory of rationality, it is rational for each person to pursue his overall good: to act on some variant of the principle of prudence. Many people who believe the self-interest theory of rationality *think* that they also believe the theory that all practical reasons are instrumental. This combination of ideas is incoherent. The instrumental principle says nothing about our ends, so it is completely unequipped to say either that we ought to desire our overall good or that we ought to prefer it to more immediate or local satisfactions. The self-interest theory of rationality, because it is committed to the principle of prudence, *has* to go beyond the instrumental theory. Now how could the purveyors of this theory make such an obvious error? I believe that the answer lies in what I have just said. People who hold this theory assume that what a person "really wants" is her overall good, and therefore that her ends, her real ends, just *are* the things that are consistent with or part of her overall good. The standard move is to treat the possibility that someone might desire something inconsistent with her overall good as if it were an uninteresting little piece of theoretical untidiness like the possibility that she might miscalculate or make a mistake. We all know that we cannot even start a discussion of rationality until we have applied a *little* spit and polish to people's desires. (You know the sort of thing I mean: "we won't say that his desire to eat the apple provides a reason for him to do so, if it is based on his ignorance that it is made of wax . . ." etc.) Self-interest theorists treat harmonizing someone's local ends with her overall good as if it were just a part of this preliminary cleaning-up process. Following Hume (and with just as little plausibility), they might say "The moment we perceive that an end is inconsistent with our overall good our passions yield to our reason without any opposition."[26] The fans of morality could just as well stipulate that what we "really want" are things consistent with love and respect for everybody, and then they too could claim that we don't need to go beyond instrumental rationality. Nothing is gained by such devices.[27]

But Hume, unlike his would-be followers, does not build consistency with one's overall good into his notion of an end. As we have seen, he thinks we neither ought-to-want nor really-want only those ends which are consistent with our overall good. And that apparently means that he must accept the claim that local desires determine our ends, and with it, the implication that we cannot violate the instrumental principle. If we cannot violate it, then it cannot guide us, and that means that it is not a normative principle. This suggests that for Hume the desire to take the means to our ends is just a calm passion, one we have by the original constitution of our nature. Hume might say of it just what he said of the principle of prudence, that we mistake it for reason because when we are under its influence our minds are calculating and cool.

One way to rescue the normativity of the instrumental principle is open to Hume. We might argue that the principle that distinguishes "my end" from "whatever I actually pursue" does not have to be a principle of reason. It only has to be some *normative* principle, since it has to pick out something I ought to pursue even if I don't.[28] Perhaps virtue itself picks out the ends we ought to pursue, and then the instrumental principle requires us to take the means to those. It is instructive here that although Hume denies that prudence is a rational requirement, he certainly does think it is a virtue. He says:

> What we call strength of mind, implies the prevalence of the calm passions above the violent; tho' we may easily observe, there is no man so constantly possess'd of this virtue, as never on any occasion to yield to the sollicitations of passion and desire. (*Treatise* 2.3.3, 418)[29]

The parallel claim, about the instrumental principle, would be that resoluteness in the pursuit of our ends is itself a virtue, and that this accounts for the normativity of the instrumental principle. We can be guided by it insofar as we can be motivated to pursue an ideal of virtue.[30] But it would have to be resoluteness in the pursuit of *virtuous* ends, for, otherwise, there would be no way to distinguish cases of resoluteness from any other actions. We would not say, except as a kind of joke, that Howard exhibits the virtue of resoluteness in steadfastly rejecting the medical treatment that he needs, or that my other exemplar displays it in slinking timidly away from the roller coaster she longs to ride. If the theory we are now constructing on Hume's behalf works, we will call somebody 'resolute' only when he pursues ends of which we approve. The normativity of taking the means can then be derived from the normativity that our moral approval attaches to the end.[31]

But if Hume took this option, it would begin to become unclear why it should matter whether we use the words 'reason' and 'rational' to signify that normativity or whether we use 'virtue' and 'virtuous' or some other words. We will have rescued the instrumental requirement for Hume, but only at the cost of showing that the word 'virtue' simply does the work in his account of action that the word 'reason' does in his supposed opponent's accounts. Hume will have been engaging in what he supposedly despises, a verbal dispute. And he would still have to grant the central point of this argument, which is that a *normative* principle of instrumental action cannot exist unless there are also normative principles directing the adoption of ends.

Earlier, I suggested that the instrumental principle cannot function as a requirement in Hume's theory because he has no resources for distinguishing a person's ends from what she actually pursues. Another way to put the same point, which in the end comes to the same thing, is to say that Hume has no resources for distinguishing the activity of the person *herself* from the operation of beliefs, desires, and other forces *in her*. Unless Hume endorses the kind of reconstruction I have just described, his model does not allow us to see a person as guided by normative principles in her actions and choices because it leaves no room for the *person* to act and choose at all. Desire, fear, indolence, and whim shape the Humean agent's ends, and, through them, her actions. When her passions change, her ends change, and when her ends change, so do her actions. We can explain everything that she does without any reference to *her* at all. To say that reason is the slave of the passions, and to say that a person is the slave of her passions, turn out to be one and the same thing.

3 Kant and the Rationalist Account

I have suggested that the instrumental principle can be rescued only if we take "my end" to be something other than "what I actually, just now, desire." One possibility is to distinguish desire from volition, and to say that your end is what you *will*, not merely what you want.[32] This distinction is at the heart of Kant's moral psychology. In Kant's view, an inclination is a kind of attraction to something, which is grounded in our sensuous nature, and in the face of which we are passive.[33] By themselves, inclinations have no normative force; they are not reasons. But they do serve as "incentives"—which means that we are predisposed to treat them as reasons, and so to adopt maxims of acting on them. Of course Kant thinks that they are not the only incentives, for reason also generates an incentive of its own, respect for the moral law, which inclines us to act morally. Volition consists in adopting a maxim of acting on some incentive or other. When we decide to act on an inclination—to do a desired action or seek a desired end—then its object becomes an object of volition. The essential point here is that the adoption of an end is conceived as the person's own free act. Inclination proposes, but it is the person herself who disposes. Given all this, it is not surprising to find Kant's version of the instrumental principle formulated in terms of the will, not in terms of desire. In general or schematic form, the instrumental principle tells us that if we *will* an end, then we ought to will the means to that end.[34] And Kant's argument for the instrumental principle depends essentially on the fact that it is formulated that way. He says:

> How an imperative of skill is possible requires no special discussion. Whoever wills the end, also wills (insofar as reason has decisive influence on his actions) the indispensably necessary means to it that are within his power. This proposition, is, as regards the volition, analytic; for in the volition of an object as my effect, my causality as acting cause, that is, the use of means, is already thought, and the imperative extracts the concept of actions necessary to this end merely from the concept of a volition of this end. (*Groundwork* 4:417)

Kant then adds that we do need some synthetic propositions—some causal laws—to arrive at these imperatives, but not for grounding the act of the will, only for determining what the means to the end are.

In other words, the imperative derives the concept of willing the means from the concept of willing the end, with the aid of some synthetic proposition telling us what the means are. So we begin with some willed end, say, health, and a causal (and so synthetic) proposition, say, that exercise is a cause of health. From the combination of these we derive the necessity of a will to exercise. What makes the derivation possible is an "analytic proposition," namely, that whoever wills the end wills the means to that end, insofar as reason has decisive influence on his actions. This proposition is analytic because to will an end, rather than just to wish for it or desire it, is to be committed to causing that end actually to exist.[35] "In the volition of an object," Kant explains, "my causality as acting cause" is "already thought." And to cause an end is of course to take the means to it. It follows that if someone wills to be healthy, then insofar as reason has decisive control over his actions, he wills to exercise.

Now the reconstruction I just gave is vague, for I have not said exactly *how* the analytic proposition makes it possible to combine willing the end with knowledge of the means so as to arrive at the necessity of willing the means. And it turns out that there is a problem about how this is supposed to work. The problem is revealed by two glitches that infect the argument as it stands. First, the claim that whoever wills the end wills "the indispensably necessary means to it that are within his power" seems to leave something out: the person in question must *know* that these are the means. It is not true that if someone wills to be healthy, then he necessarily wills to exercise. He must also *know* that exercise is a cause of health. This point is more important than it looks, because it suggests that the agent *himself* must combine willing the end with knowing the means to arrive at the necessity of willing the means. And this recalls a point I made earlier, namely, that the rationality of action depends on the way in which the person's own mental activity is involved in its production, not just on its accidental conformity to some external standard.

So the agent himself must combine willing the end and knowing the means to arrive at the necessity of willing the means. And the analytic proposition is supposed to make this possible for him somehow. But at this point we run into the second glitch in the argument. There is a recurring caveat: the analytic proposition is that whoever wills the end wills the means *insofar as reason has decisive influence on his actions*. This caveat, as I will explain below, turns out to give rise to a problem in Kant's argument. Before explaining that, it will be helpful to consider why Kant adds the caveat.

In one sense, I think the answer is clear. At the beginning of the discussion, Kant says that imperatives are expressed by an *ought* because they are addressed to wills that are not necessarily determined by the objective laws of reason. After identifying the good with the practically necessary, Kant says, "They [imperatives] say that to do or to omit something would be good, but they say it to a will that does not always do something just because it is represented to it that it would be good to do that thing" (*Groundwork* 4:413). In other words, imperatives are addressed to beings who may follow them or not. And this is true of the instrumental principle as well as of the others.

Now if this is right, it must be possible for a rational being (one who is subject to the instrumental principle) to disobey, resist, or fail to follow that principle. It must be possible for someone to will an end, and yet to fail to will the means to that end. And this means, once again, that there will be different ways to explain what happens when someone *apparently* fails to take the means to her end, or to what she says is her end.

Suppose someone claims that she wills an end: she asserts that all things considered, she has decided to pursue this end. And yet, when a means to this end is at hand she always fails to take it, even when it is expressly pointed out to her that it would promote or realize the end she has chosen. Timid Prudence says she has resolved to lead a more adventurous life, but when the opportunity for adventure knocks, Prudence always says "tomorrow." How are we to explain her conduct? One possible explanation of course is that she does not really will to lead a more adventurous life. When she says that she does, she is self-deceived or she is lying to the rest of us. We finally say to Prudence in disgust, "You really mean to live on the safe side of the street, and you had better just admit it." Notice that in this case we imply that she is guilty of insincerity rather than of instrumental irrationality. If she doesn't really will to have an adventurous life, it is not irrational of her to let these opportunities go by, although it is insincere for her to pretend she has resolved upon adventure.

A second possible explanation appeals to the fact that the instrumental principle is hypothetical, and says that *if* you will an end you must be prepared to take the means. The hypothetical character of the principle implies that you can actually conform to it in either of two ways: you may take the means, or you may cease to will the end. It matters here that willing, unlike desiring, is an act, one we can decide to refrain from, or to cease to do. Sometimes, when we see what taking the means to an end will involve, we cease to will the end, deciding that all things considered it is not worth the trouble or the price. There is no irrationality in this, and it may be what happens to Prudence. Perhaps she believes that the means to adventure which are pointed out to her will be so painful or terrifying that she decides that, all things considered, an adventurous life is not worth it after all. So she gives the idea up. Prudence says: "Well, I had resolved on leading a more adventurous life, but if I take any of the ways open to me right now, I am likely to end up in jail. I'd like to have more adventure, but it isn't really worth going to jail for." Again she is not guilty of any irrationality.

Both of those explanations say that Prudence doesn't really will to have adventures after all. This being so, she has not violated the instrumental principle, which only instructs her to take the means to those ends which she does will. The third explanation is that she does violate the instrumental principle, and fails to take the means to her end, because something is interfering with her susceptibility to reason. This might happen, for instance, because she has been rendered inert by depression, or paralyzed by terror, or because the means are painful and, although she judges the end to be worth the pain, she is simply unable to face it. Now we can say that she is violating the instrumental principle, and is guilty of irrational willing.[36]

Although we may not be sure which of these explanations is the best, the third one must be possible if the instrumental principle is a rational requirement. And it is worth noticing that there are cases where this third explanation seems to be the best in any case. Consider a standard scene of horror in Western or Civil War movies. The doctor must saw off Tex's leg in order to save his life, and there is no anesthetic or even any whiskey left in the house. Tex screams "No, no, don't"; he tries to escape from the men holding him down; he tries to push the doctor away. Yet if the doctor asks "Tex, don't you want to live?" Tex will of course say "yes." It would be stupid to say that because Tex rejects the means he is being insincere and doesn't really want to live, or that as the saw approaches he reconsiders his situation and makes a decision that all things considered, living isn't worth it. The right thing to say is that fear is making Tex irrational. After all, the judgment that someone is irrational doesn't have to be a criticism. The government of reason, like any other, requires certain background conditions in order to maintain its authority. Faced with the prospect of having his leg sawed off, Tex's sensible nature is quite understandably in revolt.

Kant, unlike the followers of Hume, recognizes that we cannot be guided by an imperative unless we can also fail to be guided by it. The caveat is necessary, then, because it must be logically possible for someone to fail to follow the instrumental principle, that is, to will an end but fail to will the means. The proposition is supposed to be analytic, so if we don't put the caveat in, failure to take the means to one's end will be logically impossible. But that means that without the caveat, the proposition can't be true after all.

But this in turn gives rise to the glitch I mentioned earlier, for it creates a problem about *how* the analytic proposition is supposed to make it possible for the agent to combine willing the end with knowing the means to *arrive at* a rational requirement of willing the means. On the model suggested by Kant's account, the agent arrives at the requirement by plugging himself in, so to speak, to a syllogism, of which the analytic proposition is the first premise:

Whoever wills the end wills the means.
I will the end.
∴ Therefore I will the means.

The trouble with this suggestion is obvious. As we have just seen, the principle "whoever wills the end wills the means" isn't true. This shows up in the fact that the syllogism puts the modal operator in the wrong place: its conclusion is not that I must will the means, but rather that it must be the case that I will the means, which is false. The only proposition which Kant can claim is an analytic truth is the one with the caveat in it: the proposition that "whoever wills the end wills the means insofar as reason has decisive influence over his actions." So it looks as if the first premise of the syllogism must include the caveat. Then it goes like this:

Whoever wills the end wills the means insofar as he is rational.
I will the end.
∴ Therefore I will the means insofar as I am rational.
∴ Therefore I *ought* to will the means.

(Recall that imperatives are expressed by an *ought*, according to Kant, because they are addressed to wills that do not necessarily do what reason demands: that's how this last step is made.)

But we cannot in any non-trivial way invoke this second syllogism to explain *why* the agent finds it rationally necessary to take the means to his end, for this syllogism's first premise trivially incorporates the claim that taking the means to one's ends is rationally required.

I believe that there is an historical explanation for what has gone wrong here. At the time he wrote the *Groundwork*, Kant apparently identified our capacity to resist the dictates of reason with the imperfection of the human will, for he asserts rather confusingly that a perfectly good will, although it would "stand under" the laws of reason, would not be necessitated to follow them and so would not be addressed in imperative form and in an *ought*. The reason for this is supposed to be that human beings are subject to incentives of inclination as well as those generated by reason itself, while a perfectly good will is moved only by the incentives generated by reason. Kant says: "Hence no imperatives hold for the *divine* will and in general for a holy will; the *ought* is out of place here, because volition is of itself necessarily in accord with the law" (*Groundwork* 4:414). This idea is picked up again in the third section of the *Groundwork*, when Kant claims that if we had only an intelligible existence (and so were perfectly rational) the moral law would be a "would" for us rather than an "ought" (*Groundwork* 4:454).[37] The structure of argument suggested by these remarks is this: God *does* so-and-so (or, a perfectly rational being does so-and-so) and therefore I *ought* to do so-and-so. This structure of argument is indeed found in the writings of dogmatic rationalists such as Leibniz and Clarke.[38] And it seems to be the model evoked in the second syllogism above: a perfectly rational being *would* take the means to his ends, therefore I *ought* to take the means to my ends. The model suggests that the normativity of the *ought* expresses a demand that we should emulate more perfect rational beings (possibly including our own noumenal selves) whose own conduct is not guided by normative principles at all, but instead describable in a set of logical truths. And this in turn suggests that rationality is a matter of conforming the will to standards of reason that exist independently of the will, as a set of truths about what there is reason to do. That is, it implies an essentially realist theory of reasons, and, as I am about to argue, a realist theory cannot provide a coherent account of rationality.[39]

According to dogmatic rationalism, or realism more generally, there are facts, which exist independently of the person's mind, about what there is reason to do; rationality consists in conforming one's conduct to those reasons. According to *moral* realism, facts about the rightness or wrongness of actions support those reasons; according to what we might call *instrumental* realism, facts about the instrumentality of actions to our ends support those reasons. The difficulty with this account in a way exists right on its surface, for the account invites the question why it is necessary to act in accordance with those reasons, and so seems to leave us in need of a reason to be rational. I have an end, and out there in the universe is a law saying what I must do if I have an end (take the means), but the reason why I must obey this law has not yet been given. To put the point less tendentiously, we must still explain why the person finds it *necessary* to act on those normative facts, or what it is about *her* that makes them normative *for her*. We must explain how these reasons get a grip on the agent. The dogmatic rationalist's inability to do that is illustrated by the impossibility of forming a syllogism that shows, in any illuminating way, how the agent manages to *arrive at* the rational necessity of taking the means to her ends.

Now the *moral* realist may be tempted to try to overcome this problem by appeal to the extended version of the instrumental principle which I mentioned earlier, the one that sees the application of a concept as a limiting case of the discovery of a means. We would first have to assume (or produce an argument to show) that doing what is right is a necessary end for a rational agent. (This parallels the social scientific strategy, which we looked at in section 2, of assuming that pursuit of the overall good is a necessary end for a rational agent.) With such an argument in hand, it might seem that we could connect the alleged normative facts about the right to the person's practical reason by way of the extended version of the instrumental principle. Consider: my end is to do what is right, in these circumstances *this* is the right action, therefore I shall do *this*. The extended instrumental principle in this way is supposed to lend *its* normative or motivational character to the independent facts about the rightness of certain actions.

But there are two problems with this strategy. The first and more obvious problem is that all the philosophical work has been transferred to the (missing, or anyway unspecified) argument that is supposed to show that doing what is right is a necessary end for a rational agent. (Just as, in the social scientific case, all the work is really done by the missing argument that shows that we what we "really want" must be consistent with our overall good.) The second problem concerns the instrumental principle itself. If it is to provide the needed connection between the rational agent and the independent facts about reasons, it cannot in turn be based on independent facts itself. Suppose it is just a fact, independently of a person's own will, that an action's tendency to promote one of her ends constitutes a reason for doing it. Why must she care about *that* fact? We cannot now appeal to the instrumental principle itself to explain how that fact gets a grip on the agent, for that is the principle we are trying to ground. You can see this by considering how the argument would have to go: doing whatever promotes your own ends is a necessary end for a rational being; this action promotes one of your ends; therefore it promotes your end of doing what promotes your ends; and therefore you have reason to do it. The circularity, or infinite regress, is obvious.[40] The instrumental principle cannot be an evaluative truth that we apply in practice, because it is essentially the *principle of application* itself: that is, it is the principle in accordance with which we are operating *when* we apply truths in practice. So if we are to use the extended instrumental principle to make the connection between the rational agent and the external facts about reasons, we cannot give the instrumental principle a realist foundation. But if we cannot give a realist account of the instrumental principle, it seems unlikely that we will end up giving realist accounts of the other principles of practical reason.

Another way to understand the argument I have just given goes like this: moral realism (or for that matter, realism about reasons of prudence) may be criticized on the grounds that it fails to meet the internalism requirement. The moral realist I am imagining tries to overcome that problem by tapping into the supposedly incontrovertible internalism of instrumental reason. The problem is that, on a realist interpretation, astonishingly enough, the instrumental principle *itself* fails to meet the internalism requirement. For all we can see, an agent may be indifferent to the fact that an action's instrumentality to her end constitutes a reason for her to act.

Now while that way of understanding the argument has some advantages, I have come to think that there is a problem with thinking of these issues in terms of the internalism requirement. The internalism requirement is concerned only with whether a consideration that purports to be a reason is capable of motivating the person to whom it applies. And I think the real question is not only whether the consideration can motivate the person, but whether it can do so while also functioning as a requirement or a guide. This, after all, is what is wrong with the empiricist account treated in section 2: the empiricist *can* explain how we can be motivated by instrumental thoughts, but at the price of not being able to explain how we could see such thoughts as embodying a requirement or a guide. The dogmatic rationalist account does show how the instrumental principle can guide us. But it does not show why we must be motivated to follow that guide. The theory I just examined tries to patch together an empiricist account of instrumental reason with a rationalist account of morality and prudence, in order to patch together the motivational force of the one with the guiding force of the other.[41] But it ends up with neither, and that is revealed in the fact that the first of the two problems with the proposed strategy still stands: the patchwork account makes no progress towards showing *why* a rational agent must care about doing what is right.

There is one way in which the realist strategy still might seem to work. We could simply *define* a rational agent as one who responds in the appropriate way to reasons, whatever they are, and we could then give realist accounts of all practical reasons, including instrumental ones. There is a set of normative facts, about which reasons there are, and a rational agent is *by definition* someone whose actions are motivated by these reasons. But this proposal falls prey to a problem we looked at before. If all we mean is that the person is reliably caused to act in accordance with reasons, we fail to capture what is rational about the person. His actions may be rationally appropriate, but not because he sees that they are so: it seems to be a sort of accident that his motivational wiring follows the pathways of reason. On the other hand, if what we mean when we say that the person's actions are motivated by reasons is that the person is caused to act by his *recognition* of certain considerations *as* reasons, then we must say *what it is* that he recognizes.[42] And the argument I have just given shows that what it is that he recognizes cannot be that "whoever wills the end wills the means" is an analytic proposition. Because, as I have just argued, it is not. We seem to be back where we started, with Kant's argument, interpreted in a dogmatic rationalist way, having achieved nothing.

The point here is that we need a reciprocal account of rationality—as some sort of human function or capacity—and of reasons. We need an account that shows what those two things have to do with each other. The dogmatic rationalist's strategy is to first identify reasons—by asserting them to be parts of reality—and then to define rationality in terms of reasons: a rational being is by definition one who responds to reasons in the right way. This strategy necessarily leads to a purely definitional account of rationality, and can tell us nothing substantive about what function or power of the human mind rationality is. The alternative and more truly Kantian strategy is to first give an account of rationality—as we will see, as the autonomy of the human mind—and then to define reasons in terms of rationality, say, as that which can be autonomously willed, or as those considerations which accord with the principles of autonomous willing.

In other words, the dogmatic rationalist is unable to explain how reasons get a grip on the agent, because he supposes that reasons exist independently of the rational will, and as a result he misconceives the relationship between rational principles and the will. The dogmatic rationalist pictures that relationship this way: the person is willing something, so to speak *anyway*, and, inspired by an ambition to be rational, consults the principles of practical reason to see what restrictions they impose on his willing. When we translate this picture into Kantian terms it looks like this: I make a maxim, and *then* I see whether it meets the three standards of reason by determining first whether my action is a means to my end, then whether the pursuit of my end is consistent with my overall good, and finally whether my maxim is moral, that is, universalizable. The model, as I said earlier, seems to invite the question: but suppose I don't care about being rational? What then? And in Kant's philosophy this question should be impossible to ask. Rationality, as Kant conceives it, is the human plight that gives rise to the necessity of making free choices—not one of the options that we might choose or reject.[43]

One of the benefits of focusing on the instrumental principle is that it reveals how odd the dogmatic rationalist conception of reason's relation to the will is. The idea that you could make a maxim and *then* apply the instrumental principle to it makes no sense. A maxim that does not already at least aspire to conform to the instrumental principle is no maxim at all. So the instrumental principle does not come in as a restriction that is applied *to* the maxim. Instead, the act of making a maxim—the basic act of will—conforms to the instrumental principle by its very nature. To will an end just is to will to cause or realize the end, hence to will to take the means to the end. This is the sense in which the principle is analytic. The instrumental principle is *constitutive* of an act of the will. If you do not follow it, you are not willing the end at all.

Now this sounds like one of the views I have already rejected, so care must be taken here. The act of will of which conformity to the instrumental principle is *constitutive* in the way I have just described is not the act of will third-personally conceived. If we took willing an end to be equivalent to actually pursuing or trying to pursue the means to that end, then we would get the paradox I have been insisting on all along. No violation of the instrumental principle would be possible, and it therefore could not function as a requirement or guide. If willing an end just amounted to actually attempting to realize the end, then there would be, so to speak, not enough distance between willing the end and willing the means for the one to *require* the other.[44] The dogmatic rationalist view, in which one conforms to a principle independent of the mind, achieves that distance, and so allows the principle to function as a guide. But as we have seen it gives rise to a new problem. Essentially, dogmatic rationalism conceives willing an end as being in a peculiar mental state or performing a mental act which somehow logically necessitates you to be in another mental state or perform another mental act, namely, willing the means. But we've just seen that this does not work either, for no mental state or act can logically necessitate you to be in *another* mental state or perform another mental act.[45] So willing the end is neither *the same as* being actually disposed to take the means nor as being in a particular mental state or performing a mental act that is *distinct from* willing the means. What then can it be?[46]

The answer is that willing an end just is *committing* yourself to realizing the end. Willing an end, in other words, is an essentially first-personal and normative act.[47] To will an end is to give oneself a law, hence, to govern oneself. That law is not the instrumental principle; it is some law of the form: realize this end. That of course is equivalent to "Take the means to this end." So willing an end is equivalent to committing yourself, first personally, to taking the means to that end.[48] In willing an end, just as Kant says, your causality—the use of means—is already thought. What is constitutive of willing the end is not the outward act of actually taking the means but rather the inward, volitional act of prescribing the end along with the means it requires to yourself.

Let me make the same point in another way. In my discussion of Hume, I contrasted two formulations of the instrumental principle. The first was "if you *have a reason to pursue* an end, then you have a reason to take the means to that end" and the second was "if you are *going* to pursue an end, then you have a reason to take the means to that end." I argued that the second of those two formulations is defective because it attempts to derive an *Ought* from an *Is* (a reason from what you are *going* to do) and any imperative that attempts to do that cannot be followed because it cannot be violated. What about Kant's own formula? If it is to be like my first formulation, the one that works, then we get this result: for the instrumental principle to provide you with a reason, you must think that the fact that you will an end *is a reason* for the end. It's not exactly that there has to be a *further* reason; it's just that you must take the act of your own will to be normative for you.[49] And of course this cannot mean merely that you are *going* to pursue the end. It means that your willing the end gives it a normative status for you, that your willing the end in a sense makes it good. The instrumental principle can only be normative if we take ourselves to be capable of giving laws to ourselves—or, in Kant's own phrase, if we take our own wills to be *legislative*.

For this, of course, is almost already the third formulation of the categorical imperative, which Kant associates with "the concept of every rational being as one who must regard himself as giving universal law through all the maxims of his will" (*Groundwork* 4:433).[50] The only difference is that the conception of oneself as a lawmaker required for the instrumental principle does not yet (or not obviously) involve universalizing over every rational agent.

Then what does it mean to say I take the act of my own will to be normative? Who makes a law for whom? The answer in the case of the instrumental principle is that I make a law *for me*.[51] And this is a law that I am capable of obeying or disobeying. At this moment, now, I decide to work; at the next moment, at any moment, I will certainly want to stop. If I am to work I must *will* it—I must resolve to stay on its track. Timidity, idleness, and depression will exert their claims in turn, will attempt to control or overrule my will, to divert me from my work. Am I to let these forces determine my actions? At each moment I must say to them: "I am not you; my will is this work." Desire and temptation will also take their turns. "I am not a shameful thing like terror," desire will say, "follow me and your life will be sweet." But if I give in to each claim as it appears *I* will do nothing and I will not have a life. For to will an end is not just to cause it, or even to allow an impulse in me to operate as its cause, but, so to speak, to consciously pick up the reins, and make *myself* the cause of the end. And if I am to constitute *myself* as the cause of an end, then I must be able to distinguish between *my* causing the end and some desire or impulse that is "in me" causing my body to act. I must be able to see *myself* as something that is distinct from any of my particular, first-order, impulses and motives. So the reason that I must conform to the instrumental principle is that if I don't conform to it, if I *always* allow myself to be derailed by timidity, idleness, or depression, then I never really *will* an end. The *desire* to pursue the end and the desires that draw me away from it each hold sway in their turn, but *my will* is never active.[52] The distinction between my will and the operation of the desires and impulses in me does not exist, and that means that I, considered as an agent, do not exist. Conformity to the instrumental principle is thus constitutive of having a will; in a sense it is even what gives you a will.[53]

Now I need to clarify these remarks in one important way. In the above argument I appealed to the possibility of being tempted away from the end on another, temporally later occasion. But the argument does not really require the possibility of a temporally later occasion. It only requires that there be two parts of me, one that is my governing self, my will, and one that must be governed, and is capable of resisting my will. The possibility of resistance exists even now, on this occasion. The possibility of self-government essentially involves the possibility of its failure; and the principles of reason are therefore ineluctably normative.[54]

It is worth pointing out that an exactly parallel argument could be made about believing. We are neither inevitably inclined nor logically necessitated to believe the logical implications of our beliefs. The rational necessity of believing the logical implications of our beliefs cannot be explained by our plugging ourselves into a syllogism, like this: "No one who believes X also believes ~X. I believe X, therefore I do not believe ~X." The first premise of such a syllogism is false, and if we add the caveat—that no one who is rational believes both of these things—then the syllogism cannot provide a non-trivial explanation of why it is irrational to believe a contradiction. The rational necessity of believing the implications of our beliefs can only be explained if we regard believing itself as a normative act. To believe something is not to be in a certain mental state, but to make a certain commitment. It is, we might say, to be committed to constructing one's view of the world in one way rather than another.

And trying to persuade someone who actually doubted the instrumental principle that she should act on it would be like trying to persuade someone who actually doubted the principle of non-contradiction that he should believe it. It would be *exactly* like that. When Aristotle said that trying to persuade someone of the principle of non-contradiction is like trying to argue with a vegetable, he was not just being abusive (*Metaphysics* 4.4 1006a15). A person who denies the principle of non-contradiction asserts that anything may follow from anything, and that therefore he is committed to nothing. And if he commits himself to nothing there is nothing he believes, and so no point from which to start the argument. This is why Aristotle says that if you can just get him to assert something, you have already won the argument. A person who rejects the principle of non-contradiction does not reject a particular restriction on his beliefs. Since he commits himself to nothing, he rejects the very project of having beliefs.[55] And parallel points can be made about someone who denies the instrumental principle. This is why it matters that, as I pointed out at the beginning, the instrumental principle can naturally be extended so that it seems to be the principle of self-conscious action quite generally. A rejection of the instrumental principle is a rejection of self-conscious action itself.[56]

On reflection, it looks as if no other solution is possible. We are trying to justify a norm, a principle, which claims to govern a certain activity. Why must we conform to the instrumental principle? Here we come to an important distinction, between norms that are constitutive of, and so internal to, the activities that they claim to govern, and norms that are external to those activities. If I say "bake a cake, and make it taste good" and you ask *why* you should make it taste good, we may think that you don't know what baking cakes is all about. But if I say "bake a cake, and make it ten feet high" and you ask *why* you should make it ten feet high, your question is perfectly in order. External norms give rise to further questions, and space for skeptical doubt. But if we can identify something as an internal norm, the question why you should conform to the norm answers itself. And some norms, unlike the norm of making cakes taste good, come not from the desired product of the activity, but from the nature of the activity itself. "Put one foot in front of the other" is a norm of walking, and "a sentence must contain both a subject and a verb" is a norm of linguistic action.[57] And yet, you can try to walk, fail to put one foot in front of another, and trip; and, as all of us who grade student papers know, you can try to take linguistic action, and yet founder for want of a verb. Although these norms are constitutive, they are still norms, and not *mere* descriptions of the activities in question. They are, as it were, instructions for performing the activities in question. And so there's no room to ask why you should follow them: if you don't put one foot in front of the other you will not be walking and you will get nowhere; if you don't have both a subject and a verb you will not be speaking and you will say nothing. The instrumental principle is, in this way, a constitutive norm of willing, of deliberate action. If you are going to act at all, then you must conform to it.[58] And, being human, you have no choice but to act.

Although of course I cannot give the argument for it here, it is important now to recall that, on Kant's view, the moral law *just is* the law of an autonomous will. To say that moral laws are the laws of autonomy is not to say that our autonomy somehow requires us to *restrict* ourselves in accordance with them, but rather to say that they are constitutive of autonomous action. Kant thinks that insofar as we are autonomous, we just *do* will our maxims as universal laws. What I have argued in this essay is that this is also true of the principle of instrumental reason.[59] Kant therefore has a *unified* account of practical rationality: to be guided by reason just is to be autonomous, to give laws to oneself.[60]

Now let me go back to my other point. I claimed before that what my argument showed was that hypothetical imperatives cannot exist without categorical ones, or anyway without principles which direct us to the pursuit of certain ends, or anyway without *something* which gives normative status to our ends. Does this account support that claim? The long answer to that question is another essay, but the short answer will do for now. If I am to will an end, to be and to remain committed to it even in the face of desires that would distract and weaknesses that would dissuade me, it looks as if I must have something to *say to myself* about why I am doing that—something better, moreover, than the fact that this is what I wanted yesterday. It looks as if the end is one that has to be *good*, in some sense that goes beyond the locally desirable. I have to be able to make sense to myself of effort and deprivation and frustration, and it is hard to see how the reflection that this *is* what I wanted yesterday can do that by itself, especially when I want something else today. I do not have an argument that shows that this is *impossible*. I suppose that through some heroic existentialist act, one might just take one's will at a certain moment to be normative, and commit oneself forever to the end selected at that moment, without thinking that the end is in any way good, and perhaps for no other reason than that some such commitment is essential if one is to have a *will* at all. But it is hard to see how a self-conscious being who must talk to herself about her actions could live with that solution. To that extent, the normative force of the instrumental principle does seem to depend on our having a way to say to ourselves of some ends that there are reasons for them, that they are good.[61] However that may be, though, even the heroic existentialist is committed to the view that an act of his own will is the source of a reason—and *that* reason cannot possibly be derived from the instrumental principle. So the conclusion in any case follows—the view that all practical reason is instrumental is incoherent, for the instrumental principle cannot stand alone.

4 Epilogue

I won't attempt to sum up the long and complex argument of this essay. But by way of conclusion, it may be useful to say something about where, if my argument is correct, it leaves us.[62] What do I suppose I've shown, and if I'm right, what is both still necessary and still possible in the theory of practical reason?

First, as I've just said, I think the argument shows that the instrumental principle cannot stand alone. Unless something attaches normativity to our ends, there can be no requirement to take the means to them. Of course, even if our ends lack such normativity, so long as they continue to be the ends we have in view, or the ones we effectively want most, we may certainly be inspired by instrumental thoughts to take the means to them: that is, instrumental thoughts may *cause* us to *want* to take those means. This is how it is with intelligent but non-rational animals, and, if Hume were right, this is how it would be with us. Indeed, this kind of instrumental *intelligence* seems pretty clearly to be a prerequisite for instrumental *rationality*, and, to that extent, this *is* how it is with us. But no account of a *requirement* of taking the means to our ends can be derived from the mere fact that we possess this kind of intelligence. If there is a principle of practical reason which *requires* us to take the means to our ends, then those ends must be, not merely ones that we happen to have in view, but ones that we have some reason to keep in view. There must be unconditional reasons for having certain ends, and, it seems, unconditional principles from which those reasons are derived. So now two further questions arise: have I done anything towards showing whether there are any such principles, or what they would have to be like?

In one sense, the answer to the first question, whether I have shown that there are unconditional principles, is no. The conclusion of this essay is hypothetical: the argument shows that *if* there are any instrumental requirements, then there must be unconditional requirements as well. Conversely, if there are unconditional requirements to adopt certain ends, then there are also requirements to take the means to those ends, since a commitment to taking the means is what makes a difference between willing an end and merely wishing for it or wanting it or thinking that it would be nice if it were realized. But these arguments show only that unconditional and conditional requirements are mutually dependent. Complete practical normative skepticism is still an option, although its price is high—a point I will come back to.[63]

The answer to the second question—"does this argument show us anything substantive about the unconditional principles of practical reason, about what they would have to be like?"—is also no. At least I have shown nothing so far about the *content* of those principles. As far as the argument of this essay goes, they could be principles of prudence, or moral principles, or something else. In fact, as the possibility of the heroic existentialist I described at the end of section 3 shows, the reason to pursue the end which is needed to support the reason to take the means can be as thin and insubstantial as the agent's arbitrary will, his raw and unmotivated decision that he will take a certain end to be normative for himself, for no other reason than that he wills it so.

Yet even my heroic existentialist is autonomous, and this leads me to the more positive side of the argument: for I think that the argument of section 3 establishes not only that instrumental principles depend on unconditional ones, but also that particular instrumental requirements must be self-given laws, grounded in our autonomy. This raises the further question whether the unconditional reasons on which hypothetical reasons depend must also be, according to my argument, grounded in autonomy, or whether we could give, say, a dogmatic rationalist account of the unconditional reasons for having certain ends.[64] I believe that the argument does show that unconditional reasons, as well as hypothetical ones, must be grounded in autonomy. This is because the arguments of section 3, both those against dogmatic rationalism, and those in favor of the view that the principles of practical reason are constitutive norms of autonomy, are not specific to the principle of instrumental reason. They are concerned with the question how we can account for the normativity of practical reasons generally. The point of focusing on the instrumental principle is really just that this conclusion is, in its case, more unexpected and striking.

But if the argument shows that our unconditional principles must be laws of autonomy, then it brings us back home to the old Hegelian question: can any substantive requirements be derived from the mere fact of our autonomy? How much determinate content do the constitutive norms of autonomy have? And does this content coincide with, or include, morality? For this is the real question behind the familiar worry whether Kant's Formula of Universal Law has content. As I see it, then, only three positions are possible: either (i) the Kantian argument that autonomy commits us to certain substantive principles can be made to work; or (ii) we are left in the position of the heroic existentialist, who must ultimately define his will through acts of unconditional commitment that have no further ground; or (iii) complete practical normative skepticism is in order.

My own view is that the Kantian argument can be made to succeed, but that of course is another story—if I am right, it is *the* other story, where practical reason is concerned.[65] But it's worth saying something here about what's left to choose between existentialism and complete practical normative skepticism, if the Kantian project does not work out. And this brings us back to the question of the price of complete practical normative skepticism.

The argument of this essay makes a strong connection between having a will and being bound by the principles of practical reason—or, at least, by the principle of instrumental reason. Conformity to the principle of instrumental reason—prescribing to oneself in accordance with this principle—is constitutive of having a will. And having a will, I believe, is constitutive of being a person. As I have argued in both section 2 and section 3, a person who does not conform to the instrumental principle becomes a mere location for the play of desires and impulses, the field of their battle for dominance over the body through which they seek satisfaction.[66] The price of complete practical normative skepticism, then, is nothing short of the loss of personal identity. The existentialist, however arbitrarily, does preserve his will and so his identity. It's important to see that the practical form in which I'm putting these claims—the skeptic *loses* his identity; the existentialist *preserves* his will—is not a mistake or a literary conceit. With realism denied, the question becomes a practical one. It is not the question whether we really have such wills as are constituted by these principles, but whether we are to conduct ourselves so as to have such wills, by acting in accordance with these principles. The final answer, then, to the question—what gives the instrumental principle its normativity?—is this: conformity to the instrumental principle is an essential part of what makes you a person. There is no position from which you can reject the government of instrumental reason: for if you reject it, there is no you.[67]

5 Afterword, 2008

This complicated essay has particular resonance for me, because it set the agenda for much of the work I have done since. The moment it struck me to add note 53, in which I note the similarity between my view that the instrumental principle unifies and constitutes the will and Plato's view that justice unifies and constitutes the soul was the moment when I conceived the idea for my book *Self-Constitution: Agency, Identity, and Integrity* [Oxford: Oxford University Press, 2009]. But the purpose of this afterword is to notice the way in which I didn't quite come to the end of my thought in this essay—or rather, I did, but somehow I only managed to mention it as an afterthought in note 60. One of the conclusions I draw in this essay is that the instrumental principle cannot stand alone—there is no normative instrumental principle unless there are normative principles directing us to adopt certain ends. That, I now believe, is not the proper way to describe the conclusion. In fact, there are two things wrong with the way I described my conclusion in this essay. First, the instrumental principle is not a principle of practical reason that is separable from the categorical imperative: rather, it picks out an *aspect* of the categorical imperative: the fact that the laws of our will must be practical laws, laws that constitute us as agents by rendering us efficacious. Second, the categorical imperative is not a principle of practical reason that tells us to have certain ends, and that is separable from the principle that tells us to take the means to those ends. Practical principles govern the will, and a principle that governs the will must tell us to *do* something—even if it is just, indeterminately, to do whatever we can (legitimately) do in the pursuit of certain ends. It cannot tell us simply to *have* certain ends. To describe the categorical imperative as a principle governing ends is to fail to take the full force of Kant's view, in the *Critique of Practical Reason*, that to be a good in the normative sense—an "object of practical reason" as he calls it—is to be "an effect possible through freedom" (*2nd Critique* 5:57). So let me here state the conclusion of my argument properly. There is only one principle of practical reason, and it is the categorical imperative.

Notes

1. See, e.g., Bernard Williams in "Internal and External Reasons," in Williams, *Moral Luck* (Cambridge: Cambridge University Press, 1981), essay 8, pp. 101–113 [this volume, chap. 1]. For a thorough discussion of the varieties of internalism, see Robert Audi, "Moral Judgment and Reasons for Action," in *Ethics and Practical Reason*, G. Cullity and B. Gaut, eds. (Oxford: Oxford University Press, 1997). Audi's focus, however, is on the internalism of moral judgments, while I am talking about the internalism of reasons or reason judgments more generally. In recent years, the literature on internalism has become increasingly intricate, and the point of settling the question whether a given type of consideration is "internal" or not has become somewhat obscure. In my own view, practical reasons *must* be internal in the sense given in the text, and therefore the point of settling the question whether moral considerations or judgments are internal is that they cannot be regarded as *reasons* unless they are. As I will argue in section 3, however, showing that a consideration is internal, although necessary, is not sufficient to show that it is a reason.

2. Kant also called the technical imperative an imperative of skill, so one might put the point I am making here this way: the instrumental principle is now seen as requiring us to exercise not merely skill, but also judgment, in the pursuit of our ends. But any self-conscious action must be guided by judgment. Some of Aristotle's examples of practical syllogisms are explicitly like the example in the text. Consider for example: "I want to drink, says appetite; this is drink, says sense or imagination or thought: straightaway I drink" (*Movement of Animals* 701a33–34). Or consider the notorious "dry food" syllogism of *Nicomachean Ethics* 7, in which Aristotle toys with the idea that incontinence occurs in a man who believes that "Dry food is good for any man" when he reasons that "I am a man" and "such and such food is dry," but then fails to exercise the knowledge that "this food is such and such" (1147a1–10). In these cases, there is no question of using technical means, but simply of the application of a principle to a case or a concept to a particular. This fact throws light on what Aristotle meant when he said that practical reasoning is not about ends but about what contributes to them (*Nicomachean Ethics* 3 1112b12): in particular, it suggests that this remark is not meant to imply *any* limitation in the scope of practical reasoning. See also my "From Duty and for the Sake of the Noble: Kant

and Aristotle on Morally Good Action," reprinted in *The Constitution of Agency* (Oxford: Oxford University Press, 2008).

3. This is a difficulty, I think, in the strategy Williams adopts in "Internal and External Reasons," in *Moral Luck* [this volume, chap. 1]. His argument seems to show that only natural extensions of the instrumental principle can meet the internalism requirement, but he is prepared to extend the instrumental principle so far that this turns out to be no limitation at all. See my "Skepticism about Practical Reason," *Journal of Philosophy* 83 (1986): 5-25 [this volume, chap. 2]. Interestingly, however, the view I defend in this essay also tends to break down the distinctions among the different principles of practical reason. See note 60.

4. As others have noticed, we use the term 'prudence', confusingly, to refer both to attention to self-interested reasons and to attention to one's future reasons, whether or not they are self-interested (see Nagel, in *The Possibility of Altruism* [Princeton: Princeton University Press, 1970], p. 36). Since I am not taking a stand on the formulation of the principle of prudence here, I don't bother to sort through this issue in the text. For further discussion, see my "The Myth of Egoism," reprinted in *The Constitution of Agency*.

5. Parfit, *Reasons and Persons* (Oxford: Oxford University Press, 1984), esp. chap. 6, section 45.

6. Kant's other (and I think better) reason for regarding the imperative of prudence as hypothetical is that it holds only conditionally—it may be overridden when duty demands that we do something contrary to our interest. As some of the things I will say later suggest, I think that there are problems about understanding the principle of prudence as a hypothetical imperative and that Kant's account of this principle is in need of revision. Unfortunately I cannot give full treatment to the complex question of the status of prudence here. For further discussion, see my "The Myth of Egoism."

7. As suggested for instance by John Mackie, in *Ethics: Inventing Right and Wrong* (Harmondsworth: Penguin, 1977).

8. Butler, *Fifteen Sermons Preached at the Rolls Chapel*, especially Sermons 1-3; and Nagel, *Possibility*. A parallel between the two problems is also suggested by Sidgwick in *The Methods of Ethics* (Indianapolis, IN: Hackett, 1981), pp. 418–419, and, following him, by Parfit in *Reasons and Persons*, pp. 307ff.

9. The clearest statement of this view is again that of Williams in "Internal and External Reasons" [this volume, chap. 1]. The cumbersome phrase in the text is an attempt to do justice to Williams's attempt to express this theory in a way that leaves it open what forms of practical reason there are.

10. The rationalist may of course speculate or stipulate that insofar as we are rational we must be motivated by the (alleged) principles of reason, and in this way

meet the internalism requirement, but this leaves their power to motivate us essentially inexplicable. I discuss the difficulties with this sort of stipulation in section 3. I believe that in "Skepticism about Practical Reason" [this volume, chap. 2], I may give the impression that I think a stipulation of this kind sufficient to meet the worries of those who complain that moral principles do not meet the internalism requirement. I don't believe that, although I now think, as I will explain later, that the real worry behind the internalism requirement is inadequately expressed by that requirement. In fact this shows up in the fact that the internalism requirement may be met by such a stipulation, but that this does not resolve the real worry.

11. It is also partly dictated by the unavailability (at least as far as I know) of detailed discussions of the instrumental principle by the dogmatic rationalists themselves.

12. At the end of section 2, I will argue that even within the confines of a reconstructed Humean account, the normativity of the instrumental principle must be traced to the agent's self-government, specifically to his capacity to be motivated to shape his character in accordance with an ideal of virtue. So this is actually not just a point about how a Kantian account of reason works.

13. I have in mind Nagel's account, in *Possibility*, although his view more strictly speaking is that we can be directly motivated by beliefs about other people's *reasons*.

14. Nagel, *Possibility*, pp. 33–34 [this volume, 198–199].

15. This point is related to an idea which Michael Smith emphasizes in "A Theory of Freedom and Responsibility," in G. Cullity and B. Gaut, eds., namely, that part of what is involved in regarding and interacting with someone as a person who has and is responsible for his beliefs is attributing to him the capacity to recognize and respond appropriately to the norms that govern belief. See especially p. 296.

16. I characterize this as a preliminary formulation since I am ultimately going to argue that a rational agent is guided by herself, that is, that being governed by reason amounts to being self-governed.

17. I don't of course mean to imply that a rational agent in fact actively entertains all of the logical consequences of her beliefs, since not all such consequences are presented as necessary, or presented at all.

18. Kant holds that a moral agent's actions are not merely in accordance with duty but done *from* it (*Groundwork* 4:397). One way to put the point of this paragraph is to say that a rational agent must act not merely in accordance with reason but *from* it. The rational agent has a conception of her actions as rational or at least as required, called for. The debate between the rationalists and the empiricists about rationality could then be constructed as proceeding in the way their debate about the relative merits of acting in accordance with duty and acting from it actually did.

For an account of that debate, see my "Kant's Analysis of Obligation: The Argument of *Groundwork I*," reprinted in *Creating the Kingdom of Ends* (Cambridge: Cambridge University Press, 1996). For more on the idea that a rational agent acts not merely in accordance with reason but from it, see my "Acting for a Reason," reprinted in *The Constitution of Agency*.

19. Some readers may be tempted to think that Hume's special notion of causality is at fault here: rationality must be something "inside" of the rational agent; causal judgments, as Hume understands them, are in the eye of the beholder, and therefore rationality cannot be reduced to a certain way of being caused, on Hume's conception. But (one might think) this doesn't show that rationality cannot be a certain way of being caused on some other, more objective, conception of causality. Now I don't think that this is right. The main argument of this part of the essay, as the reader will see, does not depend in any way on Hume's special notion of causality. But something close to it is right: namely, that causal judgments are essentially third-personal, and rational ones are essentially first-personal. (For more on this point, see my *Sources of Normativity* [Cambridge: Cambridge University Press, 1996], 1.2.2, pp. 16–18.) This is what prevents the empiricist reduction of rationality to a form of causality. So what matters here is not, so to speak, where the cause operates, but the point of view from which we make the judgment that it operates.

It's worth noticing that a parallel argument could be constructed for theoretical reason, suggesting that Hume doesn't believe in that either. I don't take this to be a problem for my account, for I don't think that Hume believes in rational belief any more than he does in rational action. His view is that beliefs are sentiments that are caused in us by perceptions and habits. Reason doesn't really enter into it.

20. In *Possibility*, Nagel appeals to exactly this sort of belief—a belief about future desires/pleasures/reasons—to show how odd the belief/desire model is. His point is that it would be bizarre to think that we needed a special desire to give motivational or normative force to a belief about a reason we will have later. Although for different reasons, Hume would agree.

21. This makes Hume sound perverse, but in fact, given his account of belief, it is a tautology. If you thought that the thing were going to affect you then you would believe in its existence; that is, that's more or less what believing it amounts to. Even apart from Hume's theory, this doesn't seem completely crazy. One plausible, if rather idealistic (in the philosophical sense) account of what is meant by claiming that something exists is that it could conceivably affect you.

22. Unless, perhaps, a sacrifice of one's personal interests is required by some yet more stringent principle of reason, such as a moral principle. Hume, however, does not think that this possibility is likely to arise. See the *Enquiry Concerning the Principles of Morals* 9, 278–284.

23. Later Hume will argue that moral considerations cannot be based on reason, because reason does not motivate and moral considerations do (*Treatise* 3.1.1, 457).

This suggests that he accepts internalism about moral considerations. Of course, it also suggests that he thinks reason cannot motivate us, generally speaking, and that may make the interpretative proposal in the text look implausible: if Hume doesn't think reason motivates, why should he suppose that considerations of prudence must motivate in order to be reasons? The answer, I think, is that Hume is an internalist about requirements, and the argument quoted above is supposed to show that reason cannot make prudence a requirement, and, more generally, that reason does not yield requirements. As we'll see later, Hume does think prudence is a requirement of virtue.

24. "Skepticism about Practical Reason," pp. 11–15 [this volume, 57–60].

25. Readers of earlier drafts of this essay have alerted me to the importance of making it clear what I am saying about Hume at this point. My primary target in this part of the essay is actually empiricists who endorse the view that the instrumental principle is the only principle of practical reason and who claim Hume for the founding father of their view. I am arguing that Hume could not have held such a view. I do not mean, however, to suggest that Hume himself tried to hold this view and failed: I do not believe that he thought the instrumental principle was a principle of reason. In note 39 below, however, I argue that Hume's arguments for the normativity of virtue may depend on the normativity of prudence, and I think that a parallel and related point can be made about the normativity of the instrumental principle. Of course some interpreters also deny that Hume is trying to establish the normativity of virtue, but this is not the line that I have taken. For my interpretation of Hume's account of the normativity of morality, see my *Sources*, 2.2.1–2.2.7, pp. 51–66. I thank Annette Baier and Barbara Herman for prodding me to be clearer on this point.

26. As Plato points out in the *Protagoras*, one idea that drives this position is the idea that the objects of desire are commensurable. If the choice is between getting $5 or 5 units of pleasure now, and $12 or 12 units of pleasure next week, it is a *little* more plausible to say that passion will conform *automatically* to the dictate of prudence—although only a little. But if the choice is between six weeks of passion with a charming scapegrace now, and a lifetime of marriage to a man of sweet reason, the claim that passion will yield *automatically* to prudence seems absurd. Economists, of course, do tend to assume commensurability.

27. For further discussion, see my "The Myth of Egoism."

28. I owe this suggestion to Erin Kelly; I would also like to thank Charlotte Brown and Andrews Reath for discussions of this point.

29. But there is a deep incoherence here. In Hume's moral theory, prudence is supposed to be a virtue because we approve of it from the general point of view. From this point of view, we approve of those qualities that are useful or agreeable to an agent himself or his associates. Hume identifies prudence as one of the virtues that

is supposed to be good (because useful) for the agent who has it. But if an agent himself has no reason to prefer his greater good to the satisfaction of his local desires, then I do not see why we should think it is good for him to prefer it, and therefore why we should count it as a virtue. The real trouble, I think, is that Hume uses the word 'good' to describe the sum of satisfactions or pleasures over the course of a person's whole life without explaining either what entitles him to that usage or what follows from it. If the word 'good' is supposed to import normativity, it may seem like a raw contradiction to say an agent has no reason to prefer his greater good. Or to make the same point in reverse, if we have no reason to care about future pleasures and satisfactions, then there is no content to the idea that adding them up makes a "greater good."

30. Notice that if this reconstruction works, it traces normativity to self-government, and in that sense, anticipates the view I will argue for in section 3. But there are problems about the extent to which Hume can give a satisfactory explanation of this kind of motivation. These problems are explored in Charlotte Brown, "Is Hume an Internalist?" (*Journal of the History of Philosophy* 25 [1988]: 69–87) and "From Spectator to Agent: Hume's Theory of Obligation" (*Hume Studies* 20 [1994]: 19–35).

31. In ordinary discourse we move freely between characterizing ends as real and characterizing them in normative terms, for our practices of psychological attribution are themselves normatively loaded in a rather deep way. Suppose a graduate student comes to your office and says, in despair: "I'm going to give it up and leave graduate school, I am getting nowhere, it is all hopeless and I'd better just bag it and go to law school." You might reply "You don't *really want* to do that." You're only partly talking about psychic reality—you are also guiding, giving a pep talk, *trying to create* psychic reality, and you and your student *both* know that. You mean something like: "Don't give up: you are still capable of being what you think it's best for you to be." Or suppose a man asks "what do I really want?" and someone replies "to kill your father and make love to your mother." At least outside of the psychoanalytic context, this answer is a kind of category mistake; the man is not asking about the actual condition of his id. It is important, I think, to recognize how pervasive this normative use of psychological language is. "You can do it!" we cheer from the sidelines of one another's lives. "You're a reasonable person" I begin my argument, looking steadily into my opponent's eyes. In one sense, this sort of thing may seem to be, to use Bernard Williams's term, bluff. But if it is, then we ought to have a lot of respect for bluff. It plays an essential role in our efforts to hold ourselves and each other together, to stay on track of our projects and relationships in the face of the buffeting winds of local temptation and desire. See Williams, "Internal and External Reasons," in *Moral Luck*, p. 111 [this volume, 47].

32. This possibility wasn't canvassed in section 2 because it is not open to Hume or other empiricists. Hume thinks the will is merely the impression that accompa-

nies voluntary action (*Treatise* 3.1.1, 399); other empiricists think it is merely the last desire that emerges from deliberation. Either way, volition does not provide a distinctive account of what it means to be an end.

33. There are of course objections to this view, which I have discussed in section 3 of the Reply in my *Sources*, pp. 238–242.

34. Kant talks about both "the" categorical imperative and categorical imperatives plural; but he does not talk about "the" hypothetical imperative. I do not think that anything important turns on this fact: in this, as in much else in this part of the essay, I am in agreement with Thomas Hill, Jr., in his paper "The Hypothetical Imperative," essay 1 in *Dignity and Practical Reason* (Ithaca, NY: Cornell University Press, 1992). Yet there's a possible issue here, for we can imagine someone interpreting the asymmetry along these lines: "Kant thinks that although we can violate particular hypothetical imperatives, we could not in general violate 'the' hypothetical imperative and still count as beings with rational wills, and, that being so, 'the' hypothetical imperative isn't really an imperative. We can, however, violate the categorical imperative in general and still count as beings with rational wills, so it really is an imperative."

According to this view, the hypothetical imperative is merely descriptive of a rational will, while the categorical imperative is normative for but not descriptive of it, and so in effect represents a restriction on the will. It will emerge in due course that I think this view is wrong, both in fact, and as an interpretation of Kant's more considered position; but also that I think Kant had some tendency to fall into it in the *Groundwork*. As I will explain later, I think that both requirements, strictly speaking, represent procedures for constructing maxims rather than restrictions applied to them, and as such they are both constitutive and normative for the rational will. See note 60 for more on this topic.

35. I am using 'wish' here in an ordinary sense, to refer to a sort of idle desire. In *The Metaphysical Principles of Virtue*, Kant uses the term *Wunsch* (6:213), translated by both Mary Gregor and James Ellington (in his translation in *Ethical Philosophy* [Hackett, 1983]) as 'wish', to describe the state in which an end is rationally endorsed, as a morally good end, but in which the agent sees no way to pursue it. In that sense of 'wish', a wish does involve a commitment to taking the means, should they arise. There Kant says that willing includes both "choice"—an immediate determination to try and bring the object about—and "wish." See note 47.

36. Peter Railton also emphasizes the necessity of allowing for this kind of case in "On the Hypothetical and Non-Hypothetical in Reasoning about Belief and Action," in G. Cullity and B. Gaut, eds., pp. 72–73.

37. This remark gives rise to serious problems, for since our actions spring from our intelligible nature, it seems to make the existence of immoral actions a mystery. I take these problems up in "Morality as Freedom," reprinted in *Creating the Kingdom of Ends*. For a somewhat different resolution of the problem presented directly by

the passage at hand—the seeming implication that the laws of reason are not normative for purely rational beings—see note 28 of "Creating the Kingdom of Ends: Reciprocity and Responsibility in Personal Relations," reprinted in *Creating the Kingdom of Ends*, especially pp. 218–219. Despite what I say here, that note suggests that there are ways of reading almost all of Kant's remarks that makes them come out true on what I believe is his more considered view.

38. See, for instance, the selections from Samuel Clarke's *A Discourse Concerning the Unchangeable Obligations of Natural Religion, and the Truth and Certainty of the Christian Revelation*, The Boyle Lectures, 1705, in D. D. Raphael, ed., *British Moralists 1650–1800*, Volume 1 (Indianapolis, IN: Hackett, 1991), especially p. 199, Raphael paragraph 231.

39. In his later ethical works, in particular in the *Critique of Practical Reason* and *Religion Within the Limits of Reason Alone*, Kant rejects the claim that susceptibility to sensuous incentives is what makes the will imperfect. In the *Religion*, he denies the claim that sensibility is a source of evil (6:34–35). In the *Critique of Practical Reason*, he acknowledges the possibility of noumenal evil (see 5:96–100). He does not explicitly give up the view that the will's imperfection is what makes us subject to an *ought*, but it seems to me that he should have, for imperfection is a red herring here. Even a perfectly rational will cannot be conceived as *guided* by reason unless it is conceived as capable of resisting reason. It may be true, as Kant insists, that a divine will is not subject to temptation and so just would do what reason requires, but it is not true, as he seems to infer, that no *ought* applies to the divine will. There are a number of places where Kant suggests that we should only use 'ought' or 'duty' when the agent is necessitated *and* that this can only happen when the agent might want to resist the claim, some of them in the later writings. For example, in the *Metaphysical Principles of Virtue*, Kant says that we cannot have a duty to pursue our own happiness because we inevitably want it anyway (6:386). Obviously, one of the central ideas of this essay is that we can be subject to normative principles only if we can resist them, because without that possibility they cannot function as guides. But I do not agree with Kant that the absence of any specific temptation to resist them removes the possibility of resistance in the sense needed for normativity. It is not imperfection that places us under rational norms, but rather freedom, which brings with it the needed possibility of resistance to, as well as of compliance with, those norms.

40. Peter Railton makes the same point in "On the Hypothetical and Non-Hypothetical in Reasoning about Belief and Action," pp. 76–77.

41. Leaving aside the argument in the text, I am inclined to treat such eclectic proposals as prima facie objectionable. But not everyone would agree that we should expect to give parallel accounts of the normativity of all of the principles of practical reason. To take one example, in *A Theory of Justice* (Cambridge, MA: Harvard University Press, 1971), Rawls suggests that the principles of justice are chosen or (in

Rawls's later terms) constructed, while the principles of goodness are not (section 68). In Rawls's later work he avoids or anyway can avoid taking a position on this; constructivism is adopted only for political purposes and we do not need to say anything about general theories of rationality or the good.

42. For further discussion, see my "Acting for a Reason."

43. See my *Sources*, 3.2.1–3.2.3, pp. 92–98, for more on this point.

44. In other words, the rationalist who takes "trying to get" as a criterion of volition runs into exactly the same problem as the empiricist who takes "trying to get" as a criterion of the strongest desire. The problem might seem even more likely to arise for the rationalist, for "trying to get" is a more tempting criterion for volition than for the strongest desire. But if we make it our criterion of volition we can give no account of rationality.

45. This is just another way of saying that the analytic principle is false without the caveat.

46. A large part of the inspiration for this essay came from an occasion when Warren Quinn pressed me very hard on this point, and I am grateful to him for making me see the difficulty. Peter Railton takes on what is essentially the same problem that I am examining here in his "On the Hypothetical and Non-Hypothetical in Reasoning about Belief and Action." If we say that willing the means is *constitutive* of willing the end then irrationality is impossible, while if we say that willing the means is not constitutive of willing the end then there is room for a skeptic to ask why he must do it. Thus there seems to be no possibility of identifying a prescription which we must, but do not inevitably, follow. Obviously something has gone wrong.

47. One of the advantages of this account is that it makes it possible to explain how wish (*Wunsch*), as a species of rational willing, in the sense described in note 35 above, is possible. If willing were just the third-personal or objective act of *trying to get*, we could not make sense of this idea.

48. Willing an end is in this respect like making a promise, and, accordingly, the contortions Hume undergoes when he tries to discover what act of the mind "making a promise" is are relevant here (*Treatise* 3.2.5, 516–517). Hume ends by deciding that there is no such act, and this is not surprising, given that only third-personal options are available to him. Nietzsche's characterization of a promise as requiring a "memory of the will" is, by contrast, right on target. (See Walter Kaufmann and R. J. Hollingdale, trans., *On the Genealogy of Morals* in *On the Genealogy of Morals and Ecce Homo* [New York: Random House, 1967], p. 58.)

49. This is the basis of my account of Kant's argument for the Formula of Humanity in *Sources*, 3.4.7–3.5.0, pp. 120–125; and in my "Kant's Formula of Humanity," reprinted in *Creating the Kingdom of Ends*. The argument begins from

our commitment to the conception of our own ends as good, which is traced to the conception of ourselves as ends-in-ourselves, which is in turn traced to the view of our own wills as legislative.

50. It's worth noticing that here and elsewhere, Kant doesn't formulate the categorical imperative as a standard that is to be applied to our maxims, but rather as a way of regarding one's maxims or even of constructing them. But of course Kant does sometimes speak, in the *Groundwork*, as if the categorical imperative were a test we applied to our maxims after formulating them. On my reading, what this test shows is whether we are actually succeeding in performing an act of free will. Obviously, this requires more argument, but it is implied by Kant's view that the moral law *just is* the law of a free will. For an explication of this point, see my "Morality as Freedom," especially pp. 162–167; and *Sources*, 3.2.3, pp. 97–98.

51. This remark may arouse Wittgensteinian worries, associated with the private language argument, about whether I can make a law (just) for me. As I understand it, Wittgenstein's argument does not show that I cannot make a language which only I in fact understand, but rather that I cannot make a language that only I can understand. Any language I make for myself must be in principle teachable to others. The parallel point here would be that I cannot bind myself to a hypothetical imperative which no one else could be bound by, and this does have ethical implications, for it means that I cannot make something my end whose value cannot be communicated to others. This provides one route to one of the conclusions of this essay, namely, that hypothetical imperatives cannot exist unless there are also principles of reason determining our ends, since it means that nothing can be my end unless I can explain the reasons why I value it to others, and to do this I must have some reasons for valuing it. I have explored these points, albeit tentatively, in lecture 4 of *Sources* and in "The Reasons We Can Share: An Attack on the Distinction between Agent-Relative and Agent-Neutral Values," reprinted in *Creating the Kingdom of Ends*. I am grateful to Tamar Schapiro for alerting me to the possible relevance of this issue here.

52. A story: Jeremy settles down at his desk one evening to study for an examination. Finding himself a little too restless to concentrate, he decides to take a walk in the fresh air. His walk takes him past a nearby bookstore, where the sight of an enticing title draws him in to look at a book. Before he finds it, however, he meets his friend Neil, who invites him to join some of the other kids at the bar next door for a beer. Jeremy decides he can afford to have just one, and goes with Neil to the bar. When he arrives there, however, he finds that the noise gives him a headache, and he decides to return home without having a beer. He is now, however, in too much pain to study. So Jeremy doesn't study for his examination, hardly gets a walk, doesn't buy a book, and doesn't drink a beer. If your reply is that Jeremy is a distractible adolescent, and following desire is not always like this, Kant's reply in turn will be that it is only an *accident* when it is not.

The Normativity of Instrumental Reason

53. This is not the place to spell this thought out, but I also take the view I have put forward here to be essentially the same as the view that Plato advances in the *Republic*: namely, that the normativity of the principles of practical reason springs from, or reflects the fact that, the soul that does not follow them ultimately disintegrates. See also *Sources* 3.3.1, pp. 100–102. If one of the central arguments of this essay is also correct—that there can be no instrumental norms unless there are also unconditional norms—then this lends support to Plato's claim that a completely unjust soul would also be incapable of "achieving anything as a unit" (*Republic* 1.351e–352a). David Velleman's remark that "unless we can commit ourselves today in a way that will generate reasons for us to act tomorrow, we shall have to regard our day-old selves as either beyond the control of today's decisions or as passive instruments of them" makes a similar point to the one I am making in the text—that without the power of commitment implicit in conformity to the instrumental principle, the autonomous self shatters into a sequence of time slices (see "Deciding How to Decide," in G. Cullity and B. Gaut, eds., p. 46).

54. The last two paragraphs are lifted almost verbatim from section 1 of my Reply in *Sources*, pp. 219–233; see especially pp. 230–231.

55. Peter Railton makes a parallel point—that someone who rejects the requirement that his beliefs be true is rejecting the project of having beliefs—in his "On the Hypothetical and Non-Hypothetical in Reasoning about Belief and Action," pp. 56–59.

56. Recent work in the philosophy of mind and action has been hampered by the presupposition that belief and desire are analogous states, the one demanding that the mind match the world, and the other demanding that the world match the mind. As the view in the text suggests, I think that the analog of belief is volition or choice; desire is more properly construed as the analog of perception. Of course, the view advanced in the text—that belief and choice must be understood as first-personal commitments if we are to make sense of rationality—has important implications for the philosophy of mind.

57. I owe the linguistic example to Barbara Herman.

58. I also discuss the idea of constitutive norms in *Sources*, section 2 of the Reply, pp. 234–237, and in "Self-Constitution in the Ethics of Plato and Kant," reprinted in *The Constitution of Agency*.

59. If, contrary to the argument of this essay, the instrumental principle were the only norm constitutive of rational action, then rational action would essentially be production, and action that was good qua action would be action that achieved its end. Aristotle explicitly rejects that view in book 6 of the *Nicomachean Ethics*, and this is part of his reason for thinking that actions are subject to special standards—ethical standards—that mere productions as such are not. For a discussion of the

similarity between Aristotle and Kant on this point, see my "From Duty and for the Sake of the Noble: Kant and Aristotle on Morally Good Action."

60. This remark will naturally evoke the question what then becomes of Kant's claim that the moral law is synthetic, while the instrumental principle is analytic. In fact, on my reading, it may seem unclear what distinction is marked by those terms. In one way, I make it sound as if both the moral principle and the instrumental principle are analytic, for both are, if Kant's arguments succeed, constitutive of rational agency. In another way, I make it sound as if both the moral principle and the instrumental principle are synthetic, for both depend on the freedom inherent in the deliberative standpoint, and this parallels the way that synthetic principles of the understanding depend on the spatio-temporal structure of intuition. Choices are presented to us *in* freedom, just as objects are presented to us *in* space and time. On the other hand, Kant's more mundane point still holds: the necessity of taking the means is analytically derivable from our commitment to the end, while our commitment to the end is not in that way analytically derivable from anything. On my reading, however, this difference throws little important light on the source of their normativity. I am not certain what to say on this point, but I am inclined to think that my argument shows the distinction to be less important than Kant thought. I am indebted here to a discussion with Sidney Morgenbesser.

I also want to thank Sidney Morgenbesser, Joseph Raz, and Michael Thompson for pointing out a related and in a way more radical implication of the argument here, which is that it tends to break down the distinction between the different principles of practical reason described at the outset of this essay. If the argument of this essay is correct, moral or unconditional principles and the instrumental principle are both expressions of the basic requirement of giving oneself a law, and bring out different implications of that requirement. This lends support to Onora O'Neill's claim, in "Reason and Politics in the Kantian Enterprise," that the categorical imperative is the supreme principle of reason in general (see O'Neill, *Constructions of Reason* [Cambridge: Cambridge University Press, 1989], essay 1). But it also raises issues about the distinguishability of different kinds of practical rationality and irrationality. I am inclined to think that the right thing to say about this parallels what I take to be the right thing to say about Aristotle's theory of the unity of the virtues. There is really only one virtue, but there are many different vices, different ways to fall away from virtue, and when we assign someone a particular virtue, what we really mean is that she does not have the corresponding vice. In a similar way, there is only one principle of practical reason, the categorical imperative viewed as the law of autonomy, but there are different ways to fall away from autonomy, and the different principles of practical reason really instruct us not to fall away from our autonomy in these different ways.

61. In his "On the Hypothetical and Non-Hypothetical in Reasoning about Belief and Action," pp. 62ff., Peter Railton distinguishes between "High Brow" accounts of practical reasoning, according to which rational agents necessarily aim at the

good, and "Low Brow" accounts, like Hume's, according to which rational agents may aim simply at the satisfaction of their desires or ends. Because I have argued that the instrumental principle cannot stand alone, my argument favors High Brow views. The case of the heroic existentialist, however, shows that the sense in which it does so is rather thin. The heroic existentialist's ends are not merely the objects of his desires, but rather of his will, so he is not merely given them by nature: he has endorsed them, and to that extent he does see them as things he has reason to pursue. But since he has not endorsed them for any further reason, it would be a bit of a stretch to say that he thinks they are good. The claim in the text—that the heroic existentialist's position is hard to live with—shows why I think that my argument also gives rise at least to pressure towards a more substantively High Brow view. I say a little more about this in the Epilogue below.

62. I have been pressed on this point by quite a few people who read or heard drafts of this essay, but I would particularly like to thank Allan Gibbard.

63. See also *Sources*, 4.4.1–4.4.2, pp. 160–164.

64. Here again I would especially like to thank Allan Gibbard.

65. The question whether there are substantive, constitutive norms of autonomy, and whether those coincide with moral norms, is a complex question that may be divided into a number of different parts, responsive to different ways in which the claim can be challenged. For an account of these different challenges, and of my own attempts to respond to them, see *Sources*, section 1 of the Reply, pp. 220–222.

66. See section 2, pp. 216–217, and section 3, p. 228. This is part of the reason why Plato thinks that the soul completely ungoverned by reason ultimately becomes "tyrannical." See note 53 above and *Republic*, book 9.

67. This essay leaves me with many debts. Final revisions were made while I was a Fellow at the University Center for Human Values in Princeton, for whose support I am deeply grateful. I discussed the essay or parts of the essay with audiences at the Twenty-First Annual Meeting of the Hume Society, with commentary by Charlotte Brown; the St. Andrews conference on Ethics and Practical Reason, with commentary by Ralph Wedgwood; at the Central Division Meetings of the American Philosophical Association, with commentary by Allan Gibbard; at the Fellows Seminar at the Center for Human Values in Princeton, with commentary by Michael Thompson; at the Philosophy Departments at Bowling Green University, the University of California at Irvine, the University of California at Los Angeles, the University of Michigan, and the University of Reading; at the Columbia Legal Theory Workshop; and at the New York University Colloquium in Law, Philosophy, and Political Theory. I am grateful to all of these audiences, and my commentators especially. I also received generous and extremely helpful written comments from Annette Baier, Kurt Baier, Alyssa Bernstein, Barbara Herman, Brad Hooker, Peter

Hylton, Arthur Kuflik, Andrews Reath, Tamar Schapiro, Allen Wood and the editors of *Ethics and Practical Reason*, in which it first appeared, Garrett Cullity and Berys Gaut. I also received excellent written comments in addition to their presented commentaries from Charlotte Brown and Allan Gibbard. I would also like to thank John Broome, Erin Kelly, Edward McClennan, Sidney Morgenbesser, John Rawls, Joseph Raz, and Michael Robins for useful remarks made in discussion, and Barbara Herman for extensive discussion in addition to her written comments. I thank all of these people for their incisive criticisms, many of which I have not been able to answer, and for their interest and support. Finally, I would like to reiterate my gratitude to the late Warren Quinn for pressing me to clarify Kant's account of the hypothetical imperative.

11 The Possibility of Practical Reason

J. David Velleman

Suppose that reasons for someone to do something must be considerations that would sway him toward doing it if he entertained them rationally.[1] And suppose that the only considerations capable of swaying someone toward an action are those which represent it as a way of attaining something he wants, or would want once apprised of its attainability.[2] These assumptions, taken together, seem to imply that the only considerations that can qualify as reasons for someone to act are considerations appealing to his antecedent inclinations[3]—that is, his desires or dispositions to desire.[4]

This conclusion amounts to an admission that reason really is, as Hume put it, the slave of the passions,[5] and Hume's conclusion is one that many philosophers hope to avoid. Some try to avoid the conclusion by rejecting one of the premises from which it appears to follow.[6] Others prefer to keep the premises while arguing that the conclusion doesn't actually follow from them.[7]

In my view, the question whether reasons do or do not depend on an agent's inclinations should simply be rejected, because it embodies a false dichotomy. This dichotomy has recently come to be formulated in terms introduced by Bernard Williams.[8] In Williams's terminology, 'internal' reasons are those which count as reasons for someone only by virtue of his antecedent inclinations; 'external' reasons are those which count as reasons for someone independently of his inclinations.[9] The Humean conclusion implies that all reasons are internal, in this sense, and it is therefore called internalism; its denial is called externalism.[10] My thesis is that we do not in fact have to choose between the two.

Christine Korsgaard has pointed out that the foregoing argument doesn't necessarily yield any constraint on what counts as a reason for acting.[11] It may instead yield a constraint on who counts as a rational agent.

The first premise of our argument doesn't entail that if a consideration fails to influence someone, then it isn't a reason for him to act; it entails that if a consideration fails to influence someone, then either it isn't a reason for him to act or he hasn't entertained it rationally. The inclinations that would make an agent susceptible to the influence of some consideration may therefore be necessary—not to the consideration's being a reason for him—but rather to his being rational in entertaining that reason. And our premises may consequently imply that an agent's inclinations determine, not what he has reason for doing, but whether he is rational in his response to the reasons he has.

Korsgaard favors the latter conclusion over the former.[12] In denying the dependence of reasons on inclinations, she qualifies as an externalist, in Williams's terminology.[13]

Korsgaard's critique of Williams suggests a version of externalism that goes something like this.[14] Being a rational agent entails having various motives, including a preference for one's own greater good[15] and an acceptance of moral principles.[16] A rational agent is influenced by a reason for doing something when, for example, he considers some respect in which doing it is morally required; and this consideration can influence him because an inclination to abide by moral requirements is partly constitutive of his rationality. If an agent lacks this inclination, its absence won't prevent him from having moral reasons for acting: moral requirements will still count as reasons for him to act. Rather, lacking an inclination to abide by moral requirements will render the agent irrational, by making him insensitive to this particular kind of reason.

The Externalist's Burden of Justification

One liability of this model is that it must identify particular features of an action as constitutive of reasons for taking it, whether an agent cares about them or not, and it must then criticize an agent as irrational if he should fail to care about those features. The model thus incorporates specific normative judgments, to the effect that one ought to be inclined toward courses of action with the features in question.

What entitles the externalist to build these normative judgments into his model of practical reason? As Williams puts it, "Someone who claims the constraints of morality are themselves built into the notion of what it is to be a rational deliberator cannot get that conclusion for nothing."[17]

Korsgaard does not try to get this conclusion for nothing, however. On the contrary, she insists that the normative judgments built into her conception of practical reason will require an "ultimate justification," which the externalist hopes to provide.[18] Indeed, the possibility of such a justification is the centerpiece of her paper.

Korsgaard's quarrel with Williams, after all, is that he prematurely discounts the possibility of justifying externalism. In assuming that an agent's imperviousness to a consideration impugns its status as a reason, rather than the agent's rationality, Williams assumes that its status as a reason cannot be established independently. For if a consideration could be certified as a reason for someone irrespective of whether he's susceptible to it, then his lack of susceptibility would thereby come to impugn his rationality instead. Yet certifying something as a reason for someone irrespective of his susceptibilities would amount to showing that it is an external reason, and hence that externalism is true. When Williams presupposes the impossibility of such a showing, he is presupposing the impossibility of justifying externalism. His case for internalism thus rests on antecedent skepticism about the alternative.

So Korsgaard argues—cogently, I believe. Yet even if she is right that the case for internalism rests on skepticism about externalism, the question remains whether we aren't entitled to be skeptical. What are the prospects for showing that something is a reason for someone whether or not he has the inclinations to which it would appeal? How will the externalist demonstrate that there are considerations by which any agent ought to be moved?

One might think that an externalist could avoid this burden of justification by avoiding the identification of any particular considerations as reasons, or of any particular inclinations as rational. But I doubt whether this strategy can work.

The version of externalism outlined above incurs a burden of justification because it judges an agent to be irrational unless he is inclined to be swayed by particular, substantive features of actions, whose value or importance may be open to question. All that externalism needs to say, however, is that the inclination responsible for the influence of reasons is one that's essential for the agent's rationality. Does this inclination have to be an inclination to be swayed by particular considerations, specified by their substance? Maybe it can be an inclination to do whatever is supported by reasons as such, or whatever is rational as such.

The inclination that's now being proposed isn't an inclination to do things with any particular features, other than the feature of being favored by reasons (whatever they may consist in) or the feature of being rational (whatever that is). Hence the claim that this inclination is essential to an agent's rationality doesn't call for any justification. For how could rationality fail to require an inclination to do what's rational, or what's favored by reasons?

Unfortunately, this version of externalism doesn't ultimately succeed in shedding the burden of justification, since it doesn't avoid the need to specify what counts as a reason or a rational action. To be sure, all it requires of a rational agent is that he be inclined to act in accordance with reasons or rationality as such. But in order for reasons to influence an agent by way of this inclination, he must recognize them as reasons, or as evidence of rationality, and so he needs some criterion of what counts as a reason or as a rational action. And until such a criterion is supplied, the proposed version of externalism will be nothing but the trivial assertion that rationality is a disposition to be influenced by reasons.

What's needed to save this version of externalism from triviality is a criterion specifying what it is about an action that makes it rational or constitutes a reason for taking it. And this criterion will once again require justification.

At this point, the externalist may attempt to repeat his earlier evasive maneuver. He is committed to the existence of a criterion by which an agent can recognize reasons or rational actions; but is he committed to its being a substantive criterion, which would have to be justified? Maybe an agent can recognize reasons or rational actions by their satisfying the generic concepts of what it is to be a reason or a rational action as such.[19]

Yet this strategy of continually postponing controversy is unlikely to help. Asking the agent to identify a rational action under the guise of rationality as such, or to identify a reason for acting under the guise of a reason as such, would be somewhat like asking him to hunt for something described only as 'the quarry', or to play a game with an eye to something described only as 'winning'. It would be to assign him a task with a formal object but no substantive object—and hence with no object at all.

The Object of Practical Reasoning

The formal object of an enterprise is a goal stated solely in terms of, or in terms that depend on, the very concept of being the object of that enterprise.[20] Thus, for example, winning is the formal object of a competitive game, since winning just is the concept of succeeding in competition.

Similarly, the formal object of a search or hunt is the quarry, and the formal object of a question is the answer.

Any enterprise that has a formal object must have a substantive object as well—that is, a goal that is not stated solely in terms that depend on the concept of being the object of that enterprise.[21] In the case of a competitive game, there must be a substantive object of the game, something that constitutes winning but cannot simply consist in winning, so described. A game whose object was specifiable only as 'winning' wouldn't have an object—that is, wouldn't have any object in particular. And if a game had no particular object, then there would be no such thing as winning it, and so it wouldn't be a fully constituted competitive game. Similarly, a hunt whose object was specifiable only as 'the quarry' wouldn't be a fully constituted search, and the question "What is the answer?" isn't by itself a fully constituted question.

Since practical reasoning is an enterprise at which one can succeed or fail, it must have an object against which success or failure can be measured. What, then, is the object of practical reasoning?

One might suggest that practical reasoning has the object of figuring out what to do, or answering the question "What shall I do?" But this suggestion either misstates the object of practical reasoning or states it in merely formal terms.

The statement that practical reasoning has the object of figuring out what to do may simply mean that it has the object of arriving at something to do or of issuing in an action. So interpreted, however, the statement is mistaken, since issuing in an action—some action or other—is not the object of practical reasoning. Issuing in an action may be what makes reasoning practical, but the object of such reasoning is, not to issue in just any action, but to issue in some actions rather than others.

The object of practical reasoning must therefore be to arrive at a privileged action or an action in some privileged class. And when 'figuring out what to do' is interpreted as expressing this object, it turns out to be a merely formal specification, since 'what to do', so interpreted, simply means the correct or privileged thing to do, the thing whose discovery is being attempted. Hence there must be a further, substantive specification of the action or kind of action that practical reasoning aims to identify. A mode of reasoning whose goal was specified solely as 'figuring out what to do' would be like a search whose object was specified solely as 'figuring out where to look', or a question whose object was specified solely as 'figuring out how to reply'.

Similar remarks apply to the notion that practical reasoning aims at figuring out the best thing to do.[22] This notion is correct if 'the best thing to do' means 'the privileged action'—that is, the action that uniquely satisfies the standard of success for this very reasoning. But in that case, it merely expresses the formal object of the enterprise. There can be an enterprise of figuring out the best thing to do, in this sense, only if that enterprise also has a substantive standard of success, just as there can be an enterprise of figuring out the best way to reply only if there is a substantive question, and there can be an enterprise of figuring out the best place to look only if there is a substantive quarry.

Of course, 'the best thing to do' might be interpreted, alternatively, as already expressing a substantive value: it might mean, for example, 'the action that's optimific', in the sense that it contributes most to the agent's welfare or to the welfare of everyone. But in that case, the notion that practical reasoning aims to figure out the best thing to do will once again express a value judgment that calls for justification.

What, then, about rational action or reasons for acting? Can the object of practical reasoning be to identify a rational thing to do, or a thing that one has reason for doing?

The concepts of rational action and reasons for acting are potentially confusing in that they can have both generic and specific uses. If we specify a substantive kind of action as the object of practical reasoning, then we can grant it the honorific 'rational', so that the phrase 'rational action' names actions of the specified kind. Similarly, if we specify substantive features that practical reasoning looks for in an action, we can grant the honorific 'reasons for acting' to those features. Practical reasoning will then turn out to aim at the rational thing to do, or at what there is reason for doing, but only because 'rational' and 'reasons' are names for substantive objects.

What cannot be the aim of practical reasoning is rational action merely as such—that is, action conceived as rational in the generic sense, rather than in a sense defined by a specific standard. The generic concept of rational action is just the concept of action that would issue from competent practical reasoning. Until there is something that counts as competence in practical reasoning, nothing counts as a rational action in the generic sense. And competence in practical reasoning can be defined only in relation to the object of the enterprise, since competence is a disposition toward success. To be indicative of competent practical reasoning is to be indicative of practical reasoning that's well suited to achieving its object. Defining the object of practical reasoning as action that's rational in this sense would thus be to string definitions in a circle, leaving the object of practical reasoning still undefined. It would be like trying to teach someone a game by telling him that the object was to make a competent showing; whereas what counts as a competent showing always depends on the substantive object of the game.[23]

Similarly, the sole aim of practical reasoning cannot be action supported by reasons merely as such—that is, reasons conceived under the generic concept expressing what it is to be a reason. The generic concept of a reason for acting is the concept of something that warrants or justifies action. And to justify something is to show or indicate it to be just—that is, in accordance with a *jus*, or rule of correctness. Until there is something that constitutes a correct conclusion or a correct inference, there can be nothing that constitutes justifying a conclusion or an inference, and so there can be nothing that constitutes a reason for a conclusion or an inference, in the generic sense. So, too, until there is something that constitutes correctness in actions, or in outcomes of practical reasoning, there can be nothing that satisfies the generic concept of a justification for action, or a justification in practical reasoning; and so there can be nothing that satisfies the generic concept of a reason for acting.

Justifying a Substantive Conception of Reasons

This argument suggests that the externalist cannot indefinitely postpone giving substantive characterizations of rationality or reasons. The externalist must at some point provide practical reasoning with a substantive standard of success, which will either consist in or give rise to a substantive account of the features that constitute reasons for an action. The externalist will then have to justify his normative judgment that an agent ought to be swayed by consideration of the specified features.[24]

What's more, the requisite justification is unlikely to emerge from an analysis of concepts such as *reason* or *rational action*. As we have seen, these are formal concepts that have no application except in relation to a substantive object or standard of success. Because these concepts implicitly require such a standard to be supplied, we can hardly expect to deduce it from them, any more than we should expect to deduce the object of a game from the mere concept of winning, or the object of a hunt from the mere concept of a quarry.[25]

I cannot prove that the task of justifying an externalist conception of reasons is impossible, but I think it's going to be awfully hard. I'm just a fainthearted externalist, I guess. Being fainthearted, however, I want to consider whether the benefits of externalism can be obtained without the burdens. I shall therefore turn to an alternative conception of practical reason, which straddles the line between internalism and externalism.

Outline of an Alternative View

Suppose that we want to frame a conception of reasons that isn't relativized to the inclinations of particular agents. That is, we want to identify particular things that count as reasons for acting simpliciter and not merely as reasons for some agents rather than others, depending on their inclinations.

One way to frame such a conception is to name some features that an action can have and to say that they count as reasons for someone whether or not he is inclined to care about them. The problem with the resulting conception, as we have seen, is that it entails the normative judgment that one ought to be inclined to care about the specified features, on pain of irrationality, and this normative judgment requires justification.

The advantage of internalism is that it avoids these normative commitments.[26] It says that things count as reasons for someone only if he is inclined to care about them, and so it leaves the normative question of whether to care about them entirely open. Yet if we try to leave this question open, by defining things as reasons only for those inclined to care about them, we'll end up with a definition that's relativized to the inclinations of particular agents—won't we?

Not necessarily. For suppose that all reasons for acting are features of a single kind, whose influence depends on a single inclination. And suppose that the inclination on which the influence of reasons depends is, not an inclination that distinguishes some agents from others, but rather an inclination that distinguishes agents from non-agents. In that case, to say that these features count as reasons only for those who are inclined to care about them will be to say that they count as reasons only for agents—which will be to say no less than that they are reasons for acting, period, since applying only to agents is already part of the concept of reasons for acting. The restriction on the application of reasons will drop away from our definition, since it restricts their application, not to some proper subset of agents, but rather to the set of all agents, which is simply the universe of application for reasons to act.

The foregoing paragraph is an outline for a conception of reasons for acting—a bare outline that needs filling in. The remainder of this article will be devoted to filling it in, at least to some extent, though not, I admit, to the extent that's needed. I shall begin by making a digression into the subject of theoretical reasoning. My hope is that we can understand reasons for acting by analogy with reasons for belief.[27]

The nature of reasons for belief, and the inclination that mediates their influence, are fairly clear. The object of theoretical reasoning is to arrive at true belief;[28] and since true belief needn't be defined in terms of success in theoretical reasoning, it constitutes a substantive rather than formal standard of success.[29] Reasons for a particular belief are recognized by their perceived relevance to this substantive standard of success, as considerations that appear to guarantee or probabilify the truth of the belief.[30] And these considerations influence a person's beliefs by virtue of an inclination to believe what seems true. Here, then, are considerations of a single kind and a single inclination to mediate their influence.

Perhaps we should ask whether the absence of this inclination would undermine the existence of reasons for belief or would alternatively undermine the believer's claim to rationality.[31] The answer to this question would determine whether reasons for belief were internal or external reasons. If someone weren't inclined to believe what seemed true, would signs of truth in a proposition no longer count as reasons for him to believe it? Or would he no longer qualify as a rational believer?

Both, I think—which goes to show that the question incorporates a false dichotomy. I shall argue that the dichotomy should be replaced with a subtler account of theoretical reasoning, along the following lines.

If someone isn't inclined to believe what seems true on a topic, he is no longer subject to reasons for believing things about it; but he is no longer subject to reasons for belief about it, I shall argue, because he is no longer a believer about it at all, and a fortiori no longer a rational believer.[32] He isn't in the business of forming beliefs on the topic, to begin with, unless he is inclined to believe what seems true about it.

Thus, reasons for believing something apply only to those who are inclined to believe what seems true on the topic, and so they are like internal reasons; but to say that they are reasons only for those who are so inclined is just to say that they are reasons only for potential believers on the topic—which is to say no less than that they are reasons for believing, period. Reasons for belief can therefore be identified independently of the inclinations of individuals, and so they are like external reasons, too.

The foregoing paragraph is a bare outline for an account of theoretical reasoning, and this outline also needs filling in. In order to fill it in, I shall have to explore the sense in which being inclined toward the truth is essential to being a subject of belief. I therefore turn to a different thesis associated with the name of Bernard Williams, the thesis that belief is an attitude that "aims at the truth."[33]

The Constitutive Aim of Belief

The grounds for this thesis emerge when we try to distinguish belief from the other propositional attitudes. One difference between belief and other attitudes is that it entails regarding its propositional object as true.

The difference between believing that P and desiring that P, for example, is that the former attitude treats P as a report of how things are, whereas the latter treats P as a mandate for how things are to become.[34] Desire takes its propositional object as representing *facienda*—things that aren't the case but are to be brought about. By contrast, belief takes its propositional object as representing *facta*—things that are the case and in virtue of which the proposition is true.[35]

This conception of belief is correct as far as it goes, but it doesn't go far enough. It's incomplete because regarding a proposition as true is involved in many cognitive attitudes, including not only belief but also other attitudes from which belief must still be distinguished. Assuming a proposition—say, for the sake of argument—entails regarding it as a report rather than a mandate, as a truth rather than something to be made true. Even imagining that P entails regarding it as a completed rather than a to-be-completed truth. One hasn't imagined that P unless one has regarded P as reflecting how things are, and hence as true. Yet to assume that P or imagine that P is not to believe it, and so regarding a proposition as true must not be sufficient for belief.[36]

Of course, there is a sense in which things that are merely assumed or imagined are not regarded as really true. But the relevant sense is not that they aren't regarded as true at all; it's rather that they are regarded as true but not really—regarded as true, that is, but not seriously or in earnest. What distinguishes a proposition's being believed from its being assumed or imagined is the spirit in which it is regarded as true, whether tentatively or hypothetically, as in the case of assumption; fancifully, as in the case of imagination; or seriously, as in the case of belief.

What's the difference between seriously regarding a proposition as true and doing so in some other spirit? Here is the point at which belief is distinguished from other attitudes by its aim.

The sense in which fantasies and assumptions aren't serious is that they entail regarding a proposition as true—or accepting the proposition, as I shall put it—without sensitivity to whether one is thereby accepting the truth. We assume a proposition when we regard it as true for the sake of thereby framing a possibility to be entertained in argument or inquiry and when we can therefore be said to accept it for polemical or heuristic purposes. We imagine a proposition when we regard it as true for the sake of thereby stimulating or vicariously satisfying our desires and when we can therefore be said to accept it for recreational or motivational purposes. But we believe a proposition when we regard it as true for the sake of thereby getting the truth right with respect to that proposition: to believe something is to accept it with the aim of doing so if and only if it really is true.

Thus, the purpose or aim with which a proposition is regarded as true is partly constitutive of the resulting attitude toward the proposition. It determines whether the proposition is being accepted hypothetically, as in assumption; playfully, as in imagination; or seriously, as in belief. These attitudes can therefore be conceived as having two tiers. The first tier, which they share and by virtue of which they differ as a group from the conative attitudes, is the attitude of regarding a proposition as true—the attitude of bare acceptance. The second tier, in which the various cognitive attitudes differ among themselves, encompasses the different aims with which a proposition can be accepted.[37]

To say that our attitude toward a proposition is partly constituted by the aim or purpose with which we accept the proposition is not to say that the aim is itself an attitude of ours, or that acceptance is an action. This point cannot be overemphasized.[38] Acceptance is a mental state whose aim may be emergent in the cognitive mechanisms by which that state is induced, sustained, and revised. For example, if our acceptance of a proposition is regulated by mechanisms performing their function of therein framing a possibility to be tested, then our acceptance may have a heuristic aim whether or not we have heuristic motives or take any action toward heuristic ends. Similarly, if our acceptance of a proposition is regulated by mechanisms performing their function of therein tracking the truth of the proposition, then it may have an epistemic aim whether or not we have or act on such an aim.[39] In short, our acceptance of a proposition may be aimed at the truth by our cognitive faculties rather than ourselves.

This possibility suggests that one can have beliefs—aimed, as required, at the truth—while also being indifferent, at another level, to the truth of those beliefs. There are two ways of being indifferent to the truth, of which only one is an obstacle to believing.

To begin with, I can accept a proposition in a manner indifferent to its truth, thereby forming an assumption or fantasy rather than a belief. I am not then proceeding with indifference to the truth of a belief; I'm proceeding with indifference to the truth of what I accept, thereby falling short of belief altogether.

In another sense, however, I can be indifferent to the truth of something conceived as a belief. I cannot believe something without accepting it seriously—in an attempt, by me or my cognitive faculties, to arrive at acceptance of the truth—but I can still have further, second-order goals with respect to this attempt. For example, I can try to ensure that an attempt to accept what's true with respect to a proposition will lead to acceptance of that proposition whether it's true or not. This second-order attempt, to manipulate the outcome of a first-order attempt to accept what's true, is precisely what I undertake when I try to get myself to hold a particular belief irrespective of its truth. And in this case I am indifferent to the truth specifically of a belief, because my indifference is directed at the success of something conceived as an attempt at accepting the truth.[40]

I can thus fail to care about the truth of my beliefs. Yet if indicators of truth in a proposition are reasons for believing it, then indifference to the truth of my beliefs would seem to leave me insensitive to reasons, and hence irrational. My conception of theoretical reason would thus seem to resemble externalist conceptions of practical reason, in mandating a particular concern or inclination as required for rationality.

But this appearance is misleading. The conception of reasons for belief as indicators of truth doesn't imply that indifference to the truth of my beliefs would be irrational. Indifference to the truth of my beliefs would not in fact make me insensitive to the associated reasons for believing.

Of course, evidence for the truth of some belief may not sway me toward wanting or getting myself to hold that belief, if I'm indifferent to its truth. But we don't necessarily think that indicators of truth are reasons for such second-order measures as wanting or getting myself to hold beliefs. We identify them as reasons for *believing*, which are simply reasons for accepting something in the course of an attempt to arrive at acceptance of what's true. And insofar as I or my cognitive faculties attempt to arrive at the truth on a topic, that attempt will already make me potentially sensitive to indicators of the truth; whereas if no such attempt is in the works, the topic will be one on which I am not in the business of holding beliefs, in the first place.

What provides my sensitivity to reasons for believing, then, is not a second-order aim of having true beliefs but rather the first-order aim that makes my acceptance of something into a belief. And if this first-order aim is lacking from my approach to some topic, then I am not irrationally insensitive to reasons for belief about it; I am out of the business of having beliefs about it altogether, and so I am no longer subject to reasons for belief about it at all. Thus, my conception of theoretical reason doesn't condemn this form of indifference as irrational, either.

In identifying something as a reason to believe a proposition, we are implicitly identifying it as a reason for a potential believer, someone who is in a position to believe or disbelieve the proposition at issue. Now, someone can be in a position to form a belief even though he lacks an interest in the truth of that belief—the second-order interest in the success of this attempt at accepting what's true. But he is not prepared to believe or disbelieve a proposition if he isn't prepared for an attempt to accept what's true with respect to it. Thus, he is not a potential believer with respect to a proposition—and hence not subject to reasons for believing it—in the absence of an inclination that would cause him to be swayed by indicators of its truth.

So when we say that indicators of truth are reasons for belief, we aren't making a normative judgment about whether to be inclined toward the truth; we're saying that they're reasons for someone only if he is inclined toward the truth, since we're identifying them as reasons of a kind whose universe of application is the set of potential believers, who are constitutively truth inclined. The question whether to be inclined toward the truth on some topic—and hence whether to be subject to reasons for belief about it—is left entirely open.

In some sense, theoretical reasoning now seems to fit the model of internalism. Indicators of truth count as reasons for someone to believe only if he has a cognitive inclination that makes him susceptible to their influence. And reasons that apply to someone only if he's susceptible to their influence are supposed to be internal reasons.

At this point, however, the distinction between internal and external reasons is out of its depth, so to speak. Reasons for belief are dependent on a particular inclination, all right, but they're dependent on that inclination which makes one a believer. They don't depend on one's peculiar inclinations *as* a believer—on one's second-order attitudes toward or preferences among beliefs.

Indeed, the dependence of theoretical reasons on a cognitive inclination does not justify relativizing them to particular believers at all. The inclination on which these reasons depend is constitutive of belief itself, and to that extent they are reasons simply *for belief* rather than for any particular person to believe.[41] If something counts in a particular epistemic context as a reason to believe that P, then it counts in that context as a reason simply to believe that P, and not just for this or that believer to do so, since all potential believers of P are alike in the cognitive inclination that gives application to such a reason.

The question of whether reasons for belief are internal or external reasons thus presents a false dichotomy. Reasons for belief are like internal reasons in that they exist and exert an influence only in relation to a particular inclination; but they are like external reasons in that the inclination on which they depend is embedded in the attitude of belief, so that they can count as reasons for belief per se, in abstraction from motivational differences among individual believers.

Maybe the way to understand the status of reasons for belief is to consider an analogy between belief and another enterprise that's partly constituted by a substantive aim. Consider reasons for sacrificing a pawn in the game of chess.

Reasons for sacrificing a pawn depend for their existence on a goal or aim, and in this respect they look like internal reasons. But the goal on which reasons for this move depend is partly constitutive of the move itself, because sacrificing a pawn is by definition a move in the game of chess, which is partly defined by its object; and because the move is by definition a sacrifice, which it can be only in relation to the object of the game. Reasons for sacrificing a pawn therefore exist in abstraction from the temperament of any particular player: they are reasons simply for the move itself, and in this respect they look like external reasons, too.

A player may have second-order aims with respect to his success or failure in a particular game of chess. He may even have the goal of losing a game—if his opponent is a sensitive eight-year-old, for example. But in order to lose a game of chess, he must stay in the game, by continuing to pursue its object, however insincerely or ineffectually. And so long as he is pursuing that object, he will have the inclination that answers to reasons for sacrificing a pawn.

A player can lose his susceptibility to those reasons only by giving up the associated object—moving his pieces around aimlessly, for example. In that case, he will in effect have quit the game: his opponent will say, not just "You're letting me win," but "You're not playing any more." Once the player has quit the game of chess, however, he has quit the only game in which pawns can be sacrificed, and his resulting insensitivity to reasons for sacrificing a pawn will not make him irrational. To someone who isn't playing chess, reasons for sacrificing a pawn simply don't apply.

In sum, reasons for sacrificing a pawn apply to anyone with the capacity to do so, irrespective of his inclinations about how to exercise that capacity. They apply to him only because he has an inclination that lends them an influence, of course, but the requisite inclination is the one that makes him a chess player, not one that determines his individual style of play.

Applying the Analogy to Practical Reasoning

I think that practical reasoning occupies the same middle ground between internalism and externalism. That is, reasons for acting apply to someone only because he has an inclination that lends them an influence, but the requisite inclination is the one that makes him an agent, not one that determines his individual course of action.

This account of practical reason simply follows the structure of theoretical reason, as analyzed above. That analysis began with the claim that belief is distinguished from other cognitive states by a substantive goal, and then it claimed that an inclination toward this goal creates the susceptibility necessary to the application of reasons for believing. Perhaps, then, action can be distinguished from other forms of behavior by a substantive goal, and an inclination toward this goal can create the susceptibility necessary to the application of reasons for acting. In that case, reasons for acting would be considerations relevant to the constitutive aim of action, just as reasons for believing are indicators of truth, which is the constitutive aim of belief. And anyone who wasn't susceptible to reasons for acting, because he had no inclination toward the relevant aim, wouldn't be in a position to act, anyway, and therefore wouldn't be subject to reasons for acting; just as anyone who has no inclination toward the truth isn't in a position to believe and isn't subject to reasons for belief.

The account rests, of course, on the initial claim that behaviors qualify as actions by virtue of having a particular aim. Let me say a word about the philosophical point of such a claim.

The point of specifying which behaviors qualify as actions is not, I think, to delineate the extension of 'action' or 'to act' as used in ordinary language. These terms are used quite loosely, in application not only to paradigm cases of action, in which human agency is exercised to its fullest, but also to marginal cases, in which agency is exercised only partially or imperfectly. The fundamental question in the philosophy of action is not how imperfect an exercise of agency can be while still qualifying as an action. The question is the nature of agency itself, and agency, like any capacity, fully reveals its nature only when fully exercised. We therefore want to know what makes for a paradigm case of action, a full-blooded action, an action par excellence.

I claim that what makes for an action, in this sense, is a constitutive aim. This claim sounds odd, to say the least. We may think that a full-blooded action must have some goal or other;[42] but we tend to think that its status as an action doesn't depend on what goal it has. Action, we tend to think, is just behavior aimed at some goal, any goal.

In my opinion, however, we are mistaken in assuming that behavior approaches full-blooded action by having a goal of the sort that varies from one action to another. Simply being goal-directed is not a mark of action.

Consider a case of unintentional behavior. An old friend unexpectedly walks into your office, and surprise lights up your face: your eyes widen, a smile flashes, an exclamation escapes your lips. These reactions just happen to you, and they may even hit you with an aftershock of surprise. Now suppose, instead, that you encounter your friend on the quad, recognizing him as he approaches. You are moved to the same reactions, but you now have a chance to modulate them or compose them into an intentional expression of surprise.

Take another case of unintentional behavior. Say, a child accidentally brushes a glass off of the table, and your hand shoots out to catch it. Everything happens so fast that you see your hand catching the glass before you fully realize that the glass is falling. Now suppose, finally, that another child—an older and sassier child—hefts the glass with a smirk and calls, "Here, catch!" You then undertake the same behavior, but as a fully intentional action.

The first instance in which you catch the glass is an instance of behavior directed at a goal, but it isn't a full-blooded exercise of your agency. Unlike your reflexive expression of surprise, which springs *out of* the emotion of surprise but not *toward* any purpose or goal, the reflexive extension of your hand is aimed at something—namely, preventing the glass from smashing on the floor.⁴³ Despite being goal-directed, however, this behavior still lacks some element that's necessary to full-blooded action. So what makes for action is not simply being goal-directed.

The question is what's missing from this goal-directed behavior. In my view, what's missing is some additional goal that every action shares, no matter what its other, contingent goals may be.

There is an ancient thesis along these lines, to the effect that action, no matter where it aims, must thereby aim at the good.⁴⁴ This thesis identifies a constitutive goal of action—the good—and it thus implements the strategy of analysis that I favor. But in this implementation, the strategy fails to achieve its purpose, since it doesn't avoid the twin pitfalls of internalism and externalism.⁴⁵

The thesis that action constitutively aims at the good can be interpreted in at least two ways. It may simply mean that an action must aim at something, which consequently counts as good in the sense of being that whose attainment will make the action a success. But this sense of the word 'good' is a formal sense, denoting whatever is the aim of an action. It identifies no particular thing at which every action must aim, and hence no particular kind of consideration as capable of influencing anyone insofar as he is an agent. If the thesis uses this formal sense of the word 'good', then the considerations that it classifies as reasons will vary along with the good being aimed at. Reasons will then depend for their application on one's inclinations as an agent, as they do under internalism.

In order to avoid this consequence of internalism, the ancient thesis would have to identify a substantive goal for action, by saying that every action aims at something conceived as good in a sense independent of its being the aim. But when the thesis uses a substantive sense of the word 'good' in this manner, it characterizes action as necessarily well-intentioned, thus ruling out various kinds of perversity. To those who believe, as I do, that behavior can still qualify as action even if its end-in-view is conceived as bad, the thesis will now appear to be burdened with controversial normative commitments, like the version of externalism considered above.⁴⁶

The ancient thesis goes wrong, I think, in treating the constitutive aim of action as something shared or jointly promoted by all of an agent's other ends-in-view, as if it were an ultimate or all-encompassing end. If action is to be constituted by an aim, however, that aim cannot be an end at all.

An end is something conceived by an agent as a potential object of his actions. It is therefore something that one cannot have unless one already is an agent, in a position to act, and so it cannot be something that one must already have in order to occupy that position. If action is to be constituted by an aim, that aim must be, so to speak, subactional or subagential—something that a subject of mere behavior can have, and by having which he can become an agent, as his behavior becomes an action.

This subactional aim can be discerned, I think, in our contrasting pairs of behaviors. It is that which the unintentional behaviors are missing in comparison with the corresponding full-blooded actions.

Intuitively speaking, what these behaviors lack is that, while directed *at* various things, they are not directed *by* you. When the glass is brushed off the table, for example, behavior aimed at arresting its fall is initiated and completed before you know it, and so you have no chance to take control of that behavior. In the intentional instance, the same goal-directed behavior occurs, but it occurs under your control.

The kind of control at issue here is not the sensorimotor process that adjusts ongoing behavior in light of perceived progress toward a desired outcome. That process of real-time adjustment is simply eye-hand coordination, which occurs in both the intentional and the reflexive cases. What's missing from the reflexive case is conscious direction on your part, which is something other than eye-hand coordination. When goal-directed behavior proceeds under this conscious control, it becomes a full-blooded action, rather than a well-coordinated reflex.[47] And behavior that isn't directed at a goal can become an action in the same fashion. The smile that springs spontaneously from your emotion of surprise isn't aimed at any result, but it, too, can be transformed into a full-blooded action if it is brought under your conscious control.

Now, if an action comprises behavior of which you take control, then taking control of your behavior cannot itself be an action; otherwise, a vicious regress will ensue. Yet controlling your behavior is indeed an activity: it's something that you do. The reason why the falling glass leaves you no time to perform a full-blooded action is that, although it leaves you time to stick out your hand, it doesn't leave you time to do something else that's essential to a full-blooded action—that is, to exercise conscious control of your catch. Hence when you catch the glass intentionally, you must be doing two things: extending your hand in order to avert a mishap and exercising control over that behavior.

Let me reiterate that I am using the noun 'activity' and the verb 'to do' in senses that do not imply the performance of a full-blooded action. To suggest that an action comprises behavior on which you perform the action of exercising control would be absurd. But you do many things that aren't actions—such as when you reflexively stick out your hand to catch a falling glass or smile out of surprise. And exercising conscious control over your behavior is indeed something that you do, in this thin sense of the verb.

I therefore suggest that our ordinary concept of a full-blooded action is in fact the concept of two, hierarchically related activities. Action is like the corporate enterprise of work performed under management: it's behavior executed under conscious control. And just as the corporate enterprise includes both a basic work activity and the higher-order activity of managing that work (neither of which is itself a corporate enterprise), so full-blooded action comprises both a basic activity and the higher-order activity of controlling it (neither of which is itself an action).

This analysis of action suggests how action might have a constitutive goal. According to the analysis, various actions involve various behaviors—directed, in many cases, at various goals—but they also share an additional, higher-order activity, the activity of consciously directing these behaviors. This activity is constitutive of action, in the sense that its addition is what makes a full-blooded action out of a merely reflexive or unintentional movement. If this higher-order activity entails the pursuit of a goal, then there may indeed be a constitutive goal of action.[48]

What I have in mind here is not an ulterior goal or aim toward which behavior is consciously directed, as a corporation's work activity might be managed toward the end of maximizing profits. The executive officers can still manage the work of a corporation without having the goal of profit maximization, in particular, and so this goal is not itself essential to work's being performed under management. Similarly, a goal toward which behavior is consciously directed may not be essential to the behavior's being consciously directed, insofar as behavior might be consciously directed at other goals or no goal in particular.

What I have in mind is a goal that must be pursued if behavior is to be consciously directed at all. This goal will not be one of the agent's ends-in-view, nor will it be something on which those ends converge. Rather, it will be something whose pursuit is ancillary to theirs—something whose pursuit transforms them, from outcomes sought unconsciously or reflexively, into ends at which action is consciously directed.

The Constitutive Goal of Action

What is this goal? A hint lies in the fact that consciously controlling one's behavior is not something that one can do without aiming to.[49] Maybe, then, the aim without which there is no conscious control of behavior is simply the aim of being in conscious control of one's behavior. If so, then the constitutive aim of action will turn out, in Kantian fashion, to be autonomy.[50] And considerations will turn out to qualify as reasons—also in Kantian fashion—by virtue of their relevance to our autonomy rather than their relevance to our interests or our good.[51]

These remarks are merely suggestive at best, and this is not the place to develop them into a full account of autonomy or its role as the constitutive goal of action.[52] I can only sketch how they might be developed.

My sketch begins with the conception of autonomy as conscious control over one's behavior. Consciously controlling one's behavior involves two elements: being conscious of one's behavior and controlling it. How are these elements connected?

One possibility is that they aren't connected at all. Conscious control might just be the sum of two independent elements, control over what one is doing and consciousness of what one is doing. Another possibility is that exercising control over one's behavior is what brings it to consciousness. One might control what one is doing and thereby become conscious of that behavior.

The problem with these possibilities is that they would leave an agent's knowledge of his behavior dependent on the usual inbound channels, such as perception of the behavior itself or introspection on the process by which it is directed. And as many philosophers have noted, an agent's knowledge of his behavior is not receptive knowledge: an agent knows what he is doing, as they say, without observation.[53]

The work of these philosophers points to a third possibility for the relation between self-control and self-awareness. Maybe consciousness of what one is doing is that by which one exerts control. Consciously controlling one's behavior would then be—not just controlling it and also, or thereby, becoming conscious of it—but rather having a *controlling consciousness* of one's behavior, a guiding awareness of what one is doing. This possibility would account not only for an agent's self-control but also for the quality of his self-awareness, since his knowledge of what he was doing would be, so to speak, directive rather than receptive knowledge.[54]

But how can knowledge be directive? For the answer, let me return to my earlier account of cognition. (I'll give the answer in this section and then illustrate it in the next.)

Consciousness or knowledge must be a cognitive state, and so it must involve regarding propositions as true rather than as to be made true. It must also be a serious cognitive state, regarding propositions as true in an attempt thereby to get the truth right. Indeed, the success that's implied in the concept of consciousness or knowledge is success in this very attempt, to regard as true what really is true.

But there are two ways of attempting to regard as true, or accept, what really is true. One way is to accept a proposition in response to its being true; the other is to accept a proposition in such a way as to make it true. Note that the latter method does not entail regarding the proposition as *to be made* true. It entails attempting to make the proposition true by regarding it as such, but attempting to make a proposition true by regarding it as true is quite different from regarding it as to be made true. The proposition is regarded as fact, not *faciendum*, and so it is accepted, in a cognitive rather than conative attitude. What's more, the proposition is accepted seriously, not hypothetically or frivolously. For in attempting to accept something so as to make it true, one attempts to reach the position of accepting a genuine truth, no less than when one attempts to accept something in response to its being true. In either case, one's acceptance aims at correspondence between what's regarded as true and what is true, and so it is a serious cognitive attitude, whose success deserves to be called knowledge.[55]

How can one regard a proposition as true in such a way as to make it true? Well, when one accepts a proposition in response to its truth, one registers the influence of evidence and other reasons for belief, thereby manifesting an inclination to conform one's acceptance to the facts. Accepting a proposition in such a way as to make it true would simply require a converse inclination, to conform the facts to one's acceptance. And one can indeed be inclined to conform the facts to one's acceptance, if the proposition accepted is about one's own behavior. One need only be inclined to do what one accepts that one will do. If one has this inclination, then accepting that one will do something can be a way of making this proposition true, and it can therefore be an attempt at accepting the truth.

This admittedly convoluted proposal can be applied to the contrast between your reflexively and intentionally catching that glass. In both cases, your desire to save the glass causes your hand to extend. In both cases, you're aware of this causal sequence, since you're aware of extending your hand in order to save the glass. But in only one of the cases is your knowledge directive, or your behavior autonomous.

When you extend your hand reflexively, you react before you know it, but then you observe your reaction. Extending your hand in order to save the glass causes you to accept the proposition that you're doing so. When you react intentionally, however, acceptance precedes behavior: you accept that you'll extend your hand to save the glass, and this acceptance is what prompts you to do so.

In the latter case as well as the former, your acceptance is an attempt to accept something true. You're not just hypothesizing or fantasizing that you'll extend your hand: you're seriously regarding it as true that you will extend it. Of course, your acceptance of this proposition is not an attempt to accept something that's true antecedently; it's an attempt to accept something whose truth will follow as a result. But it is not therefore less serious as an attempt to accept a truth. If the proposition accepted comes true, then its acceptance is a cognitive success—an instance of directive knowledge.

In sum, instead of reacting before you know it, you react after and because you know it, and that's what makes your behavior an autonomous action. You act autonomously because you extend your hand in, and out of, a knowledge of what you're doing.

But why would your extending a hand to save the glass result from your accepting that you would do so?

Suppose that you have an inclination toward being in conscious control of your next move. This inclination will inhibit you from doing anything out of other motives until you've accepted that you're going to—precisely so that you'll do it only after and because you know it, and hence under conscious control. Once you accept that you're going to do something, however, the inclination toward being in conscious control will reinforce your other motives for doing it, since doing what you've accepted you'll do is what puts consciousness in control. Your inclination toward conscious control is thus converted, from an inhibition against doing something into a motive in favor of doing it, by your accepting that you'll do it. Accepting that you'll extend your hand to save the glass can therefore prompt you to do so.

Here, then, is how autonomy can serve as the constitutive goal of action. The goal-directed movement of your hand comes under your conscious control because it is prompted by your accepting that you will perform such a movement. And it is prompted by that acceptance because of your inclination toward conscious control of what you're doing—which is just an inclination toward autonomy. Your movement thus becomes autonomous precisely by manifesting your inclination toward autonomy; and in becoming autonomous, it becomes a full-blooded action. A full-blooded action is therefore behavior that manifests your inclination toward autonomy, just as a belief is a cognitive attitude that manifests your inclination toward the truth.

My view is that your inclination toward the constitutive goal of action also mediates the influence of your reasons for acting, just as your inclination toward the truth mediates the influence of your reasons for belief. Your reasons for acting can be displayed as the premises of a practical inference:

I want to save that glass.
I could save the glass by extending my hand.
So I'll extend my hand.

Since the premises of this inference are about how to fulfill a desire of yours, they sound like reasons that Williams would call internal. But in my view, they don't influence you in quite the way that internal reasons are supposed to.

    Here is how internal reasons are supposed to work. The first premise of your inference is about a desire of yours: "I want to save that glass." The second premise is about the means to the object of that desire: "I could save the glass by extending my hand." The desire mentioned in the first premise and the belief expressed in the second combine to motivate the action mentioned in your conclusion: "So I'll extend my hand." According to the internalist tradition, this process of motivation is the very process whereby reasons for acting exert their influence as reasons.

    This conception of how reasons exert their influence encourages a particular reading of the statements displayed above. Since the influence of reasons is conceived as the motivational influence of desire and belief, and since the second premise expresses the operative belief, the first premise is read as expressing the associated desire.[56] Similarly, the conclusion is sometimes read as expressing—or standing in for—the action itself, which is said to be the real conclusion of your inference.[57] The three displayed statements are thus interpreted as expressions of your reasons and of the action that they influence you to perform.

I don't dispute the traditional account of how desire and belief motivate behavior. My quarrel is with the claim that when desire and belief motivate behavior, they exert the influence of reasons.[58] You extend your hand, I agree, out of a desire for something and a belief about how to attain it. But you can extend your hand out of a desire and belief even when you do so reflexively, without knowing what you're doing or why, and hence without the benefit of practical reasoning.

In my view, extending your hand out of a desire and belief is the underlying behavior over which you may or may not exercise conscious control—the underlying work that may or may not come under your executive management. And practical reasoning is the process by which you exercise conscious control over this activity in some cases but not others. If you extend your hand without any guiding knowledge of what you're doing, then even though your behavior is motivated by a desire and belief, it isn't under your conscious control, and so it isn't a full-blooded action. Your behavior amounts to a full-blooded action only when it is performed in, and out of, a knowledge of what you're doing—or, as I have said, after and because you know it.[59]

This view of practical reasoning encourages a different interpretation of the statements displayed above. The first premise expresses a desire-based reason, in my view, but the reason expressed is not the desire itself. The reason expressed by "I want to save that glass" is your recognition of the desire.

This recognition is a reason because, together with the belief expressed in your second premise, it forms a potentially guiding awareness of what you would be doing in extending your hand. The awareness that you want to save the glass, and that extending your hand would save it, puts you in a position to frame a piece of directive knowledge—"I'm extending my hand in order to save the glass"—a proposition that you can now make true by accepting it. Your awareness of the desire thus presents the behavior of extending your hand in a form prepared for your conscious control, as a potential object of your directive grasp. It presents the behavior, if you will, as fit for (en)action, given the constitutive aim of action, just as theoretical reasons present a proposition as fit for belief, given the constitutive aim of belief.

This view of practical reasoning requires far more elaboration and defense than I can offer here. Its only relevance to this article is that it implements the compromise that I favor between internalism and externalism. For according to this view, even desire-based reasons for acting derive their influence from an inclination other than the desires on which they are based.

The reasons displayed above are desire-based in the sense that they mention your desire to save the glass and the means to fulfilling that desire. Yet their influence as reasons is not mediated by the desire that they mention.

Your desire to save the glass does exert a motivational influence in this example. But its influence as a motive contributes to the underlying activity of extending your hand in order to save the glass—the activity that comes under the control of your practical reasoning. And the contribution of your reasons to the control of this activity is distinct from the contribution of your motives to the activity itself.

What exerts the influence of a reason in this example is the recognition that you want to save the glass. And this recognition doesn't influence you by engaging your desire to save the glass. Wanting to save the glass is a motive that can be engaged by considerations about how to save it, not by the recognition that you want to. The recognition that you want to save the glass engages a different inclination, your inclination toward autonomy—toward behaving in, and out of, a knowledge of what you're doing. And it thereby exerts a rational influence distinct from the motivational influence of the desire that it's about.

Now, if desire-based reasons derive their influence from something other than the desires on which they are based, then perhaps the same influence is available to considerations that aren't based on desires at all. Perhaps considerations that aren't about your inclinations can still provide potentially directive knowledge.

Such considerations would still have the influence of reasons, by virtue of their capacity to engage your inclination toward autonomy. But they wouldn't depend for their influence on the inclinations that differentiate you from any other agent, and they wouldn't be about such inclinations, either. They might therefore be reasons that Williams would call external.

My thesis, in any case, is that reasons for acting shouldn't be classified as external or internal, since they don't conform to the assumptions underwriting the use of these terms. A reason applies only to those whom it can influence, but its application is not therefore limited to agents of a particular temperament. The inclination that makes one susceptible to a reason for acting is just the inclination that makes one an agent.

Acknowledgments

I am grateful to Sonja Al-Sofi, Stephen Darwall, Jennifer Church, Paul Boghossian, Alfred Mele, Elijah Millgram, Derek Parfit, Peter Railton, Sigrún Svavarsdóttir, Nicholas White, Bernard Williams, Stephen Yablo, and several anonymous referees for helpful discussions of the issues raised in this article. Earlier versions of the paper were presented to the philosophy departments at New York University, Stanford University, the University of Illinois at Urbana-Champaign, and the University of Houston; and to the philosophy faculty colloquium at the University of Michigan. Some of the material was also presented to Michael Bratman's 1993 National Endowment for the Humanities seminar on intention. I have benefited from comments received on all of these occasions, especially the comments of Frances Kamm, Fred Dretske, Rachel Cohon, Allan Gibbard, Sally Haslanger, David Hills, Tomis Kapitan, Jeff McMahan, Patrick Hays, and David Phillips. Finally, I received many helpful comments from participants in a graduate seminar taught at the University of Michigan in the winter of 1993. Work on this article was supported by the Edna Balz Lacy Faculty Fellowship at the Institute for the Humanities, University of Michigan.

Notes

1. This principle is meant to apply only to complete sets of reasons, not to reasons taken individually. That is, if a particular consideration counts as a reason only in the context of a larger set or series of considerations, then it need not be capable of swaying the agent unless it is considered in that context. The assumption that 'reasons' denotes complete sets of reasons will be in force throughout the following discussion. I shall also rely on the success-grammar of the word 'considerations': considerations are, by implication, true considerations—or, as I shall sometimes call them, facts.

2. The last clause is meant to account for cases like this: "It may be true of me that were the aroma of fresh apple pie to waft past my nose I would be moved to discover its source and perhaps to try to wangle a piece. It does not follow from this, however, that before I smell the pie I desire to eat it or to eat anything at all" (Stephen L. Darwall, *Impartial Reason* [Ithaca, N.Y.: Cornell University Press, 1983], p. 40). Here apple pie is something that the agent doesn't yet want but will want once he considers its attainability, and so considerations about how to obtain it are capable of influencing him in the requisite way. I take it that this mechanism is what David Hume regarded as the first of the two ways in which reason can influence action: "Reason . . . can have an influence on our conduct only after two ways: Either when

it excites a passion by informing us of the existence of something which is a proper object of it; or when it discovers the connexion of causes and effects, so as to afford us means of exerting any passion" (*A Treatise of Human Nature*, ed. L. A. Selby-Bigge [Oxford: Clarendon, 1978], p. 459).

3. Note that I am not using the word 'inclination' in its Kantian sense. I am using it as the generic term for conative or motivational states of all kinds.

4. The argument presented here is discussed at length in Darwall, *Impartial Reason*, esp. chaps. 2 and 5.

5. Hume, p. 415. I do not claim that the argument offered above for Hume's conclusion should necessarily be attributed to Hume.

6. The most frequent target has been the second assumption, which is sometimes called the Humean theory of motivation. See, e.g., Thomas Nagel, *The Possibility of Altruism* (Princeton, N.J.: Princeton University Press, 1970); John McDowell, "Are Moral Requirements Hypothetical Imperatives?" in *Proceedings of the Aristotelian Society, Supplementary Volume* 52 (1978): 13–29; Darwall, *Impartial Reason*, chap. 5; Rachel Cohon, "Are External Reasons Impossible?" *Ethics* 96 (1986): 545–556. For arguments defending this assumption, see Michael Smith, "The Humean Theory of Motivation," *Mind* 96 (1987): 36–61; and Alfred Mele, "Motivational Internalism: The Powers and Limits of Practical Reasoning," *Philosophia* 19 (1989): 417–436. Arguments against the first assumption are rare, although some philosophers have argued against a related assumption applied to moral requirements rather than reasons for acting. See, e.g., William Frankena, "Obligation and Motivation in Recent Moral Philosophy," in *Essays on Moral Philosophy*, ed. A. I. Melden (Seattle: University of Washington Press, 1958), pp. 40–81; and David Brink, *Moral Realism and the Foundations of Ethics* (Cambridge: Cambridge University Press, 1989), chap. 3.

7. See Christine Korsgaard, "Skepticism about Practical Reason," *Journal of Philosophy* 83 (1986): 5–25 [this volume, chap. 2].

8. Bernard Williams, "Internal and External Reasons," in *Moral Luck* (Cambridge: Cambridge University Press, 1981), pp. 101–113 [this volume, chap. 1]; "Internal Reasons and the Obscurity of Blame," in *Making Sense of Humanity and Other Philosophical Papers* (Cambridge: Cambridge University Press, 1995), pp. 35–45; "Replies," in *World, Mind, and Ethics: Essays on the Ethical Philosophy of Bernard Williams*, eds. J. E. J. Altham and Ross Harrison (Cambridge: Cambridge University Press, 1995), pp. 185–224 [this volume reprints pp. 186–194 as chap. 4].

9. Here I am choosing one of two possible readings that have occasioned considerable confusion in the literature. The confusion can be traced to the casual manner in which Williams introduces the term 'internal reason'. Williams carefully defines what he calls the 'internal interpretation' of the statement 'A has reason to ϕ'. Interpreted internally, the statement implies that A has some motive that can be

served by his φ-ing. Williams then says "I shall also for convenience refer sometimes to 'internal reasons' and 'external reasons'" ("Internal and External Reasons," p. 101) [this volume, 37]. But Williams never explains how a scheme for interpreting reason-attributions can be transformed into a scheme for classifying reasons themselves.

Two different schemes of classification have suggested themselves to philosophers writing in this area. One scheme classifies as internal any reason that can engage one of the agent's motives so as to sway him toward doing that for which it is a reason. The other scheme classifies as internal only those reasons whose status as reasons depends on their capacity to engage the agent's motives in this way. An internal reason, on this latter scheme, is one that wouldn't be a reason if the agent didn't have a motive that it could engage. The difference between these schemes of classification can be illustrated by the case of an agent who has both a reason and a corresponding motive. According to the first scheme, this reason is definitely internal, since the agent has a motive corresponding to it. According to the second scheme, however, this reason could still be external, if it would remain a reason for the agent whether or not he had the motive.

Only the latter scheme captures the entailment that distinguishes Williams's internal interpretation of reason-attributions. For on the former scheme, the agent's having a reason doesn't require him to have a motive. If he lacks a corresponding motive, then his reason doesn't necessarily cease to be a reason, on this scheme; it simply ceases to be internal. Yet under the internal interpretation of reason-attributions, the agent must have the motive in order for it to be true that he has a reason at all. I therefore prefer the latter scheme of classification.

10. Note that this usage differs somewhat from that of other philosophers, for whom the term 'internalism' refers to our first premise, requiring reasons to have the capacity of exerting an influence.

11. Korsgaard, "Skepticism about Practical Reason" [this volume, chap. 2]. For other discussions of Williams, see Cohon, "Are External Reasons Impossible?" and Rachel Cohon, "Internalism about Reasons for Action," *Pacific Philosophical Quarterly* 74 (1993): 265–288; Martin Hollis, *The Cunning of Reason* (Cambridge: Cambridge University Press, 1987), chap. 6; Brad Hooker, "Williams' Argument against External Reasons," *Analysis* 47 (1987): 42–44; John McDowell, "Might There Be External Reasons?" in Altham and Harrison, eds., pp. 68–85 [this volume, chap. 3]; Elijah Millgram, "Williams' Argument against External Reasons," *Noûs* 30 (1996): 197–220.

12. See also Michael Smith, "Reason and Desire," *Proceedings of the Aristotelian Society* 88 (1988): 243–258. Smith seems to think (pp. 248–252) that he and Korsgaard disagree, but I think that they don't. In particular, Smith believes that Korsgaard rejects the second premise, that considerations can influence an agent only in conjunction with his conative attitudes. But I don't interpret Korsgaard as rejecting this premise. Korsgaard never claims that a consideration, or belief, can move an agent

without the help of a conation or motive; what she claims, I think, is that the desires and values mediating the influence of a consideration need not be ordinary motives, of the sort that are directed at the agent's ends, since they can instead constitute his virtue of rationality.

Williams responds to this argument but seems to misunderstand it. He seems to think that if all rational agents have, say, a motive for doing what's right, then the fact that an action is right will turn out to be an internal reason for them, after all: "If this is so, then the constraints of morality are part of everybody's [motivational set], and every correct moral reason *will be* an internal reason" ("Internal Reasons and the Obscurity of Blame," p. 37). But here Williams adopts a sense of the phrase 'internal reason' that fails to capture his own internal interpretation of reason-attributions, as I have explained in n. 9, above. In this sense, an internal reason is one with the capacity to engage an agent's motives, but not necessarily one whose very status as a reason depends upon that capacity.

I believe that Korsgaard is working with the alternative (and, to my mind, preferable) sense of 'internal reason', according to which an internal reason is one whose status as a reason depends on its capacity to engage the agent's motives. And what Korsgaard envisions is that reasons for behaving morally will qualify as reasons whether or not people have motives that such reasons can engage. Even if people happen to have the relevant motives, reasons for behaving morally will still be independent of them, in Korsgaard's view, and such reasons should be classified as external.

For a misinterpretation similar to Williams's, see John Rawls, *Political Liberalism* (New York: Columbia University Press, 1993), p. 85, n. 33.

13. I do not mean that Korsgaard would call herself an externalist, since she uses the term in a somewhat different sense. See n. 10 above.

14. I don't mean to claim that Korsgaard holds this version of externalism. Korsgaard's "Skepticism about Practical Reason" seems designed to be independent, in many respects, of her larger metaethical project. It therefore leaves open various versions of externalism that Korsgaard herself would not necessarily endorse. Indeed, I suspect that the version of externalism discussed here in the text corresponds to what Korsgaard rejects under the label 'dogmatic rationalism' in "The Normativity of Instrumental Reason," in *Ethics and Practical Reason*, eds. G. Cullity and B. Gaut (Oxford: Oxford University Press, 1997) [this volume, chap. 10].

15. Korsgaard, "Skepticism about Practical Reason," p. 18 [this volume, 63].

16. Ibid., p. 22 [this volume, 66].

17. Williams, "Internal Reasons and the Obscurity of Blame," p. 37.

18. Korsgaard, "Skepticism about Practical Reason," p. 22 [this volume, 66].

19. I believe that Korsgaard proposes this very strategy ("Skepticism about Practical Reason," pp. 20–21) [this volume, 65–66]. And I believe that there may be a way—a

distinctively Kantian way—of making the strategy work. I discuss this Kantian version of the strategy briefly in n. 25, below. Note, then, that the present argument does not purport to prove that the strategy in question is unworkable. It's meant to justify doubts about the strategy, by showing just how difficult it will be to carry out.

20. I suspect that the argument offered in this section is related to the argument offered by Williams on pp. 109–110 of "Internal and External Reasons" [this volume, 44–45]. Because I don't fully understand the relevant passage, however, I hesitate to attribute the argument to Williams.

21. The distinction between the formal and substantive aims of practical reason is discussed by Derek Parfit in *Reasons and Persons* (Oxford: Clarendon, 1984), pp. 3, 9, 37. As David Gauthier has pointed out ("Rationality and the Rational Aim," in *Reading Parfit*, ed. Jonathan Dancy [Oxford: Blackwell, 1997]), Parfit is less than clear on the relation between these aims; in particular, Parfit doesn't appear to believe that the substantive aim of practical reason, as identified by a particular theory, is a specification of the formal aim. Like Gauthier, I prefer to use the phrase 'substantive aim' for that which specifies what it is to achieve the formal aim.

22. This notion is, for example, the basis of Donald Davidson's conception of practical reasoning. See his *Essays on Actions and Events* (Oxford: Clarendon Press, 1980). The problems mentioned here are discussed further in the text accompanying n. 45 below.

23. Of course, we could introduce a substantive conception of competent practical reasoning—a substantively specified procedure, adherence to which constitutes good reasoning. In that case, however, the definition of rational action as that which would issue from competent practical reasoning will become a substantive concept, which once again requires justification.

24. The notion that practical reasoning is framed by a criterion of success for actions is discussed by David Gauthier in "Assure and Threaten," *Ethics* 104 (1994): 690–721. I discuss Gauthier's treatment of this notion in my "Deciding How to Decide," in G. Cullity and B. Gaut, eds.

25. Kant's conception of practical reason, as I understand it, is an attempt to circumvent this problem, by using the concept of a reason, not to identify which features are reasons, but rather to identify which features aren't, and by replacing the rule of acting for reasons with a rule of not acting for nonreasons. On Kant's conception, as I understand it, the object of practical reasoning is to act on any consideration but one whose being a reason would entail a contradiction. It's like a hunt whose object is to locate anything but that which could not possibly be a quarry. Perhaps the generic concepts of a quarry or a reason can indeed serve this modest role.

26. I don't mean to imply that internalism avoids all normative commitments. In "Skepticism about Practical Reason" [this volume, chap. 2], Korsgaard suggests that the instrumental principle of adopting the means to one's ends is a substantive norm; she defends this point at length in "The Normativity of Instrumental Reason" [this volume, chap.10]. But even if internalism has to justify requiring us to care about the means to what we already care about, it avoids the further and heavier burden of justifying any requirements to care about particular things.

27. The analogy between theoretical and practical reason is being pursued independently by my colleague Peter Railton, with somewhat different results. See his "What the Noncognitivist Helps Us to See the Naturalist Must Help Us to Explain," in *Reality, Representation, and Projection*, ed. John Haldane and Crispin Wright (New York: Oxford University Press, 1993), pp. 279–300, pp. 292ff.; "A Kind of Nonsubjective Reason?" in *Essays in Honor of Kurt Baier*, ed. J. Schneewind (La Salle: Open Court, 1996); and "On the Hypothetical and Non-Hypothetical in Reasoning about Belief and Action," in G. Cullity and B. Gaut, eds. David Gauthier also discusses the analogy, but he ultimately rejects it ("Assure and Threaten," pp. 699–702).

28. Some may be inclined to think that the object of theoretical reasoning is not true belief but empirically adequate and explanatorily fruitful belief, or belief of some other kind. My argument doesn't depend on the outcome of this disagreement. What matters for my purposes is that theoretical reasoning aims at some outcome specified substantively (i.e., not in terms of its being the object of theoretical reasoning or belief).

29. The claim that truth isn't defined in terms of success in theoretical reasoning is potentially controversial. It must be rejected by those who hold a pragmatist conception of truth as the eventual deliverance of rational inquiry. In my view, however, the pragmatist conception renders theoretical reasoning vacuous, like a game whose only object is winning.

30. In the case of inductive reasoning, of course, we may have trouble saying what relevance reasons have to the truth of a belief. Nevertheless, such reasons count as reasons for a belief because they make it seem true, even if we cannot say how or why. (An alternative way of handling this case would be to point out that inductive reasons satisfy a substantive procedural criterion of correctness in inductive inference. See n. 23 above.)

31. Williams raises this question and seems to suggest that the absence of an inclination toward the truth would undermine the existence of reasons for belief ("Internal Reasons and the Obscurity of Blame," p. 37). This is, of course, the internalist answer to the question.

32. I believe that Korsgaard makes a similar point ("The Normativity of Instrumental Reason," p. 42) [this volume, 229]. In passages such as this, where Korsgaard

seems to be pursuing a strategy like the one I am developing here, I begin to doubt whether she really is an externalist, in Williams's sense of the term. My reasons for this doubt will be explained in the text, below, when I explain why I do not regard the present strategy as a version of externalism.

33. Bernard Williams, "Deciding to Believe," in *Problems of the Self* (Cambridge: Cambridge University Press, 1973), 136–151.

34. This difference between belief and desire can be obscured by the fact that desiring that P entails desiring P to be true, just as believing that P entails believing it to be true. These locutions obscure the difference between belief and desire because they use the infinitive 'to be', which is required for indirect discourse, to replace what would be different moods of the copula in direct speech. In believing P to be true, one believes in its completed truth, as would be expressed by the indicative statement that P is true; whereas in desiring P to be true, one desires its to-be-completed truth, as would be expressed by the optative that it *be* true. Thus, although we can speak either of believing or of desiring P to be true, transposing these statements from *oratio obliqua* to *oratio recta* reveals an underlying difference in the relation that P is taken as bearing to the world.

35. The language used in this contrast should not be overinterpreted. To say that belief involves regarding a proposition as true, or that desire involves regarding it as to be made true, is simply to articulate our concepts of belief and desire as propositional attitudes. We express the fundamental similarity among these content-bearing mental states by describing them as ways of regarding propositional contents, and we express the differences among them by differentiating among the ways in which those contents can be regarded. The resulting locutions should not be understood as positing any particular mental architecture, least of all an inner eye that squints at propositions or raises its eyebrow at them so as to regard them in different ways. Rather, these locutions simply translate our terms for propositional attitudes into a common vocabulary, in which their similarities and differences can be clearly expressed. To say that belief entails regarding a proposition as true is therefore not to commit ourselves to any particular theory about which physical, neurological, or otherwise subdoxastic states make up the mental state of belief. It commits us only to a view about what such states must amount to if they are to constitute belief—namely, that they must amount to the state of regarding a proposition as true. For recent discussions of this phenomenon, commonly called 'direction of fit', see Lloyd Humberstone, "Direction of Fit," *Mind* 101 (1992): 59–83; and G. F. Schueler, "Pro-attitudes and Direction of Fit," *Mind* 100 (1991): 277–281. Note that I understand direction of fit somewhat differently from these and other authors. For a fuller treatment of the differences, see my "The Guise of the Good," *Noûs* 26 (1992): 3–26; and n. 55 below.

36. For related discussions of the similarities and differences among these cognitive states, see Jennifer Church, "Judgment, Self-Consciousness, and Object Indepen-

dence," *American Philosophical Quarterly* 27 (1990): 51–60; and Mark Leon, "Rationalising Belief," *Philosophical Papers* 21 (1992): 299–314.

37. An example that can help to illustrate this conception of the propositional attitudes appears in Bernard Williams's discussion of "Imagination and the Self" (in *Problems of the Self*, pp. 29–31). Williams compares two men who imagine assassinating the Prime Minister in the person of Lord Salisbury. One man imagines assassinating the Prime Minister but falsely believes that Lord Salisbury occupies that position; the other man, who knows that Lord Salisbury isn't Prime Minister, nevertheless imagines him to be, while also imagining a similar assassination. "On the purely psychological level," Williams remarks, "the same visualisings, the same images, could surely occur in both cases. The difference lies rather in how the story is meant" (p. 31). According to my account, "how the story is meant" should be understood in terms of the aim with which it is regarded as true that Lord Salisbury is Prime Minister. Each subject includes this identification in his "story," and thereby regards it as true. But one subject regards it as true for the sake of correctly identifying the Prime Minister, whereas the other regards it as true for the sake of his own entertainment.

38. The point will be lost on those who believe that any goal-directed movement, mental or physical, automatically qualifies as an intentional action. I reject this view, as will become clear on pp. 715ff [this volume, 264ff.]. My reasons for rejecting it are developed more fully in my "Guise of the Good" and "What Happens When Someone Acts?" *Mind* 101 (1992): 461–481. In any case, the present account of belief will be misunderstood if aims are assumed to be necessarily agential.

39. As David Phillips has pointed out to me, the mechanisms whose function is to track the truth may employ assumptions or even fantasies along the way. Thus, whether a particular instance of acceptance is an hypothesis, fantasy, or belief cannot depend on the ultimate aim toward which it is directed. Rather, the nature of each acceptance must depend on its immediate aim, as I have tried to indicate with the words 'therein' and 'thereby': to assume that P is to accept P for the sake of thereby formulating a possibility to be tested, whereas to believe that P is to accept P for the sake of thereby accepting the truth with respect to P. (Peter Railton raises the same problem in his "Truth, Reason, and the Regulation of Belief," *Philosophical Issues* 5 [1994]: 71–93.)

40. As Williams noted in "Deciding to Believe," this account of indifference to the truth of a belief explains the difficulty of acting on that indifference. In order to end up believing the proposition that I want to believe, I must accept it in the course of an attempt to accept what is true, not an attempt merely to accept this proposition. Indifference to the truth must not seep into my first-order attempt from my second-order attitude toward its success or failure. Some psychological partitioning is therefore necessary. On the difficulty of manipulating beliefs, see also Leon, "Rationalising Belief."

41. Of course, reasons for belief are also relative to an informational context, and insofar as different people are in possession of different information, they will be subject to different reasons. But if the informational context is held constant, the relativity of reasons to persons disappears.

42. See, e.g., Jay Wallace, "How to Argue about Practical Reason," *Mind* 99 (1990): 355–385, p. 359: "To act intentionally . . . is necessarily to be in a goal-directed state"; see also Smith, "The Humean Theory of Motivation."

43. The idea that some actions spring out of motives without being directed toward any ends or goals is defended by Michael Stocker, "Values and Purposes: The Limits of Teleology and the Ends of Friendship," *Journal of Philosophy* 78 (1981): 747–765.

44. This view is echoed by Donald Davidson in "How Is Weakness of the Will Possible?" in *Essays on Actions and Events*, pp. 21–42, p. 22.

45. This problem was foreshadowed in the text accompanying n. 22, above.

46. In adopting an evil end, the perverse agent may of course be said to make evil his good, as Satan does in *Paradise Lost* (bk. 4, line 110). But Satan makes evil his good only in the formal sense that its attainment will be the criterion of his success. The fact that even Satan's actions aim at the good in this formal sense doesn't help us to identify a substantive aim that constitutes them as actions. G. E. M. Anscombe discusses this passage (*Intention* [Ithaca, N.Y.: Cornell University Press, 1963], p. 75), and I have elsewhere criticized her discussion ("Guise of the Good," pp. 18ff.).

47. I do not mean that every part or aspect of the behavior must come under your conscious control in order for the behavior to constitute a full-blooded action. How you execute the catch may still be left to those reflexes which make up your skill as a catcher; that you execute a catch, however, must come under your control, or the catch won't be an action in the fullest sense.

48. I have elsewhere presented an independent argument for this thesis ("What Happens When Someone Acts?"). The idea that practical reason has motives of its own, directed at the control of one's behavior, is contained in the theory of motivation attributed to Plato by John Cooper, "Plato's Theory of Human Motivation," *History of Philosophy Quarterly* 1 (1984): 3–21.

49. Bernard Williams has pointed out to me that one can consciously control one's behavior while aiming not to—as, for example, when one unsuccessfully tries to let one's reflexes or instincts take over. But this point strikes me as compatible with my claim that one cannot consciously control one's behavior without aiming to. Trying not to control one's behavior involves a second-order goal, of relaxing one's first-order efforts at control. If one continues to control one's behavior while trying not to, the reason is that one continues to aim at controlling it while trying not to

persist in that aim. (Remember that the aims under discussion here may be subagential. See pp. 716–717, above [this volume, 265–267].)

50. Thanks to Chris Korsgaard for publicly daring me to express this thought.

51. Stephen Darwall has proposed a similar conception of reasons, under the name 'autonomist internalism' ("Autonomist Internalism and the Justification of Morals," *Noûs* 24 [1990]: 257–268). Of course, considerations may be relevant to our autonomy because of their relevance to our interests. The point is that their relevance to autonomy will be what makes them reasons for acting.

52. See my *Practical Reflection* (Princeton: Princeton University Press, 1989); and "The Story of Rational Action," *Philosophical Topics* 21 (1993): 229–254.

53. See Anscombe, *Intention*; Stuart Hampshire, *Freedom of the Individual* (Princeton: Princeton University Press, 1975), chap. 3; Brian O'Shaughnessy, *The Will: A Dual Aspect Theory* (Cambridge: Cambridge University Press, 1980), chap. 8. See also Ludwig Wittgenstein, *Philosophical Investigations*, trans. G. E. M. Anscombe (Oxford: Blackwell, 1967), sections 627ff.

54. Compare the ancient and medieval notion of "practical knowledge," which is "the cause of what it understands" (Aquinas, *Summa Theologica*, Ia IIae, Q3, art. 5, obj. 1). Anscombe discusses this notion in the last two paragraphs of her paper "Thought and Action in Aristotle" (in *New Essays on Plato and Aristotle*, ed. R. Bambrough [London: Routledge & Kegan Paul, 1965], pp. 143–158), thereby picking up a theme that was left undeveloped in *Intention*, pp. 1–5, 56–58, 87. See also David Pears, *Motivated Irrationality* (Oxford: Clarendon, 1984), chap. 8; and Arthur Danto, "Action, Knowledge, and Representation," in *Action Theory*, eds. M. Brand and D. Walton (Dordrecht: Reidel, 1976), pp. 11–25.

55. Here I am expanding on two themes that I have discussed elsewhere. First, I am expanding an earlier critique of the traditional notion of direction of fit (in my "Guise of the Good"). In my view, this notion conflates two different distinctions. One is the distinction between the cognitive and the conative—the distinction between accepting, or regarding as true, and approving, or regarding as to be made true. The other is a distinction between the receptive and the directive, which are two different ways of attempting to accept what's true—namely, by accepting so as to reflect the truth, and by accepting so as to create the truth. If these distinctions are conflated under the heading 'direction of fit', then one and the same mental state can appear to have two different directions of fit, since a subject can attempt to accept what's true by accepting something so as to make it true. The resulting state is cognitive rather than conative, but directive rather than receptive: it's directive cognition. I would claim that this state of directive cognition is the state of intending to act. This is the second theme on which I am currently expanding. In the past, I have said that an intention is a self-fulfilling and self-referring belief

(*Practical Reflection*, chap. 4; see also "How to Share an Intention," *Philosophy and Phenomenological Research* 57 [1997]: 29–50). The present discussion explains why I call it a belief, but also why I can dispense with that label. What matters is that intention is a state of directive cognition, not whether that state should be called belief.

56. See Davidson, "Intending," in *Essays on Actions and Events*, pp. 83–102, p. 86. Because Davidson thinks that this premise should express your desire, he would reformulate it, from "I want to save that glass" to "Saving that glass would be desirable."

57. Davidson, "How Is Weakness of the Will Possible?" p. 32; and "Intending," pp. 98–99.

58. This quarrel is a continuation of my "Guise of the Good" and "What Happens When Someone Acts?"

59. Note that in my account, your autonomy isn't an ability to control the motions of your hand; it's an ability to control your behavior, which is bodily motion psychologically understood, in terms of its motivation. Even a robot can control whether its hand moves. It takes an autonomous agent to control whether he moves his hand out of a desire to save a glass. The object of autonomous control is thus the entire behavior, comprising motivation as well as movement. The same point can be put in (somewhat) Kantian terms, as follows. Acting autonomously isn't just moving in accordance with one's idea of a movement; it's acting in accordance with one's idea of a law—in this case, the law of motivation.

12 Velleman's Autonomism

Philip Clark

People sometimes think they have reasons for action. They think, that is, that there is some reason why they should do one thing rather than another. It is worth asking just what it takes for such thoughts to be true. On a certain naive view, what makes them true is a connection between the action and the agent's good life. Thus, if safety, or excitement, or glory is something you have reason to pursue, this will be because safety, or excitement, or glory would be a good thing in your life. And if you have reason to be cooperative, this will be because it is good to be cooperative, and so on.

In a recent article, David Velleman argues for replacing this view with a more Kantian line, on which reasons are reasons in virtue of their connection with autonomy.[1] As Velleman notes, his view has points in common with the "autonomist internalism" of another Ann Arbor ethicist, Stephen Darwall, and with Christine Korsgaard's gloss on Kant's autonomism.[2] But despite the current popularity of Kantian ethics, direct criticism of the naive view remains rare. Thus Velleman's remarks provide a rare opportunity for some straight talk across party lines.

The aim in what follows is to defend the naive view. I shall first raise some problems for Velleman's proposal and then fend off the objection that serves as his rationale for braving the depths of Kantianism. Velleman's starting point is Humean motivational skepticism. He seeks to explain the connection between reasons for action and motivation without relativizing reasons to the desires agents just happen to have. His solution is to ground reasons in a desire that is nonoptional for practical reasoners, namely, the goal of acting autonomously. This is not a desire that reasoners just happen to have, he says. It is one that all agents have simply in virtue of being agents. But Velleman goes this way because he sees no hope for "externalism," the view that there are reasons for action that do not owe their status as reasons to desires. I want to defend an externalist version of the naive view by showing that Velleman has not justified his pessimism about externalism.

On the principle that the best defense is a good offense, let us begin with a look at the Kantian line Velleman ultimately adopts. I shall raise an objection, namely, that Velleman's view makes it impossible to criticize any fully intentional action as being contrary to the weight of reasons.

Velleman wants an answer to the question with which we began. He wants to know what makes a reason a reason, in the case of reasons for action. In the case of reasons for belief, he takes the answer to be fairly clear: reasons for belief qualify as reasons in virtue of their connection with the constitutive goal of belief, which is to believe the true. A constitutive goal, for Velleman, is something at which one must aim in order to count as doing the thing in question, in this case believing: "I cannot believe something without accepting it seriously—in an attempt, by me or my cognitive faculties, to arrive at acceptance of the truth" (p. 710) [this volume, 260]. To believe is necessarily to aim at truth. Moreover, what qualifies a consideration as a reason for belief is that it "appear[s] to guarantee or probabilify the truth of the belief" (p. 706) [this volume, 257]. This suggests a strategy for answering the question about reasons for action. If reasons for belief qualify as reasons in virtue of their connection with the constitutive goal of belief, then perhaps reasons for action qualify as reasons in virtue of their connection with the constitutive goal of action. But does action have a constitutive goal?

Velleman thinks so. He suggests that the constitutive goal of action is "conscious control of one's behavior" or, simply, autonomy. This will be the practical analogue of truth, and considerations will qualify as reasons in virtue of their connection with this goal.

In support of his choice, Velleman offers the following stretch of objection and reply. One might doubt that action has a constitutive goal at all. One might agree that every action has to be aimed at something, without agreeing that there is any one thing that is always sought. On Davidson's view, for instance, action just is behavior aimed at a goal.[3] But there is no particular goal at which one must aim in order for one's behavior to count as action. Velleman replies that in order to see that action has a constitutive goal, we must look at central, or "full-blooded," cases of action. Some behavior that Davidson would count as action is not full-blooded action, on Velleman's view. Here is Velleman's example: "Say, a child accidentally brushes a glass off of the table, and your hand shoots out to catch it. Everything happens so fast that you see your hand catching the glass before you fully realize that the glass is falling" (p. 715) [this volume, 264].

This is behavior aimed at a goal, but it is not full-blown action, as the next case is intended to show: "Now suppose, finally, that another child—an older and sassier child—hefts the glass with a smirk and calls, 'Here, catch!' You then undertake the same behavior, but as a fully intentional action" (p. 715) [this volume, 264]. The mark of fully intentional action, Velleman says, is that in it the agent takes conscious control of her behavior: action is not fully intentional unless it is autonomous. But taking control of one's behavior is something one cannot do without aiming to do it. Thus, in fully intentional action one necessarily has the aim of being in conscious control of one's behavior: "If so, then the constitutive aim of action will turn out, in Kantian fashion, to be autonomy. And considerations will turn out to qualify as reasons—also in Kantian fashion—by virtue of their relevance to our autonomy rather than their relevance to our interests or our good" (p. 719) [this volume, 268]. And so we arrive at the autonomist alternative to the naive view.

To see how this view differs from the naive view, it will be useful to consider the implications of Velleman's position. To begin, it is important to see that the argument just rehearsed has two parts. First we are to see that nothing counts as full-blown intentional action unless it is executed under conscious control. Then we are to notice that exercising control is one of those things that you can't do, logically can't do, without aiming to do it. And from this we are to conclude that nothing counts as full-blown intentional action unless, in it, the agent aims to exercise conscious control over her behavior.

One noteworthy implication of Velleman's position, then, is that no fully intentional action can fail to achieve the constitutive aim of action. The constitutive aim is autonomy, but as we've just seen, it is a premise of the argument that every fully intentional action is autonomous. So unlike belief, which, however full-blown, can and often does fall short of its constitutive aim, fully intentional action never exhibits the practical analogue of falsehood.

This makes it difficult to see how a fully intentional action could ever be rationally criticizable, on Velleman's view. One thing that seems to happen on a regular basis is this: someone does a fully intentional action, but the weight of reasons is against it. This happens with beliefs too. Some people believe, for instance, that certain well-documented genocides never happened. We would like to be able to say that the weight of the evidence is on the other side. And on Velleman's view, we can say this. But notice how the explanation goes. We can say the weight of reasons is against a belief, because we can say having the contrary belief is better suited to belief's constitutive goal, that is, the goal of believing the true. This explanation would not be available, however, if it were not possible for belief to fall short of its constitutive goal. For in that case, the beliefs of those who deny the genocide would be as well suited to the goal as any other.

For the same reason, Velleman cannot invoke the parallel explanation in the case of action. He cannot say, of some fully intentional action that someone is doing, like strangling one's next-door neighbor, that some other course of action is better suited to the constitutive goal of action. For by hypothesis, any fully intentional action reaches that goal. Any fully intentional action is, literally, perfectly well suited to the goal. Consequently, Velleman must deny that any fully intentional action is contrary to the weight of reasons.

We are now in a position to see the contrast between the autonomist view and the naive view. On the naive view, what qualifies something as a reason is not its relation to conscious control but its relation to the agent's good. What qualifies safety, excitement, and glory as reasons, if they are reasons, is that they are desirable, that is, that they are things it makes sense to want in one's life. On the face of it, the pursuit of the good is not identical with the pursuit of autonomy. To exhibit full-blown agency is not necessarily to choose well. A fully intentional action, such as purchasing a gun, say, might still be unwise, and its demerit, on the naive view, would consist in a lack of fit with certain desirable ends, like safety, or with the sort of person it makes sense to want to be. Indeed Velleman appears to agree that autonomy can fall short of the good, for he holds that "behavior can still qualify as action even if its end-in-view is conceived as bad" (p. 716) [this volume, 265]. If he is willing to add that in some of these cases the end-in-view is correctly conceived as bad, then it looks as though he holds that conscious control is no sure path to good choice. This impression is reinforced by Velleman's references to the actions of Satan as examples of genuine agency. Velleman thinks, reasonably enough, that Satan's deeds can be both fully intentional and bad.

If it is right that autonomy and the good are distinct objectives, then autonomism and the naive view are distinct views, since they give different answers to the question of what makes a reason a reason. Velleman's departure from the naive view comes when he refuses to stake reasons to the good and, instead, stakes them to the goal of conscious control.

By now the initial preferability of the naive view should be obvious. On the naive view, fully intentional action is not automatically successful from the point of view of reason. Rational assessment requires that we ask a further question, namely, whether the action is consistent with the agent's good. This is how it can turn out that a fully intentional action is contrary to the weight of reasons. On Velleman's view, however, the goal that serves as the standard of rational assessment is automatically achieved in fully intentional action. Every autonomous action is a complete success from the point of view of practical reason. This leaves us with nowhere to turn to assess whether the weight of reasons favors or disfavors the action.

One thing an autonomist might do, to save the day, is drop the idea that every fully intentional action is one in which the goal of conscious control is achieved. There is a long-standing philosophical tradition according to which "real" control is understood to exclude actions done from perverse motives that are in some way foreign to one's true self. Thus, the addict's crimes, though fully intentional, are not autonomous, since they are done from motives that are alien to the addict's true self. This move will allow the autonomist to criticize some fully intentional actions as being contrary to the weight of reasons. For reasons, as before, are pinned to the goal of autonomy. Fully intentional action will now be what parallels belief, and autonomy will serve, like truth, as a target that can be missed.

This maneuver is problematic for two reasons. First, while the new view does allow for some actions to count as contrary to the weight of reasons, it doesn't allow for enough. Actions done from motives that are not foreign to the agent's true self will still lie beyond the pale of rational criticism. For instance, Truman's decision to use nuclear weapons against Japan remains a topic of debate. A theory of reasons should not preempt that debate just on the ground that Truman's desire to save the lives of American soldiers was in complete harmony with his true self.[4] One might respond by expanding the notion of autonomy still further and counting as autonomous only those actions that are done from motives that are in harmony with the weight of reasons. But now, clearly, we are using reasons as the test of autonomy rather than the other way around. The difficulty lies in finding a conception of autonomy that is not parasitic on the notion of a reason but that also does not unduly restrict the range of actions that can be contrary to the weight of reasons.[5]

The second difficulty is this: if Velleman were to separate fully intentional action from autonomous action, he would lose his argument that autonomy is a constitutive aim of fully intentional action, as truth is a constitutive aim of belief. The argument, recall, is that in fully intentional action, the agent exerts conscious control, and conscious control can only be exerted by someone who is aiming to exert it. Thus, no behavior counts as intentional unless, in it, the agent aims to exert control over the behavior. But if we say that autonomy is something over and above the control that is exerted in just any fully intentional action, then we lose the argument that the goal of autonomy is constitutive of intentional agency. Why should we think that a fully intentional action must be aimed at some kind of control over and above what is exerted in any fully intentional action? Why should we think that in stealing a purse, the addict must be aiming at any greater control than is necessary to get that next vial?

None of this, of course, impugns Velleman's claim that fully intentional action has conscious control as a constitutive goal.[6] Perhaps he is right that we cannot act intentionally without trying to exert and succeeding in exerting control over our behavior. But if that is so, the lesson to be drawn is not that conscious control is the standard of rational assessment for actions. At most, what we learn is that to act intentionally is to succeed at something. It is to succeed in bringing one's behavior under one's conscious control. Since fully intentional actions can run contrary to the weight of reasons, the standard of rational assessment for actions must be something else. It must be a target that can be missed. That target, according to the naive view, is the good. My fully intentional actions can depart from the weight of reasons, because they can depart from the sort of life it is good to live or the sort of person it is good to be.

But whatever the fate of his autonomism, it is clear that Velleman thinks the good will not do as the target of practical reasoning. His interest in the idea of a goal of practical reasoning springs from the hope of answering Humean motivational skepticism. He acknowledges that one might try to answer the Humeans by saying "practical reasoning aims at figuring out the best thing to do."[7] But he argues that this strategy is caught in a dilemma. It will either take on an undesirable burden of justification or it will fail to identify a substantive aim for practical reasoning. In the space that remains, I want to explain why the naive view is not, in fact, caught in this dilemma.

To see how the dilemma is supposed to arise, we need to understand the project on which Velleman is embarked. He wants to answer a certain familiar skeptical argument, which he presents as follows: "Suppose that reasons for someone to do something must be considerations that would sway him toward doing it if he entertained them rationally. And suppose that the only considerations capable of swaying someone toward an action are those which represent it as a way of attaining something he wants, or would want once apprised of its attainability. These assumptions, taken together, seem to imply that the only considerations that can qualify as reasons for someone to act are considerations appealing to his antecedent inclinations—that is, his desires or dispositions to desire" (pp. 694–95) [this volume, 249]. This is an argument for "internalism," the view that every reason for someone to act is an internal reason, in the sense that it owes its status as a reason to the person's antecedent inclinations. The "externalist," by contrast, holds that there are external reasons, that is, reasons that do not depend on the inclinations of the person for whom they are reasons. Velleman notes that an externalist might keep both of the argument's assumptions but deny that the conclusion follows.[8] What really follows, one might say, is that if there are any external reasons, then there are desires that we can count on agents to have insofar as they entertain considerations rationally. The externalist can grant the assumptions but hold that certain desires just come with the territory of being a rational agent.

But are there really desires that just come with the territory of being a rational agent? Here Velleman says there are two ways the externalist can proceed. One way is to pick some specific conception of the sorts of considerations that qualify as reasons and claim that the corresponding inclinations are partly constitutive of an agent's rationality. For instance, one might identify considerations of justice and benevolence as external reasons and then claim that inclinations to justice and benevolence are part and parcel of being a rational agent. But Velleman sees a problem here. The claim that, insofar as one is rational, one will have inclinations to justice and benevolence is a normative claim. It is a claim about what one ought rationally to want and therefore stands in need of justification. The externalist will have to show that, whatever one's antecedent inclinations, one ought rationally to have inclinations in those specific directions. And Velleman is pessimistic about the prospects of justifying any such claim.

Alternatively, though, the externalist might try to escape this "burden of justification" by appealing to "an inclination to do whatever is supported by reasons as such." This would be a desire whose object was not given by any specific idea about what sorts of things are reasons. It would be a desire to follow reasons "whatever they may consist in." The naive view, as I understand it, follows this tack. It posits, as a condition on rationality, an inclination whose object is generic rather than specific. The object is to do what is best, whatever that may be.

But the flight to the generic, according to Velleman, only postpones the problem. For as long as one tries to make do with generic descriptions, he says, one fails to identify a "substantive" target: "Asking the agent to identify a rational action under the guise of rationality as such, or to identify a reason for acting under the guise of a reason as such . . . would be to assign him a task with a formal object but no substantive object—and hence with no object at all" (p. 700) [this volume, 252]. Consider, for example, the claim that rational agents aim, in their practical reasoning, at the good. This might seem to identify an inclination that is part and parcel of being a rational agent, namely, an inclination to the good. And the externalist might seek to avoid the burden of justification by reading 'the good' generically. But to read it generically, Velleman reasons, is to read it as expressing the "formal object" of an episode of practical reasoning. And read that way, it does not, in fact, identify any particular inclination as part and parcel of being a rational agent.

Velleman is right, I think, that the externalist cannot use a formal object to identify any particular inclination as partially constitutive of rationality. The error is in the previous step. To read an expression like 'the good' or 'the action supported by reasons' generically is not necessarily to read it as expressing a formal object. To see this, we need to look at what Velleman means by 'formal'.

Velleman defines the formal object of an enterprise as "a goal stated solely in terms of, or in terms that depend on, the very concept of being the object of that enterprise" (p. 700) [this volume, 252]. And he defines a substantive object as one that is not formal, that is, "not stated solely in terms that depend on the concept of being the object of that enterprise." Thus, when we say that in searching one aims at the quarry, or that in competing one aims to win, or that in posing a question one asks for the answer, we are giving the formal objects of a search, a contest, and a question, respectively. The objects are formal because 'the quarry', 'winning', and 'the answer' are just names for whatever is sought in a search, attempted in a contest, and asked for in posing a question. They are defined in terms of the very idea of being the object of the enterprise. By contrast, 'the source of the Nile', 'catching the most fish', and 'the cube root of 27' express substantive objects, because they are not just names for whatever is sought, attempted, and asked for.

One might think the difference is that there is no such thing as the quarry, taken just like that, whereas there is such a thing as the source of the Nile. But interestingly, this is not right. A description need not be satisfied in order to express a substantive object in Velleman's sense. Assuming the earth is round, there is no such thing as the edge of the earth. But 'the edge of the earth' still expresses a substantive object for a search. This is because the description is not defined in terms of the notion of being the object of a search. If it expressed the formal object of a search, then just as one can transform something into the quarry just by searching for it, so one could transform something into the edge of the earth just by searching for it. But plainly one cannot do this. I can turn my keys into the quarry just by searching for them. But I can't turn them into the edge of the earth just by searching for them. This suffices to show that 'the edge of the earth' is not defined, as 'the quarry' is, in terms of being the thing sought. The mark of the substantive, therefore, is not that anything actually satisfies the description. It is, rather, that the description has what we might call a semantic life of its own, apart from the notion of being the object.

On the naive view, as I understand it, expressions like 'the good' and 'the best action' do have a semantic life of their own and so are substantive in Velleman's sense. On this view, it does not go without saying that whatever sort of life one pursues will thereby be a good one. Satan, for instance, cannot take it that the sort of life he has in mind will be a good one, just so long as he pursues it. "Evil be thou my goal" is not a tough assignment. Satan can make evil his goal just by pursuing it. But "Evil be thou my good" suggests a Satan who expects to make it the case, by making evil his goal, that in pursuing evil he acts well. On the naive view, it does not go without saying that making evil his goal would have that effect. But that would go without saying if 'good' expressed the formal object of practical reasoning.

Likewise, Truman cannot take it for granted that the means best suited to whatever he pursues will thereby be the best thing to do. He can't just assume that if he makes winning on the smallest possible budget his sole objective, say, and ignores all other considerations, then whatever it takes to achieve that objective will thereby be a good action. But if 'good action' expressed the formal object of practical reasoning, then he could assume this. One can make 3 the answer, simply by asking for the cube root of 27. And one can make Paris the place to look just by setting out to find the Eiffel Tower. This is because 'the answer' and 'the place to look' are defined in terms of the notions of what is asked for and what is sought. But on the naive view, one cannot make a nuclear attack the best thing to do by adopting just any goal to which it is indispensable. Thus 'the best thing to do', on this view, is not defined in terms of the notion of what is pursued. It expresses a substantive object.

By Velleman's lights, this should commit the naive theorist to a specific reading of 'good'. To succeed in identifying an inclination whose object is substantive, Velleman argues, the externalist must move from the generic to the specific. That is, she must offer up some specific conception of what sorts of actions are rational, or best, or what things are good, or what sorts of considerations are reasons, and hold that rational agents can be relied upon to have an inclination whose object is given by that specific conception (p. 702) [this volume, 254]. And that reintroduces the burden of justification, because the claim that rational agents will be inclined in those specific directions is a normative one.

But why should we think that just because 'the good' expresses a substantive object, it must express some specific conception of what things are good? Why can't it be used to express an object that is both generic and substantive? To see how it could, we need to look at the distinction between using a description to express a generic object and using it to express a specific object.

Suppose I ask you to bring me the best gumshoe in town. On one possible scenario, what I have in mind is that you should bring me the smartest gumshoe in town. Perhaps I even add, "and by that I mean the smartest." In that case you will have done as I asked if and only if you bring me the smartest gumshoe in town. Even if, as it happens, the smartest detective is not the best, the assignment is to bring the smartest. On another scenario, what I have in mind is that you should bring me the best gumshoe in town, whatever other characteristics he or she may have. In that case you will have done as I asked if and only if you bring me the person who is, in fact, the best gumshoe in town. On the first scenario, I use the description 'best gumshoe' to express a specific object. On the second, I use it to express a generic object. The mark of the specific is that one has in mind some object that one does not conceive merely under the description itself, and one uses the description to express the goal of achieving that object whether it satisfies the description or not.

Notice, moreover, that one can use a description to express a generic object even if one has views about what sort of thing is apt to satisfy the description. Perhaps I expect the best gumshoe to be the smartest, and I have confidence in you, so I fully expect you to bring me the smartest. It doesn't follow that I am telling you to bring me the smartest gumshoe in town, whether that person is the best or not. It may be that I want you to take the description 'best gumshoe' as your guide and not my expectations, which, after all, might be wrong.[9]

Notice, finally, that one can use a description to express a generic object even if one has views about how that object is to be analyzed. It might seem that if the naive theorist endorses some analysis of 'good', then when she says rational agents want good lives, she must be expressing a specific object, namely, the object given by her preferred analysis. If that were so, then the appeal to a generic object would bar the naive theorist from endorsing any analysis of 'good'. But one can endorse an analysis of 'good', and still use 'good' to express a generic object.

Suppose, for example, that you urge your son to live a good life. And suppose he knows you accept a certain philosophical analysis of 'good', on which 'good' means 'loved by the gods'. Eager to grant your request, he makes contact with the gods and finds that they love it when people let their talents rust, neglect their health, and have no meaningful relationships. He lives accordingly. Has he satisfied your request that he lead a good life? One might conclude, instead, that the analysis was wrong. "If this is what the gods love," one might say, "then the analysis does not capture the meaning of 'good' after all." Perhaps what you had in mind was that your son should follow the description 'good life' in its actual meaning, not that he should follow your preferred analysis, correct or not. In that case, you were giving him a generic object, even though you did endorse an analysis of that object. (This resembles the case where, knowing I assume the best detective to be the smartest, you bring me the smartest, and that person turns out to be inexperienced, indiscreet, and easily intimidated. It doesn't follow that you've satisfied my request for the best gumshoe in town. Perhaps my request was generic.) So the appeal to a generic object does not bar the naive theorist from endorsing an analysis of that object. In saying rational agents want good lives, the naive theorist can be saying they want good lives as such. She need not be saying they want the life of her preferred analysis, correct or not.

To return to our question, we were asking why 'the good' could not be both substantive and generic. Drawing on the foregoing discussion, we can put the question like this: Why would using 'good life' to express a substantive object require that we have in mind some object not conceived merely under the description itself? As a general matter, there seems to be no such requirement on the expression of substantive objects.

Consider, for example, the Eighth Amendment prohibition on "cruel and unusual punishments." As Ronald Dworkin points out, it is not plausible to read this as a prohibition on what the authors took to be cruel and unusual.[10] The authors wrote in a time when brutal public floggings were commonplace, and most of them did not think public floggings were cruel. "But *that*," Dworkin observes, "is no evidence that they meant to say that only the punishments they believed cruel and unusual were to be unconstitutional" (p. 135). The authors could simply have listed the punishments they thought of as cruel or codified their opinions in some precise formula.

The fact that they chose highly abstract language instead, Dworkin argues, is evidence that they meant to prohibit cruel and unusual punishment as such, and not cruel and unusual punishment as they saw it. They meant to leave it up to us to figure out which punishments were cruel and unusual. He also notes that the parties had their working papers burned, "so that their detailed opinions would never be known" (p. 136). Dworkin's point, then, is that the object of the prohibition is generic.

But the object of the prohibition is also substantive. The formal object of a prohibition is the thing prohibited. But 'cruel and unusual' in the mouths of the authors does not mean 'the class of punishments we hereby prohibit'. If it did, the authors could prohibit cruel and unusual punishments by prohibiting just any class of punishments. But of course it was not that easy. They had to come up with the right language for what they wanted to make unconstitutional. And that shows that 'cruel and unusual' does not express the formal object of a prohibition. It is not defined in terms of the concept of being the object of a prohibition.

The claim that 'cruel and unusual' expresses a substantive object for a prohibition might seem to imply the normative claim that some punishments are cruel and unusual, which would then stand in need of justification. But this appearance is mistaken. As we have seen, a description can express a substantive object even if nothing satisfies the description. If I tell you not to give your baby too many kisses, and it turns out that no number of kisses is too many, this does not show that the object of the prohibition was formal. 'Too many kisses' has a semantic life of its own. It expresses the general idea of "overdoing it." It does not just mean 'the number I hereby prohibit'. If it did, I could transform two kisses into too many by telling you not to give more than one. Likewise, the claim that 'cruel and unusual' has a semantic life of its own does not imply that some punishments cross the line into that category. Some punishments are cruel and unusual, of course. The point is just that this cannot be inferred from the fact that the description expresses a substantive object. One has to argue it by pointing to specific punishments.

There is no apparent obstacle, then, to the idea that some objects are both generic and substantive. If there could not be such objects, the externalist would indeed be in serious trouble. For then, just as Velleman says, the flight to the generic would be a flight to the formal. And the externalist cannot use a formal object to answer the Humean argument. A formal object places no constraints on the goals a rational agent can pursue in her reasoning and, consequently, places no constraints on the desires a rational agent can have. Any agent can "pursue the good," in this sense, as long as she has some desires that can drive episodes of reasoning. But the externalist strategy is precisely to place constraints on the desires a rational agent can have. The idea is to hold out for external reasons by saying there are certain desires that are just part and parcel of being a rational agent. So if generic objects could only be formal, there would be no choice but to move from the generic to the specific and accept the burden of justification. The externalist would be caught between a view that affords no relief from the Humean argument and one that takes on "controversial normative commitments." But the wise externalist will refuse to make that choice. The wise externalist will describe the inclination that comes with the territory of being a rational agent as one whose object is both generic and substantive.

The moral is that Velleman's pessimism about externalism and, by extension, about the naive view, is premature. He has not shown that the externalist cannot answer motivational skepticism. For it remains open to proceed as follows. First, accept the two assumptions of the Humean argument for internalism. Second, note that the argument needs an additional premise, to the effect that every desire is rationally optional, in the sense that a rational agent could fail to have it. Third, reject that premise, on the ground that only someone who is estranged from reason could fail to want a good life, where the object of this desire is understood generically.[11] Velleman is right that 'good life' must be taken substantively, if this is to work. But he has given us no reason to suppose that this will commit the externalist to normative claims that stand in need of justification. If generic objects could not be substantive, then the externalist would be forced to offer up a specific conception of what is good. But there is no apparent reason to think generic objects cannot be substantive.

Velleman will have to say more than he has said, then, if he is to put externalism on the ropes. One strategy at this point would be to argue that descriptions like 'living well' and 'the best thing to do' simply do not have a semantic life of their own, apart from the notion of being the object of a piece of practical reasoning. But that will take some arguing. The claim that 'good' is formal does not comport well with the way we ordinarily think and talk about value. We do not ordinarily think that whatever we pursue will thereby be good or that any action uniquely well suited to its end will thereby be the best thing to do.[12] Strangling one's neighbor might be uniquely well suited to dispatching her quietly, but it does not follow that strangling her as a way of dispatching her quietly would be a good idea. By contrast, we have to think that whatever we seek will thereby be the quarry and that any place uniquely well suited to finding the quarry is the place to look. So much is a matter of the meanings of the words. This suggests that the naive view is on firm ground in treating 'the good' as expressing a substantive object. We cannot infer from that alone, however, that there are good things. That will have to be argued by looking at particular cases, just as one must argue by an appeal to cases that some punishments are cruel and unusual.[13]

Conclusion

The naive view has the advantage over Velleman's s autonomism because the good is a target that can be missed. Autonomy, as Velleman conceives it, is a goal that is achieved in every fully intentional action and so cannot serve as the standard of rational assessment for action.

But the deep rationale for Velleman's autonomism is motivational skepticism about external reasons. Velleman doubts that the externalist can mount a satisfactory reply to the Humean argument. At the same time, he wants to avoid the skeptical implications that go with the Humean picture. His solution is to accept the conclusion of the argument but reject the skeptical implications. He accepts the conclusion that reasons owe their status as reasons to inclinations but seeks to ground reasons for action in a goal that is constitutive of action. There is nothing about this strategy that commits Velleman to autonomy per se as the goal of action. But Velleman's rationale for pursuing the strategy in the first place is that the externalist is caught in a dilemma. And as we have seen, Velleman has not shown that the externalist is caught in any dilemma. The externalist does not have to take the object of practical reasoning either formally or specifically. The wise externalist will take descriptions like 'the action supported by reasons' and 'the best thing to do' as expressing an object that is both substantive and generic.

Acknowledgments

For helpful comments on earlier drafts, I thank Kai Draper, John Exdell, Sean Foran, James Hamilton, Philip J. Ivanhoe, David Silver, David Velleman, and two anonymous referees for *Ethics*.

Notes

1. David Velleman, "The Possibility of Practical Reason," *Ethics* 106 (1996): 694–726 [this volume, chap. 11]. All subsequent references in the text are to this work.

2. Stephen Darwall, "Autonomist Internalism and the Justification of Morals," *Noûs* 24 (1990): 257–268; Christine Korsgaard, *The Sources of Normativity* (Cambridge: Cambridge University Press, 1996).

3. See Donald Davidson, "Actions, Reasons, and Causes," in *Essays on Actions and Events* (Oxford: Clarendon Press, 1980), pp. 3–19.

4. I do not aim here at the truth about Truman's motives.

5. A discussion of attempts by contemporary Kantians to overcome this difficulty would take us too far afield. It is worth noting, however, that one common complaint against autonomism in general is that it unduly limits the range of actions that can be criticized. See, e.g., G. A. Cohen, "Reason, Humanity and the Moral Law," in Korsgaard, *Sources*, pp. 167–188.

6. Velleman says an earlier draft of this article has convinced him that autonomy is not the constitutive aim of action. See the introduction to his collection, *The Possibility of Practical Reason* (Oxford: Clarendon Press, 2000), esp. pp. 19 and 30 and nn. 27 and 37. But I have raised no objection to his argument that agents necessarily aim, in their actions, at conscious control. My claim is that even if this argument works, conscious control cannot be the standard of rational assessment for action, because conscious control comes too cheap. My suspicion is that Velleman is persuaded that autonomy comes too cheap and infers that autonomy is not something at which agents necessarily aim in their actions. But that would be his inference, not mine. Moreover, he is left with the task of explaining what is wrong with his argument that agents necessarily aim at conscious control.

7. Velleman describes this as the basis of Davidson's conception of practical reasoning. See Davidson, *Essays on Actions and Events*.

8. Velleman reads Korsgaard, I think correctly, as pursuing this strategy. See Christine Korsgaard, "Skepticism about Practical Reason," *Journal of Philosophy* 83 (1986): 5–25 [this volume, chap. 2].

9. See Ronald Dworkin, *Life's Dominion* (New York: Knopf, 1993), pp. 132–144.

10. Ibid., pp. 135–136.

11. Notice that this way of defending externalism does not commit the naive theorist to the idea that action is "necessarily well-intentioned" (p. 716) [this volume, 265]. Suppose someone pursues some goal she sees as having no place in what is for her a life well lived. Perhaps it is the very badness of the end that appeals to her. What follows on the present view is not that her behavior is not action but that her behavior does not issue from the desire for a good life. That might be because she lacks that desire and is in that respect estranged from reason. Or it might be because, though she has that desire, she also has other desires, perverse ones, from which she sometimes acts. The externalist response to the Humean argument

requires that there be a desire that comes with the territory of practical rationality. It does not require that, to count as acting, one must act from that desire.

12. See Warren Quinn, "Putting Rationality in Its Place," in *Morality and Action*, ed. Philippa Foot (Cambridge: Cambridge University Press, 1993), pp. 228–255 [this volume, chap. 8]. Quinn argues that mere pursuit cannot "rationalize choice."

13. Perhaps it will be argued that, unlike *cruel*, *good* is a thin concept and so cannot be "world-guided" (Bernard Williams, *Ethics and the Limits of Philosophy* [Cambridge, Mass.: Harvard University Press, 1985], p. 140). But it begs the question to introduce the contrast as one between concepts that are world-guided and concepts that are not. On the naive view as developed both by Aristotle and by contemporary authors, the contrast is between evaluative concepts that are immediately world-guided and evaluative concepts whose grip on the world is mediated by the thick concepts that give them content. See Elizabeth Anderson, *Value in Ethics and Economics* (Cambridge, Mass.: Harvard University Press, 1993), chap. 5; Philippa Foot, "Moral Arguments" (pp. 96–109) and "Moral Beliefs" (pp. 110–131), both in *Virtues and Vices* (Berkeley: University of California Press, 1978); and Susan Hurley, *Natural Reasons* (Oxford: Oxford University Press, 1989).

IV Alternatives

13 Beyond the Error Theory

Michael Smith

In *Ethics: Inventing Right and Wrong*, published just over 30 years ago, John Mackie famously argued for the error theory (Mackie 1977). Though the argument initially met with considerable skepticism (see, e.g., Blackburn 1993; McDowell 1985), in the years that followed many theorists came to the conclusion that Mackie had things more or less right (see e.g., Lewis 1989; Garner 1994; Joyce 2001). But which of these views is correct? Should we all be error theorists? Or is the renewed admiration for Mackie's argument itself mistaken? To anticipate, my somewhat tentative suggestion will be that Mackie's argument fails. Since I have been tempted to believe the error theory myself in the past (Smith 2006), this represents something of a shift in my own thinking.

1 An Outline of Mackie's Argument

Mackie's argument for the error theory proceeds in two stages. He begins by pointing out that our concept of a moral value is the concept of a feature of things that is at once both objective and prescriptive. But, he then goes on to argue, general reflections of a metaphysical and epistemological kind show that nothing has such a feature: the concept of an objective and prescriptive feature isn't instantiated. As we will see, the reasons he offers make it seem that the conclusion would have to be necessary, so the upshot, if the argument works, is not just that nothing has moral value, but that nothing could have such value.

As even this briefest of outlines makes clear, the real power of Mackie's argument is that it is addressed to people who are antecedently engaged in ordinary moral thought and talk in blissful ignorance of the error that it is the aim of his argument to lay bare. His strategy is to get those people to agree first to the conceptual claim—this fixes what it is that they are thinking and talking about—and then to the substantive reasons he offers for supposing that there could be nothing like that. Mackie's argument is thus an internal critique of morality: it purports to show that someone who is committed to morality shouldn't be so committed, and it purports to show this on terms that that person can himself recognize. Let's consider the two stages of the argument in more detail.

Mackie's defense of the conceptual claim consists in a rehearsal of what he sees as "the main tradition of European moral philosophy from Plato onwards," a tradition which, he tells us.

> ... has combined the view that moral values are objective with the recognition that moral judgments are partly prescriptive or directive or action-guiding. Values themselves have been seen as at once prescriptive and objective. In Plato's theory the Forms, and in particular the Form of the Good, are eternal, extra-mental, realities. They are a very central structural element in the fabric of the world. But it is held also that just knowing them or "seeing" them will not merely tell men what to do but will ensure that they do it, overruling any contrary inclinations. . . . Similarly, Kant believes that pure reason can itself be practical, though he does not pretend to be able to explain how it can be. Again, Sidgwick argues that if there is to be a science of ethics—and he assumes that there can be, indeed he defines ethics as "the science of conduct"—what ought to be "must in another sense have objective existence: it must be an object of knowledge and as such the same for all minds"; but he says that the affirmations of this science "are also precepts," and he speaks of happiness itself as "an end absolutely prescribed by reason." (Mackie 1977, pp. 23–24)

Though Mackie seems to think that these diverse formulations are all in some sense equivalent, in what follows I will focus on just one of them, namely, Sidgwick's.

In Sidgwick's terms, Mackie's claim that our concept of moral value is the concept of an objectively prescriptive feature of things amounts to the claim that to conceive of (say) happiness as a moral value is to conceive of happiness itself as having the feature of *being an end that is absolutely prescribed by reason*.

Mackie's argument from this conceptual claim about moral value to the conclusion that there is no such value is brevity itself. He dubs it 'the argument from queerness' and he tells us that it

> ... has two parts, one metaphysical, the other epistemological. If there were objective values, then they would be entities or qualities or relations of a very strange sort, utterly different from anything else in the universe. Correspondingly, if we were aware of them, it would have to be by some special faculty of moral perception or intuition, utterly different from our ordinary ways of knowing everything else. These points were recognized by Moore, who spoke of non-natural qualities, and

by the intuitionists in their talk about a "faculty of moral intuition." Intuitionism has long been out of favour, and it is indeed easy to point out its implausibilities. What is not so often stressed, but is more important, is that the central thesis of intuitionism is one to which any objectivist view of values is in the end committed: Intuitionism merely makes unpalatably plain what other forms of objectivism wrap up. Of course the suggestion that moral judgements are made or moral problems solved by just sitting down and having an ethical intuition is a travesty of actual moral thinking. But, however complex the real process, it will require (if it is to yield authoritatively prescriptive conclusions) some input of this distinctive sort, either premises or forms of argument or both. (Mackie 1977, p. 38)

Though Mackie goes on to consider various replies to this argument, he doesn't really say anything more to spell it out beyond what he says in this passage. So what exactly is the argument?

Let's begin by restating Mackie's argument in Sidgwickian terms. Though we believe that happiness has the feature of being an end that is absolutely prescribed by reason, Mackie seems to be saying, the idea that happiness is such an end is both metaphysically and epistemologically queer. Why is it metaphysically queer? Mackie doesn't explicitly say, but we can imagine what he is thinking. Ends are the sorts of things that each of us has, in so far as we aim at, or desire, different things. But while it is therefore true that some of us have happiness as an end, as some of us do desire happiness, the claim that happiness has the feature of being an end absolutely prescribed by reason, "the same for all minds," would have to be made true by some further fact about happiness, a fact beyond this purely descriptive psychological fact. Yet what further fact is there?

At this point, Mackie seems to just throw up his hands. He cannot see what further fact there could be. Or, more accurately, he cannot think of anything beyond its being a brute further fact, a Moorean non-natural fact the like of which he can make no sense (Moore 1903). This seems to be the metaphysical queerness he has in mind. Moreover, since he can make no sense of what kind of fact would make true the claim that happiness is an end absolutely prescribed by reason, he cannot think of any way in which we might come to know about such a further fact either. Or, more accurately, he cannot think of anything beyond our possessing a special faculty which enables us to detect non-natural features, a faculty the like of which he can make no sense either. This seems to be the epistemological queerness that he has in mind.

I said earlier that the reasons Mackie gives for thinking that there are no moral values would, if they were successful, make the conclusion necessary. We can now see why this is so. The problem with Moorean non-natural qualities isn't that there aren't any such things as a matter of contingent fact. The problem is that we can literally make no sense of them: there are no possible worlds in which objects have such qualities (though see Shafer-Landau 2003). Since Mackie appears to think that the existence of objectively prescriptive features requires the existence of such non-natural qualities, it follows, if he is right, that there could be no objectively prescriptive features either.

To sum up: Mackie's argument from queerness consists in an analysis of the concept of moral value together with a pair of challenges which purport to show that we can make no real sense of how that concept could be instantiated. We are therefore left with the conclusion that there is nothing beyond facts like the purely descriptive psychological fact that some of us do indeed have happiness as an end. Suppose we were antecedently committed to morality. Mackie's argument purports to show that we shouldn't be. Moreover, it purports to show this on terms that we can ourselves recognize. If we are to respond to his argument then we must therefore either take issue with his analysis of value or else provide answers to the metaphysical and epistemological challenges.

2 Value or Obligation?

Let's begin with an initial worry about the analysis. Mackie's conceptual claim, which focuses on the concept of moral value, is framed in rationalist terms. He tells us that to say that happiness is a moral value is to say that happiness has the feature of being an end absolutely prescribed by reason. But insofar as they go in for conceptual analysis at all, the concept most rationalists seek to analyze is not the concept of moral value, but rather the concept of moral obligation. Do things look any better if we restate Mackie's argument in terms of the concept of moral obligation, rather than the concept of moral value? It might initially be thought that they do.

Rationalists typically tell us that the concept of a moral obligation is the concept of a certain sort of reason for action. Thus, for example, if we assume that act utilitarianism is the correct theory of what we ought to do—and from here on, in deference to the earlier decision to focus on Sidgwick's analysis of value, I will assume this for ease of exposition—then many rationalists claim it follows from this that there is a reason, perhaps conclusive perhaps non-conclusive (for there are stronger and weaker forms of rationalism), for each of us to maximize happiness and minimize suffering. One question to ask is whether rationalists mightn't just stop at this point. Or is there meant to be something metaphysically and epistemologically queer about the concept of a reason for action as such? Do reasons for action presuppose the existence of Moorean non-natural qualities? (Relatedly, we might ask whether there is meant to be something especially queer about *moral* obligation, or *moral* reasons, or whether the queerness is supposed to attach to the idea of there being anything at all that we ought to do, or any reasons for action at all.)

The answer is that Mackie's argument from queerness, if it works at all, establishes that the concept of a reason for action invoked by the rationalists is metaphysically and epistemologically queer as well. There are various ways to bring this out, but for present purposes the following observation should suffice. If we add to rationalism—understood as a claim about the link between moral obligations and reasons for action—the following "Williams-Korsgaard" thesis about the nature of reasons for action (Williams 1981; Korsgaard 1986) [this volume, chaps. 1 and 2]:

WK: If an agent has a reason to ϕ then she would want herself to ϕ if she engaged in a suitable course of deliberation,

then it follows that claims about what we morally ought to do entail claims about what we would desire ourselves to do after a suitable course of deliberation. But since a suitable course of deliberation is simply one in which the deliberator is maximally informed and then forms his desires on the basis of that information in accordance with the requirements of rationality—this is something about which both Bernard Williams (a Humean) and Christine Korsgaard (a Kantian) agree—it further follows that claims about what we morally ought to do entail claims about what we would want ourselves to do after forming our desires in the light of full information and the requirements of rationality. (See also Smith 1994.) Mackie's two challenges thus re-emerge, but this time about the possibility that our concept of a moral obligation is instantiated.

Why do Mackie's two challenges re-emerge? They re-emerge because, if he is right that there is something metaphysically and epistemologically queer about the idea that happiness is an end absolutely prescribed by reason, then there is something equally metaphysically and epistemologically queer about supposing that desiring to maximize happiness and minimize suffering is absolutely prescribed by reason. This, after all, is what we must be supposing if we think that we would each desire ourselves to maximize happiness and minimize suffering if we formed our desires in the light of full information and the requirements of rationality. If the former presupposes the existence of Moorean non-natural qualities, then so must the latter. Given WK, the argument from queerness is thus equally an objection to the rationalist's traditional analysis of the concept of moral obligation in terms of the concept of a reason for action. (Indeed, this suggests that the argument from queerness equally calls into question not just the existence of moral obligations, but there being anything we ought to do and the existence of any reasons for action.)

Nor, for the record, should this be in the least surprising. For a natural way to understand what it is to have a reason for action is in terms of the value produced by the action that we have reason to perform. As Davidson puts it, an action we have reason to perform must have certain "desirability characteristics" (Davidson 1963). The WK condition that must be satisfied by our moral obligations, if our moral obligations give rise to reasons for action, is thus much the same as the condition that must be satisfied by the states of affairs brought about by our actions if those states of affairs have moral value, given the Sidgwickian account of what it is for something to have moral value. In each case what's required is that there is some desire, or end, absolutely prescribed by reason. In the case of moral value, the desire in question concerns a state of affairs. In the case of a reason for action, the desire in question concerns the action of bringing that state of affairs about. There's no surprise here given that it follows from the fact that we have a reason to do something that our doing that thing will bring about something of value.

This detour is, however, helpful, as it enables us to focus more clearly on how we might respond to Mackie's two challenges. First of all, remembering once again our simplifying assumption about what we are morally obliged to do, we must explain either what the world would have to be like or what the requirements of rationality would have to be like for it to be the case that we would each desire ourselves to maximize happiness and minimize suffering if we formed our desires in the light of full information and the requirements of rationality. Second, we must show that it is plausible to suppose that the facts about the world, or the requirements of rationality, are like that. And third, on the assumption that we can know what's of moral value or what we have reason to do, we must make explicit how it is that we are able to acquire knowledge of the relevant facts about the world and requirements of rationality.

In what follows I will describe and assess what I take to be the four main approaches to responding to Mackie's two challenges. The discussion will of necessity be incomplete, as each approach can be developed in different ways, some of which are more promising than others. My main aim, however, is not to say the last word about any of these approaches, but rather to put all four on the table for further discussion. My own view, to anticipate, is that only the fourth has any chance of showing what's wrong with Mackie's argument. Though I am tempted by the fourth approach, I must confess to a sense of unease about it.

3 The Instrumental Approach

According to what I will call the 'Instrumental Approach', only one requirement of rationality governing the formation of desires is needed to underwrite the truth of the claim that we would each desire ourselves to maximize happiness and minimize suffering if we formed our desires in the light of full information and the requirements of rationality. The requirement is some variation on the following, fairly uncontroversial, requirement of means-ends rationality (note that hereafter 'RR' is short for 'Reason requires that'):

ME: RR (if a subject has an intrinsic desire that p and a belief that he can bring about p by bringing about q, then he has an instrumental desire that he brings about q).

This is because all of the work is done by a crucial empirical fact, one that we would each come to appreciate if we had full information, about the means by which we will get what we intrinsically desire, no matter what we intrinsically desire. (For a related argument see Gauthier 1986.) Before we get to that, however, let's focus for a moment on ME itself.

If the Instrumental Approach is to succeed, then we will have to explain what sort of fact ME is and we will also have to explain how it is possible for us to come by knowledge of this fact, in so far as we have knowledge of moral values and reasons for action. My own view is that ME is best understood in much the same way as we understand claims like "It ought to be the case that knives cut well." This 'ought'-claim derives from the metaphysically mundane fact that *knife* is a functional kind. Since what a knife is is something whose function is to cut, it follows that knives can be ordered according to how well they serve that function: knives that cut serve that function better than knives that don't; knives that cut more efficiently serve that function better than knives that cut less efficiently; and so on. As I see things, the claim that it ought to be the case that knives cut well is simply an efficient way of saying that this raft of evaluative claims is true. No Moorean non-natural qualities are thus required to underwrite the truth of this claim.

Similarly, it seems to me that ME derives from the metaphysically mundane fact that intrinsic desires and means-end beliefs are psychological states possessed by agents, where the psychology of an agent is also a functional kind. The psychology of an agent is something whose function is, inter alia, to produce action. Psychologies too can thus be ordered according to how well they serve their function: those in which intrinsic desires combine with means-end beliefs in the way required to produce action—for this is what happens when they combine in such a way as to produce an instrumental desire (indeed, in my view, instrumental desires just are intrinsic desires that have suitably combined with means-end beliefs [Smith 2004])—better serve the function of the psychology of an agent than do those in which intrinsic desires and means-end beliefs do not combine in this way; psychologies in which intrinsic desires and means-end beliefs reliably combine in this way serve that function better than those in which they combine in this way albeit unreliably; and so on. ME, which is just an 'ought'-claim about the relationship between desires and means-end beliefs, is simply an efficient way of saying that this raft of evaluative claims is true.

Understood in this way, ME states a fact that is as metaphysically mundane as the claim that knives ought to cut well, and our knowledge of ME, much as our knowledge of the claim that knives ought to cut well, is mundane knowledge too. Just as the 'ought'-claim about knives implied nothing about Moorean non-natural qualities, neither does ME. There is, however, one crucial difference between claims about the function of a knife and claims about the function of the psychology of an agent. Since knives are a human invention, the function of a knife can be traced in some loose way to human purposes. The psychology of an agent, by contrast, is not a human invention, so its function cannot be traced to human purposes. So what does fix the function of the psychology of an agent? Human psychologies are, of course, the causal product of a process of evolution, so it might be thought that the function of the psychology of an agent is fixed by the contingencies of that process. But the fact that a human psychology is the product of a process of evolution is not an essential feature of a human psychology *as a psychology*. ME purports to tell us something about the proper functioning of every possible psychology of an agent, including those that spring into existence willy-nilly, not just something about the contingencies of an evolved human psychology. Indeed, a human psychology might evolve in ways that make it flout ME. So, to repeat, what does fix the function of the psychology of an agent?

My own view is that we must think of the psychology of an agent as a privileged kind in reality—a Lewisian elite property, if you like (Lewis

1984)—and that we must suppose that knowledge of the function of the psychology of an agent is purely speculative knowledge of a thing of that kind. We gain knowledge of the function of the psychology of an agent a priori by reflecting on the nature of psychology and agency, much as we gain knowledge of causation, persistence, freedom, and the like, by reflecting on their natures. At this point, my suggestion is, when we reflect on the nature of the psychology of an agent we learn that that is something that has a function captured, inter alia, by ME. A crucial question that will need to be addressed, in attempting to respond to Mackie's argument, is whether we need to have a richer account of what it is for the psychology of an agent to function properly or whether this is all that needs to be said.

With this account of the metaphysics and epistemology of ME in place, the Instrumental Approach holds that what's been said is all that needs to be said. It holds that we need to appeal to just one further fact in order to explain why we would each desire ourselves to maximize happiness and minimize suffering—again, remember our simplifying assumption—if we formed our desires in the light of full information and the requirements of rationality. The further fact in question is a crucial empirical fact: namely, that acting so as to maximize happiness and minimize suffering is an all-purpose means to the satisfaction of *whatever* desires agents happen to have. This is what full information would reveal to us, or so the Instrumental Approach tells us. Morality is an all-purpose means to our ends. In that case, no matter what people desire, so long as they have full information, and hence true beliefs about means, and so long as they go on to form their instrumental desires in accordance with the requirements of means-ends rationality in the light of these true beliefs, they will acquire an instrumental desire to maximize happiness and minimize suffering.

What should we make of this response to Mackie's argument?

The Instrumental Approach certainly succeeds in showing that there is a lacuna in Mackie's argument. Whereas Mackie says that the existence of desires that are absolutely prescribed by reason would require the existence of Moorean non-natural qualities, the Instrumental Approach shows that no such qualities are required. All that's required is ME and a crucial empirical fact. Unfortunately, however, the alleged empirical fact—the fact, given our simplifying assumption, that maximizing happiness and minimizing suffering is an all-purpose means to the satisfaction of whatever desires anyone happens to have—seems to be no empirical fact at all. And nor would it help if we were to eschew the simplifying assumption and make different assumptions about what we are obliged to do, and hence different assumptions about what the all-purpose means to our ends are. For whatever we are in fact obliged to do, it seems not to be an empirical fact that our doing that is an all-purpose means to the satisfaction of whatever desires we happen to have.

Some may balk at this. Couldn't God see to it that doing what we are obliged to do is an all-purpose means to the satisfaction of our desires, whatever desires we happen to have? Couldn't he institute a set of rewards for doing what we are obliged to do and punishments for our failing to do what we are obliged to do, where these rewards and punishments are in turn a matter of our getting whatever it is that we happen to want or be averse to? If so, and if God exists and sets up such a system of rewards and punishments, then the Instrumental Approach shows that he would thereby have seen to it that there exist features that are both objective and prescriptive. I said earlier that Mackie's argument purports to show that there could only exist objectively prescriptive features if there were Moorean non-natural features, something we can literally make no sense of. But, it might be thought, we now see that his argument shows no such thing. For the existence of moral value would be equally secured by the existence of God, on the assumption that God can indeed set up a system of rewards and punishments as described. However I am not persuaded that this last crucial assumption is plausible.

Suppose (for reductio) that God exists and sets up the required system of rewards and punishments in some possible world. So far, so good. Now let's ask a question about that possible world. Had there been someone whose intrinsic desires are not satisfied by his doing what's morally obligatory, would he have had moral obligations? This is a legitimate question to ask, because moral obligations, if they exist at all, are possessed not just by actual people, but also by those who would have existed had things been otherwise. And the answer is surely that he would still have had moral obligations. Imagine, for example, someone whose every intrinsic desire is for some X where X does not come about by means of whatever it is that we are imagining it is morally obligatory for him to do. That person, by hypothesis, has moral obligations. But, given our analysis of moral obligation, he too would have to be rationally required to desire to do whatever it is that we are imagining he has a moral obligation to do. Yet if ME is the only requirement of rationality governing the formation of desires, we have imagined his having desires that make this condition impossible to satisfy. If this is right then the upshot is that not even God can help the Instrumental Approach explain the existence of moral obligations.

Let me sum up. If we take the Instrumental Approach, then, though we don't commit ourselves to the existence of Moorean non-natural qualities, we do land ourselves with the error theory nonetheless. We land ourselves with the error theory because it is incoherent to suppose that our doing what we are morally obliged to do is an all-purpose means to the satisfaction of our desires whatever we happen to desire: that's what the possibility of someone with desires like those just described shows. But the failure of the Instrumental Approach teaches us an important lesson. Imagine that everyone who is obliged to maximize happiness and minimize suffering would indeed desire themselves to so act if they formed their desires in the light of full information and the requirements of rationality. In that case there would have to be something irrational about someone whose every intrinsic desire is for some X where X doesn't come about by means of whatever it is that we are imagining we have an obligation to do. We thus have no alternative but to suppose that such intrinsic desires themselves are subject to rational requirements. Thus, the question to which we require an answer, given our simplifying assumption, is whether we mightn't be rationally required to intrinsically desire that we maximize happiness and minimize suffering. The remaining approaches all proceed by attempting to answer this question in the affirmative without presupposing the existence of Moorean non-natural qualities.

4 The Universalization Approach

If our intrinsic desires themselves are subject to rational requirements, then there must be rational requirements beyond ME. But what might such requirements of rationality be like?

One possibility is that, in order to be rational, our intrinsic desires must meet certain formal constraints, formal constraints that weed out all but the desire to maximize happiness and minimize suffering and those intrinsic desires whose satisfaction is consistent with the satisfaction of such a desire. The most obvious such constraint is some variation on the following requirement of universalization:

U: RR (if a subject has an intrinsic desire that p, then either p itself is suitably universal or the satisfaction of the desire that p is consistent with the satisfaction of desires whose contents are themselves suitably universal).

The rationale for U is not hard to provide. (For a related argument see Kant 1786/1948.) If there are any norms of rationality governing desires at all, then, since no particulars have a privileged status in the rational order of things, it must be possible to state the norms in purely universal terms. There is an obvious analogy here with laws of nature. Because laws of nature assign no particulars a privileged role in the causal order, it follows that it must be possible to state them too in purely universal terms. According to U, this means that, to be rational, our intrinsic desires must have contents that are themselves suitably universal—they must mention no particulars—or, at any rate, their satisfaction must be consistent with the satisfaction of desires whose contents are themselves suitably universal. (From here on I will omit this qualification.)

According to the Universalization Approach, however, there is a further argument that takes us from U to the conclusion that the only desires concerning particulars that are rational are those either derived from or consistent with the desire to maximize happiness and minimize suffering. But what exactly the further argument is supposed to be is very much a moot point. The best known argument for something like this conclusion is that given by R. M. Hare (1981). (Having said that, however, it must immediately be added that Hare himself didn't accept U, which purports to state a requirement of rationality. According to Hare, though universalization is a condition of *morality*, it is not a condition of *rationality*. Hare therefore rejects the Sidgwickian analysis of value in terms of certain desires being absolutely prescribed by reason; this is where he parts company with Mackie. Let's, however, leave Hare's reasons for rejecting the Sidgwickian analysis of value, an analysis which Mackie accepts, to one side.) Hare did, however, argue that the only intrinsic desire that is suitably universal is a desire much like the intrinsic desire that there is as much happiness as possible. According to Hare, the only intrinsic desire that passes the universalization test is the desire that there is as much desire satisfaction as possible.

But now look at what happens if we put U together with Hare's views about the power of universalization arguments. We get the conclusion that, if we have any intrinsic desires at all, then, if we formed our intrinsic desires in the light of full information and the requirements of rationality, we would all desire that we maximize desire satisfaction. It might therefore be thought that the Universalization Approach provides us with a response to Mackie's two challenges all by itself. U is hardly metaphysically queer, after all. Much like ME, it is a principle that tells us what must be the case for the psychology of an agent to function properly. According to U, the psychology of an agent functions properly only if the desires that issue in action are themselves suitably universal. No Moorean non-natural qualities there. Nor is there any epistemological queerness either—not, at any rate, if Hare's arguments succeed in showing that the only intrinsic desire that passes the universalization test is the desire that there be as much desire satisfaction as possible. As I said, however, what the argument is supposed to be that establishes this conclusion is very much a moot point. Let me briefly explain why.

Hare thinks, plausibly enough, that U would require us, in whatever situation we happen to find ourselves, to find something that we want to obtain in every possible situation identical in universal respects to this situation. Let's suppose that we find ourselves in a situation, which we will call 'S', in which there are three people interacting in a certain way. In S: we desire that p, a second person desires that q, and a third person desires that r. In figuring out what we can want to obtain in every possible situation identical in universal respects to S, Hare suggests that we need to put together three distinct desires concerning three distinct ways things could be that are none the less identical in universal respects to S. The first is our desire that p and it concerns S itself. The second is the desire that we would acquire if we were fully to imagine ourselves in the possible situation identical in universal respects to S, but in which we ourselves occupy the position of the second person. According to Hare, this is the desire that, in the possible situation in which we occupy the second person's position, q. And the third is the desire that we would acquire if we were to fully imagine ourselves in the possible situation identical in universal respects to S, but in which we occupy the position of the third person. According to Hare, this is the desire that, in the possible situation in which we occupy that position, r. The upshot, according to Hare, is that we have three conflicting desires concerning three possible situations all of which are identical to S in purely universal respects. In forming a desire for one thing to obtain in all of these situations, he thinks that there is therefore only one rational course, and that is to desire whatever will maximally satisfy our three conflicting desires concerning these situations. This in turn, he thinks, is equivalent to our desiring to maximally satisfy the desires of all three parties involved in S.

There are many things to say about this argument, but for present purposes it will suffice to focus on just one. To repeat, Hare thinks that if we were fully to imagine ourselves occupying the position of (say) the second person, who desires that q, then we would acquire the desire that, in the possible situation in which we occupy that position, q. There are two ways to understand what he has in mind. One is that there is a necessary connection between belief and desire: when we form the belief that there is some possible situation in which we desire that q then that entails that we also form the desire that, in that possible situation, q. But since it is plainly false that there is such a necessary connection between belief and desire—it is at least possible for someone to believe that there is a possible situation in which she desires that p while being indifferent or averse to p's being the case in that situation—the argument, so interpreted, isn't very plausible. The other possibility is that Hare is positing a normative connection between belief and desire. He might be thinking that reason requires us, when we believe that there is some possible situation in which we desire that q, to desire that, in that possible situation, q. We may of course have the belief but lack the desire, but only at the cost of flouting the normative requirement. The trouble with this interpretation of Hare's argument, however, is that it posits a rational principle independent of U. Whereas U tells us that there is a normative constraint on the form of our desires—our desires must have contents that are suitably universal—this rational principle tells us that the contents of our beliefs put normative constraints on the contents our desires. Understood in this way, Hare's argument isn't a version of the Universalization Approach at all. It is a version of a quite different approach, the one that I will consider next.

This brief consideration of the Universalization Approach hardly establishes that every variation on that approach is flawed. Perhaps a more plausible version can be found in Kant's own much more extensively discussed version of the Universalization Approach (Kant 1786/1948), though the ink spilled explaining why Kant's various arguments don't work strongly suggest otherwise (see, most recently, Parfit 2011). My own view, however, is that this is unlikely to be so. When you look closely at them, all versions of the Universalization Approach seem to share the crucial feature of Hare's just identified. Though it may be plausible to suppose that universalization is a condition of rationality, all versions of the Universalization Approach appeal to something beyond mere universalization in order to establish that some particular intrinsic desire is rationally required. Mackie's two challenges thus remain. In these terms, his challenge is to dispel the sense that there is something metaphysically and epistemologically queer about the further thing to which appeal is made in such arguments. Perhaps universalization itself doesn't presuppose the existence of Moorean non-natural qualities, but the further thing to which appeal is made does.

5 The Reasons Approach

In *What We Owe to Each Other*, Thomas Scanlon explicitly rejects the idea that goodness is a Moorean non-natural quality. He claims that what it is for something to be of value is for there to be a reason to want it, or to appreciate it, or to have some other attitudinal response towards it, where the different attitudinal responses are markers of different kinds of value (Scanlon 1998). This is his well-known "buck-passing" account of value. On the plausible assumption that the existence of a reason to want something entails that wanting that thing is absolutely prescribed by reason, his account entails Sidgwick's.

Derek Parfit concurs and elaborates on the nature of the reasons that we have for wanting things when the value in question is intrinsic value (Parfit 2011). Parfit says that what it is for something to be intrinsically good is for that thing to have intrinsic features that provide us with reasons to want intrinsically that those very features be realized. This suggests the following alternative account of the principles of rationality governing our intrinsic desires.

Remembering once again our simplifying assumption, the idea would have to be that the intrinsic nature of the states of affairs in which there is as much happiness as possible provides us with a reason to intrinsically desire that that state of affairs obtains, and hence a reason to desire that we bring that state of affairs about. If this claim about the reasons that exist for intrinsically desiring is correct, then that in turn suggests that our intrinsic desires are subject to the following rational principle:

BD: RR (if a subject believes that a state of affairs has the intrinsic nature of that state of affairs in which there is as much happiness as possible, then he intrinsically desires that that state of affairs obtains).

The idea, in other words, is that subjects are rationally required to form the beliefs and desires that there are reasons for forming when they believe that those reasons obtain; they are, in other words, rationally required to be sensitive to such reasons as they can appreciate. Let's call this the 'Reasons Approach'.

How plausible is it to suppose that there are rational principles of the kind that the Reasons Approach posits? In answering this question we must remember that the question isn't whether BD itself is plausible. The question is the more general one whether rational principles with BD's form are plausible. In other words, the question is whether it is plausible to suppose that, for some p and some q, there is a basic rational principle of the form:

RR (if a subject believes that p then she has an intrinsic desire that q).

Moreover, it is important to emphasize that the question concerns *basic* rational principles of this form because, on plausible assumptions, we can derive at least one principle with the same form as BD from a mere commitment to the existence of rational principles governing desires. This would not, however, be a vindication of the Reasons Approach. Let me explain why.

Assuming that desires, like beliefs, are indeed subject to rational requirements, it follows that, no matter what form the rational requirements on desires take—whether the requirements are like those posited on the Instrumental Approach, the Universalization Approach, or the Reasons Approach—those who have the capacity to reflect on the rational standing of their desires may, as a result of their reflection, form beliefs about what they would desire if their desires conformed to such rational requirements. But now imagine someone who does indeed form such beliefs. Let's suppose he forms the belief that he would intrinsically desire that q if his desires conformed to the rational requirements to which they are subject. It seems that we thereby imagine someone who is under rational pressure either to acquire the intrinsic desire that q or to give up his belief that that is indeed what he would desire if his desires conformed to rational requirements. In other words, we seem thereby committed to supposing that the following is a further requirement of rationality:

RR (if a subject believes that she would intrinsically desire that q if her desires conformed to all rational requirements then she has an intrinsic desire that q),

where this principle has exactly the same form as BD; it is that instance where p is the proposition that she would intrinsically desire that q if her desires conformed to all rational requirements. Given that we think our desires are subject to some rational requirements or other, it therefore seems that we're committed to their being subject to an *additional* rational requirement: a requirement that our desires match our beliefs about what our desires should be, given those rational requirements (Smith 2001).

Nor is it surprising that our desires should be subject to such an additional requirement of rationality, for what we imagine, when we imagine someone who has the capacity to form beliefs about the rational standing of his desires, and indeed his beliefs too for that matter, is someone who doesn't just have beliefs and desires that are subject to rational requirements, but someone who can bring about what are, by his own lights, rational improvements in his beliefs and desires, taken as a whole. This capacity to reflectively manage one's beliefs and desires is a distinctive rational capacity, one that presupposes rational requirements that govern the self-management itself, rational requirements with the same form as BD. But, of course, these rational requirements are not themselves basic in the sense we're after. They piggy-back on our commitment to more basic rational requirements that govern our beliefs and desires in the first place, those about which we form beliefs when we engage in the process of self-management.

We now have a new way of putting the question we asked initially. How plausible is it to suppose that a principle of the kind to which we are committed on the Reasons Approach—BD—is both true and explanatorily basic in the sense of not piggy-backing on our commitment to more basic rational requirements?

It might be thought that our discussion of the Universalization Approach already suggests a positive answer to this question. After all, when we described Hare's version of the argument from U to the conclusion that the only desire that is suitably universal is the desire that there is as much preference satisfaction as possible, we saw that his argument made crucial appeal to the following principle:

RR (if someone believes that there is some possible situation in which she desires that q, then she desires that, in that possible situation, q).

This principle, which has the same form as BD, tells us in effect that a certain consideration—the nature of the possible situation in which we desire that q—provides us with a reason to form a certain desire, namely, the desire that, in that situation, q. The fact that Hare's argument made crucial appeal to this principle was, I suggested, symptomatic of the failure of the Universalization Approach. That's because, as we can now see, he was really offering a version of the Reasons Approach. To the extent that his argument has any appeal at all, its appeal rests entirely on the assumption that the principle just described expresses an explanatorily basic requirement of rationality.

In fact, however, as we will shortly see, not only could this principle *not* be explanatorily basic, it seems doubtful that any such principle could be explanatorily basic. To see why this is so we need to reflect for a moment on what would have to be the case for such a principle to be explanatorily basic, so consider a slightly different case. Why should we suppose that the following is an explanatorily basic rational principle governing our beliefs?

B: RR (if someone believes that p and believes that if p then q, then she believes that q).

The answer to this question may seem to run parallel to what we have already said about BD. We should believe that this principle is true and explanatorily basic, we might say, because the facts that p and that *if p then q* are reasons to believe that q, and rationality is a matter of sensitivity to reasons; that is, it is a matter of forming the beliefs that we have reason to believe when we believe that those reasons obtain. But in fact the answer in the case of B has an extra and important feature over and above anything that we can say about the principle to which we are committed on the Reasons Approach.

Suppose someone asks why the facts that p and that *if p then q* are reasons for believing that q. I take it that this is a legitimate question and that we can answer it by saying something about the way in which the facts that p and that *if p then q* bear upon the truth of q. This is because what these considerations are reasons for is the attitude of *believing*, where believing is in turn an attitude whose nature we need to explain in terms of its having the aim of truth. The facts that p and that *if p then q* are reasons for *believing* q because, inter alia, belief aims at the truth and there are truth-supporting relations between p, *if p then q*, and q. If this is right, however, then the worry with BD can be stated rather simply. The worry is that we cannot say anything in defense of BD remotely similar to what we just said in defense of B.

Suppose we ask why the fact that a state of affairs has the intrinsic nature of a state of affairs in which there is as much happiness as possible is a reason for *intrinsically desiring* that that state of affairs obtains. If the answer to this question were to run in parallel to the answer we just gave in the case of reasons for belief, then we would have to answer it by appealing to the aim of desire. But what is the aim of desire? The aim of desire obviously isn't truth. That is the aim of belief. Nor would it help to suggest that the aim of desire is something like satisfaction, given our beliefs. That plainly won't help us explain why the fact that a state of affairs has the intrinsic nature of a state of affairs in which there is as much happiness as possible is a reason for intrinsically desiring that that state of affairs obtains. This, at any rate, is what we learned from the failure of the Instrumental Approach. The only answer that seems likely to do the required work is that the aim of desire is the good. But the trouble with this answer is that the Reasons Approach is itself derived from the Scanlon/Parfit buck-passing account of the good, an account according to which the good is simply that which there is reason to desire. There therefore isn't a good independent account of what there is reason to desire that could play the role of explaining what makes the considerations that are reasons to desire reasons to desire. It would be viciously circular to explain why a consideration is a reason for desiring in terms of the fact that the good is the aim of desire and then to immediately go on and explain the good in terms of what there is reason to desire.

The upshot, it seems to me, is that if we adopt the buck-passing account of the good then we simply cannot explain why the fact that a state of affairs has the intrinsic nature of a state of affairs in which there is as much happiness as possible is a reason for intrinsically desiring that that state of affairs obtains in a way that parallels the explanation that we give of why the considerations that are reasons for beliefs are reasons for beliefs. But if this is right then it turns out that the basic relation out of which the Reasons Approach is constructed—the relation of a consideration's being a reason for desiring—is a relation whose nature is (so far, at any rate) utterly opaque to us. We literally have no idea what would make one consideration rather than another a basic reason for *desiring*.

This discussion of the Reasons Approach helps us better understand Mackie's original metaphysical challenge to the existence of value. As I said earlier, Mackie says that if happiness is of value then it follows that happiness has the feature of being an end absolutely prescribed by reason, "the same for all minds." We can now see that Mackie's argument really poses a dilemma. If happiness is an end absolutely prescribed by reason then, at least if we take the Reasons Approach, it follows that there must be some consideration that provides us all with a reason to desire happiness. But in order to understand what it would be for some consideration to be a reason to desire happiness we would have to have some independent conception of the good as the aim of desire. We might suppose that this is why Mackie thinks that we are led inevitably to Moorean non-naturalism about the good with its attendant metaphysical and epistemological difficulties. This is one horn of the dilemma. There is, however, another horn on which we deny the existence of Moorean non-natural qualities and follow instead the buck-passers in conceiving of the good as that which there is reason to desire. On this horn, however, the problem is that we can give no explanation at all of what it is for certain considerations, as distinct from others, to be reasons for *desiring* at all. On this horn, the idea of there being reasons for desiring literally makes no sense.

The Reasons Approach must therefore be rejected. This is not to say that we must reject BD, the principle to which we are committed on the Reasons Approach. BD may well be true, for all that's been said. But if BD is true, then that will be because we have derived it in some way from something else that is itself explanatorily more basic. But what else is there to derive it from?

6 The Constitutivist Approach

To avoid the error theory, it seems that we must explain why certain intrinsic desires are rationally required without presupposing that there are explanatorily basic reasons for desiring, since such reasons do presuppose the existence of Moorean non-natural qualities. But how might we do this?

The only untried possibility I can imagine is that we might suppose that certain desires are constitutive of being fully rational. In other words, remembering once again our simplifying assumption about the substance of morality, we might suppose that the following is an explanatorily basic principle of rationality:

C: RR (people intrinsically desire that there is as much happiness as possible).

Let's call this the 'Constitutivist Approach'. (Parfit considers views of this kind when he discusses the "critical" versions of the present aim theory [Parfit 1984].) To anticipate, it seems to me that we are better placed to respond to Mackie's metaphysical and epistemological challenges to the existence of value if we take the Constitutivist Approach than if we take any of the others.

As with the other approaches, C states a condition on the proper functioning of the psychology of an agent. It says, in effect, that if it is to function properly, an agent's psychology must include the desire that there is as much happiness as possible. C is thus metaphysically innocent. It does not presuppose the existence of any Moorean non-natural qualities and it doesn't presuppose unexplained reason relations either. C thus differs crucially from BD, the principle to which we are committed on the Reasons Approach. BD assumes that we can explain why a fully rational person would desire that there is as much happiness as possible in terms of reasons that exist for desiring. BD thus falls foul of the need to explain what it would be for a consideration to be a reason for desiring: this is what gives rise to the need to appeal to Moorean non-natural qualities and the attendant metaphysical and epistemological queerness. Since C makes no such assumption, it avoids this charge of metaphysical and epistemological queerness.

Even so, note that C would, if it were true, explain the truth of BD. After all, if it is constitutive of being rational that we desire that there is as much happiness as possible then it follows that we are rationally required, when we believe that a state of affairs has the intrinsic nature of a state of affairs in which there is as much happiness as possible, to intrinsically desire that that state of affairs obtains. We might even express this by saying that the intrinsic nature of happiness provides us with a reason to intrinsically desire happiness. What's crucial, however, is that BD, so understood, would not be explanatorily basic. What's explanatorily basic is rather C itself: the claim that we are rationally required to desire happiness. But how plausible is it to suppose that this is so?

In answering this question it is once again important to remember that the question isn't whether this particular rational principle. C, is itself plausible. The question is the more general one whether it is plausible to suppose that, for some p, there is a rational principle of the form:

RR (people intrinsically desire that p).

Moreover, it is also important to remember that this is a metaphysical question and that epistemological questions are therefore orthogonal. The principle to which we are committed on the Constitutivist Approach is a principle that captures what the psychology of an agent has to be like if it is to function properly. We thus mustn't suppose that the principle purports to state some sort of obvious analytic truth about rationality. C itself may be no such thing. But the mere fact that it is far from obvious that C is true is neither here nor there given that C purports to be a metaphysical thesis, rather than an analytic truth about rationality. To be sure, if C is true then it is something that we can discover simply by thinking about what the psychology of an agent is like if it is to function properly, but it may be difficult and non-obvious for all that.

So let's now face the question fairly and squarely. How plausible is it to suppose that there are rational principles like those to which we are committed on the Constitutivist Approach? Here is where matters get tricky. Those who urge the Constitutivist Approach upon us will insist that, to the extent that we are convinced by Mackie's conceptual claim, we just have to admit that each and every moral judgment we make commits us to a corresponding judgment that some desire or other is constitutive of being rational. The judgment that it is morally obligatory to keep some promise in certain specific circumstances, for example, commits us to the judgment that desiring to keep that promise in those specific circumstances is the product of some intrinsic desire that is constitutive of being rational plus facts about how keeping that promise leads to the satisfaction of that intrinsic desire; the judgment that it is morally obligatory to return a borrowed book in certain specific circumstances commits us to the judgment that the desire that we return the borrowed book in those circumstances is the product of some intrinsic desire that is constitutive of being rational plus facts about how returning that book leads to the satisfaction of that intrinsic desire; and so we could go on. It thus seems that our moral beliefs commit us to the conclusion that there are rational principles of the kind to which we are committed on the Constitutivist Approach.

The question, however, is whether we can rest content with this commitment. Mackie might say that we cannot. The commitment to these principles is, he might say, grist for his mill. Since we know, ex ante, that no desires are constitutive of being rational, the upshot is thus that we have to do a modus tollens and give up our moral beliefs. But the other possibility, of course, is that we can indeed rest content with the commitment. On this alternative way of thinking, the response we just imagined Mackie giving begs the question. For even if we were disposed to think that no desires are constitutive of being rational ex ante, after being convinced that our moral beliefs commit us to the conclusion that there are such desires, and after seeing that the supposition that there are such desires is metaphysically innocent, we should simply revise that belief. Our moral beliefs commit us to the conclusion that there are rational principles of the kind to which we are committed on the Constitutivist Approach, so that's that.

I must confess that I find it difficult to say which of these two responses is correct. Should we think that one way of figuring out what the psychology of an agent is like when it functions properly is by engaging in ordinary moral reflection? If so, then we should conclude that ordinary moral reflection provides us with insight into which desires are constitutive of being rational. Or should we instead suppose that our ex ante beliefs about the nature of rationality are themselves true? If so then, if we are indeed disposed, ex ante, to deny that there are any desires that are constitutive of being rational, then we should conclude that our moral beliefs are all false. My somewhat tentative suggestion is that the first supposition is more plausible than the second. But I say this mindful of the fact that I thereby merely express a hunch rather than the conclusion of a reasoned argument.

Once the suggestion that our moral views provide us with insight into the nature of rationality is on the table, an obvious way of figuring out which desires are constitutive of being rational presents itself. We figure out which desires are constitutive of being rational in exactly the same way as we figure out what the most fundamental moral principles are (compare Gilbert Harman on the autonomous approach to morality in Harman 1985). In other words, we should believe C, as opposed to some alternative claim about the desires constitutive of being rational, for much the same reason that we should believe that the principle of utility is the most fundamental moral principle, if indeed we should believe either of these things at all.

We figure out what the most fundamental moral principles are by engaging in a certain canonical method of reasoning: the process of reflective equilibrium (Rawls 1951; Daniels 1979). We try to get our considered judgments about what our moral obligations are in specific cases into equilibrium with our reflective judgments about the most general moral principles that govern those specific cases. Similarly, the suggestion goes, we can figure out which desires are constitutive of being rational by getting our considered judgments about what reason requires us to desire in specific cases—where, remember, our commitments about this can simply be read off from our moral judgments about the specific cases, as the one entails the other—into equilibrium with our reflective judgments about what the most general intrinsic desires constitutive of being rational are that stand behind these more specific desires.

Suppose that, via the process of reflective equilibrium, we are led to the conclusion that the intrinsic value of happiness and disvalue of suffering best explain and justify our more specific judgments of moral obligation. In that case it seems that that same process of reasoning will inevitably lead us to conclude that intrinsically desiring that there is as much happiness as possible is constitutive of being rational. The upshot is thus that, on the Constitutivist Approach, our ability to vindicate the truth of a candidate rational principle such as C, in the sense of being rationally justified in believing it to be true, goes hand in hand with our ability to provide a similar vindication of the principle of utility itself. Moral theorizing and theorizing about the nature of rationality are one and the same. What can we say to those who disagree with us about what our moral obligations are if we take the Constitutivist Approach? Let's suppose that they have the beliefs and desires of someone with a firm commitment to commonsense morality, whereas we have the beliefs and desires of a committed utilitarian. One thing we can say is that, as we see things, they lack the desire that is constitutive of being rational, whereas we possess that desire. But it is worth adding that the account we have just given of how we come by knowledge of what our obligations are and which desires are constitutive of being rational shows that they may be liable to a different kind of charge as well. Those who do not believe the principle of utility may be such that, if they were to engage in the reflective equilibrium process, they would come to the conclusion that the principle of utility is the most fundamental moral principle, and in that case we can criticize them for being irrational in the further sense of having epistemically unjustified beliefs. Moreover, given that the belief they would have, if their beliefs were epistemically justified, commits them to the conclusion that they would desire to maximize happiness and minimize suffering if they had the desires constitutive of being rational, it follows that such agents are liable to a further charge of irrationality as well. For if they had epistemically justified beliefs, rationality would be on the side of their having a matching desire to maximize happiness and minimize suffering. In this way the Constitutivist Approach allows that there may be many different grounds on which we might criticize those with whom we have moral disagreements.

And what can we say to someone who disagrees with us about the nature of rationality? Imagine someone who agrees that moral beliefs commit those who have them to the conclusion that certain desires are constitutive of being rational—to this extent they follow the Constitutivist Approach—but who then goes on to insist that, since there are no desires that are constitutive of being rational, it follows that all moral beliefs are false. Perhaps he goes on to add "That's why I have never had any moral beliefs." What are we to say to him? As I have already indicated, the only thing to say to such a person is that we quite reasonably take our moral beliefs to provide us with insights into the nature of rationality, insights that he evidently lacks. Unfortunately, this means that we will be unable to convince him that his views about the nature of rationality are mistaken. But it could hardly be a requirement on any philosophical view that you have to be able to convince the arbitrary person that that view is correct. It is surely enough that we are able to convince ourselves of the reasonableness of our own view.

Let me sum up. The Constitutivist Approach seems to me to offer the most promising way of responding to Mackie's metaphysical and epistemological arguments for the error theory. Let's grant that Mackie is right that something is of moral value just in case desiring that thing is, as Sidgwick says, "absolutely prescribed by reason." It turns out that all that this requires is that desiring that thing is constitutive of being fully rational. Controversial though this claim is, the important point is that there is nothing metaphysically queer about it. It presupposes neither Moorean non-naturalism nor an unexplained reason relation. To be sure, we may not be able to convince everyone of the truth of this claim. But who would have thought that we could?

Acknowledgments

An earlier draft of this paper was given at the Symposium on Moral Rationalism at the annual Australasian Association of Philosophy Conference held in Melbourne in 2008. I am grateful for helpful comments made by my co-symposiasts—Charles Pigden and François and Laura Schroeter—and by members of the audience, especially Daniel Cohen, Simon Keller, Norva Lo, and Geoffrey Sayre-McCord. I am also especially grateful for written comments I received from Richard Joyce and Simon Kirchin. Though they saved me from many errors, I fear that all too many remain. Finally, I would like to thank the anonymous referee who suggested that I fix my tortured prose.

References

Blackburn, S. 1993. Errors and the phenomenology of value. In his *Essays in Quasi-Realism*, 149–165. New York: Oxford University Press.

Daniels, N. 1979. Wide reflective equilibrium and theory acceptance in ethics. *Journal of Philosophy* 76:256–282.

Davidson, D. 1963. Actions, reasons, and causes. *Journal of Philosophy* 60: 685–700.

Garner, R. 1994. *Beyond Morality*. Philadelphia: Temple University Press.

Gauthier, D. 1986. *Morals by Agreement*. Oxford: Clarendon Press.

Hare, R. M. 1981. *Moral Thinking*. Oxford: Oxford University Press.

Harman, G. 1985. Is there a single true morality? In *Morality, Reason, and Truth*, ed. D. Copp and D. Zimmerman, 77–99. Totowa: Rowman & Allanheld.

Joyce, R. 2001. *The Myth of Morality*. Cambridge: Cambridge University Press.

Kant, I. 1948 [1786]. *Groundwork of the Metaphysics of Morals*. Trans. H. J. Paton. London: Hutchinson.

Korsgaard, C. 1986. Skepticism about practical reason. *Journal of Philosophy* 83:5–25.

Lewis, D. 1984. Putnam's paradox. *Australasian Journal of Philosophy* 62:221–223.

Lewis, D. 1989. Dispositional theories of value. *Proceedings of the Aristotelian Society, Supplementary Volume* 63:113–137.

Mackie, J. L. 1977. *Ethics: Inventing Right and Wrong*. London: Penguin.

McDowell. J. 1985. Values and secondary qualities. In *Morality and Objectivity*, ed. T. Honderich, 110–129. London: Routledge & Kegan Paul.

Moore, G. E. 1903. *Principia Ethica*. Cambridge: Cambridge University Press.

Parfit, D. 1984. *Reasons and Persons*. Oxford: Clarendon Press.

Parfit, D. 2011. *On What Matters*. Oxford: Oxford University Press.

Rawls, J. 1951. Outline of a decision procedure for ethics. *Philosophical Review* 60:177–197.

Scanlon, T. M. 1998. *What We Owe to Each Other*. Cambridge, MA: Harvard University Press.

Shafer-Landau, R. 2003. *Moral Realism: A Defence*. Oxford: Oxford University Press.

Smith, M. 1994. *The Moral Problem*. Oxford: Blackwell.

Smith, M. 2001. The incoherence argument: Reply to Shafer-Landau. *Analysis* 61:254–266.

Smith, M. 2004. Instrumental desires, instrumental rationality. *Proceedings of the Aristotelian Society, Supplementary Volume* 78:93–109.

Smith, M. 2006. Is that all there is? *Journal of Ethics* 10:75–106.

Williams, B. 1981. Internal and external reasons. In his *Moral Luck*, 101–113. Cambridge: Cambridge University Press.

14 Rationality and Virtue

Philippa Foot

This paper is about the rationality of moral action, and so about a problem that is as old as Plato but which still haunts moral philosophy today. It is about the rationality of following morality: of refraining from murder or robbery for instance, and being faithful in keeping contracts and promises even where this seems to be against our interest and contrary to what we most desire. The problem of the rationality of morality arises most obviously over such actions and therefore has to do particularly with the virtue of justice, because it is here that self-interest and morality often seem to clash. Then Reason may represent itself as on the side of self-interest and the fulfilment of present desire; so unless it can be shown that acting justly is a necessary part of practical rationality, cynics like Thrasymachus will always say that there is no good reason to pass up an advantage for the sake of acting justly, and plenty of reason not to pass it up.

A great deal is at stake here. For if Thrasymachus is right the just person will often act irrationally, and we take it for granted that there is something *wrong* with doing that; so that someone who acts irrationally does not act well. And because it is in the concept of a virtue that it makes its possessor's action good, the status of justice as a virtue is being questioned by Thrasymachus, as he himself said with a sneer.[1]

By what strategy should this problem about the rationality of morality be addressed? It may be at this point, when strategy is determined, that a crucial error is very often (even usually) made. It is assumed that our task is to reconcile the requirements of justice with a preconceived theory of practical rationality; as if we had to show that despite appearances it always is in our interest to act justly, or that that is the way to get what we presently want most. Such attempts have, in my opinion, always foundered on the case of the "tight corner," where someone might be able to save his life only by ruthlessly ignoring other people's interests and rights. This kind of example obviously raises difficulties if practical rationality is taken to be self-interested action. And other more strictly Humean doctrines are not in any better case. If, for instance, practical rationality consisted in the pursuit of the maximum satisfaction of *present* desires, there would still be, at best, a contingent coincidence between rational action and morality, and even that would be hard to make out.

It is natural therefore to ask whether the intractability of this problem may not be due to something in the strategy by which we try to solve it. In pursuit of that thought I want, in a sense, to turn the problem on its head: to start out not from a theory of practical rationality but from the idea that justice is a virtue. This may sound like the most outrageous question-begging, given that the status of justice is exactly what is in doubt; but there can be nothing wrong with exploring such a hypothesis, and I shall now do that.

To discover the implications of the idea of justice as a virtue we must ask what a virtue is. It is said to be an excellence, but that does not take us very far when we want to think not about the virtue of sharpness in a knife, or meticulous carefulness in a scholar, but about the putative virtues of human beings, and of human beings as such. These excellences, which we often call moral virtues, are supposed to make their possessors good. But in what respect? The answer to this is somewhat controversial, since some say that virtues "rectify" passions as well as actions, and others do not. I shall bypass this controversy by pointing out that it is agreed on all sides that virtues, whatever else they do, must make their possessors' actions good. So we shift our attention to the concept of *good action*. An action is something done by a human being, which may come to grief for irrelevant reasons like non-culpable ignorance or lack of physical strength, but can also be judged as bad *as an action*. So what exactly does a virtue, in the sense in which justice is supposed to be a virtue, do? What distinguishes a just person from one who is unjust? The fact that he keeps his contracts? That cannot be right, because circumstances may make it impossible for him to do so. Nor is it that he saves life rather than killing innocent people, for by mischance it may be the latter rather than the former that he does. "Of course," someone will say at this point, "It is the just person's intention not what he actually brings about that counts." But why not say, then, that it is the distinguishing characteristic of the just that *for them certain considerations count as reasons for action*? (And as reasons of a certain weight.) Will it not be the same with other virtues, as, e.g., of charity, courage, and temperance? Those who possess these characteristics possess them by virtue of the fact that they recognize certain considerations as powerful, and in many circumstances compelling, reasons for acting, and that their actions reflect their views.

The description 'just' as applied to a man or woman speaks of how it is with them in respect of the acceptance of a certain group of considerations as reasons for action. So if justice is a virtue, it is this that justice makes to be good: the just are good in that they recognize and act on certain reasons. Which is to say—since it can hardly be one thing to be practically rational in a certain area and another thing to be as one should be there so far as the recognition and following of reasons is concerned—that if justice is a virtue this is because it takes care of a certain area of practical rationality. Possession of a virtue makes a person *do well* in respect of acting on reasons, and justice would make him do well where the reasons are about, e.g., promises, property rights, or respect for life. This is not a surprising conclusion, given that it was recognized earlier that the status of justice as a virtue was at stake in the dispute with Thrasymachus. All we have done in the preceding paragraphs is to spell out the reason why if justice is a virtue just action must be rational action, and so why if the latter is not the case the former cannot be true.

It seems, therefore, that we have arrived at a point at which it is crucial to decide whether justice is a virtue or not. Does someone act well—is his action so far forth good—if he is just? This is a weighty question, to which I suppose there is as yet no satisfactory answer. But it will be useful here to advert to some considerations already familiar from the work of various moral philosophers.

In the first place I should like to pick up Peter Geach's use of the idea of 'good' as an "attributive" adjective; that is one that applies to individuals only in conjunction with another description.[2] Geach thus drew a distinction between predicates such as 'large', 'genuine', and 'good' on the one hand and 'red' on the other. The former, but not the latter, need, he said, to be attached to an individual via a certain concept: something that is to be called 'large' can only be judged large in a particular class of things; and a genuine van Meegeren is not a genuine Vermeer. Similarly, a book that is a good soporific may or may not be a good book; the evaluation is of an individual, but by criteria that are given by the concept under which it is being judged. Geach insisted that when we call an action 'good' the word is being used attributively, and so not like the word 'red' in 'This book is red'. In evaluating, we are thus not predicating a quality in the way that G. E. Moore's writings suggested when he took 'X is good' as the primary form of a "judgement of value." Nor, says Geach, does moral judgement say that something or other is "a good thing" or that "It is good that" something or other is the case; he is suggesting that without further explanation such utterances have uncertain sense.

This seems to me to be both right and important. I shall therefore take our question to be whether just action is good *action*, not whether justice is good, whether it is good that people are just, or whether a state of affairs in which there is more justice is so far forth better than one in which there is less. (Whatever, if anything, any of that might mean.)

What difference will it make if we pay attention to 'good' as an attributive adjective in something like Geach's sense, and think of moral judgement as having to do with good *action*? At once, we see it as belonging, at least superficially, with a set of evaluations whose correctness or incorrectness is to be judged by more or less determinate criteria. Already we seem to be far away from the 'boos' and 'hurrays', and even the feelings and attitudes referred to in expressive accounts of judgements of good and bad. No one thinks that calling a knife a good knife, a farmer a good farmer, a speech a good speech, a root a good root, necessarily expresses or even involves an attitude or feeling towards it. And even a description such as 'good for my purposes' has to be judged, objectively, by reference to the purposes that I have. This is not, however, the point that I want to stress here. It is rather that even the most adventitious list of attributive uses of 'good' will contain examples differing from each other in striking respects. Thus the last example contained an explicit reference to the purposes of a particular person, not necessarily wanting what others want; whereas an object's being a good knife (*tout court*) must be judged by reference to cutting; while a root's being a good root depends on something to do with nourishment or anchorage for a plant; and a farmer is a good farmer only if he looks after his soil, his animals, or his crops.[3]

Now suppose, for the sake of argument, that the judgement of an action as a good action belongs somewhere in the extension of such a list. Where would it come? It would come, I shall argue, in a range of attributions of goodness that could be called 'autonomously species-dependent'. So let us see what this might mean. It concerns, as the words suggest, evaluations of individual living things, and of their characteristics and operations; and this without reference to interests that we may have in them.[4] This is what the word 'autonomous' is doing in the description of the mode of evaluation. How species-dependence comes in must be the subject of further discussion, which may begin with the faculties of animals, and with certain things the animals do.

Take the operation of sight or hearing for instance, or the power of locomotion. An individual animal which is well or badly endowed in respect of these things is fitted to operate correspondingly badly or well.[5] But it is obvious that it is only by reference to its species that we can so evaluate an individual. It is only *as the endowment of a such and such* that the perception or other capacity of any individual can be judged. Nor is it just that in respect of sight moles are not to be judged by the standards of hawks; as if there were one thing, good sight, which different kinds of animals could be expected to have in different degrees. The example of owls puts us on to the fact that it is the way of life of the species that determines what the better or worseness of sight consists in for an individual. And it is, of course, this rather than the circumstance it itself happens to be in. For an individual put into a special environment, like a wild animal in a zoo, may have what is no less a defect because it happens to fit its special life. Expressions such as 'good sight' have reference to a species in their meaning. If we want to talk about the kind of sight that *happened* to be advantageous to a particular individual in a special environment, or even in its own, we can always do so; but then we are talking not of good sight but of something else.

Thus, where excellences and defects of animals are concerned, it is by reference to the life of the species that the evaluation is made. But what does 'life of the species' mean here? It does not include everything characteristic of members of the species, but only that which has some function in that life. There is, as far as I know, no distinction to be made (in species-dependent goodness) between leaves that rustle badly and those that rustle well.

This may begin to give some idea of what is meant by saying that autonomous species-dependent goodnesses and defects derive from the life of the species. But how is that to be worked out? The key notion is, I believe, the concept of *need* appearing in various constructions; as when we say what a plant or animal of a certain species *needs* to have, both in itself and in its environment, and what it itself, and its operative features, such as roots, leaves, hearts, and lungs, *need* to do. Good eyes are the eyes a particular kind of creature needs; good roots the ones a particular kind of plant needs; and so on. And since the idea is that the organisms cannot flourish without the parts, features, organs, and operations that things of this kind need, the notion of need is roughly the one described, most helpfully, by David Wiggins as 'absolute need'.[6] Wiggins defines this as the notion of need that depends on a conditional to the effect that something or other is necessary for the avoidance of *harm*. This is not exactly what I want here because an organism can be defective in lacking something necessary for reproduction, as an animal is if it loses the mating instinct, and perhaps this does not exactly count as harm, unless a species itself can be said to be harmed in this way. There is, however, a more important difference between what Wiggins has (and needs) for his purposes and what I need for mine. I am interested in species-dependent goodness, and therefore in what is needed (absolute need) by a member of a particular species *as such*. He, on the other hand, is interested in claims of need, and therefore as much with individuals as with species. An example which shows the difference is that a fly in a fly-bottle, which will starve if it does not find the exit, has an absolute need to do this on Wiggins's definition of absolute need. But as fly-bottles are not part of the natural habitat of flies, and it is no part of the survival mechanism of flies to distinguish direct and refracted light, this is not, in my sense, one of the things that "flies need to do." No doubt many tricky questions can be raised here about adaptation to new environments, but this introduces a dynamism into the model: a dynamism from which notions such as *good eyes* and *good roots* must abstract.

Autonomous species-dependent goodness is therefore intertwined with a particular notion of need; needs being based, at least in the case of plants and animals, not only on what is necessary for the health and survival of individual members of a species but also for the continuance of the species itself. A further distinction is to be made which depends on the answer to the question "Where does the harm occur if the need is not met?" For while a defect of sight, or hearing, or instinct, most often rebounds on the one who has it—whom we may call the subject of the evaluation—this is not always so. If a gull cannot distinguish its own offspring's cry in the cacophony of the colony it will be the chick that dies; and the cubs die, not the lioness, if she fails to teach them to hunt. There are many such examples. One thinks, for instance, of members of the species of dancing bees, who dance a complex dance that directs *other bees* to a source of nectar. Or again of any species of stinging bee. It is necessary that bees have stings (they need to sting): so that predators learn to fear bees, and for the protection of the hive. Bees need to sting. So does this individual bee need to sting, in spite of the fact that it itself will die if it does? It does not matter exactly how we choose to speak at this point. What does matter is that the evaluation of an individual—of its features and operations—may depend on harm, public or private, which threatens others rather than itself.

Rationality and Virtue

Let us turn now to human beings. Are their excellences and defects likewise species-dependent, despite the fact that there is so much greater diversity in the way they live? First of all, what about such things as defects of sight or hearing with which we opened this discussion? It is important, of course, that human beings can sometimes choose their way of life, and can deliberately modify their environment. What they need in the way, e.g., of sight may depend somewhat on chosen surroundings. Moreover, for human beings there are greater diversities of lives within a given habitat, as for instance in a single city, and this will have to be taken into account. Nevertheless, a very great deal is in common to all human beings. None of us need the eyesight of a gannet; not having a gannet's diving capacity, and having other ways of catching fish. But we all need sight that allows us to recognize faces; and ears to hear, tongues to sound, and brains to process, speech. To be sure, some particular professions need specialized capacities, as a scholar needs a specialized memory. But there are some things quite apart from language that human beings as such need to be able to remember, like the distinctive physiognomy of friend or foe.

One would want to stress, however, that a great change has come over the conceptual scene with the move from animals (other animals) to humans, and that we shall have to look afresh at the necessities standing behind the evaluation in their case. To begin with, we now have to deal with the much larger number of harms, and here also of deprivations, that can be suffered: deprivations that belong to the world of imagination and understanding for instance. On the most simple level, and leaving aside such things as art and science, one notices that a human being who is unable to follow a tune or a dance is deprived, and therefore does not have what a human being needs for the good things that human beings enjoy. Although the notion of deprivation is elastic and difficult, it is right to speak of such human beings as poorly endowed. But it depends again on human life, on the human capacity to find things interesting, amazing, and marvellous that we understand the idea that someone is deprived if he does not have many things that are not necessary for life or even for health. Flourishing, for human beings, encompasses the enjoyment of many good things. Anyone is deprived if he does not have some measure of this enjoyment; and if the deprivation is due to some incapacity in him rather than to external factors then this is one source of adverse evaluation. I hope that it will be enough for the purpose of this paper to follow the ordinary use of 'deprivation' and 'need': the one we all understand when it is said that human beings *need* affection, or that lack of affection is itself a deprivation, as hardship is not.

Much of what has to be said here will depend on a feature of the operation of human beings to which Aquinas drew attention, when he said that while animals perceive things that are good and go for them, human beings go for what they *see as good*.[7] This idea can seem extremely puzzling if one thinks that seeing something as good ought to be like seeing it with a halo. In fact the truth, and great importance, of what Aquinas said comes out in the recognition of the whole conceptual structure belonging to the idea of human action and desire; as for instance in the fact that they can say why they want something, can conduct practical reasoning, and defend a choice. It is also important for the question of absolute needs of human beings that there is second-order evil in human life, meaning for instance the misery that comes from the consciousness of being disregarded, lonely, or oppressed.

It seems clear that in spite of the greater range of considerations that are relevant to the determination of absolute need in human beings, the evaluation of such things as locomotion, sight, and memory, has the same conceptual structure in animals and men. There is much more flexibility in our judgement, and variation in the background, but nevertheless physical and mental health, good sight, etc. are judged here in a species-dependent way. And the tenor of this paper is to suggest that the same is true when the subject is the goodness or badness of human action. If it is so, and if, moreover, action is evaluated in relation to human needs, as the things bees do are evaluated by what bees need, this will be highly relevant to the status of justice as a virtue. Is the behaviour of an unjust person defective, we should ask, for the same reason, broadly speaking, as is the behaviour of a free-riding non-dancing dancing bee, or a lioness who does not teach her cubs to hunt?

On the pattern of the evaluation of other operations in animals and in men we now need to point to the good served by justice. But surely we can do that? For the teaching and observing of rules of justice is as necessary a part of the life of human beings as hunting together in packs with a leader is a necessary part of the life of wolves, or dancing part of the life of the dancing bee. As Elizabeth Anscombe has said about one aspect of justice—the keeping of promises—a great deal of human good hangs on the possibility that one man can bind the will of another by getting him to promise to do something. As she says, the institution of promise-making and -keeping is "an instrument whose use is part and parcel of an enormous amount of human activity and hence of human good; of the supplying both of human needs and of human wants so far as the satisfactions of these are compossible. . . . It is scarcely possible to live in a society without encountering it and even being involved in it."[8] Why then will it seem, to most philosophers, impossible to infer from this kind of consideration, that a human being who refuses to count "I promised to do *A*" as in itself a good and rationally compelling (though not of course always overriding) reason to do *A*, is defective precisely in practical rationality? Why will the analogy with defective behaviour in animals seem so ridiculous to many moral philosophers?

First of all this may be because the analogy seems to give us a picture of morality as blind adherence to some norm for a species to which we happen to belong. But to think this is a mistake. For while in a wolf, or a dancing bee, appropriate hunting or dancing (as opposed to free-riding) is all that is needed for them to be behaving well in this respect, mere conformity to rules would indeed be *blind* obedience in one of us. To advert again to what Aquinas said, human beings not only go for what *is* good but for what they *see as* good. So it is not surprising if practical rationality requires the *understanding* of reasons for acting; which is why we criticize some people's following of social norms as "merely conventional" behaviour. It may be objected that most people do not understand why they should act according to justice, or to other virtues. But this is not true. For this understanding is not something acquired only by study and debate. On the contrary it is just that which is expressed by any one of us when we say, e.g., "How would we get on if people did not keep their promises?" or "What if no one helped anyone; where would we be then?" This type of answer can readily be given to the question "Why should one act justly?"; that is, "Why does one have reason to do so?" By contrast, similar answers could not be given, or not successfully defended, if the question were about the rationality of obeying just any old rule, as, e.g., a duelling rule or a merely snobbish rule of etiquette. It was because I myself failed to see that this was crucial to the discussion of reasons for action that I made such a mess of things in an article called "Morality as a System of Hypothetical Imperatives."[9] Still more or less in the grip of a desire-based theory of practical rationality I looked everywhere but where I now think it is right to look for the difference, in the matter of practical rationality, between one who follows any old rule and one who follows morality.

It may be objected that the kind of thing that people naturally say about justice or charity does not draw on the idea of the human *species* which plays so prominent a part in the argument of the present paper. But this is not true. I have already quoted Elizabeth Anscombe on the need that human beings have for binding each other's wills in an enormous number of their enterprises. The reason why we need mutual aid is also easy to see. If people did not get ill or in other trouble some at one time and some at another, and if they were not able to give aid without themselves falling into the same trouble, then there might be no good reason to consider benevolence a virtue and to perform kindly action just because of that. I remember that this thought about how different things would be for a race of beings who could only *exchange* trouble among themselves, so that one person could be got out of a pit only if someone else fell in, was one of the ideas that first put me on to the possibilities of a species-dependent account of virtue.

A second objection may, however, seem to be more powerful. It has to do with a shameless individual, concerned perhaps only about his own power, wealth, and comfort, who says that nothing said here has given him any motive for acting justly when such action is unlikely to pay off in his terms. But my argument was not supposed to show that such a man would have a motive for just action, if 'motive' means, e.g., what the detective looks for after a crime. What I was arguing was that since it is part of practical rationality, every human being has *reason* to be charitable and just. If our shameless immoralist says that *he* has no reason so to act he is simply begging the question. He has, to be sure, nothing that he *recognizes* as a reason; but that, if my argument is correct, is because he fails to recognize the truth. Any idea that if he does not have a motive he cannot act justly is of course ridiculous. No one says this unless he is influenced by bad philosophy, perhaps of the kind that interprets 'motive' half in the ordinary way and half as 'whatever it is that moves us to action', thinking that there must always be such a "moving force." Considerations such as "I promised" or "It is his property" do very generally move people to action. If they did not they could not play the part in human life which they do. By hypothesis they do not move the totally selfish, shameless man, and perhaps there is no way in which we can touch his life. But it is an advantage, not a disadvantage, in an account of reasons for action, that it leaves room for such a person. To show that there is reason for him, as for everyone else, to do what justice demands, we do not have to show how he can be *got to act*.

This concludes what I want to say here about the rationality of justice; which I believe can be applied, *mutatis mutandis* to other virtues which have to do with the good of others rather than oneself, as, e.g., charity and parental devotion. It is time, therefore, to confront the theories of practical rationality which, I suggested, were wrongly seen as preconceived structures into which we must try to fit the rationality of moral action. We have to deal with these theories—or at least with the examples of irrationality on which they relied—if the concept of practical rationality is not to break apart. We have to take account of the irrationality of self-destructiveness for instance, or with selling one's birthright for a mess of potage. And I think here of a burglar I once read of who sat down to watch television in the house he was burgling, and got caught. Here too there were good reasons for acting otherwise, whether the agent recognized them or not. Through his lack of concern for consequences he was so far forth deficient in practical rationality, so that he acted badly not only in thieving but also in this respect.

Do we then have two different kinds of rationality, with a theory for each; one to fit the examples just given and another to fit the rationality of acting justly or according to other virtues? Not at all. For if I am not mistaken, the basic ground of the rationality is in both cases the same.

Why, after all, do most of us so readily accept that a rational person takes account of his own good, weighing advantages and disadvantages of action by their effect on his future, even his distant future? To do so is a possibility for human beings as it is not, or not in the same way, for animals, because language allows us to throw our thoughts into a hypothetical future as they cannot. Moreover, human beings *need* to do this. It is part of the way they survive and flourish. Unless others looked after him, the life of one who never came to do it would be nasty, brutish, and short. Moreover, it is a feature of the way we operate—one so general that we hardly notice it—that each one of us takes special thought for his or her *own* life. Here some variation is possible. We hire doctors to tell us what to do for our future health, and might give them more power to act for us than we do. But it would obviously be ridiculous for everyone to act for everyone: no one can see more than a very little on so vast a scale. A sort of "buddy system" might be suggested, by which each person looked after one other, and was looked after by one other in his turn. But no one can plan for another human being as he can plan for himself, if only because intentions form so large a part of plans. Our behaviour would therefore be defective if we had no special care for ourselves.

There are many facets of practical rationality which seem to be based in the same kind of necessities of human life. There is, for instance, the properly careful consideration of means to ends, and the willingness to take the best means even when they are toilsome or alarming, or when they involve the denial of an urgent wish. To fail in this can be in itself a fault, as it was with the TV burglar. This does not of course imply that ends are neutral from the point of view of practical rationality.[10] If my argument is correct the burglar had two faults, both failures of practical rationality: one because he failed to see (or to act on) the fact that there is reason not to steal, and another because he failed to see (or to act on) the fact that there is reason not to risk imprisonment for half an hour's TV.

It would have been natural to end the preceding paragraph by saying that there was a *more compelling* reason for leaving the house quickly than there was for sitting down in front of the television. And it is time now to say more about the relative strength of reasons, which I have hardly touched on yet. Is this, too, determined, when determinate, by facts of human life? It seems to me that it is. It is obvious, for instance, that the fulfilment of promises must take precedence—some precedence—over the plans and interests of the promiser; otherwise the power to bind the will of another through promises would have little strength. It is obvious too why it is not a fault to give one's own serious interest, and the interest of one's family, some precedence over that of strangers; and obvious why rationality demands that in general parents put the good of their children before their own. This, one would say, reverting to the concept of absolute need, is what needs to happen for the averting of harm and provision of the kind of good without which human beings can be counted as deprived.

Nothing of this implies that such questions of precedence are always easy to answer; nor does it rule out large areas of indeterminacy. A special problem of precedence also arises from the distinction of greater and lesser human goods. Some things are important in human life, while others are less important or trivial; and wisdom, as part of practical rationality, must take account of this in governing our aims. I cannot even begin to deal with this topic here, except to notice a conceptual connexion with the concept of deprivation (as opposed to hardship). It is a reasonable assumption, however, that the idea of *importance* must depend on facts about the things that run deep in human life, however exactly that should be understood.

I would claim that in spite of many unsolved problems, the general picture is clear. The suggestion is that the notion of practical rationality is correlative to that of the goodness of action, so far as that consists in the proper following of reasons. What is "proper" or "good" here is determined by human life and its necessities, analogously to the way in which good or (proper) sight or locomotion or memory is determined in both animals and men. Thus practical rationality includes prudential self-interest, the weighing of advantages, the adoption of means to the securing of ends, but also such other-regarding matters as care for offspring, fidelity to contracts, and mutual aid. One has no reason to say that practical rationality has to do especially with the agent's own self-interest or his own desires, except when that has rational precedence, as it does sometimes but certainly not always. Nor is there any point in keeping bits of the vocabulary to signify practical rationality in one particular aspect. We could of course do so, as, e.g., by using 'irrational' to mean something like 'acting against one's own interests and desires', and 'rational' to mean 'not-irrational'. Such is, I suppose, the intention of those who are ready to speak of 'rational villains'. But this decision would make *akrasia* as such not irrational, which it is normally supposed to be. Moreover, there would be only awkward ways of expressing the contrariety to rationality of breaking promises or neglecting one's children. The suggested usage belongs, I think, with the whole idea of a preconceived, "desire-based" concept of practical rationality; which it is the intention of this paper to subvert.

The strategy I adopted was to set aside these received theories of practical rationality which raised problems about the rationality of moral action, returning to them only at the end of the paper. I argued that if justice is a virtue it must make action good by disposing its possessor to goodness in practical rationality; the latter consisting of the right recognition of reasons, and corresponding action. I then argued that justice is indeed a virtue, having introduced the idea of autonomous species-dependent goodness to show how I thought that the argument should go. Finally, I suggested that the examples of prudential and desire-fulfilling actions, on which the preconceived theories had been based, were themselves in need of the same kind of scrutiny, and could in fact be validated in the same way. We were left, therefore, not with two rival accounts of practical rationality, but with only one.

Acknowledgments

The ideas in this paper owe much to the work of Warren Quinn and Michael Thompson. I have benefited, too, from criticisms, from Rosalind Hursthouse and from participants at the Vienna Circle Institute's Conference "Norms, Values, and Society" in Sept.–Oct. 1993.

Notes

1. Plato, *Republic*, 348c2–d3.
2. P. T. Geach, "Good and Evil," *Analysis* 17 (1956): 33–42.

3. See Philippa Foot, "Goodness and Choice," *Proceedings of the Aristotelian Society, Supplementary Volume* 35 (1961): 45–60; reprinted in Foot, *Virtues and Vices* (Oxford: Blackwell, 1978; Oxford: Oxford University Press, 2002).

4. I mean by this to exclude, e.g., comfort to a rider in the evaluation of the way a horse moves.

5. Whether it actually does so depends, of course, partly on external circumstances and on other things about itself.

6. He is contrasting this with the "relative need" which would be implied if someone said that he needed money for an expensive suit. David Wiggins, "Claims of Need," in Wiggins, *Needs, Values, Truth* (Oxford: Blackwell, 1987).

7. Thomas Aquinas, *Summa Theologica*, 1a 2ae, q. 1 a. 2 (First Part of the Second Part, question 1, article 4).

8. G. E. M. Anscombe, "On Promising and Its Justice," in Anscombe *Collected Philosophical Papers* (Minneapolis: University of Minnesota Press, 1981), iii, 18.

9. Philippa Foot, "Morality as a System of Hypothetical Imperatives," *Philosophical Review* 81/3 (1972): 305–316.

10. For a powerful criticism of this Humean idea, see Warren Quinn, "Rationality and the Human Good," in Quinn, *Morality and Action* (Cambridge: Cambridge University Press, 1993).

15 Reasons and Motivation

Derek Parfit

As rational beings, we can ask:

What do we have most reason to want, and do?

What is it most rational for us to want, and do?

These questions differ in only one way. While reasons are provided by the facts, the rationality of our desires and acts depends instead on what we believe, or—given the evidence, ought rationally to believe. When we believe the relevant facts, these questions have the same answers. In other cases, it can be rational to want, or do, what we have no reason to want, or do. Thus, if I believe falsely that my hotel is on fire, it may be rational for me to jump into the canal; but I may have no reason to jump. Since beliefs aim at truth, and to be rational is to respond to reasons, it is the first question that is fundamental.

This question is about *normative* reasons. When we have such a reason, and we act for that reason, it becomes our *motivating* reason. But we can have either kind of reason without having the other. Thus, if I jump into the canal, my motivating reason was provided by my belief; but I had no normative reason to jump. I merely thought I did. And, if I failed to notice that the canal was frozen, I had a reason not to jump that, because it was unknown to me, did not motivate me.

Though we can have normative reasons without being motivated, and vice versa, such reasons are closely related to our motivation. There are, however, very different views about what this relation is. This disagreement raises wider questions about what normative reasons *are*, and about *which* reasons there are. After sketching some of these views, I shall discuss some arguments by Williams, and then say where, in my opinion, the truth lies.[1]

I

Following Williams, we can distinguish two kinds of theory.[2] According to

Internalism about reasons: All normative reasons are in this sense *internal*: for it to be true that

(R) we have a reason to do something,

it must be true that either

(D) doing this thing might help to fulfil one of our present intrinsic desires,

or

(M) if we knew the relevant facts, and deliberated rationally, we would be motivated to do this thing.

Our desire for something is *intrinsic* if we want this thing for its own sake. Facts are *relevant* if our knowledge of them might affect our motivation. We can be *motivated* to do something without being moved to do it. But, for us to be motivated, it must be true that, given the opportunity, and in the absence of contrary or competing motivations, we would do this thing.

Many Internalists believe that, if either (D) or (M) is true, that is not only necessary but also sufficient for the having of a reason. Though my remarks will often apply to this simpler view, I shall not say when that is so. Similarly, though (D) could be true while (M) is false, and vice versa, I shall here, like Williams, set (D) aside.

According to *Externalists*, at least some reasons for acting are not internal, since they do not require the truth of (M). Suppose that I have borrowed money from some poor person. This fact, some Externalists would claim, gives me a reason to return this money. In calling this reason *external*, they would not mean that I am not motivated to return this money. They would mean that I have this reason whatever my motivational state.

Consider next one of Williams's examples. Suppose that, by taking a certain medicine, someone could protect his health against some illness in the future. According to Internalists, if this person did not care about his further future, and his indifference would survive any amount of informed and rational deliberation, he would have no reason to take this medicine.[3] Most Externalists would disagree. On their view, we all have reasons to protect our health, and to prevent our own future suffering, and these reasons do not depend on whether, after informed and rational deliberation, we would care about these things.

There is now a complication. Many Externalists would claim that, if we knew the relevant facts and were fully rational, we would be motivated to do whatever we had reason to do. This claim is not, as it may seem, a concession to Internalism. According to these Externalists, if

(R) we have a reason to do something,

that entails that

(E) if we knew the relevant facts, and were fully *substantively* rational, we would be motivated to do this thing.

To be substantively rational, we must care about certain things, such as our own well-being. If Williams's imagined person were fully rational, these Externalists would claim, he would be motivated to take the medicine that he knows he needs. That could be true even if, because he is not fully substantively rational, no amount of informed deliberation would in fact motivate him.

Internalists hold a different view. On their view, more fully stated, for it to be true that

(R) we have a reason to do something,

it must be true that

(M) if we knew the relevant facts, and deliberated in a way that was *procedurally* rational, we would be motivated to do this thing.

To be procedurally rational, we must deliberate in certain ways, but we are not required to have any particular desires or aims, such as concern about our own well-being. If Internalists allowed such further requirements, then, as Williams writes, "there would be no significant difference between the internalist and externalist accounts," since Internalism would allow "anything the externalist could want."[4]

Given the difference between (E) and (M), the distinction between these views is deep. Most Internalists describe deliberation in partly normative terms. But, since their conception of rationality is procedural, it is an empirical, psychological question whether claims like (M) are true.[5] Thus we might be unable to predict whether, if Williams's imagined person were procedurally rational, he would be motivated to take the medicine that he knows he needs.[6] When Externalists appeal to (E), their claim is not empirical. It is a normative question whether, if this person failed to be motivated, that would make him less than fully rational.

There is a related difference in the way the inferences run. According to Internalists, if (R) is true, that is *because* (M) is true. The psychological fact described in (M) is, or is part of, what makes (R) true. According to Externalists, (E) is merely a consequence of (R). What gives us reasons for acting are not facts about our own motivation, but facts about our own or other people's well-being, or facts about other things that are worth achieving, or—some would add—moral requirements. Internalists derive conclusions about reasons from psychological claims about the motivation that, under certain conditions, we would in fact have. Externalists derive, from normative claims about what is worth achieving, conclusions about reasons, and about the motivation that we ought to have.

If we turn to morality, there is a similar pair of views. According to

Moral Internalism: We cannot have a duty to act in some way unless (M) is true.

This view restricts the range of those to whom moral claims apply. According to Moral Internalists, if informed and rational deliberation would not lead us to be motivated to do something, it cannot be our duty to do this thing. Those who were sufficiently ruthless, or amoral, would have no duties—and, some Internalists conclude, could not be held to be acting wrongly. *Moral Externalists* reject these claims. On the simplest version of their view, moral requirements apply to all of us, whether or not (M) is true.

We should also consider a view, not about the motivational implications of reasons or morality, but about moral reasons. According to

Moral Rationalism: Moral requirements always give, to those to whom they apply, reasons for acting.

According to those who reject Moral Rationalism, people who do not care about morality might have a duty to act in some way without having any reason to do so.

The relation between these views can be shown [as in fig. 15.1]. If we are Externalists about both reasons and morality, we may believe that we always have a moral reason to do our duty. This is view (2), or Externalist Moral Rationalism. On a stronger version of this view, if some act is our duty, that makes it what we have most reason to do.

Though Double Externalists can be Moral Rationalists, they do not have to be. According to some writers, for example, though self-interest provides external reasons, morality does not. Such people accept view (1).[7]

Reasons and Motivation

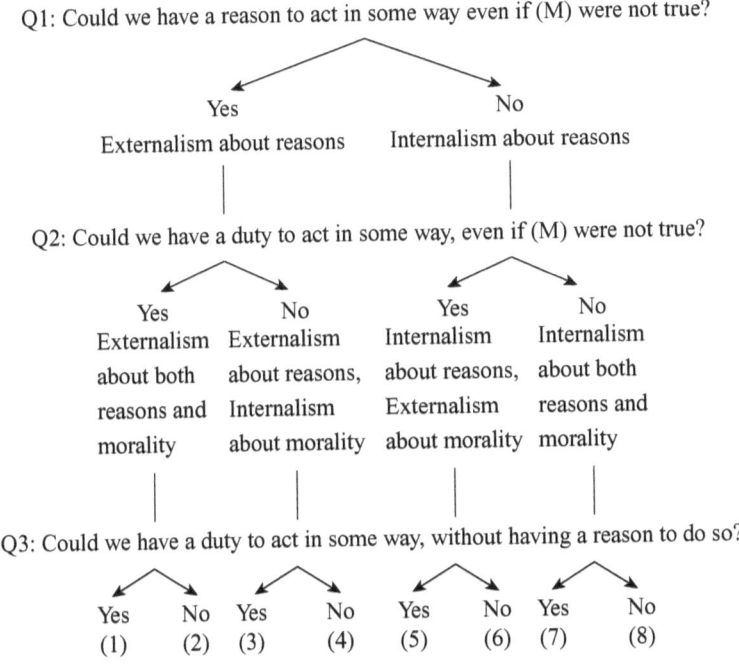

Figure 15.1

If we are Double Internalists, we are likely to be Moral Rationalists, accepting (8) rather than (7). On this view, we cannot have a duty to act in some way unless (M) is true, and we are likely to believe that (M)'s truth would, in such cases, give us a reason for acting. We would then conclude that we always have a reason to do our duty. This version of Moral Rationalism is weaker than the Externalist version, since it restricts morality to those who have moral motivation.

Even if we are Internalists about reasons, we may believe that moral requirements apply to everyone. We shall then combine Internalism about reasons with Externalism about morality. On this view, we cannot be Moral Rationalists. We preserve morality's scope at the cost of denying its reason-giving force. Though we believe that people can have duties whatever their motivational state, we must admit that, on our view, people may have no reason to do their duty. Since this view implies (5), (6) is untenable.

The remaining views are (3) and (4), which combine Externalism about reasons with Internalism about morality. Though not incoherent, these views are too implausible to be worth discussing.

Consider now, not our *having* some reason for acting, but our *believing* that we have some reason. According to

Belief Internalism: Beliefs about reasons necessarily involve motivation. We cannot believe that we have a reason to do something without being motivated to do this thing.

Belief Externalists reject this claim. More commonly appealed to is another, more restricted view. According to

Moral Belief Internalism: Moral beliefs necessarily involve motivation. We cannot believe some act to be our duty without being motivated to do it.

On a stronger version of this view, we cannot have a moral belief without being moved, if the opportunity arises, to act upon it.[8]

Consider next some views about motivation. According to

the Humean theory: No belief could motivate us unless it is combined with some independent desire.

Such a desire is *independent* when it is not itself produced by our having this belief.

As Nagel and others claim, we can reject this theory.[9] When we come to have some belief—such as the belief that some aim is worth achieving—that might cause us to have some wholly new desire. Such a belief could not all by itself cause us to have this desire, since we would have to be *such that*, if we came to have this belief, that would cause us to have this desire. But this disposition may not itself be a desire. On a variant of this anti-Humean view, whenever a belief moves us to act, we can he truly said to have wanted to act as we did; but this desire may not be a distinct mental state, since it may consist in our being moved by this belief. In either of these ways, reason might have the power that Hume denied. By giving us such beliefs, reason might motivate us without the help of any independent desire.

Humeans might retreat to the view that, for beliefs to motivate us, they must be combined with desires, even if these beliefs themselves produce these desires. But, with this revision, the Humean theory would lose most of its significance. According to Hume, reason is, and must be, wholly inert or inactive, as must be anything that reason alone could produce.[10] We could not claim that reason cannot be active on the ground that, though it might motivate us, it could do that only by producing some new desire. That would be like claiming that some bomb cannot be destructive because, though it might destroy us, it could do that only by producing some explosion.

Consider finally two Humean arguments. According to some non-cognitivists:

(A) If we have some moral conviction, we must be motivated to act upon it.
(B) If moral convictions were beliefs, (A) could not be true.
Therefore
(C) Moral convictions cannot be beliefs.

In defending (B), these non-cognitivists appeal to the Humean theory. They might say: "If moral convictions were beliefs, they could not motivate us without the help of some independent desire, so it would be conceivable that we might have some moral conviction without being motivated to act upon it. Since that is inconceivable, moral convictions must themselves be desires, or pro-attitudes."

If we are cognitivists about morality, and wish to deny (B), it would not be enough to show that we can reject the Humean theory. Even if moral beliefs *could* motivate us without the help of some independent desire, that would not explain how such beliefs *necessarily* involve motivation. To reject (B), we might appeal to

the Platonic theory: Moral knowledge necessarily motivates.

Or we might claim that, unless we cared about morality, we would not be able to have moral beliefs. But, for cognitivists, both claims are hard to defend and explain.[11]

We may find it easier to question (A), or Moral Belief Internalism. Or we might try to show that, in the sense in which (A) is true, it does not support non-cognitivism. Thus we might claim that, while moral beliefs are not called 'convictions' or 'sincere' unless they involve motivation, those who lack such motivation might still know that their acts were wrong. Such knowledge may imply belief in the sense that cognitivism requires.

According to another Humean argument:

(D) When moral convictions motivate us, they can do that without the help of any independent desire.
(E) No belief could have this property.
Therefore
(C) Moral convictions cannot be beliefs, but must themselves be desires.

This argument is weaker. Unlike (A), (D) has little intuitive appeal.[12] And, to deny (E), it *is* enough to reject the Humean theory.

My description of these views differs from those that are sometimes given. Several writers, for example, conflate my four versions of Internalism. That leads them to overlook important possibilities. Consider next what Korsgaard calls

the internalism requirement: "Practical reason claims, if they are really to present us with reasons for action, must be capable of motivating rational persons."[13]

My Externalists could accept this requirement. Some would make the stronger claim that, if we believe that we have a reason to do something, and we are fully practically rational, we *must* be motivated to do this thing.

Korsgaard also says that, according to externalists, an act's rightness is not a reason for doing it.[14] Several other writers make such claims.[15] This use of 'externalist' conflicts with mine. It is my Double Externalists who can most easily be Moral Rationalists, since they can regard morality as always giving everyone reasons for acting. Why do these writers claim that, if we are externalists, we shall deny that an act's rightness is a reason for doing it? They may assume that, even if we are Externalists about morality, or moral beliefs, we must be Internalists about reasons.[16] Or they may conflate normative reasons and motivating states.[17]

We can now draw some more distinctions. According to Internalists, for it to be true that

(R) We have a reason to do something,

it is necessary—and, some add, sufficient—that

(M) if we deliberated on the facts in a procedurally rational way, we would be motivated to do this thing.

This view can take at least three forms:

Analytically Reductive: When we assert (R), what we mean is (M).

Non-Analytically Reductive: Though these claims do not mean the same, when (R) is true, that normative fact is the same as, or consists in, the fact reported by (M).

Non-Reductive: The facts reported by (R) and (M) are very different. While (M) is psychological, (R) is an irreducibly normative truth.

Reductive Internalism is a form of naturalism. Non-Reductive Internalism is a form of non-reductive normative realism.

Reasons and Motivation

There is another form of Internalism that is, in a weak sense, non-reductive. According to some non-cognitivists, since (R) is a normative claim, it cannot be, in a strong sense, true. If we claim that (R) requires (M), we are expressing some kind of attitude.[18]

Similar remarks apply to Externalism. Thus, according to most Externalists,

(P) We have a prudential reason to act in some way

if and only if

(S) this way of acting would promote our own well-being.

(P) and (S) might mean the same, or report the same fact in two different ways, or report two very different facts, or this Externalist view might consist in the holding of some attitude.

That completes my proposed taxonomy. I shall now begin to suggest why, as I believe, we should be non-reductive normative realists, and should regard all reasons as external.

II

In the articles that have done most to clarify and to show the importance of these questions, Williams argues that there are no external reasons.

Williams's main objection is that Externalists have not explained what such reasons could be. He considers someone who maltreats his wife, and whose attitudes and acts would not be altered by informed and rational deliberation. If we are Externalists, we might claim that, despite this man's motivational state, his wife's unhappiness gives him reasons to treat her better. In rejecting this claim, Williams asks:

> what is the difference supposed to be between saying that the agent has a reason to act more considerately, and saying one of the many other things we can say to people whose behaviour does not accord with what we think it should be? As, for instance, that it would be better if they acted otherwise?[19]

We might answer: "The difference is that, if we merely said that it would be better if this man acted more considerately, we would not be claiming that, as we believe and you deny, he has reasons to do so."

Williams's ground for rejecting this claim is that he finds it "quite obscure" what it could mean. As he writes elsewhere, Externalists do not "offer any *content* for external reasons statements."[20]

Williams may here be assuming Analytical Internalism.[21] On this view, in claiming that

(1) this man has reasons to treat his wife better,

we would mean that

(2) if he deliberated rationally on the facts, he would be motivated to treat her better.

If (1) meant (2), and we knew that (2) was false, it would indeed be obscure what, in claiming (1), we could mean. *Non*-Analytical Internalists would not find our claim so obscure. Such Internalists believe that, though (1) is true only if (2) is true, these claims have different meanings. These Internalists would understand—though they would reject—the view that, despite this man's motivational state, he has reasons to treat his wife better.

Discussing another, similar example, Williams asks:

What is gained, except perhaps rhetorically, by claiming that A has a reason to do a certain thing, when all one has left to say is that this is what . . . a decent person . . . would do?[22]

This question seems to assume that, if our claim about A does not have the sense described by Analytical Internalists, there is nothing distinctive left for it to mean. We couldn't mean that, despite A's motivational state, A has a reason to do this thing. If we could mean that, there would be a simple answer to Williams's question. We might be saying something that was both distinctive and true.

Williams continues:

it would make a difference to ethics if certain kinds of *internal* reason were very generally to hand . . . But what difference would external reasons make? . . . Should we suppose that, if genuine external reasons were to be had, morality might get some leverage on a squeamish Jim or priggish George, or even on the fanatical Nazi? . . . I cannot see what leverage it would secure: what would these external reasons do to these people, or for our relations to them?

These remarks assume that, for external reasons to make a difference to ethics, such reasons would have to get *leverage* on people, by motivating them to act differently. This conception of ethics is, I believe, too utilitarian. When we believe that other people have reasons for caring, or for acting, we do not have these beliefs as a way of affecting those people. Our aim is, not influence, but truth. Similar remarks apply to morality. Someone might say:

What difference would it make if it were true that the Nazis acted wrongly? What leverage would that moral fact have secured? What would the wrongness of their acts have done to them?

Reasons and Motivation

Even if moral truths cannot affect people, they can still be truths. People can be acting wrongly, though the wrongness of their acts does not do anything to them.

After asking what external reasons would do to such people, Williams writes:

> Unless we are given an answer to that question, I, for one, find it hard to resist Nietzsche's plausible interpretation, that the desire of philosophy to find a way in which morality can be guaranteed to get beyond merely *designating* the vile and recalcitrant, to transfixing them or getting inside them, is only a fantasy of *ressentiment*, a magical project to make a wish and its words into a coercive power.[23]

Williams has a real target here. Many philosophers have hoped to find moral arguments, or truths, that could not fail to motivate us. Williams, realistically, rejects that hope.

Note however that, in making these remarks, Williams assumes that claims about reasons could achieve only two things. If such claims cannot get inside people, by inducing them to act differently, they can only designate these people. On the first alternative, these claims would have motivating force. On the second, they would be merely classificatory, since their meaning would be only that, if these people were not so vile, or were in some other way different, they *would* act differently. As before, however, there is a third possibility. Even when such claims do not have motivating force, they could be more than merely classificatory. They could have *normative* force. Perhaps these people *should* act differently.

We should remember next that Externalists need not be Moral Rationalists. Some Externalists would agree with Williams that those who act wrongly may have no reason to act differently. These people are Externalists in their beliefs about prudential reasons. Return to Williams's imagined person who needs some medicine to protect his health, and whose failure to care about his future would survive any amount of informed and procedurally rational deliberation. Such a person, Williams writes, would have no reason to take this medicine.[24] He might ask:

> What would be gained by claiming that this person has such a reason? What would that add to the claim that, if he were prudent, he would take this medicine?

This claim would add what Williams denies. This person, these Externalists believe, ought rationally to take this medicine. He has reasons to care about his future; and, since these are reasons for caring, this person's failure to care does not undermine these reasons. Such claims, I believe, make sense, and might be true.

Williams suggests several arguments against their sense and truth. According to one such argument:

(A) Normative reasons must be able to be motivating reasons. It must be possible that we should act *for these reasons*.

(B) Motivating reasons must be internal, since our acts must be in part explained by our desires, or other motivating states.

Therefore

(C) Normative reasons must be internal.[25]

If we reject the Humean theory of motivation, we might question (B). Some of our acts, we might claim, are fully explained by our beliefs.

We can also claim, that in the sense in which (A) is true, it does not support (C). Suppose that, unlike Williams's imagined person, I care about my future. As Internalists would then agree, if it is true that

(3) I need some medicine to protect my health,

this fact would give me a reason to take this medicine. For (3) to give me such a reason, it must be possible, as (A) claims, that I should act for this reason. That condition would be met if, when asked why I took this medicine, I could truly answer, "Because I need it to protect my health." The normative reason provided by (3) could then be said to *be* my motivating reason. But, though these reasons would be in that sense the same, they would still differ in at least two ways. First, for (3) to have given me my motivating reason, I must have believed (3). But, even if I had not had this belief, (3)'s truth would have given me a normative reason to take this medicine. We can have reasons of which we are unaware.[26] Second, I would have had this same motivating reason even if my belief had been false.[27] But, if (3) had been false, I would have had no normative reason to take this medicine: I would have merely thought I did. So, while motivating reasons require that we have some belief, whether of not this belief is true, normative reasons are provided by some truth, whether or not we believe it.

Return now to the argument sketched above. Perhaps, for (3) to have given me my motivating reason, I must have wanted to protect my health, or had some other relevant desire. That might make this reason internal. But that would not show that my normative reason must have been internal. As we have just seen, normative and motivating reasons are not identical. Though motivating reasons require that we have some belief, that is not true of the corresponding normative reasons. Since an appeal to (A) could not show that, to have some normative reason, we must have some belief, it cannot show that, to have some normative reason, we must have some desire, or other motivating state. Externalists are free to claim that, even if I had not cared about my health, and my indifference would have survived procedurally rational deliberation, I would have had a normative reason to take the medicine that I need.[28]

Consider next someone who has no internal reason to act in some way. Let us call this person *Jack*, and this way of acting *X*. Suppose we claim that

(4) Jack has some external reason to do X.

Williams writes that, if Jack comes to believe (4), "he will be motivated to act; so coming to believe it must, essentially, involve acquiring a new motivation. How can that be?"[29] These remarks suggest that, if we are Externalists, we cannot explain the truth of Belief Internalism.

There is, I believe, nothing to explain. Belief Internalism is most clearly false when applied to people who accept Reductive Internalism. Suppose that such a person comes to believe that

(5) if he knew certain facts, and deliberated rationally, he would be motivated to act in some way.

As a Reductive Internalist, this person may conclude that he has a reason to act in this way. But, because he doesn't yet know these facts, he might not be motivated to do so. People often try to avoid learning certain facts because they want to avoid the motivation which, as they predict, that knowledge would arouse in them.

Externalists need not claim that, if Jack came to believe (4), that would guarantee that he would be motivated to do X. But they might claim that, if Jack were rational, his coming to have this belief would motivate him. For that to be so, Williams writes, (4) "will have to be taken as roughly equivalent to, or at least as entailing," the claim that

(6) if Jack "rationally deliberated, then, whatever motivations he originally had, he would come to be motivated" to do X.

But, if (4) entails (6), Williams continues,

it is very plausible to suppose that all external reason statements are false. For, *ex hypothesi*, there is no motivation for the agent to deliberate *from*, to reach this new motivation.

If Jack did become motivated to do X, as a result of such deliberation, Jack's new motivation would have to have been reached *from* some earlier motivation. But "in that case," Williams objects, "an *internal* reason statement would have been true."[30]

If we are Externalists, we could give three replies. First, this objection seems to assume the Humean theory. As I have said, we can reject this theory. When Jack comes to believe (4), that might produce in him some wholly new desire.[31] For that to happen, Jack would have to be such that, if he came to believe (4), he would develop this new desire; but that disposition may not itself be a desire, or other motivating state. Since Jack would not be deliberating *from* some earlier motivation, it is doubtful whether, before he developed this desire, he would have had an internal reason to do X.

Second, even if Jack would have had such a reason, that would not show it to be false that

(4) Jack has some external reason to do X.

(4) does not imply that Jack has no internal reason to do X. (4) means that Jack has a reason to do X that is not provided by, and does not require, the motivational fact—(M)—to which Internalists appeal. Jack may have this external reason even if, because (M) is true, he also has an internal reason to do the same thing.[32]

Third, when Williams refers to *rational* deliberation, he uses 'rational', as we have seen, in a procedural sense. For our deliberation to be procedurally rational, we must avoid "errors of fact or reasoning," and we must meet certain other conditions; but there are no substantive requirements on the motivation with which we begin. If that is the sense of 'rationally' used in (6), Externalists can deny that (4) entails (6). On that reading, the claim that (4) entails (6) assumes Internalism; so it cannot be an argument for this view. And if this entailment seems plausible, Externalists can say, that is because (6) has a different reading. (6) could be taken to mean

(7) If Jack deliberated on the facts, and were fully substantively rational, he would be motivated to do X.

To be substantively rational, we must want, and do, what we know that we have most reason to want and do. If what (4) entails is (7), it is irrelevant whether, after informed and procedurally rational deliberation, Jack would be motivated to do X. What (4) would entail is that, if Jack were substantively rational, his awareness of this external reason would motivate him. This claim, which Externalists could happily accept, is not challenged by the argument that we are now discussing.[33]

Williams sometimes appeals to a weaker form of Internalism. On this view, for it to be true that we have a reason to do something, it need not be true that, after a certain process of deliberation, we *would* become motivated to do this thing. What is required is only that, by deliberating in this way, we *could rationally* come to have such motivation.[34]

When stating this view, Williams often applies it, not to our becoming motivated, but to our deciding to act. For such a decision to be rational, as Williams notes, we must believe that we have *most* reason to act in some way. According to what we can call

Weak Internalism: For it to be true that

(A) X is what we have most reason to do,

it must be true that

(B) there is "a sound deliberative route," starting from our "existing motivations," by which we could rationally decide to do X.

According to the rival view, which we can call

Strong Externalism: If it is true that

(A) X is what we have most reason to do,

it must be true that

(C) we could rationally decide to do X, for this reason, *whatever* our existing motivations.[35]

In rejecting Strong Externalism, Williams calls it "unattractive." What objection might he have in mind?

Strong Externalists assume that, given certain ways of specifying X, (A) could be true whatever our existing motivations. Williams would reject this assumption, since he believes that, for (A) to be true, (B) must be true. But, since this belief assumes Weak Internalism, it cannot provide an argument for preferring Weak Internalism to the rival, Strong Externalist view.

Such an argument must allow us to suppose that, whatever our existing motivations, (A) might be true. The argument must claim that, even if we come to believe truly that

(A) X is what we have most reason to do,

that, by itself, would not make it rational for us to decide to do X. For such a decision to be rational, we must have reached it by a deliberative route that appealed to some motivation that we already had.[36]

There seem to be two ways to defend these claims. Weak Internalists might say that, even if (A) is true, we could not rationally come to believe

(A) except by deliberating from some earlier motivation. Or they might say that even if, in some other way, we have rationally come to believe (A), that would not make it rational for us, whatever our earlier motivations, to decide to do X.

Both these claims can be plausibly denied. If it is true that we have most reason to act in some way, it could be rational to come to believe that truth by some process of deliberation that did not start from facts about our existing motivations. When we consider certain other facts or arguments, we may rationally change our view about which aims are worth achieving, and we may thus be rationally led to some new belief about what we have reason to do.[37] And, if we believe both rationally and truly that we have most reason to act in some way, that must make it rational for us, whatever our earlier motivations, to decide to act in this way. That is an understatement. If we know that we have most reason to act in some way, it would be irrational for us *not* to make that decision.

Weak Internalists might now reply that, if we decide to do X because we come to believe (A), we must have been deliberating *from* one of our earlier motivations. Williams includes, among what he counts as motivations, "dispositions of evaluation."[38] Since our deliberation has led us to believe (A), and to decide to do X, we must have been such that, given such deliberation, we might come to reach that belief and make that decision. We must, that is, have had a disposition to reach this evaluative conclusion. And that might be held to show that, as Weak Internalists claim, any rational decision to act must be reached by deliberation from some pre-existing motivation.

Williams would not, I believe, give this reply. It would achieve nothing. No Externalist would mind conceding that, if our deliberation leads us to make some decision, we must have been such that our deliberation might lead us to make this decision.[39]

Return now to Williams's objections to the weaker form of Externalism. Williams suggests one other argument against this view. Externalists might say, he writes,

that the force of an external reason statement can be explained in the following way. Such a statement implies that a rational agent would be motivated to act appropriately, and it can carry this implication because a rational agent is precisely one who has a general disposition . . . to do what (he believes) there is reason for him to do.[40]

Such a claim, Williams objects,

merely puts off the problem . . . *What* is it that one comes to believe when he comes to believe that

[(1)] there is reason for him to do X.

if it is not the proposition, or something that entails the proposition, that

[(2)] if he deliberated rationally, he would be motivated to act appropriately?

We were asking how any true proposition could have that content; it cannot help, in answering that, to appeal to a supposed desire which is activated by a belief which has that very content.[41]

Since Williams believes that (1) could be true, and that (1) either means or entails (2), the problem that he mentions cannot be how propositions with that content could be true. But his objection may be this. If we claim that (1) means (2), and we use 'rationally' in (2) in Williams's preferred procedural sense, that gives (1) a determinate content. It is an empirical question whether, if someone deliberated in this way, he would be motivated to act. But, if (2) is to give the content of a claim about some *external* reason, it would have to use 'rationally' in the other, substantive sense: the sense in which, to be fully rational, we must be motivated by our awareness of any reason. On such a view, in claiming that

(1) someone has a reason to do X,

we would mean that

(3) if this person deliberated on the facts, and he would be motivated to do whatever he knew that he had a reason to do, he would be motivated to do X.

This account would be vacuously circular. It would be like the view that, in claiming

(4) We have a duty to do Y,

we mean

(5) Y is what, if we always did our duty, we would do.

Even Kant needed to assume more than that.

Externalists can reply that, even if (1) entails (3), that is not all that (1) means. Return to Williams's imagined person who does not care about his further future, and whose indifference would survive any amount of Internalist deliberation. When we claim that such a person has reasons to care about his future, and to take the medicine that he needs, we do not merely mean that, if he were fully rational, he *would* care, and *would* take this medicine.

What, then, *do* we mean? We are back with Williams's main objection. As he later wrote: "I do not believe . . . that the sense of external reason statements is in the least clear."[42]

III

Williams's objection has great force. It is not, however, an objection to Externalism. Some Externalists hold analytically reductive views. For example, they might say that, in claiming that this person has a reason to take this medicine, we mean that he needs this medicine, or that it would promote his well-being. Such proposed analyses are as clear as the one that Williams suggests.

Williams's objection applies to all views that are not analytically reductive. Some Internalists hold such views, since they believe that, even though claims about reasons must be supported by claims about the agent's motivation, that is not what they mean. If we hold such a view, and we were asked what 'reason' means, we would find this hard to explain. Reasons for acting, we might say, are facts that *count in favour* of some act. But 'counting in favour of' means 'giving a reason for'. Or we might say that, if we have *most reason* to act in some way, that is what we *ought rationally* to do, or—more colloquially—what we *should* do. But we could not understand this use of 'should' unless we had the concept of a reason.

These two concepts—that of a normative reason, and the concept that is expressed by this use of 'should'—cannot I believe be helpfully explained, since they cannot be explained in non-normative terms. This fact is not surprising. Normative concepts form a fundamental category—like, say, temporal or logical concepts. We should not expect to explain time, or logic, in non-temporal of non-logical terms. Similarly, normative truths are of a distinctive kind, which we should not expect to be like ordinary, empirical truths. Nor should we expect our knowledge of such truths, if we have any, to be like our knowledge of the world around us.

To defend such a view, we must answer several objections, and we must show that other views are, in various ways, inadequate. I hope to do that elsewhere.[43] I shall end, here, with some brief and oversimplified remarks.

Reductive Internalism, as I have said, is a form of naturalism. According to analytical naturalists, normative statements mean the same as certain statements about natural facts. That cannot be true, Moore argued, since we could believe the latter but intelligibly question the former. Analytical naturalists rightly reply that some definitional truths can be, because they are not obvious, intelligibly questioned.

Non-analytical naturalists reject Moore's argument as irrelevant. Such writers often appeal to analogies drawn from science, such as the discoveries that water is H_2O or that heat is molecular kinetic energy. These identities were not implied by the existing concepts of water and heat. In the same way, these writers claim, though normative and naturalistic statements do not mean the same, some pairs of such statements may turn out to refer to the same properties, or to report the same facts.

I believe that we should reject all forms of naturalism. Though we cannot helpfully explain what normative concepts mean, we can sufficiently explain what they do not mean. And we can thereby show that, if there are normative truths, these could not be the same as, or consist in, natural facts. These two kinds of fact are as different as the chairs and propositions that, in a dream, Moore once confused.

It may seem that, by appealing to claims about normative concepts, we could at most refute analytical naturalism. Since non-analytical naturalists do not appeal to claims about meaning, their views may seem immune to this kind of argument.

That, I believe, is not so. Reductive views can be both non-analytical and true when, and because, the relevant concepts leave open certain possibilities, between which we must choose on non-conceptual grounds. But many other possibilities are conceptually excluded. Thus it was conceptually possible that heat should turn out to be molecular kinetic energy. But heat could not have turned out to be a shade of blue, or a medieval king. In the same way, while it may not be conceptually excluded that experiences should turn out to be neurophysiological events, experiences could not turn out to be patterns of behaviour, or stones, or irrational numbers.

Similar claims apply, I believe, to Reductive Internalism, and to all other forms of naturalism. Since normative facts are in their own distinctive category, there is no close analogy for their irreducibility to natural facts. One comparison would be with proposed reductions of necessary truths—such as the truths of logic or mathematics—to certain kinds of contingent truths. Given the depth of the difference between these kinds of truth, we can be confident, I assume, that such reductions fail. There is a similar difference, I believe, between normative and natural truths.[44]

Compare, for example, these two claims:

(1) There are acts that maximize happiness.

(2) There are acts that are right.

According to Reductive Utilitarians, even if (1) and (2) have different meanings, they report the same fact. One objection to this view is that it makes morality trivial. We already knew that some acts maximize happiness; and it could not be significant that this fact could be redescribed by calling these acts right. For morality to be significant, it must claim that, when acts have certain natural properties, something *else* is true: these acts are *right*. These must be *different* properties, and *different* facts.⁴⁵

Return next to Reductive Internalism. Suppose that, because my hotel really is on fire, I know that

(A) Jumping into the canal is my only way to save my life.

Given my rational desire to live, I decide to jump. According to Reductive Internalists, if I accepted their view, my practical reasoning could be this:

(B) Jumping is what, after rationally deliberating on the truth of (A), I am most strongly motivated to do.

Therefore

(C) As another way of reporting (B), I could say that I have most reason to jump.

On this view, I believe, normativity disappears. If there are normative truths, they could not be facts like (B). When I believe that I have most reason to jump, I am believing that I *should* jump, and that, if I don't, I would be acting irrationally, or making a terrible mistake. That, if true, could not be the same as the fact that, after such deliberation, jumping is what I most want to do.

Reductive Internalists, or other naturalists, might give the following reply. When we claim that we have some reason for acting, what we appeal to is very often some natural fact. Thus, in our example, my reason to jump might be the fact that

(A) jumping is my only way to save my life,

or—less plausibly—the fact that

(D) jumping is my only way to get what I most want,

or—least plausibly—the fact described by (B). If any of these facts *is* my reason to jump, that reason, naturalists might claim, is a causal or psychological fact.

Such facts can indeed be claimed to be reasons for acting. But, if that is all we say, such claims are seriously misleading. They suggest that, in believing that there are normative reasons, and normative truths, we can avoid any commitment to non-natural properties and facts. That, I believe, is not so. We must distinguish between the fact that

(A) jumping is my only way to save my life,

and the fact that

(E) the truth of (A) gives me a reason to jump.

Though (A) has *normative significance*, (A) is not a normative fact. The normative fact is (E), or the fact *that* (A) has such significance. That is not, like (A) itself, an empirical or natural fact.

Naturalists would now reply that their view sufficiently preserves normativity. Thus, when discussing Analytical Internalism, Williams writes:

> It is important that even on the internalist view, a statement of the form 'A has reason to do X' still has what may be called *normative force*. Unless a claim to the effect that an agent has a reason to do X can go beyond what that agent is already motivated to do . . . then certainly the term will have too narrow a definition. 'A has reason to do X' means more than 'A is presently disposed to do X'.[46]

Williams's point may here be this. When we say that you have a reason to do something, we intend to be giving you advice. If our claim merely meant that you were already disposed to do this thing, that would hardly be advice. Things are different if we mean, not that you are *now* disposed to do this thing, but that you *would become* so disposed if you knew certain facts. As Williams later writes, in saying what someone has reason to do, we are allowed to correct this person's factual beliefs, and "that is already enough for the notion to be normative."[47]

That, I believe, is not so. On this view, if we claimed

(F) You have a reason to jump,

we would mean

(G) If you believed the truth, you would want to jump.

(G) could indeed be used to give you advice. You may rightly assume that, if (G) is true, you must have a reason to jump. But that does not make (G) normative. (G) is like

(H) This building is on fire,

which could also be used to give advice. These cannot be normative claims, since they do not even use a normative concept.

It may be said that, though (G) is not explicitly normative, this claim has normative *force*. Have I not just admitted that (G) could be used to give you advice? But this fact does not, I believe, answer this objection. In claiming (G), we may be implying that you have a reason to jump. But, for such advice to be implied, it must be able to be explicitly stated. We must be able to think about what we have reason to do, or what we ought rationally to do. To be able to think such thoughts, we must understand the normative concepts *ought* and *reason*. And, if (F) meant (G), the concept of a reason would not be normative. If we had no concepts with which we could directly state or understand normative claims, we could not imply such claims by making other non-normative claims, even ones with normative significance.

Williams's own view appeals, not to mere knowledge of the facts, but to *rational* deliberation. On his proposed account, statements about reasons are explicitly normative. But, as I have begun to suggest, they are still not *relevantly* normative. On this view, the fact that

(R) we have a reason to do something

is the same as the fact that

(M) after informed and procedurally rational deliberation, we would be motivated to do this thing.

However we answer the normative question of which kinds of deliberation are procedurally rational, (M), if true, is a psychological fact. Though such facts can have normative significance, they are not normative facts. And, if these were the only kinds of fact to which our view appealed, we could not understand their normative significance. Similar objections apply, I believe, to all forms of normative naturalism, including those that are not analytically reductive.

These objections, which I shall try to defend elsewhere,[48] assume a certain view about normativity. Many people, I should admit, hold very different views.

One difference is this. Many people, I believe mistakenly, regard normativity as some kind of motivating force. For example, Korsgaard writes that, if a certain argument "cannot motivate the reader to become a utilitarian then how can it show that utilitarianism is normative?"[49] Railton writes: "there is no need to explain the normative force of our moral judgments on those who have no tendency to accept them and who recognize no significant community with us. For that is not a force that we observe in moral practice."[50] McNaughton writes that, when externalists deny that moral beliefs necessarily motivate, they "deny the authority of moral demands."[51] Scheffler writes that, even if wrong-doing were always irrational, that would not give morality "as much authority as some might wish," since it would not "guarantee . . . morality's *hold* on us."[52]

Consider next some remarks of Mackie's. Since Mackie is an *error theorist*, who believes that ordinary moral thinking is committed to peculiar non-natural properties, we might expect that he at least would give a non-reductive account of the normativity that he rejects. Mackie writes that, according to some cognitivists, a moral judgment is "intrinsically and objectively prescriptive," since it "demands" some action, and implies that other actions are "not to be done." These phrases look normative. But Mackie later writes that, in response to Humean arguments for non-cognitivism, cognitivists might

> simply deny the minor premiss: that the state of mind which is the making of moral judgments and distinctions has, *by itself*, an influence on actions. [They] could say that just seeing that this is right and that is wrong will not tend to make someone do this or refrain from that: he must also *want* to do whatever is right.

If cognitivists made such claims, Mackie continues, they would "deny the *intrinsic* action-guidingness of moral judgments," and they would "save the objectivity of moral distinctions . . . only by giving up their prescriptivity." Mackie here assumes that, in claiming moral judgments to be action-guiding and prescriptive, we mean that such judgments can, by themselves, *influence* us, or tend to *make* us act in certain ways. So, even when describing the view that he rejects—or the "objectively prescriptive values" that he calls "too queer" to be credible—Mackie takes normativity to be a kind of motivating force.[53]

Normativity, I believe, is very different from motivating force. Neither includes, or implies, the other. Other animals can be motivated by their desires and beliefs. Only we can understand and respond to reasons.

Internalists could accept these claims. Some Internalists believe that, when we have some reason for acting, that is an irreducibly normative truth. But, as I shall also argue, we should reject even Non-Reductive Internalism.

If we consider only reasons for acting, Internalism may seem to be broadly right, or to contain most of the truth. But the most important reasons are not merely, or mainly, reasons for acting. They are also reasons for having the desires on which we act. These are reasons to want some thing, for its own sake, which are provided by facts about this thing. Such reasons we can call *value-based*.

Since Internalist theories are desire-based, they cannot recognize such reasons. On such theories, all reasons to have some desire must derive from other desires. Thus we might have reason to want something to happen because this thing would have effects that we want, or because we want to have this desire, or because we want the effects of having it. But we cannot have reasons, provided by the nature of some thing, to have an intrinsic desire for that thing. Such a reason would have to be provided by our wanting this thing; but the fact that we had this desire could not give us a reason for having it. So, on desire-based theories, any chain of reasons must end with some desire that we have no reason to have.

Such a view, I believe, misses most of the truth. According to many Internalists, all reasons are provided by desires. There are, I believe, no such reasons. It is true that, in most cases, we have some reason to fulfil our desires. But that is because, in these cases, what we want is in some way worth achieving. We can also have reasons that *depend* on our desires, since our having some desire may affect what is worth achieving, or preventing—as when it makes some experience enjoyable or frustrating. But the fact that we have some desire never, by itself, provides reasons.[54]

Why has it been so widely thought that all reasons must be provided by desires, since we cannot have value-based reasons to have these desires?

There are some bad arguments for this view. Thus Hume claimed that, since reasoning is entirely concerned with truth, and desires cannot be true or false, desires cannot be supported by or contrary to reason. If this argument were good, it would show that, since acts cannot be true or false, acts cannot be supported by or contrary to reason. Most Internalists would reject that conclusion. And Hume's argument is not good. Hume assumed that there is only one kind of reason: reasons for believing. He said nothing to support the view that we cannot have reasons either for caring or for acting.

Of the other grounds for ignoring, or rejecting, value-based reasons to have desires, one is especially relevant here. On Internalist theories, the source of all reasons is something that is not itself normative: it is the fact that we have some desire, or the fact that, if we knew more, we would be motivated to act in some way. On Externalist theories, the source of any reason is something normative. These theories appeal, not to facts about our actual or counterfactual desires, but to facts about what is relevantly worth achieving or preventing. Such alleged normative truths may seem to be metaphysically mysterious, or inconsistent with a scientific world view.

The important distinction here is not, however, between Internalism and Externalism. It is between reductive and non-reductive theories. For Internalist theories to be about normative reasons, they must, I have claimed, take a non-reductive form. Even if all reasons were provided by certain motivational facts, the fact that we have some reason could not be the same as, or consist in, such a motivational fact. Internalists must claim that, because some motivational fact obtains, something *else* is true: we have a reason for acting. In making that claim, they are committed to one kind of irreducibly normative truth. That undermines their reason to deny that there can be such truths about what is worth achieving, or preventing.

According to normative Internalism:

(A) Some acts really are rational. There are facts about these acts, and their relations to our motivation, which give us reasons to act in these ways.

According to normative Externalism:

(B) Some aims really are worth achieving. There are facts about these aims which give us reasons to want to achieve them.

(B), I believe, is no less plausible than (A). (B) has metaphysical implications, since it implies that there are irreducibly normative properties, or truths. But the same is true of (A).

Reasons for acting, I believe, are all external. When we have a reason to do something, this reason is not provided by, and does not require, the fact that after Internalist deliberation we would want to do this thing. This reason is provided by the facts that also give us reason to have this desire. We have reason to try to achieve some aim when, and because, it is relevantly worth achieving. Since these are reasons for *being* motivated, we would have these reasons even if, when we were aware of them, that awareness did not motivate us. But, if we are rational, it will.

Notes

1. Given the size of this territory, my map will have to be rough. I must make some claims which, unless further qualified, could not have a hope of being true. In writing this paper, I have been helped by several people, especially Bernard Williams, Jonathan Dancy, John Broome, Jeff McMahan, Ingmar Persson, Roger Crisp, Julian Savulescu, Brad Hooker, Jerry Cohen, Susan Hurley, Tim Scanlon, Jonathan Bennett, Philippa Foot, David McNaughton, Sigrún Svavarsdóttir, Mary Coleman. Ken O'Day and Sophia Reibetanz.

2. Williams drew this distinction in his "Internal and External Reasons," henceforth *IER*, reprinted in his *Moral Luck* (Cambridge: Cambridge University Press, 1981) [this volume, chap. 1]. He returned to it in "Internal Reasons and the Obscurity of Blame," henceforth *IROB*, in *Making Sense of Humanity* (Cambridge: Cambridge University Press, 1995); and again in *World, Mind, and Ethics*, henceforth *WME*, ed.

J. E. J. Altham and Ross Harrison (Cambridge: Cambridge University Press, 1995), pp. 186–194 [this volume, chap. 4] and 214–216.

3. Williams discusses this example in *IER*, pp. 105–106 [this volume, 41]. (To make the case more plausible, I have added the reference to the further future.)

4. *IROB*, p. 36.

5. More precisely, while it is a normative question which kinds of deliberation are procedurally rational, it is an empirical question whether, if we deliberated in such a way, we would be motivated to act.

6. As Williams writes: "I take it that insofar as there are determinately recognisable needs, there can be an agent who lacks any interest in getting what he needs. I take it, further, that lack of interest can remain after deliberation" (*IER*, p. 105) [this volume, 41].

7. This view was suggested, for example, in Philippa Foot's "Morality as a System of Hypothetical Imperatives," *Philosophical Review* 81/3 (1972): 305–316.

8. In drawing these distinctions, I follow Stephen Darwall, *Impartial Reason* (Ithaca, NY: Cornell University Press, 1983), p. 54.

9. *The Possibility of Altruism* (Princeton: Princeton University Press, 1970), chap. V [this volume, chap. 9]. Of the other authors who challenge this theory, I have learnt most from Jonathan Dancy, *Moral Reasons* (Oxford: Blackwell, 1993), chaps. 1 to 3, and "Why There Is Really No Such Thing as the Theory of Motivation," *Proceedings of the Aristotelian Society*, New Series 95 (1995):1–18; and Francis Snare, *Morals, Motivation, and Convention* (Cambridge: Cambridge University Press, 1991), chaps. 1 to 5.

10. In Hume's words, "an active principle can never be founded on an inactive," *A Treatise of Human Nature*, ed. L. A. Selby-Bigge (Oxford: Clarendon Press, 1896), p. 457.

11. We would also need to extend the Platonic theory so that it covered even false moral beliefs.

12. Though it might be claimed that (D) is implied by (A).

13. "Skepticism about Practical Reason," *Journal of Philosophy* 83: 5–25 [this volume, chap. 2].

14. "Kant's Analysis of Obligation: The Argument of *Groundwork I*," p. 43, reprinted in *Creating the Kingdom of Ends* (Cambridge: Cambridge University Press, 1996).

15. See, for example, David Brink, *Moral Realism and the Foundations of Ethics* (Cambridge: Cambridge University Press, 1989), pp. 37–43, and Michael Smith, *The Moral Problem* (Oxford: Blackwell, 1994), pp. 62–63.

16. Thus David McNaughton writes that, according to externalists, "someone who has no concern for human welfare may still recognize that inflicting unnecessary suffering on others is morally wrong. But that recognition is held not to be in itself sufficient to give him a reason to desist from causing such suffering. If he lacks the appropriate desires then he has no reason to act in accordance with moral requirements" (*Moral Vision* [Blackwell, 1988], pp. 48–49). My Externalists can deny that reasons presuppose desires.

17. Thus McNaughton also writes that externalism regards "moral questions as factual ones but distances them from *motivation* in its claim that moral commitments do not, in themselves, provide the agent with *reason* to act"; in contrast, on "an internalist account of moral *motivation*," there are facts awareness of which "will supply the observer with *reason* to act" (ibid., pp. 49 and 105, my italics).

18. Cf. Allan Gibbard, *Wise Choices, Apt Feelings* (Oxford: Oxford University Press, 1990). I must here ignore such views.

19. *IROB*, pp. 39–40.

20. *WME*, p. 191, my italics [this volume, 93].

21. As he seems to do elsewhere. Thus he writes: "I think the sense of a statement of the form 'A has a reason to *phi*' is given by the internalist model" (*IROB*, p. 40). See also *IER*, pp. 109–110 [this volume, 44], and *IROB*, p. 36. In his most recent discussion, however, in *MWE*, p. 188 [this volume, 90], Williams rejects Analytical Internalism.

22. *WME*, p. 215.

23. *WME*, p. 216.

24. *IER*, 105–106 [this volume, 41].

25. This argument, which Williams may not intend, is suggested by remarks in *IER*, pp. 102 and 106–107 [this volume, 38 and 42–45], and in *IROB*, p. 39.

26. As Williams would agree. See, for example, *IER*, pp. 102–103 [this volume, 39].

27. As Williams writes: "The difference between false and true beliefs on the agent's part cannot alter the *form* of the explanation which will be appropriate to his action" (*IER*, p. 102) [this volume, 38].

28. It may be objected that, if I had not cared about my health, and my indifference would have survived such deliberation, it would not have been possible, as (A) requires, that I should have acted for this reason. But, in the sense in which (A) is uncontroversial, it means only that, if certain facts are claimed to provide normative reasons, it must be true that "*people sometimes* act for these reasons" (*IER*, p. 102, my italics) [this volume, 38]. The kind of reason that (3) provides meets that requirement. People sometimes take medicine that they know they need. This last

objection takes (A) to mean that, for it to be true that some particular person has some normative reason, it must be possible that, on *this* occasion, and *without* any further change in this person's motivational state, *this* person should act for this reason. So interpreted, (A) could not support an argument for Internalism, since it would merely restate this view.

Much more needs to be said about motivating reasons. Such reasons can be acceptably regarded in two ways. On the *psychological account*, motivating reasons are beliefs and/or desires, when these explain our decisions and our acts. On the *non-psychological account*, motivating reasons are *what* we believe and/or *what* we want. Thus, when asked, "Why did he jump?," we might truly claim: "Because the hotel was on fire," or "Because he believed the hotel was on fire," or "To save his life," or "Because he wanted to save his life."

Since both accounts are acceptable, we should accept both, and should thus conclude that there are two kinds of motivating reason: one kind are mental states, the other are the contents or objects of these states. These two kinds of reason always go together. For some purposes, especially normative discussion, the non-psychological account is more natural; for others, such as causal explanation, we must appeal to the psychological account. The acceptability of both accounts can, however, cause confusion. On one account, motivating reasons are the true or apparent normative reasons belief in which explain our decisions and our acts. On the other account, motivating reasons are motivating states. Since *motivating* reasons can thus be regarded *both* as normative reasons *and* as motivating states, that may suggest that *normative* reasons are motivating states. That, I believe, is a grave mistake.

29. *IER*, p. 108 [this volume, 44].

30. *IER*, p. 109, my italics [this volume, 44–45].

31. Williams himself writes that "reason, that is to say, rational processes, can give rise to new motivations" (*IER*, p. 108) [this volume, 44]. The argument that we are now discussing must, however, assume that Jack could not rationally become motivated to do X except by deliberating from some earlier motivation. Without that assumption, (4) might both entail (6) and be true.

32. As before, Williams himself notes that claims about internal reasons do not conflict with claims about external reasons (*IER*, p. 108) [this volume, 43]. This suggests that I am misinterpreting the first full paragraph on *IER*, p. 109 [this volume, 44–45]. Williams's argument may instead be this:

(i) Since (4) entails (6), Jack cannot have an external reason to do X unless it is true that, if he rationally deliberated, he would become motivated to do X.
(ii) Jack could not rationally become motivated to do X unless he were deliberating from some earlier motivation.
(iii) In that case, Jack would have had an internal reason to do X.
(iv) *Ex hypothesi*, however, Jack had no such reason.

Therefore

(v) Jack cannot have an external reason to do X.

As I have just implied, and shall argue further below, we can reject (ii).

33. As Williams points out, (4) could not always entail (7), since what Jack has reason to do may in part depend on facts about him that would not have obtained if he had been fully substantively rational (*WME*, p. 190) [this volume, 92].

34. *IER*, p. 105 [this volume, 41], and *IROB*, p. 35.

35. I take my description of these views from *WME*, pp. 186–187 [this volume, 89]. The phrase 'we could rationally' here means 'it would not be irrational for us'.

36. The argument might then claim that, if (A) doesn't entail (C), we should drop our assumption that, even if (B) is false, (A) might be true.

37. For what may be a different view, which appeals to a "non-rational" change of mind like that involved in "conversion," see John McDowell, "Might There Be External Reasons?," (*MWE*, pp. 72–78) [this volume, 76–83].

38. *IER*, p. 105 [this volume, 41].

39. Suppose that we are *not* such that, if we deliberated in this way, we might come to believe (A), and for that reason decide to do X. According to Weak Internalists, (A) would then be false. According to Strong Externalists, (A) might still be true. Strong Externalism might here be claimed to violate the principle that 'ought' implies 'can'. Though I believe that this objection is unsound, I have no space to argue that here.

40. *IER*, p. 109 [this volume, 45].

41. *IER*, pp. 109–110 [this volume, 45] (I have substituted 'do X' for 'phi').

42. *IROB*, p. 40.

43. In my *On What Matters* (Oxford: Oxford University Press, 2011).

44. For strong objections to both of these reductive views, see Thomas Nagel, *The Last Word* (Oxford: Oxford University Press, 1996).

45. Note that, for this objection to be good, it need not assume that there *are* any moral truths. It assumes only that, *if* there are such truths, they could not be in this way trivial. (Nor does this objection assume that moral naturalism is trivial. If morality were trivial, that fact would not be trivial.)

46. *IROB*, p. 36.

47. *IROB*, p. 36.

48. In my *On What Matters*, op. cit.

49. *The Sources of Normativity* (Cambridge University Press, 1996), p. 85.

50. Peter Railton, "What the Non-Cognitivist Helps Us to See," in *Reality, Representation, and Projection*, eds. J. Haldane and C. Wright (Oxford: Oxford University Press, 1993). Though Railton is here describing what other people might claim, he seems to endorse this claim.

51. *Moral Vision*, p. 48.

52. Samuel Scheffler, *Human Morality* (Oxford: Oxford University Press, 1992), p. 76.

53. J. L. Mackie, *Hume's Moral Theory* (Routledge and Kegan Paul, 1980), pp. 54–55. For another discussion of this view of normativity, see Stephen Darwall, "Internalism and Agency," in *Philosophical Perspectives* 6 (1992): 155–174.

54. For defenses of this view, see Warren Quinn, "Putting Rationality in Its Place," in his *Morality and Action* (Cambridge: Cambridge University Press, 1993) [this volume, chap. 8], and Thomas Scanlon, *What We Owe to Each Other* (Cambridge, MA: Harvard University Press, 1998), chap. 1.

Bibliography

Bond, E. J. *Reason and Value*. Cambridge: Cambridge University Press, 1983.

Bratman, M. Cognitivism about practical reason. *Ethics* 102 (1991): 117–128.

Brewer, T. The real problem with internalism about reasons. *Canadian Journal of Philosophy* 32 (2002): 443–474.

Brink, D. Kantian rationalism: Inescapability, authority, and supremacy. In *Ethics and Practical Reason*, ed. G. Cullity and B. Gaut. Oxford: Oxford University Press, 1997.

Brink, D. *Moral Realism and the Foundations of Ethics*. Cambridge: Cambridge University Press, 1989.

Brink, D. The significance of desire. *Oxford Studies in Metaethics* 3 (2008): 5–45.

Broome, J. Can a Humean be moderate? (1993). Reprinted in J. Broome, *Ethics Out of Economics*. Cambridge: Cambridge University Press, 1999.

Broome, J. Does rationality consist in responding correctly to reasons? *Journal of Moral Philosophy* 4 (2007): 349–374.

Broome, J. Reasons and motivation. *Proceedings of the Aristotelian Society, Supplementary Volume* 71 (1997): 131–146.

Chang, R. Can desires provide reasons for action? In *Reason and Value: Essays on the Moral Philosophy of Joseph Raz*, ed. R. J. Wallace, P. Pettit, S. Scheffler, and M. Smith. Oxford: Oxford University Press, 2004.

Clark, P. Velleman's autonomism. *Ethics* 111 (2001): 580–593.

Cohon, R. Are external reasons impossible? *Ethics* 95 (1986): 545–556.

Cohon, R. Internalism about reasons for action. *Pacific Philosophical Quarterly* 69 (1993): 99–116.

Dancy, J. *Practical Reality*. Oxford: Oxford University Press, 2000.

Darwall, S. Autonomist internalism and the justification of morals. *Noûs* 23 (1990): 257–267.

Darwall, S. Internalism and agency. *Philosophical Perspectives* 6 (1992): 155–174.

Darwall, S. *Impartial Reason*. Ithaca, N.Y.: Cornell University Press, 1983.

Darwall, S. *The British Moralists and the Internal "Ought": 1640–1740*. Cambridge: Cambridge University Press, 1995.

Dreier, J. Humean doubts about the practical justification of morality. In *Ethics and Practical Reason*, ed. G. Cullity and B. Gaut. Oxford: Oxford University Press, 1997.

Dreier, J. Rational preference: Decision theory as a theory of practical rationality. *Theory and Decision* 40 (1996): 249–276.

Finlay, S. The obscurity of internal reasons. *Philosophers' Imprint* 9 (2009): 1–22.

Fitzpatrick, W. J. Reasons, value, and particular agents: Normative relevance without motivational internalism. *Mind* 113 (2004): 285–318.

Foot, P. *Moral Dilemmas*. Oxford: Oxford University Press, 2002.

Foot, P. Morality as a system of hypothetical imperatives (1972). Reprinted with postscript in P. Foot, *Virtues and Vices*. Oxford: Oxford University Press, 2002.

Foot, P. *Natural Goodness*. Oxford: Oxford University Press, 2001.

Foot, P. Rationality and virtue (1994). Reprinted in P. Foot, *Moral Dilemmas*. Oxford: Oxford University Press, 2002.

Foot, P. Reasons for action and desires (1972). Reprinted with postscript in P. Foot, *Virtues and Vices*. Oxford: Oxford University Press, 2002.

Foot, P. *Virtues and Vices*. Oxford: Oxford University Press, 2002.

Gauthier, D. *Morals by Agreement*. Oxford: Oxford University Press, 1986.

Gert, J. *Brute Rationality*. Cambridge: Cambridge University Press, 2004.

Goldman, A. H. Reason internalism. *Philosophy and Phenomenological Research* 71 (2005): 505–533.

Hampton, J. *The Authority of Reason*. Cambridge: Cambridge University Press, 1998.

Heath, J. Foundationalism and practical reason. *Mind* 106 (1997): 451–473.

Heuer, U. Reasons for actions and desires. *Philosophical Studies* 121 (2004): 43–63.

Hooker, B. Williams' argument against external reasons. *Analysis* 47 (1987): 42–44.

Hubin, D. C. Irrational desires. *Philosophical Studies* 62 (1991): 23–44.

Hubin, D. C. Hypothetical motivation. *Noûs* 30 (1996): 31–54.

Hubin, D. C. The groundless normativity of instrumental reason. *Journal of Philosophy* 98 (2001): 445–468.

Hubin, D. C. What's special about Humeanism? *Noûs* 33 (1999): 30–45.

Hurley, S. Reason and motivation: The wrong distinction? *Analysis* 61 (2001): 151–155.

Johnson, R. Internal reasons and the conditional fallacy. *Philosophical Quarterly* 49 (1999): 53–71.

Jollimore, T. Why is instrumental rationality rational? *Canadian Journal of Philosophy* 35 (2005): 289–307.

Korsgaard, C. *Self-Constitution*. Oxford: Oxford University Press, 2009.

Korsgaard, C. Skepticism about practical reason. *Journal of Philosophy* 83 (1986): 5–25.

Korsgaard, C. *The Constitution of Agency*. Oxford: Oxford University Press, 2008.

Korsgaard, C. The normativity of instrumental reason (1997). Reprinted with postscript in C. Korsgaard, *The Constitution of Agency*. Oxford: Oxford University Press, 2008.

Korsgaard, C. *The Sources of Normativity*. Cambridge: Cambridge University Press, 1996.

Lavin, D. Practical reason and the possibility of error. *Ethics* 114 (2004): 424–457.

Lenman, J. Belief, desire, and motivation: An essay in quasi-hydraulics. *American Philosophical Quarterly* 33 (1996): 291–301.

Mason, M. Aretaic appraisal and practical reasons. *Southern Journal of Philosophy* 44 (2006): 629–656.

McDowell, J. Are moral requirements hypothetical imperatives? (1978). Reprinted in J. McDowell, *Mind, Value, and Reality*. Cambridge, Mass.: Harvard University Press, 1998.

McDowell, J. Might there be external reasons? (1995). Reprinted in J. McDowell, *Mind, Value, and Reality*. Cambridge, Mass.: Harvard University Press, 1998.

McDowell, J. *Mind, Value, and Reality*. Cambridge, Mass.: Harvard University Press, 1998.

McDowell, J. Response to Pettit and Smith. In *McDowell and His Critics*, ed. C. Macdonald and G. Macdonald. Oxford: Blackwell, 2006.

McDowell, J. Two sorts of naturalism (1995). Reprinted in J. McDowell, *Mind, Value, and Reality*. Cambridge, Mass.: Harvard University Press, 1998.

McDowell, J. Virtue and reason (1979). Reprinted in J. McDowell, *Mind, Value, and Reality*. Cambridge, Mass.: Harvard University Press, 1998.

Millgram, E. *Practical Induction*. Cambridge, Mass.: Harvard University Press, 1997.

Millgram, E. Williams' argument against external reasons. *Noûs* 30 (1996): 197–220.

Moreau, S. Reasons and character. *Ethics* 115 (2005): 272–305.

Nagel, T. *The Possibility of Altruism*. Princeton: Princeton University Press, 1970.

Parfit, D. Normativity. *Oxford Studies in Metaethics* 1 (2006): 325–380.

Parfit, D. *On What Matters*. Oxford: Oxford University Press, 2011.

Parfit, D. Reasons and motivation. *Proceedings of the Aristotelian Society, Supplementary Volume* 71 (1997): 99–130.

Pettit, P., and M. Smith. External reasons. In *McDowell and His Critics*, ed. C. Macdonald and G. Macdonald. Oxford: Blackwell, 2006.

Quinn, W. Putting rationality in its place. Reprinted in W. Quinn, *Morality and Action*. Cambridge: Cambridge University Press, 1993.

Quinn, W. Rationality and the human good (1992). Reprinted in W. Quinn, *Morality and Action*. Cambridge: Cambridge University Press, 1993.

Railton, P. On the hypothetical and non-hypothetical in reasoning about belief and action. In *Ethics and Practical Reason*, ed. G. Cullity and B. Gaut. Oxford: Oxford University Press, 1997.

Raz, J. Agency, reason, and the good. In J. Raz, *Engaging Reason*. Oxford: Oxford University Press, 1999.

Raz, J. Incommensurability and agency (1998). In J. Raz, *Engaging Reason*. Oxford: Oxford University Press, 1999.

Raz, J. The myth of instrumental rationality. *Journal of Ethics and Social Philosophy* 1 (2005): 1–28.

Raz, J. When we are ourselves: The active and the passive (1997). Reprinted in J. Raz, *Engaging Reason*. Oxford: Oxford University Press, 1999.

Sayre-McCord, G. Deception and reasons to be moral. *American Philosophical Quarterly* 26 (1989): 113–122.

Scanlon, T. M. *What We Owe to Each Other*. Cambridge, Mass.: Harvard University Press, 1998.

Schroeder, M. *Slaves of the Passions*. Oxford: Oxford University Press, 2007.

Searle, J. *Rationality in Action*. Cambridge, Mass.: MIT Press, 2001.

Bibliography

Setiya, K. Against internalism. *Noûs* 38 (2004): 266–298.

Setiya, K. Is efficiency a vice? *American Philosophical Quarterly* 42 (2005): 333–339.

Setiya, K. *Reasons without Rationalism*. Princeton: Princeton University Press, 2007.

Shafer-Landau, R. *Moral Realism: A Defence*. Oxford: Oxford University Press, 2003.

Skorupski, J. Internal reasons and the scope of blame. In *Bernard Williams*, ed. A. Thomas. Cambridge: Cambridge University Press, 2007.

Smit, H. Internalism and the origin of rational motivation. *Journal of Ethics* 7 (2003): 183–231.

Smith, M. Beyond the error theory. In *A World without Values: Essays on John Mackie's Moral Error Theory*, ed. R. Joyce and S. Kirchin. Dordrecht: Springer, 2010.

Smith, M. Internal reasons. *Philosophy and Phenomenological Research* 55 (1995): 109–131.

Smith, M. Reason and desire. *Proceedings of the Aristotelian Society* 88 (1988): 243–258.

Smith, M. The explanatory role of being rational. In *Reasons for Action*, ed. D. Sobel and S. Wall. Cambridge: Cambridge University Press, 2009.

Smith, M. The Humean theory of motivation. *Mind* 96 (1987): 36–61.

Smith, M. *The Moral Problem*. Oxford: Blackwell, 1994.

Sobel, D. Explanation, internalism, and reasons for action. *Social Philosophy & Policy* 18 (2001): 218–235.

Sobel, D. Subjective accounts of reasons for action. *Ethics* 111 (2001): 461–492.

Svavarsdóttir, S. Evaluations of rationality. In *Metaethics after Moore*, ed. T. Horgan and M. Timmons. Oxford: Oxford University Press, 2006.

Svavarsdóttir, S. The virtue of practical rationality. *Philosophy and Phenomenological Research* 77 (2008): 1–33.

Thomas, A. Internal reasons and contractualist impartiality. *Utilitas* 14 (2002): 135–154.

van Roojen, M. Humean motivation and Humean rationality. *Philosophical Studies* 79 (1995): 37–57.

van Roojen, M. Should motivational Humeans be Humeans about rationality? *Topoi* 21 (2002): 209–215.

Velleman, J. D. *How We Get Along*. Cambridge: Cambridge University Press, 2009.

Velleman, J. D. Is motivation internal to value? (1998). Reprinted in J. D. Velleman, *The Possibility of Practical Reason*. Oxford: Oxford University Press, 2000.

Velleman, J. D. *Practical Reflection*. Princeton: Princeton University Press, 1989.

Velleman, J. D. The possibility of practical reason (1996). Reprinted in J. D. Velleman, *The Possibility of Practical Reason*. Oxford: Oxford University Press, 2000.

Velleman, J. D. *The Possibility of Practical Reason*. Oxford: Oxford University Press, 2000.

Velleman, J. D. What happens when someone acts? (1992). Reprinted in J. D. Velleman, *The Possibility of Practical Reason*. Oxford: Oxford University Press, 2000.

Vogler, C. *Reasonably Vicious*. Cambridge, Mass.: Harvard University Press, 2002.

Wallace, R. J. How to argue about practical reason. *Mind* 99 (1990): 355–385.

Wallace, R. J. Three conceptions of rational agency. *Ethical Theory and Moral Practice* 2 (1999): 217–242.

Wedgwood, R. Choosing rationally and choosing correctly. In *Weakness of Will and Practical Irrationality*, ed. S. Stroud and C. Tappolet. Oxford: Oxford University Press, 2003.

Wedgwood, R. Practical reason and desire. *Australasian Journal of Philosophy* 80 (2002): 345–358.

Wedgwood, R. *The Nature of Normativity*. Oxford: Oxford University Press, 2007.

White, S. Rationality, responsibility, and pathological indifference. In *Identity, Character, and Morality*, ed. O. Flanagan and A. Rorty. Cambridge, Mass.: MIT Press, 1990.

Williams, B. Internal and external reasons (1979). Reprinted in B. Williams, *Moral Luck*. Cambridge: Cambridge University Press, 1981.

Williams, B. Internal reasons and the obscurity of blame (1989). Reprinted in B. Williams, *Making Sense of Humanity*. Cambridge: Cambridge University Press, 1995.

Williams, B. Postscript: Some further notes on internal and external reasons. In *Varieties of Practical Reasoning*, ed. E. Millgram. Cambridge, Mass.: MIT Press, 2001.

Williams, B. Replies. In *World, Mind, and Ethics: Essays on the Ethical Philosophy of Bernard Williams*, ed. J. Altham and R. Harrison. Cambridge: Cambridge University Press, 1995.

Contributors

Philip Clark University of Toronto
James Dreier Brown University
Philippa Foot[†] University of California, Los Angeles
Troy Jollimore California State University, Chico
Christine Korsgaard Harvard University
John McDowell University of Pittsburgh
Thomas Nagel New York University
Hille Paakkunainen Syracuse University
Derek Parfit All Souls College, Oxford
Warren Quinn[†] University of California, Los Angeles
Kieran Setiya University of Pittsburgh
Michael Smith Princeton University
J. David Velleman New York University
Bernard Williams[†] University of California, Berkeley

[†] Deceased

Index

Action, constitutive aim of, 256, 263–273, 286–290, 298. *See also* Constitutivism; Rationalism, ethical
Advice model of reasons, 13–15, 91–93, 100–102, 116–121
Akrasia. *See* Weakness of will
Anscombe, G. E. M., 183, 336–338
Aquinas, St. Thomas, 336–337
Aristotle, 18–19, 24, 59–60, 62–63, 77, 91–95, 167, 170, 182, 229
Autonomy, 56, 68, 204, 225, 230–233, 268–273, 285–290, 298

Belief, 229, 257–263, 269–270, 286, 287–288, 319–320. *See also* False belief and reasons for action; Judgement internalism; Knowledge; Theoretical reason
Blackburn, Simon, 303
Brandt, R. B., 99
Butler, Joseph, 203

Carroll, Lewis, 140
Categorical imperatives, 42, 51, 56, 68–69, 130, 133–134, 137, 141, 202–205, 230–235. *See also* Kant; Kantian conceptions of practical reason; Moral reasons
Clark, Philip, 25
Clarke, Samuel, 222
Cognitivism. *See* Non-cognitivism

Coherence, 19–21, 83, 105–107, 118–119
Constitutive aim of action. *See* Action, constitutive aim of
Constitutive aim of belief. *See* Belief
Constitutivism, 226–234, 322–326. *See also* Action, constitutive aim of; Rationalism, ethical
Copp, David, 133

Daniels, Norman, 105, 325
Darwall, Stephen, 115, 285
Davidson, Donald, 16–17, 183, 286, 308
Desire, 6–7, 15–17, 41, 66, 73–74, 82, 131–133, 135–136, 138–140, 143–144, 196–197, 213–215, 320–321. *See also* Motivation
  as reason for action, 171–185, 271–273, 365–366 (*see also* Humean conception of practical reason; Instrumental Rationality; Instrumentalism; Internal reasons theory)
Dogmatic rationalism. *See* Rationalism, dogmatic
Dreier, James, 4, 18, 21, 151–152
Dworkin, Ronald, 295–296

Empiricism, 69, 203–207, 224
Epistemology. *See* Knowledge

Error theory, 168–169, 186, 303–309, 365. *See also* Mackie, J. L.
Ethical rationalism. *See* Rationalism, ethical
Ethical realism. *See* Realism, ethical
Ethical virtue. *See* Virtue, ethical
Example model of reasons. *See* Advice model of reasons
Externalism about reasons, 6, 76–86, 186, 250–257, 285–286, 290–298, 344–346, 350–360, 365–367. *See also* Internal reasons theory; Internalism about reasons
External reasons. *See* Externalism about reasons; Internal reasons theory; Internalism about reasons

Falk, W. D., 54–56
False belief and reasons for action, 3–4, 17, 19–20, 38–39, 41, 57–58, 102–103, 179–180, 212, 343, 354
Foot, Philippa, 24, 26, 130, 337
Frankena, William, 54, 62
Frege, Gottlob, 81
Function arguments, 18–22, 23–24, 309–311, 314–315, 322–323, 331–338

Garner, Richard, 303
Gauthier, David, 309
Geach, Peter, 331–332
God, 56, 222, 295, 312
Good, 21, 170–171, 174–176, 179–187, 253–255, 265, 285, 288–298, 316–322, 331–332, 336

Hare, R. M., 168, 180, 314–316, 319
Harman, Gilbert, 324–325
Hegel, G. F., 233
Hobbes, Thomas, 4, 55
Hume, David, 38, 44–45, 52–54, 57–58, 60, 64–67, 76, 86, 108–109, 116–117, 169, 186, 206–217, 220, 227, 231, 249, 348, 366. *See also* Humean conception of practical reason; Humean theory of motivation; Instrumentalism; Internal reasons theory
Humean conception of practical reason, 4, 38, 40, 64, 108–109, 127, 130–137, 158, 160–162, 169, 249, 285, 290, 296–298, 307, 330. *See also* Hume; Instrumentalism; Internal reasons theory
Humean theory of motivation, 6, 11, 19–20, 44–45, 53–54, 63–67, 76, 116–121, 130–135, 186, 205, 208–209, 249, 355–356, 365. *See also* Hume; Humean conception of practical reason; Judgment internalism; Motivation
  objections to, 16, 83–84, 195–198, 348–350
Hypothetical imperatives. *See* Instrumental rationality; Kant, Immanuel, on instrumental rationality

Instrumentalism, 21, 40–41, 52–53, 57–58. *See also* Desire; Humean conception of practical reason; Instrumental rationality; Internal reasons theory
  arguments for, 3–6, 63–65, 138–144, 147–152
  arguments vs., 60–61, 66, 157–162, 172–177, 214–215, 230–235, 271–273, 365–366
Instrumental rationality, 159–163, 201–204, 207, 212–224, 226–235, 309–313. *See also* Desire; Instrumentalism; Will
Internal reasons theory, 1–4, 37–41, 56, 73–75, 90–91, 102–103, 109–116, 249. *See also* Advice model of reasons; Desire as reason for action;

Index

Externalism about reasons; Humean conception of practical reason; Instrumentalism; Internalism about reasons; Procedural rationality
  arguments for, 5–6, 12–15, 22–24, 42–47, 63–67, 75–80, 83–85, 91–96, 249–250, 256, 354–359
Internalism about reasons, 4–5, 7–10, 14, 19–23, 54–60, 63–67, 90–91, 99–102, 201, 224–225, 249, 261–263, 265, 271–273, 344–346, 350. *See also* Advice model of reasons; Externalism about reasons; Internal reasons theory; Judgment internalism
  arguments for, 5–6, 10–12, 15–19, 22–26, 250–256, 291, 351–353
Intuitionism, 55, 67, 304–305
Irrationality, 8–9, 46–47, 79–80, 82–83, 94, 135–136, 148–149, 158, 162–164, 341. *See also* Possibility of error

Jollimore, Troy, 21–22
Joyce, Richard, 303
Judgment internalism, 5, 7, 43, 45, 54–55, 116–121, 186, 348–350. *See also* Humean theory of motivation
Justice, 1–2, 24, 147, 186, 196, 234, 291, 329–332, 336–338, 341. *See also* Moral reasons; Virtue, ethical

Kant, Immanuel, 42, 56, 58, 63, 68–69, 149, 179, 230, 233, 235, 304, 313, 316, 359. *See also* Categorical imperatives; Kantian conceptions of practical reason; Moral reasons
  on instrumental rationality, 136, 201–204, 217–222, 225–227
Kantian conceptions of practical reason, 4, 6–7, 11–12, 21, 23, 51, 54, 56, 66–69, 92, 95, 109, 129, 142, 144, 149, 268, 285–286, 307, 313–316. *See also* Categorical imperatives; Kant; Moral reasons
Knowledge, 24–26, 305, 308–311, 314–315, 324–327, 360
  practical, 268–270 (*see also* Motivation)
Korsgaard, C., 4, 6–10, 11–12, 14, 18, 21, 23, 99–101, 108, 249–251, 285, 307, 350, 364

Leibniz, G. W., 222
Lewis, David, 112, 303, 310–311

Mackie, J. L., 167–169, 186–187, 303–312, 314, 316, 321–324, 326, 365
McDowell, John, 6, 8, 11–15, 89–94, 303
McNaughton, David, 364
Mill, J. S., 55, 67
Moore, G. E., 22–24, 304–307, 309–314, 316–317, 321–322, 326, 331–332, 360–361
Moral reasons, 169–171, 222–224, 304–309, 311–314, 317, 346–347. *See also* Categorical imperatives; Justice; Virtue, ethical
  defense of, 62–69, 76–79, 84–85, 158–161, 163–164, 186–187, 230–235, 250, 322–326, 330–332, 336–341, 350, 352–353, 364–367 (*see also* Kantian conceptions of practical reason)
  doubts about, 1–2, 6–7, 26, 47–48, 73, 127–130, 133–134, 137, 140–144, 147–152, 196, 202–203, 329–330 (*see also* Humean conception of practical reason; Instrumentalism; Internal reasons theory)
Motivating reasons, 2–3, 10–11, 17, 130–137, 150–151, 338, 343, 350, 354–355. *See also* Motivation

Motivation, 15–17, 42–45, 61–64, 75–76, 80–84, 198–200, 205–206, 271–272, 344. *See also* Desire; Humean theory of motivation; Judgment internalism; Knowledge, practical; Motivating reasons

Nagel, Thomas, 2, 4, 6, 15–19, 23, 54–56, 62, 67–68, 203, 205–206, 348
Naturalism, reductive, 22–26, 304–314, 316–317, 321–322, 326, 350–352, 360–367
Needs, 5, 24, 41, 210, 216, 333–340, 353, 360
Nietzsche, Friedrich, 170, 353
Non-cognitivism, 167–170, 332, 349, 351, 365

Objective and subjective reasons, 155–159

Parfit, Derek, 22–24, 26, 111–112, 202, 316–317, 320, 322
Plato, 1, 170, 182, 234, 304, 329, 331, 349
Pleasure, 177–180, 182, 184–185
Possibility of error, 19, 57–58, 134–137, 212–215, 219–221, 226–228, 287–290, 298
Prichard, H. A., 55
Procedural rationality, 22–23, 85, 93–94, 345, 350, 355–356, 358–359, 364. *See also* Instrumentalism; Internal reasons theory
Prudence, 60–63, 128–129, 170, 195–196, 202–203, 208–212, 214–215, 339–341, 344–345, 353, 359–360

Railton, Peter, 364
Rationalism, dogmatic, 203–204, 222–226, 232–233
Rationalism, ethical, 20–25. *See also* Constitutivism

Rationality. *See* Humean conception of practical reason; Instrumental rationality; Irrationality; Kantian conceptions of practical reason; Possibility of error; Procedural rationality; Prudence; Reasons; Theoretical reason
Rawls, John, 99, 105, 325
Realism, ethical, 167, 187, 304–305, 350–351. *See also* Rationalism, dogmatic
Reasons. *See* Advice model of reasons; Desire as reason for action; False belief and reasons for action; Internal reasons theory; Internalism about reasons; Moral reasons; Motivating reasons; Objective and subjective reasons; Rationality; Universality of reasons
Reductive naturalism. *See* Naturalism, reductive
Ross, W. D., 55

Satan, 288, 293
Scanlon, T. M., 8, 316–317, 320
Scheffler, Samuel, 364
Self-interest. *See* Prudence
Shafer-Landau, 306
Sidgwick, Henry, 304–306, 308, 314, 317, 326
Smith, Michael, 13–15, 20, 22, 99, 110, 115, 116, 132, 303, 307, 310, 318
Stevenson, Charles, 168
Subjective reasons. *See* Objective and subjective reasons
Substantive rationality. *See* Procedural rationality

Theoretical reason, 21–22, 59–60, 81–83, 140–144, 153–159, 162–163, 170, 206, 229, 366. *See also* Belief; Knowledge

Universality of reasons, 14–15, 99–100, 107–116, 313–316

Velleman, J. David, 7, 9–10, 21, 24–26, 285–294, 296–298
Virtue, ethical, 12–13, 24, 46, 63, 92–93, 171, 186–187, 196, 215–216, 329–341. *See also* Justice; Moral reasons
Volition. *See* Will

Watson, Gary, 101
Weakness of will, 43, 211, 230–231, 341. *See also* Will
Wedgwood, Ralph, 20–21
White, Stephen, 8
Wiggins, David, 333–334
Will, 53–54, 68, 177, 181, 186, 202–204, 209, 217–218, 222, 225–228, 230–231, 234–235. *See also* Weakness of will
Williams, Bernard, 1–16, 21, 22, 54, 56, 99–100, 169–170, 258, 271, 273, 307, 343–345. *See also* Humean conception of practical reason; Internal reasons theory; Internalism about reasons
criticized, 6–7, 10–11, 16, 64–67, 73–86, 90, 102–116, 249–251, 351–360, 363–364

www.ingramcontent.com/pod-product-compliance
Lightning Source LLC
Chambersburg PA
CBHW051250300426
44114CB00011B/965